MASTERING THE INLAND SEAS

THEODORE J. KARAMANSKI

MASTERING
THE INLAND SEAS

HOW LIGHTHOUSES, NAVIGATIONAL AIDS, AND HARBORS
TRANSFORMED THE GREAT LAKES AND AMERICA

THE UNIVERSITY OF WISCONSIN PRESS

The University of Wisconsin Press
728 State Street, Suite 443
Madison, Wisconsin 53706
uwpress.wisc.edu

Gray's Inn House, 127 Clerkenwell Road
London EC1R 5DB, United Kingdom
eurospanbookstore.com

Printed in the United States of America

This book may be available in a digital edition.

Library of Congress Cataloging-in-Publication Data

Names: Karamanski, Theodore J., 1953- author.
Title: Mastering the inland seas: how lighthouses, navigational aids,
and harbors transformed the Great Lakes and America /
Theodore J. Karamanski.
Description: Madison, Wisconsin: The University of Wisconsin Press, [2020]
| Includes bibliographical references and index.
Identifiers: LCCN 2019039027 | ISBN 9780299326302 (cloth)
Subjects: LCSH: Navigation—Great Lakes Region (North America)—History.
| Inland navigation—Great Lakes Region (North America)—History.
| Aids to navigation—Great Lakes Region (North America)—History.
| Lighthouses—Great Lakes Region (North America)—History.
| Great Lakes Region (North America)—History.
| Great Lakes (North America)—History.
Classification: LCC HE631.G74 K37 2020 | DDC 386/.850977—dc23
LC record available at https://lccn.loc.gov/2019039027

To all my history teachers,
particularly
Robert W. McCluggage
and
the faculty of Loyola University Chicago.

Contents

Illustrations

MASTERING THE INLAND SEAS

Introduction

Deep in the North American heartland lies a vast inland sea. Along its margins are world-class cities, villages, farms, and mammoth industrial complexes. Yet far from shore, out on the dark waters, exists a wilderness more dangerous to the adventurer than the Rocky Mountain peaks or the arid expanse of Death Valley. How North Americans have learned to venture out on their truly Great Lakes and use them to build diverse societies on their shores is an unappreciated chapter in history. Critical to that story is the role lighthouses, harbors, channels, and charts played in making a maritime region out of what was, and in some ways still is, a watery wilderness. While water is essential to life, it is an alien element to a human caught in its cold embrace. Step from the warm sand of a beach into cool water or from the solid surface of a wharf and onto the heaving deck of a ship and you have entered the realm of an elemental power. Joseph Conrad understood the existential nature of the human

3

relationship with water when he wrote, "To the destructive element submit yourself, and with the exertions of your hands and feet in the water make the deep, deep sea keep you up." That quotation from Conrad's epic novel *Lord Jim* encapsulates maritime history, the story of our struggle to live and work in the world of water.[1]

This book was written far from Conrad's ocean, in the heart of a continent yet on the shore of the vast inland sea. The city of Chicago stretches for miles away from Lake Michigan, with most of its residents living out of its sight, unthinkingly taking life from its waters piped mysteriously to their faucets. Tap water is tamed of its destructive power, processed and filtered of impurities. The raw nature of the Great Lakes of North America is unappreciated in the living rooms and workplaces of the city. Only a few feet from the metropolis, with all its comforts, is a wilderness of beauty, adventure, and menace. More than three hundred years after the first ship's crew went shrieking to their deaths beneath its waves, and more than ten thousand years since the first Paleo-Indian canoe was launched, the Great Lakes are still a vast expanse of untamed primal energy, a domain alien to terrestrial life. This history is the story of the people and the technologies that have made it possible to use the wilderness of North America's inland seas for commerce, communication, and recreation.

To understand the importance of the Great Lakes, we need to appreciate them as part of the broad pattern of North American history. To do this we need to move away from retelling colorful shipwreck tales and follow the lead of the Swedish archaeologist Christer Westerdahl, who emphasized the importance of integrating both the terrestrial and the waterborne aspects of maritime history. The concept of maritime infrastructure provides the means of effecting that integration. The infrastructure of the Great Lakes consists of hardware and software. Boats and lighthouses are the oldest elements of the infrastructural hardware, but no less important are breakwaters, canals, and GPS satellites. The software of the maritime infrastructure includes nautical charts, governmental policy, and administrative agencies such as the Lighthouse Service and, later, the Coast Guard. Critical to infrastructural software are the social attitudes that shape the way the lakes are perceived, their social construction as it were. Policy has long hinged on whether the lakes are viewed as true inland seas and a national resource of international importance or dismissed as bodies of water of merely local concern. The term "navigation" in the title refers to both the technique of safely maneuvering a vessel as well as the commercial trade conducted by boats and ships. Navigational aids are the infrastructure employed to aid safe sailing. The creation and maintenance of a navigational infrastructure on the Great Lakes was a critical, if historically underappreciated, feature of North American frontier expansion. The maritime character of the inland seas required a set of federal government interventions that were unique in the trans-Appalachian West and that significantly contributed to antebellum sectional tensions and postbellum industrial expansion.[2]

The Great Lakes are boundary waters between two nations, save, of course, for Lake Michigan, which alone is solely within the U.S. There is therefore a transnational dimension to the history of the waterway. This book includes discussion of events within both Canada and the U.S. However, the complex and widely varied nature of the maritime infrastructure together with space limitations regrettably mean that the narrative unfolds with a stronger focus on the region's U.S. context.

In some ways this is an environmental history since its focus is the process by which North Americans attempted to settle a watery wilderness. While the Great Lakes remain wild, the development of charts, lighthouses, buoys, improved channels, locks, and harbors were all attempts to domesticate these great inland seas. Those features are as much a part of the process of "settlement" as such well-recognized markers of terrestrial development like roads, farms, factories, and towns. The technologies of maritime navigation were—and are—key components in integrating the Great Lakes into the larger means of production of the burgeoning capitalist economy of North America. Canals, improved channels, and harbors are examples of what environmental historian William Cronon famously dubbed "second nature," the artificial or altered landscape of human engineering. Yet while most environmental history places nature as the main narrative actor, this study looks instead at the technologies developed to harness the lakes first to build a region and then a nation and, eventually, to impact the world. The significance of navigational aids in the Great Lakes region can perhaps be made clearer through an analogy with the classic study of another, very different region. In 1931 Walter Prescott Webb tried to highlight the unique nature of the Great Plains' barren, arid environment by arguing, with a touch of hyperbole, that its settlement was made possible by the revolver, barbed wire, and the windmill. The development of the Great Lakes frontier, unmapped and with few natural harbors, with ships playing the role of the covered wagon, was made possible by the lighthouse, the nautical chart, and the building of ports.[3]

The Great Lakes, some ninety thousand square miles of open water, shape a distinct region of the North American continent, yet that region has received considerably less attention from scholars than other regions such as New England, French Canada, the Deep South, the Great Plains, or the Desert and Mountain West. Yet the communities that line its shores and are grouped into parts of eight American states and the Canadian province of Ontario share a common history of using, abusing, loving, and living with a vast fresh water resource. Historians of antebellum America have been especially guilty of lumping the communities that line the lakes with "the West," as if, by and large, Missouri and Detroit or Arkansas and Buffalo shared common economic and political goals. Historians have neglected the unique interests and shared experiences of Great Lakes people across a basin that extends 690 miles from north to south and 860 miles from west to east. Settlers of a lacustrine landscape required maritime technologies to adapt to their incomparable natural resource. The lakes were not an environment as unexpectedly different as North Americans would encounter on the arid Great Plains. The U.S. and Canada had been born as maritime nations. Settlers of the inland seas could creatively borrow from the technologies that humanity developed to make the oceans of the world highways of commerce and avenues of empire. From ship design and lighthouses to maritime engineering and navigational techniques, the lakes followed the lessons learned on saltwater. However, the people of the inland seas also were inventive in adapting their lives to the broad blue water horizon that extends from their shores. A folklore rich in weather and navigational collective knowledge developed among the sailors and fishermen and was passed on in stories, songs, and notations on charts. The lake mariner pioneered an impressive range of innovations that subsequently were adopted on the oceans of the world. More striking were the unique adaptations that were required to effect commerce on the closed but nonetheless often tempestuous waters of the inland seas—the birchbark canoe of the Anishinaabeg, Mackinaw boats and fish tugs, the clipper schooners of William Wallace Bates, the whaleback freighters of Alexander McDougall, the lighthouses of Orlando Poe, or the inventive artificial harbors designed by generations of army engineers. While this rich history is preserved in a handful of maritime museums in the region, traditional American historiography has regarded the Great Lakes as blank spaces between midwestern states, an empty void amid the terrestrial cities, farms, and factories. It is only by including the maritime dimension of regional history that the role of the heartland in continental history can be properly understood.[4]

The navigational needs of this maritime region significantly shaped the history of the U.S. Canals and urban development in the region laid the foundation for the creation of a national market and a dynamic capitalist economy. More than 90 percent of the waters of the Great Lakes system are navigable for large vessels without improvement. Yet the remaining 10 percent of connecting channels and harbors required (and still requires) engineering intervention to reach its full economic potential. In the nineteenth century, tensions over appropriations needed for the safe navigation of the Great Lakes exasperated relations between sections of the country and ensured that the communities along the inland sea would be the strongest supporters of the Union cause during the Civil War. The development of water transportation in the Great Lakes region produced a type of capitalism quite different from that which expanded into the lower Mississippi Valley in the antebellum era. Slaveholders were willing to use the federal government to expand the geographic reach of their "peculiar institution," but they abhorred the thought of the national government playing a large role in their states. On the contrary, Great Lakes boosters saw government as a necessary partner. They first looked to their state governments to improve their integration with the national economy through an extensive series of canal and road projects. The prohibitive cost of such endeavors for new commonwealths later caused them to insist on the federal government as an infrastructure partner. Union victory in the Civil War made the Great Lake states' version of a capital-government partnership the model of Gilded Age America. For the region, the most important aspect of the Reconstruction Era was the construction of long-delayed maritime infrastructure. The boom in Great Lakes development that followed that conflict fueled the industrialization of the nation. The mines, mills, and factories of the region were the arsenal of democracy through world and cold war conflicts. The lighthouses, light ships, harbor works, and ship museums left by this history are the tangible reminders of a dynamic and unique regional history and the critical role the lakes played in American life.

Lighthouses were the first and most enduring navigational improvements brought by the federal governments of the U.S. and Canada to the inland seas. Lighthouse history, therefore, occupies a central place in this book. Nothing better symbolizes the drama of humanity's ambivalent embrace of the water than a lighthouse on a storm-washed shore. As of 2013 the Great Lakes were home to more than 400 standing lighthouses, 262 on the U.S. side and 151 on the Canadian side. For centuries, a lighthouse was, for the mariner, a wayfaring marker, a beacon marking dangerous shoals, and a reminder that, when shipboard, land can be as much a danger as water. To the literary imagination, the lighthouse is a symbol of hope, an unwavering tower standing strong amid the gales of life. Something about the setting of a lighthouse on rocky shores or isolated islands against the backdrop of a watery horizon captures the artistic imagination. The overwhelming majority of books published about navigational aids are first and foremost collections of carefully composed photographs of isolated lighthouses. While the navigational utility of lighthouses has been eclipsed by newer technologies, there remains a strong desire for both government and the private sector to continue to bear the mounting costs of maintaining these structures. It is as if to lose a lighthouse a community would be severed from its connection to its maritime past.[5]

Yet rather than fill these pages with romantic tales of isolated and heroic lighthouse keepers, this volume strives to present the story of Great Lakes lighthouses and related navigational improvements within the context of the development of the American heartland. It is fundamentally a story of state formation. The settler states that emerged along the lakes between 1803, when Ohio entered the Union, and 1858, when Minnesota shed its territorial status, all began life as part of a domestic trans-Appalachian empire. Scholars have made important contributions to our understanding of the role of the federal government in dispossessing the indigenous people of the region and importing legal and land-tenure regimes that empowered white newcomers. Yet state formation in the region had a vital spatial and maritime dimension that was as crucial as American Indian conquest. The building and maintenance of a maritime infrastructure in the heart of the continent required a multigenerational commitment by the federal governments of both the U.S. and Canada. The conflict and controversy resulting from lake settlers' insistence on that support played a major role in shaping the region's politics and identity.[6]

Because this is a history of infrastructure, it necessarily tacks away from notions of American exceptionalism that exalt individualism and free enterprise economics at the expense of government. Individuals, no matter how daring or rugged, do not sail ships. It takes a crew pulling together to set sail and stand watch. Similarly, shipowners or vessel masters do not build harbors, erect and maintain lighthouses, or chart the waterways. Such indispensable maritime infrastructure requires more capital and ongoing vigilance than any farsighted capitalist can muster. A lighthouse is a symbol of a commitment to the common good. Historically, commentators from Alexis de Tocqueville to Frederick Jackson Turner to Seymour Martin Lipset downplayed the importance and power of the federal government, particularly in the nineteenth century. The history of the Great Lakes region, perhaps more than any other area of the country, counters the laissez-faire, rugged individualist myth. The establishment of a distinctive maritime province in the heart of North America occurred because of government action. From the building of the first lighthouses and harbors in the early nineteenth century to the development of radar during World War II and the maintenance of global positioning satellites and relay stations, it has taken the collective and cooperative action of the people of North America through their governments to "settle" the inland seas frontier.[7]

1

Native Waters

In August 1679 a small ship sustained by a stiff southerly breeze scudded across the dark green waters of Lake Huron. The ship was *Le Griffon*, the first ship ever to sail on the Upper Great Lakes of North America. She was on her maiden voyage and piloted by "Luke the Dane," an arrogant mariner who had scant respect for the waters that earlier French explorers had named "La Mer Douce"—the Sweet Sea—because of its lack of salt. Although he had never been on the lakes before, he kept *Le Griffon* under sail through the night, blindly plowing on into the unknown darkness. Near midnight the sound of crashing waves revealed "a great Point which jutted into the lake." The pilot had to quickly alter his course and only just succeeded in clearing safely when the little ship was hit by "a furious gale." *Le Griffon* was so buffeted by the wind and waves that all sails had to be close-reefed while the pilot desperately scanned the horizon for any sign of a safe anchorage. Through the night and into the following day the vessel was in distress. More than thirty disheartened men were aboard. Rene Robert Cavalier, Sieur de La Salle, who had commissioned *Le Griffon*, announced that their fate was now in God's hands and bade his priest to lead them all in prayers. La Salle dedicated his to Saint Anthony of Padua, the patron saint of the lost. Luke the pilot refused to join the prayers and cursed La Salle for bringing him to "a nasty freshwater lake to die, whereas he had lived long and happy navigating the ocean."[1]

Perhaps their prayers were answered because the gale abated and *Le Griffon* was able to complete its journey safely to Lake Michigan. This first European voyage on the Upper Great Lakes revealed much about the difficulty of navigating the little-known waters of the inland seas that lie at the heart of the continent. These first European navigators had no knowledge of the wind and weather patterns. They had no charts to reveal the shape of the shoreline let alone the location of shoals. Prayer and an act of contrition was the closest thing they had to a navigational aid. Through divine intervention or, perhaps, just dumb luck, La Salle and his men safely concluded their journey. Unfortunately, *Le Griffon*'s pilot learned no lessons. He did not respect "La Mer Douce"; on the return journey he ignored the gale warnings provided by Indian canoeists and promptly sailed the ship into a watery grave.[2]

When *Le Griffon* was lost, the lakes took into their depths the lives of six men and thousands of dollars' worth of property. The purpose of the ever more sophisticated systems of navigational aids that followed in the wake of this and other early shipwrecks has been to prevent the loss of life and property. It is a task that the early whale oil lamp beacons, Fresnel-lens-topped lighthouses, channel markers, and even modern radio beams and satellite-guided navigation systems can only imperfectly carry out. The deep and broad waters of the Great Lakes may be an inviting place for recreational boaters and beach lovers, and they certainly are a critical medium for cheaply transporting bulk commodities, but they have always been and will ever remain alien to terrestrial life. Every year skilled mariners and experienced fishermen die in its waters—victims of wind, waves, fog, water spouts, shoals, ill fortune, and hubris. The history of the development of navigational aids on the Great Lakes is the story of how the U.S. government has tried to modify the risks inherent in utilizing these wild, unpredictable waters. This story is intricately linked to the development of the North American heartland, the history of maritime technology, and national economic and political history.

American Indian Navigation on the Lakes

Traditionally, there were two basic types of navigation. Celestial navigation relies on the observation of heavenly objects—the sun, moon, and stars—to determine one's position on the earth. This was a method of wayfinding critical to mariners who sailed out of the sight of land, and it was developed over the centuries, from the ancient Greeks and Polynesians to the perfection of longitude in the eighteenth century. Celestial navigation was not widely practiced on the Great Lakes because of their enclosed nature. Ships were rarely long out of sight of land. Therefore, for most of its history mariners on the Great Lakes relied on what is known as geonavigation (also known as coastal piloting or dead reckoning). Simply put, sailors relied on geographic features to determine their position. This has always been the most common type of navigation, as it relies on knowledge of the waters that are being traversed more than on an ability to take readings of the stars or sun. Historically, lighthouses developed as aids to geonavigation. They were man-made features designed to enhance a mariner's ability to locate their geographic position.[3]

The first people to navigate the Great Lakes were American Indians, and they relied on geonavigation. Even before the lakes reached their current shape and size and they were still the youthful creations of the departing glaciers, men and women built watercraft and used the lakes to journey to distant parts. Dugout canoes were undoubtedly the first watercraft in the region. All around the world this type of vessel played an early and important role in enabling societies to become exploiters of the waterways. These canoes could be crudely hacked out of tree trunks, but it did not take long for experience and craftsmanship to assert itself and more seaworthy dugouts to be developed. As a tree was being hewn into shape, the builders would soak the interior in hot water to make the wood more pliable. Thwarts made of stout hardwood would then be wedged into the hull to force the sides apart and create greater width in the middle, giving the vessel both greater carrying capacity and enhanced stability. Attachments to the bow and or stern allowed for creative decoration but also served the important purpose of helping break waves and deflect them away from the canoe.[4]

The earliest evidence of a watercraft in the Great Lakes region is a dugout canoe recovered in Ohio that dates from 1500 BC. Yet it is likely that even Paleo-Indian peoples, who came to the region more than ten thousand years earlier, at a time when the lakes were still covered by ice sheets, had knowledge of watercraft. Archaic period (8000–1000 BC) Indians used canoes to travel long distances. Recent excavations of Archaic-period sites on Isle Royale indicate that related cultures felt confident enough to journey across broad stretches of Lake Superior to mine copper ore.[5]

Indigenous America's enduring contribution to the region's maritime history was the development of the birch-bark canoe. When, where, and how this craft was developed is lost to both archaeology and history. It may have been an offshoot of the skin-covered boat that enjoyed limited prehistoric use in the Great Lakes area. The bark canoe featured a cedar frame covered by large strips of paper birch bark sown together with spruce tree roots and sealed with pine pitch. Where birch bark was not available, elm bark was sometimes used. The success of the design was its lightweight yet durable character that bore wind and waves well on open water and was highly maneuverable in swift-flowing rivers. It was a craft that opened the entire Great Lakes basin—even its most remote islands—to Indigenous peoples. Birch-bark canoe journeys of hundreds of miles for hunting, warfare, and trade became common. The canoe greatly expanded the geographic range of an Indigenous family's seasonal round of economic activity. Andrew J. Blackbird, who was among the last generation of Anishinaabeg (Odawa) people to grow up in what was still a fairly traditional lifestyle, described his family's long Great Lakes journeys. "In navigating Lake Michigan they used long bark canoes in which they carried whole families and enough provisions. . . . In one day they could sail a long distance along the coast of Lake Michigan." At night they would put up wigwams made from poles and woven mats that were carried in the canoe. Some families would travel completely down the lake shore from the Straits of Mackinaw to as far as the site of Chicago.[6]

There were few navigational aids available to Indigenous mariners. They relied on dead reckoning for planning their course and intimate knowledge of the shoreline to make their way. Place-names given to coastal features, to which stories would often be attached, helped keep alive knowledge of coastal features. For example, the Anishinaabeg legend behind the naming of Sleeping Bear Dunes accounts for the prominent headland and the two islands, North and South Manitou, that help form the Manitou Passage. In the story, a raging forest fire on the Wisconsin shore drove a mother bear and her two cubs into the lake. As they swam to the safety of the Michigan shore, the two cubs became tired and drowned. The Great Spirit Manitou then created the great dune in memory of the grieving mother bear and made North and South Manitou Islands to mark were the two cubs perished. Place-names contained key navigational information. The missionary priest Father Frederic Baraga recorded that the Anishinaabeg (Ojibwe) told him that the name for Keweenaw meant "the place where they traverse a point of land by foot." In contrast, the name for the point of land near DeTour, Michigan, was the "point which we go around in a canoe."[7]

The Anishinaabeg had a detailed knowledge of the night sky, although it is unclear if this knowledge was applied for navigation purposes. They certainly knew of the North Star and noted that it did not set below the horizon. Like the ancient Greeks, they noted constellations, and traditions developed that explained their presence and preserved cultural information. The Anishinaabeg (Ojibwe) constellation Gaadidnaway represented Mishipeshu, the great, malevolent spirit panther with serpentine features that dwelled at the bottom of the Great Lakes. The constellation rises in the winter sky and is overhead Lake Superior in spring. Traditionally, this was a sign that it was time to relocate from winter hunting camps to the sugar bush as well as to warn travelers not to trust the melting ice on the lakes.[8]

Like the men aboard *Le Griffon*, Indigenous people regarded spiritual intercession as an important part of prudent navigation. The sprinkling of tobacco on the water before embarking on a journey was regarded as a gesture of respect to the Manitous that lurked beneath the waves. A more serious offering would be the sacrifice of a dog. Seventeenth-century missionary to the Anishinaabeg (Odawa) Claude Allouez, SJ, reported that "during storms or tempests, they sacrifice a dog, throwing it into the Lake. 'That is to appease thee,' they say to the latter; 'keep quiet.'" Anishinaabeg (Ojibwe) embarking from Grand Portage onto Lake Superior placed offerings at the foot of Manido Gee-shi-gance, or Spirit Little Cedar, a gnarled tree standing alone at the tip of the point. In 1794 John Tanner was part of a ten-canoe flotilla that embarked on a Lake Superior traverse. After paddling out several hundred yards, the paddlers stopped and spread tobacco on the water while the leader said this prayer to the Great Spirit: "You have made this lake, and you have made us, your children; you can now cause that the water shall remain smooth, while we pass over in safety." The old chief then sang a "religious song" while they made the crossing. In Anishinaabeg (Ojibwe and Odawa) oral tradition, the lakes were the haunt of powerful creatures that controlled the motion of the water. One of the most popular oral traditions of the Anishinaabeg (the Ojibwe and Odawa) cultural hero Nanabozho told of his attempt to kill a great serpent that dwelled in the lakes. In an act of revenge, the serpent then sent a great flood that inundated all the land. Fortunately, Nanabozho was able to reconstitute the land. Another oral tradition told of Mishipeshu and its perpetual battle with the Manitous of the sky, the revered Thunderbirds. Mishipeshu would sometimes reveal himself in the form of a sudden fog or violent storm on the lakes. Pictographs of Mishipeshu have been found on the rock walls of several lakes, most famously at Agawa Bay on the north shore of Lake Superior. Such artwork may have originated as a warning to other travelers or as an attempt to appease the lake monster. The Anishinaabeg lived in close association with the Great Lakes. It was the source of much of their subsistence, and in their canoes they traveled many hundreds of miles on it. Nonetheless, their lore concerning Mishipeshu was a recognition that the lakes were an alien element. With all their skill as watercraft builders and open water navigators, they were not masters of the lakes. In making sacrifice and observing rituals they recognized that those broad waters were beyond their control. These traditions all serve to underscore that the Anishinaabeg saw the Great Lakes as a living entity with which humans had a relationship that could at least in part be managed through ritual respect and negotiation.[9]

Fur Trade Canoes

The Iroquoian and Anishinaabeg peoples of the Great Lakes shared their knowledge of the inland waterways and canoe navigation with the first Europeans who entered the region. It was only by adopting the technology and methods of the Indians that, first, the French and, later, the English were able to reach and exploit the resources of the inland seas. The canoe was the key to early European trade on the Great Lakes, yet few of the white men ever developed the skills necessary to build their own vessels. Most canoes used in the fur trade were made by Indian men and women. The same was true of the snowshoes and tobog- gans needed for winter travel. Lob trees were one of the route- finding techniques that the fur trade voyageurs adopted from the Indigenous people in the Great Lakes region. These trees were usually prominent pines that were located near the site of portages or channels that might otherwise be hard to locate. A nimble voyageur would climb the tree and lob off its middle branches, making the crown of the tree stand out and serve as a way-finding device. Lob trees were sometimes named in honor of individuals and their names would be carved on a lower por- tion of the trunk.[10]

Fur traders did eventually adapt the Indian canoe to one more suited to their purposes. During the eighteenth century, a particu- lar type of vessel known as a *canot du maitre*, or master's canoe, was frequently employed. These birch-bark craft were usually thirty-six feet long and up to six feet wide at their midsection. They could weigh up to six hundred pounds when wet but were capable of carrying three tons of cargo. Fur traders heading west from Montreal followed interior rivers west until they reached Lake Huron and thence to Michilmackinac, where they dis- charged their cargoes, or they continued further west to the depot at Grand Portage on Lake Superior. Traders operating out of Albany, New York, used the Hudson-Mohawk River route to

Lake Erie and then paddled west along the south shore of Lake Erie to Detroit. Canot du maitre usually went west in groups known as brigades of between three and six canoes. The lead canoe would have an expert guide, knowledgeable about the terrain and hazards to be encountered on the way. Voyageurs paddled from before dawn to dusk, taking a break every hour or so for a short rest, at which time the canoe men inevitably brought out their clay pipes for a short smoke. When measuring the distance between places, fur traders often used the number of pipe breaks from one point to another. One "pipe" was figured to be between ten and twelve miles. Canoe guides had in their head a mental map of the Great Lakes in which the distance from an island to a bay, from a good camping place to a portage, would be measured by the number of "pipes."[11]

Imperial Rivalries and Navigation

By the 1670s decked sailing ships like *Le Griffon* were built on the lakes to help facilitate the fur trade and to project the military power of France's colony on the St. Lawrence River. The maritime technology of the Europeans impressed Indigenous Americans. The name given to the French by the Montagnais of modern Quebec was *ouemichtigouchiou,* "a man who works in wood, or is in a canoe or vessel of wood." In the middle of the eighteenth century the French had a virtual flotilla on Lake Ontario, with four schooner-rigged ships each armed with brass cannon. Sometime before 1735 the French also launched their first ship to sail on Lake Superior. The vessel was built about seven miles above the falls at Sault Ste. Marie, and it has been described as a barque, meaning it had at least two masts, one of which was rigged with a square sail. This ship appears to have been in use for many years thereafter. Although the French devoted time and precious resources to outfitting a small number of Great Lakes vessels and they produced several accurate general maps of the lakes, they made no attempt to chart the inland seas or to develop navigational aids. Canoes continued to be the dominant commercial vessels on the lakes. On the eve of their expulsion from the region, the commander of Fort Niagara complained that his countrymen had never even circumnavigated Lake Erie let alone made "bearings of its shores, the depths of its bays, and the anchorages that occur."[12]

In 1760 the British Empire completed its conquest of New France and began a regime that would see an expansion of commercial exploitation of the lakes and the first steps in creating navigational aids on the Great Lakes. Within a year they had two vessels—the schooner *Huron* and the sloop *Beaver*—built for duty on Lake Erie and the upper lakes. In the decade that followed, five more vessels would rise from the stocks and cast off onto the lakes. These vessels participated in making soundings of the shallow waters of Lake St. Clair, which would long plague the movement of vessels north from Lake Erie to Lake Huron.[13]

A thread that runs through the entire history of Great Lakes navigation is the reluctance of saltwater sailors to take seriously the power of the inland seas. Sometime in the late 1760s, the British schooner *Gladwin* was lost on Lake Huron largely because her master obstinately refused to take the time to properly ballast the vessel. When caught in heavy weather, the vessel capsized and took the entire crew with her. James Fennimore Cooper captured this dangerous willful arrogance in his 1840 novel *The Pathfinder, or The Inland Sea*. Set on Lake Ontario during the French and Indian War, the hero is the young lake pilot Jasper Western, nicknamed Eau Douce (freshwater) by the American Indians. He escorts a veteran mariner from the ocean to Ontario's shores. On first glance at the lake, the saltwater man blustered, "Just as I expected. A pond in dimensions and a scuttlebutt in taste." When Jasper points out that it is impossible to see from one coast of the lake to the other, the mariner says: "The coasts of the ocean have farms and cities and county-seats, and in some parts of the world, castles and monasteries and lighthouses—ay, ay—lighthouses, in particular, on them; not one of all which things is to be seen here. . . . I never heard of an ocean that hadn't more or less lighthouses on it; whereas, hereaway there is not even a beacon."[14]

The complete lack of lighthouses on Lake Ontario, let alone the Great Lakes, was remedied in 1781. Since the early eighteenth century, the French had maintained a large limestone fortress near where the Niagara River enters Lake Ontario. At its core was an imposing two-story, limestone structure the French called "Maison a Machicoulis," which later became popularly known as "the French Castle." The British captured the fort in 1759 after a nineteen-day siege. The American Revolution should have brought the fort into the control of the new U.S., but British military authorities refused to relinquish control of their posts along the Great Lakes. For thirteen years the British used the base to build military alliances with Indian tribes along the young nation's northern border. In 1781 the British built the first Great Lakes lighthouse by constructing a beacon atop the "French Castle." The location was an important one for commerce because the fort was situated at the end of the portage trail around Niagara Falls. This pioneer navigational aid was likely illuminated by a whale oil lamp. The British were prompted to construct the beacon by the disastrous loss of the two-masted man-of-war *Ontario*, which foundered amid a Halloween night gale in 1781. The wreck cost the British their largest and most powerful vessel on the Great Lakes and took the lives of 130 men. The light was maintained by the U.S. Army when the U.S. finally was able to occupy the site in 1796 following the signing of Jay's Treaty. It went dark, however, in 1803. A year later the British established a new lighthouse near their new fort on the Canadian side of the lake. In 1822 Congress voted funds to reactivate the light and to construct a new wooden tower atop the French Castle. That lighthouse remained in service until after the Civil War.[15]

The Articles of Confederation government had no real sway over the Great Lakes frontier. The leaders of this first U.S. government, however, harbored great ambitions for the West; these were expressed in the Ordinance of 1785, which established a system for the survey and sale of all the lands in the public domain. In 1787 the Congress also passed the Northwest Ordinance. This act provided a structure of administration for the lands north and west of the Ohio River and created a formula by which this territory would be divided into new states that could enter the federal union on an equal basis with the original thirteen. The ordinance did much to shape the future development of the Great Lakes region. Famously, it outlawed slavery in the region, and it provided the first legislation on Great Lakes navigation. The ordinance stipulated that the navigable waters leading to the Mississippi and St. Lawrence, and the carrying places between the same, shall be common highways forever free, as well to the inhabitants of the said territory as to the citizens of the U.S., and those of any other States that may be admitted into the confederacy, without any tax, impost, or duty therefor.

This key provision recognized that the Great Lakes constituted an interconnected system of waterways in which all states of the republic and all U.S. citizens had a stake.[16]

The occupation of the Great Lakes forts by the U.S. in 1796 was the true beginning of U.S. navigation on the lakes. Fort Niagara, Detroit, and Fort Mackinac became outposts for the projection of U.S. power into the region and bases from which merchants could enter the region's bustling fur trade. The U.S. built two vessels for public use on the Upper Great Lakes—the brig *Adams* and the much smaller sloop *Tracy*. A third ship, the *Oneida*, was operated below the falls on Lake Ontario. The *Adams* and *Tracy* were essential in transporting troops and supplies to remote outposts such as Fort Mackinac at the straits between Lakes Michigan and Huron and Fort Dearborn at the site of Chicago. A small number of private vessels also plied the lakes, carrying cargoes of furs or salted fish to the east and bringing back food and trade goods.[17]

Commerce and navigation on the Great Lakes was severely retarded by the three-way struggle for control of the region among Great Britain, the U.S., and an alliance of western Indians that included elements of the Shawnee, Miami, Odawa, Potawatomi, and Ojibwe. The British goal was to protect their new colony of Upper Canada (modern Ontario), which was largely made up of Loyalists driven from their homes by the American Revolution. Their strategy for doing this at limited direct cost was by fostering the emergence of an autonomous American Indian territory in the Great Lakes region. With some skepticism of British reliability, the Indian leaders accepted British military aid, and between 1790 and 1794, the Indian alliance successfully repulsed U.S. attempts to assert control of the area south of Lake Erie. In one stunning engagement in 1791, the allied tribes utterly destroyed a large portion of the U.S. Army, which left close to one thousand dead on the battlefield. The U.S. did not recover until

1794, when at the Battle of Fallen Timbers they were able to defeat the alliance and force the first of a series of land cessions upon
the Indians. Hostilities flared again in 1811 when a new American
Indian alliance was created by the Shawnee leader Tecumseh. It
was smaller than the previous alliance but no less determined.
The U.S. entry into the War of 1812 was fueled in part by a desire
to crush Tecumseh by capturing Upper Canada and the Indian's
British base of support.[18]

The War of 1812 must be properly seen as a war for control of
the Great Lakes region, and the most important battles of that
war were fought on and near the inland seas. At the start of the
war the British quickly captured the U.S. warship *Detroit*, which
gave them command of Lakes Michigan and Huron and allowed
a small number of redcoats and a large number of Indian allies to
capture or destroy Fort Mackinac, Fort Dearborn (Chicago), and
Detroit. Both Britain and the U.S. created makeshift fleets to contest control of Lake Erie and Lake Ontario. These fleets were
made up of converted merchant ships and new and increasingly
larger warships constructed at shipyards on the lakes. The 1813
victory by the U.S. in the Battle of Lake Erie was one of the most
significant events in American military history because it allowed
the Americans to partly recoup their losses in the West and with
that their postwar territorial claim to much of the upper Great
Lakes. After that battle, an escalating race to build larger and
more powerful fleets ensued. The Royal Navy was by far the more
skilled competitor. It is fortunate for the U.S. that peace came in
1815, as the British were on the verge of sending into battle on
the lakes several ships of the line that mounted as many as 102
cannons. The war ended on the terms of *status quo antebellum*.
The British deserted their Indian allies, and the U.S. was able to
force upon the American Indian tribes land cession treaties and,
eventually in many cases, treaties of removal from the region.

The War of 1812 essentially removed the British-Indian barrier
to the expansion of the U.S. population and commerce into the
Great Lakes region. It also ensured that the Great Lakes would
remain divided between two emerging nations. In the half century that followed the war, the region was transformed from
being a remote and dangerous frontier into a heartland for both
the U.S. and eventually Canada. The legacy of the conflict that
raged across the Great Lakes from the time of the Washington

administration through to the end of the War of 1812 was that, more than any region of the new nation, the states of the Old Northwest had benefited from the exercise of federal power. It had taken a vast sum of blood and treasure to forestall the Indian confederacies and their British allies. The national government, in particular the army, was seen by the people of the region as an effective and reliable partner in frontier development. Significantly for latter sectional conflicts, the frontier south of the Ohio River benefited much less from direct federal support. Hence the politics of that region came to cherish state autonomy. As the antebellum period began, the vast Great Lakes borderland was open to exploitation, yet for its opportunity to be realized, the people of the region once again required the active engagement of the federal government. On the cusp of a transportation revolution, the watery wilderness required navigational aids and a maritime infrastructure.[19]

2

A Transportation Revolution on the Lakes

1789–1839

Samuel Ward was both surprised and upset. He had just skippered the first boat from the Upper Great Lakes through the Erie Canal to the Hudson River and finally to New York City. His vessel was a little twenty-eight-ton schooner named the *St. Clair*. Ward had sailed her from Detroit to Buffalo, where he took down the vessel's rigging and masts and then towed her up the canal with two horses he had brought with him. On reaching the Hudson, the vessel was rerigged and Ward proudly sailed into the greatest port city in the U.S. He expected a bonus or prize of some kind. He expected to be toasted and feasted. Instead he was presented with a bill. Ward had not calculated the toll charges on what was a historic passage. Putting aside his disappointment, Samuel Ward did what he did best—dickered with Gotham's merchants to get the best deal for his cargo of potash, furs, and black walnut lumber. On the return trip, he took a cargo of manufactured goods, salt, and several passengers at fifteen dollars a head. Back in Detroit he complained of his treatment by the people of New York but nonetheless counted out a $6,000 profit.[1]

The arrival of Samuel Ward and his little schooner in New York City was just a ripple of what would become a powerful wave of commercial traffic between the Atlantic coast and the Great Lakes region. Ward was emblematic of the rising tide of economic activity in the West and the growing importance of commercial activity in the American republic. Born in Rutland, Vermont, the son of a Baptist preacher, Ward gained his first experience on the lakes during the War of 1812 when he operated a small coasting vessel that carried supplies to U.S. forces along the shores of Lake Ontario. When peace came he headed west, first to Ohio and later to Lake St. Clair in the Michigan Territory. From a log cabin home in the wilderness, Ward operated a small sailing ship engaged in what was known as the "lakeshoring trade." Essentially, this meant that Ward sailed between Lake Michigan and Detroit in search of cargoes, brokered deals as he went, and risked a great deal as he entered uncharted waters. Sometimes he carried barrels of salted fish, at other times furs, and occasionally passengers. Little schooners like the *St. Clair* also functioned as floating stores. From his deck he sold flour, sugar, tea, gunpowder, and whiskey to isolated settlers. His voyages paid well enough that he was able to expand his operations by building a small fleet of some of the earliest commercial vessels on the upper lakes. Three new schooners slid off the stocks from his own shipyard.[2]

Ward, however, was not content to be a mere mariner. He was a restless Yankee who sought profit wherever it could be found. He planted orchards around his homestead and raised herds of cattle and swine. When chinking the walls of his log cabin home, he discovered pure clay and shortly thereafter erected a kiln and established a brick-making yard. He sold brick in nearby Detroit and also erected a large brick residence that he operated as a tavern. Money flowed into his hands from his ships, his sawmill, his shipyard, his brickyard, and his tavern. When he sailed for New York City in June 1826, Ward was consciously extending his web of commercial activities to an emerging national market. In the years that followed, he invested in steamboats and railroads and eventually retired as one of the first millionaires in the Great Lakes region.[3]

Captain Samuel Ward was one of thousands of American citizens in the large commercial cities of the East and on the fringes of the western frontier who participated in a profound transformation of their nation. When Samuel Ward was born in 1784, nearly all the new nation's 3.9 million inhabitants made their living from agriculture. The bulk of their harvest was reserved for home or local consumption. The limited merchant community largely focused on trading surplus U.S. agricultural produce to the West Indies. Eighty years later, when the nation was split by a ghastly civil war, its economic life had been vastly transformed. Most Euro-Americans still lived on farms, but the orientation of those farms had shifted from home subsistence to trade in national and even international markets. Instead of merely feeding their families, their harvest provided subsistence for millworkers in Manchester, England, or Lyon, France. Instead of bartering with neighboring farmers, they dealt with elevator operators and commission house agents. Thousands of farmers' sons found work in towns and growing cities that bustled with shops and factories churning out textiles, charcoal, iron, household goods, farm machinery, wagons, and weapons. Entire new "white-collar" professions had been created to protect patents on new inventions, to insure products being transported, to invest in expansive new factories, and to finance an ever-expanding network of canals and railroads. At midcentury the transformed nation now produced more than two billion dollars in goods and services and exported more than $400 million in produce and products.[4]

The Great Lakes region played a significant role in this transformation. It was made possible not merely by dynamic individuals such as Samuel Ward but also by an effective partnership between nascent state governments that emerged from the Northwest Territory and the federal government. Together they pushed a policy of settler colonialism that displaced the native people of the region and fostered the transportation improvements that transformed the region's maritime economy. Historians have dubbed the national economic transformation that took place between the War of 1812 and the Civil War as the "market revolution" because of the tremendous escalation of commercial activity during those years and the profound impact that this growth had on the nation's social, cultural, and political life. The historiography of the market revolution emerged in the 1990s as a healthy corrective to an overemphasis on the impact of Andrew Jackson's political leadership on the period. From a Great Lakes perspective, however, market forces were less important in the initial decades of the antebellum era than government-initiated transportation improvements. Beginning with the Erie Canal, the expansion of navigation and navigational aids played a significant role in the creation of a national market.

This is in keeping with historian Daniel Walker Howe's characterization of the era as a "communications revolution." Howe argues that there were greater improvements in communication during the thirty years that followed the end of the second war with Britain than in all the previous centuries. Inventions such as the telegraph and the railroad were truly revolutionary, yet when combined with the extensive development of canals, river and harbor improvements, and the deployment of steamboats on the nation's inland and coastal waters, it is clear that a revolution occurred in the movement of people, products, and the communication of information. What was new about an individual like Samuel Ward and his relentless pursuit of profit was not that he was involved in market relations but, rather, the ease with which he could pursue a wide variety of such relations from far-off Michigan. By 1839 the number of steamboats on the Upper Great Lakes had increased from one in 1825 to sixty-one, and there were thirteen improved Great Lakes harbors with lighthouses where ten years before there had been none. On the lake frontier, such changes were revolutionary.[5]

The concept of a "communication revolution" as opposed to a largely capitalist driven "market revolution" recognizes that governmental institutions played a profound role in the building of the first national commercial market. The period after the War of 1812 saw an unprecedented influx of state and federal funding into endeavors that on the surface appeared to benefit one area or region yet when taken altogether accelerated the movement of goods and services across the nation. Yet these endeavors came in the face of considerable political opposition and, in the Great Lakes region, were haltingly executed and insufficient to the needs of a rapidly growing commerce. Throughout the period between 1815 and 1865, a large number—often a majority—of Americans took their cue from Thomas Jefferson by articulating a desire for a small government with limited resources and power. The expansion of navigation and navigational aids on the Great Lakes took place amid a burgeoning market revolution and a bitterly contested struggle to extend a communication revolution to the shores of the inland seas.

The Lighthouse Act and the Ambiguous Legacy of the Founders

For the first half of the nineteenth century, the task of improving navigation conditions on the Great Lakes was beset by controversy and sectional division. The first sign of this political division was manifested in 1789 immediately after the establishment of the federal government under the U.S. Constitution. Only one week after the House of Representatives first met in session, the issue of lighthouse construction stirred up sectional disagreement. It began when James Madison of Virginia proposed a resolution to impose a tariff duty on foreign goods entering the U.S. Madison saw this action as an essential measure to raise funds for the operation of the national government. More specifically, he argued that the duties were necessary "for support of lighthouses, hospitals for disabled seamen, and other establishments incident to commerce." The issue, however, soon became much more complicated as legislators sought to amend the bill to meet the needs of their constituents. In particular, northern commercial states sought to include duties that would protect nascent U.S. manufacturers from more cheaply made foreign goods. Southern legislators, whose states had few manufacturing interests and relied heavily on imported goods, objected. As the legislation became more controversial, it was decided to separate out the issue of lighthouse construction from the legislation to tax imports.[6]

In July 1789 Congress debated a new bill for "the Establishment and Support of Light Houses, Beacons, and Buoys, and for authorizing the several States to provide and regulate Pilots." The bill was strongly backed by northeastern legislators whose states were deeply involved in maritime commerce and whose waters presented considerable challenges for navigation. At the time, there were numerous beacons or lighthouses along the

New England coast, yet south of Chesapeake Bay, there were only two along the southeastern shore. It was no surprise, then, that South Carolina's Thomas Tucker objected to the notion of federal control of lighthouses, and he proposed an amendment that would keep lighthouses under state jurisdiction. Using rhetoric that would become all too familiar, Tucker called federal control of lighthouses "an infringement of states' rights." Northern representatives countered with a more flexible reading of the Constitution by arguing that the document gave "the regulation of commerce to Congress," and therefore, it logically "conferred every power which was incidental and necessary to it." In the Senate, concessions were made to win southern support for the bill. These included leaving the regulation of river and harbor pilots to the states and a specific provision for the construction of a lighthouse in Chesapeake Bay. A late attempt was made to include a provision in the bill for the federal government to undertake the removal of obstructions from rivers, ports, inlets, and harbors. This provision, however, failed to win broad support, and the issue of river and harbor improvements would prove one of the most divisive in pre–Civil War America. On August 7, 1789, President George Washington signed the Lighthouse Act into law.[7]

The Lighthouse Act debate revealed a fundamental problem that would impede federal action to improve interstate navigation initiatives. The Constitution provides no specific provision for federal aid for internal improvement projects. In fact, a close reading of the Constitutional Convention minutes indicates clear-cut opposition to such an idea. Early in the proceedings, Benjamin Franklin and James Madison proposed provisions that would specifically empower the U.S. government to build roads, canals, and other improvements "to secure easy communication between the States." However, their motion was defeated by a sectional vote. On that occasion, it was New England that saw no need for canals and roads, and it was southern states that wanted better access to the West. Fortunately, that vote did not settle the issue. This was because some of the new nation's most important political figures were strong supporters of an enhanced system of interstate commerce and communication.[8]

As Madison's support for the Lighthouse Act suggests, the legislator did not give up his support for internal improvements because there was no specific constitutional authority for such action. In the *Federalist No. 14*, he argued that "intercourse throughout the nation" aided by "new improvements" was critical to holding a large and geographically diverse nation together. As president he called on Congress to create "a general system of internal communication and conveyance" and specifically pointed to proposals for major navigation improvements such as a canal between the Hudson River and the Great Lakes. Yet when the time came to offer federal support for the Erie Canal, Madison balked. Thomas Jefferson in his messages to Congress also cited the benefit to national unity from improved transportation, but reflecting his adherence to a strict interpretation of the Constitution, he also called for a "corresponding amendment" before action was taken to build canals or to improve waterways. The foremost of the "founding fathers," George Washington, was a vigorous advocate for navigational improvements. He had been deeply involved in efforts to drain Virginia's Dismal Swamp and to improve the upper Potomac River so that it might serve as a commercial connection to the Ohio River valley. In his 1796 Farewell Address to the nation, he warned against "geographic discriminations—Northern and Southern, Atlantic and Western— whence designing men may endeavor to excite a belief that there is a real difference of local interests and views." The key to avoiding this problem, he suggested, was "the progressive improvement of interior communications by land and water." Thus, the founders gave to the new nation a belief that internal improvements were critical to national unity, yet they had provided a Constitution in which the legality of federal support for such a program was at best ambiguous.[9]

The erection and maintenance of lighthouses along the nation's Atlantic coast was an early and important exercise in federal state building. Under the authority of the Lighthouse Act, Congress voted to expand the handful of colonial-era beacons it had inherited into a truly national system of navigational aids. Where most colonial-era lighthouses were erected to guide vessels to a particular port, the beacons of the new republic erected at Bald Head in North Carolina, Montauk Point in New York, and Cape Henry in Virginia were coastal lights located to aid trade between states and other nations. They represented the national government's pursuit of the general good. The lighthouses were located at sites remote from existing population centers. Building and maintaining a light at such locations exceeded the capability of the local communities or colonies that had erected earlier beacons. To international shipping, the beacons became obvious symbols of U.S. national sovereignty. To American citizens they were a sign of the credibility and stability of the new republic created by the Constitution.[10]

The First Lighthouses on the Great Lakes

Although the Lighthouse Act granted the federal government responsibility for lighthouse maintenance and construction, no action was taken on the Great Lakes until 1811. In that year Congress authorized the construction of two lighthouses at strategic locations along the Lake Erie shore. Where the Buffalo River entered Lake Erie a town had developed with much loftier aspirations than its low collection of log cabins would have seemed to warrant. Yet federal officials deemed that the settlement was the appropriate place to locate a navigational aid that would guide vessels to the head of the lake. A second lighthouse was approved for the mouth of Erie Bay on the Pennsylvania shore of the lake. The site where a narrow peninsula jutted out into the lake, like a broad semicircle, offered the promise of a sheltered anchorage. Unfortunately, a sandbar partly blocked its mouth. Nonetheless, a number of merchant schooners operated out of the bay. When war broke out with Great Britain, one of those schooner men, Daniel Dobbins, traveled to Washington, D.C., to impress upon the government the strategic value of the site. His mission was responsible for Erie Bay being selected as the site where Commodore Oliver Hazzard Perry built the bulk of the fleet that won for the U.S. mastery over the upper lakes in the Battle of Lake Erie in 1813. The danger of enemy action, however, prevented either lighthouse from being constructed until the war was over.[11]

It was not until 1818 that these two lighthouses were actually erected. It is impossible to say whether it was the Erie light or the Buffalo light that had the privilege of being the first U.S. Great Lakes navigation aid, and so the two have been forced to share the honor. They also shared the fate of many other pioneers in that being first did not make them particularly successful. The Buffalo lighthouse was a conical stone tower a mere thirty feet in height. The keeper's house was likely a log cabin. The weak beam of the light together with its low height soon drew the complaints of mariners. When the Erie Canal was completed, these objections were joined in chorus by canal boat operators who could not even see the light. In 1826 Congress ordered that a replacement be built. The Erie Bay light was lit in November 1818. It was a twenty-foot-high square stone tower. The light had a serious design flaw. It was erected on unstable ground and over time it began to settle at a dangerous angle. Despite this problem, it did remain in service longer than the first Buffalo light. It was not replaced until 1858.[12]

By the time the first two Lake Erie lighthouses were constructed in 1818, there were more than twenty commercial vessels operating out of makeshift ports on the U.S. shoreline. That year the first steam-powered vessel was launched on the upper lakes. *Walk-in-the-Water* was a 138-foot-long craft with huge paddlewheels mounted amidships. In her three years in service she proved very successful. Yet in 1821 the hazards of early lake navigation claimed her. As she neared the end of a trip from Detroit to Black Rock, New York, *Walk-in-the-Water* was beset by a gale. In vain her master looked for the beacon from the Buffalo lighthouse by which he might have been able to guide the vessel into the safety of the Buffalo River. Instead, they were driven by the waves onto the beach in front of the lighthouse. The crew was able to bring off all eighteen passengers without the loss of a life. The nearby keeper's house, with its large fireplace, provided a needed refuge for the drenched survivors. Before the storm abated, however, the pioneering steamboat was mortally damaged. The first Great Lakes lighthouse had proven useless to the ship, but at least it proved a shelter for the survivors. In short order, the steam engine was removed from the wrecked vessel and installed in a second steamer—the *Superior*. In 1824 a sister ship, the *Henry Clay*, was constructed, and between them the two vessels offered regular service to the burgeoning ports of Lake Erie.[13]

A third Lake Erie lighthouse was added in 1821 on a peninsula jutting into Sandusky Bay. The fifty-foot tower and its whale oil lamps were designed to help ships locate the superb shelter

Figure 1. The wreck of the steamer *Walk-in-the-Water* with the poorly sited Buffalo Lighthouse in the background. Painting by John Lee Douglas Mathies, 1821.
Source: J. B. Mansfield, *History of the Great Lakes* (1899), 601.

afforded by the bay amid the islands and points that would otherwise obscure its mouth. It was dubbed the Marblehead Lighthouse because of the peninsula on which it sits and from which its limestone was quarried. This lighthouse has proven one of the most durable American navigational aids, and it is the oldest beacon in continuous operation on the Great Lakes.[14]

Lake Ontario, which was closer to the settled parts of the republic, was the busiest of the Great Lakes. It attracted more shipping in the years before 1812 than the other four lakes combined. In the wake of the war with Great Britain, Ontario also experienced a boom in navigation. It was on its waters that the first two Great Lakes steamboats operated, the *Ontario* on the U.S. side of the lake and the *Frontenac* on the British side. Both were in operation by 1817. The early steamboats on the Great Lakes were among the first such vessels to see regular service on open water. Before this time steam vessels were seen as practical only as harbor ferries or river boats. The *Ontario* was actually disabled on its maiden voyage by the swells of the open lake that lifted the paddle-wheel shaft out of position, leading to important design changes. It was Lake Erie's *Walk-in-the-Water*'s ability to maintain a schedule and turn a hefty profit that fully demonstrated that steam power was well suited for the Great Lakes and other open waters.[15]

Lake Ontario received its first lighthouse shortly after the pioneering beacons on Lake Erie went into service. In 1820 the first light beacon location was Galloo Island near Sackets Harbor, the leading shipbuilding port on the lake. It was followed by towers at Oswego, Genesee River, and Sodus Bay.[16] Lake Huron received its first navigation aid in 1825 when a thirty-two-foot tower was erected near the site of a U.S. Army garrison—Fort Gratiot. The site was a crucial one, for it marked the place at the southern end of Lake Huron where navigators had to adjust to the narrow confines and swift-flowing water of the St. Clair River. The contract for building the structure was originally given to Washington, D.C., favorite Winslow Lewis, who farmed it out to a subcontractor with little concern for the quality of the construction. As a result, both the tower and the keeper's house were, in the words of an officer from the fort, "a miserable piece of workmanship." The foundation was inadequate, the mortar and stone were inferior, the tower was too low for vessels to see, and the site was poorly selected on land subject to flooding and erosion. After just three years the tower collapsed. A new, properly built structure was erected in 1829. A second Lake Huron beacon was erected at the far northern end of the lake, at Bois Blanc. The initial sixty-five-foot tower was almost as poorly sited and built as the Fort Gratiot light. In 1837, only eight years after it was first lit, the light tower collapsed. Safe navigation, however, required an aid at this location that marked the eastern entrance to the Straits of Mackinac, the focus of commerce on the Upper Great Lakes. A replacement was operational by 1838.[17]

The first lighthouse on Lake Michigan was not erected until 1831, and it suffered from the same shabby design and construction as had bedeviled the pioneer beacons on Lakes Erie and Huron. The site selected was Chicago, where streams flowing into the Mississippi River system were only a few miles inland. The site was, therefore, a magnet for fur traders and emigrating agriculturalists. Although there was no harbor, lake vessels brought between ten thousand and twenty thousand new people to the site every year. Finally, Congress approved a $5,000 appropriation for a lighthouse. The site selected was a lot owned by the government adjacent to the Fort Dearborn army base and near the mouth of the Chicago River. Not for the first or last time in Chicago history, an inept contractor was selected for the job and the tower collapsed only minutes after it had been inspected and approved as finished. A second lighthouse rose near the same place in 1832 and fortunately it proved more durable. The port towns of St. Joseph, Michigan (1832), and Michigan City, Indiana (1837), also received early lighthouses. It was not until 1839 that a lighthouse was placed within the critical Manitou Passage—the route followed by most ships destined for Chicago, Michigan, or Indiana ports. In that year a rather poorly designed lighthouse with a squat wooden tower was built to mark the southern entrance to the passage and the site of South Manitou Island's Crescent Bay—the finest natural harbor on Lake Michigan.[18]

Lighthouses reached Lake Superior much later than the sister lakes to the south. The falls at Sault Ste. Marie inhibited either sail or steam navigation on its cold waters. It took the development of copper mining in the region of the Keweenaw Peninsula and on Isle Royale to catch the attention of Congress. Commercial copper mining began in 1843 and within a year a boom was in progress. Ships were the only way to reach the mines and the only way to move copper to the market. However, there were only two such vessels, and one of them, the *John Jacob Astor*, was wrecked in a storm at Copper Harbor in 1844. In 1847 Congress appropriated funds for two lighthouses on the lake, one at Copper Harbor and another at Whitefish Point. Yet when renowned journalist Horace Greeley made a trip to the region in 1848, the lights still were not built. Traveling on a steamer recently portaged around the falls, he was horrified by the navigational dangers on the lake. In an editorial in the *New York Tribune*, he complained:

> On the whole lake there is not a lighthouse nor any harbor other than such holes in the rock-bound coast as nature has perforated. Not a dollar has been spent on them. Congress has ordered a lighthouse to be erected at Whitefish Point and has provided the means; a Commissioner has located it; every month's delay is virtual manslaughter; yet the executive pays men to air uniforms

at the Sault [Army garrison Fort Brady] in absurd uselessness, and leaves the lighthouse until another season.

Goaded by Greeley's golden pen, the Whitefish Point Lighthouse was completed the following year. It guarded a stretch of lake-front that would eventually be known as the "graveyard of Lake Superior" or the "shipwreck coast." By 1848 it had already earned a reputation as a dangerous stretch of water because of the fierce north winds that whipped up waves from across the entire expanse of the lake and lashed the shores of the bay. Like many of the first lighthouses built on the other lakes, these two early Superior beacons were not long in use because of construction inadequacies or problems with siting.[19]

The expansion of lighthouses along the Great Lakes reflected a national commitment to the development of that inland maritime frontier. This entailed an implicit recognition that the Great Lakes were indeed inland seas and that they required the same navigational aids as shores lashed by the salted wave. Unfortunately, federal support for a maritime infrastructure that went beyond lighthouses to include charts, channel improvements, and harbors would be fraught with controversy. As it was, the administration of U.S. lighthouse expansion, especially on the lakes, was deeply flawed. In the 1790s when the new republic built lighthouses on the Atlantic Seaboard, they received the highest level of close scrutiny by Alexander Hamilton, secretary of the treasury—who reviewed plans for the site and the design of the tower himself. Three decades later when early Great Lakes lighthouses were constructed, the task was left to the administration of a small and incompetent bureaucracy.

Early Lighthouse Administration and Design

Even where there was a federal consensus on supporting Great Lakes maritime infrastructure, such as lighthouse construction, the execution of the national will was greatly retarded by the lack of an effective bureaucracy. For most of the early national period there were more congressmen in the capital than there were civil servants. Hence the execution of both executive orders and congressional legislation suffered, often with tragic results, such as in enforcing treaties with American Indian tribes. Worse still, the heads of executive departments operated with little direct supervision either by Congress or the president, and once entrenched in office often operated as free agents. This was the case with Stephen Pleasonton, the fifth auditor of the Treasury Department, wherein resided the Lighthouse Bureau. He was titled "General Superintendent of Lights," although he was not a maritime man, nor did he have any engineering expertise. He owed his position to a grateful James Madison, who rewarded Pleasonton for saving the Declaration of Independence from the torches of the British invaders in 1814. He was an accomplished clerk and bookkeeper, and as such he was generally more concerned with reducing costs than paying attention to the needs of mariners. Charles Wilkes, a distinguished naval officer and friend of Pleasonton, noted that although he was "not a bright man" he "was intimate with most of the leading men of his day," whom he courted with frequent dinner parties at his house. His social cache was enhanced by his wife, who was "a great belle" and who helped him attain "much influence in the intricacies of the Govt." In fairness to the man, he was also charged with overseeing all accounts of the State Department and the Patent Office. When Congress legislated for a new lighthouse, Pleasonton's bureau let the contract, set the budget, and usually provided some type of specifications, seemingly in the form of a drawing. Of course, the actual construction took place far from the seat of government. Eventually Pleasonton directed that local collectors of customs take responsibility for supervising the building of new lighthouses. While that would be fine in Boston Harbor or Chesapeake Bay, there were few treasury agents on the remote Great Lakes. Hence, in many cases, there was no supervision of the contractor's work at the site. Pleasonton's administration does not seem to have taken into account the frontier setting of the Great Lakes. The region around Lakes Erie, Huron, and Michigan was sparsely inhabited in the 1820s, and Superior was beyond the pale of settlement well into the 1840s. Workman were in short supply, let alone skilled artisans, and supplies always a problem.[20]

Over and above shoddy construction, there were serious design flaws with early Great Lakes lighthouses that became apparent shortly after their construction. Besides Pleasonton, the

Figure 2. Stephen Pleasonton, fifth auditor of the
United States and head of the U.S. Lighthouse
Administration, 1820–51.
Source: Library of Congress.

individual who deserves blame for the construction problems
was his friend and associate Winslow Lewis. Unlike the Treasury auditor, Lewis was an experienced mariner, a point he emphasized by styling himself "Captain Lewis." He had the New
England Yankee gift for practical invention, self-promotion, and
avarice. He claimed to have invented an improved light for navigational aids, and in 1812 he conned the Congress into purchasing
his patent rights and contracting with him to place his lights in
all existing American lighthouses. Not content with this accomplishment, the enterprising Lewis then snared a contract to supply
all coastal lighthouses with whale oil for the new lights and to
inspect each one on an annual basis. Pleasonton extended Lewis's
hold over U.S. lighthouses even further in 1820 by awarding him

a large percentage of the contracts for building new lighthouses. He quickly subcontracted out most of these jobs, pocketing a fine profit and giving little thought to the resulting lighthouse. Lewis was awarded the original contract for the miserably built Fort Gratiot lighthouse on Lake Huron, which had to be replaced after a mere four years in service.[21]

Winslow Lewis's poorly built light towers were only a small part of the problems he caused the Lighthouse Bureau. Every lighthouse was outfitted with his lamp. The basic design of the lamp was sound, in large part because it was the work of Frenchman François-Pierre Ami Argand and was widely used in European lighthouses. Lewis's version, however, was an imperfect copy. The lamp required parabolic reflectors to amplify light. The key to a parabolic form is that it must be curved inward in such a way as to focus the light source to maximum effect. Lewis's reflectors had a "wash basin" shape, unlike a parabolic form (such as a modern satellite dish) and, hence, American lighthouses projected a very weak beam. Lewis's reflectors were made even worse because of the thin sheets of metal he used, which became misshapen over time, and his stingy veneer of silver would quickly wear off. Sailors who visited European waters noted the difference and complaints by the hundreds were sent to Congress. Yet no action was taken.[22]

Lewis's inferior lighting system was the standard in American lighthouses for forty years, in part because of his cozy, if not corrupt, relationship with auditor Pleasonton. A shameful lack of congressional oversight further ensured that there was a basic inattention to proper engineering in lighthouse tower design during the first half of the nineteenth century. In Europe, where the input of both engineers and mariners was incorporated into the design, it was noted that on coastlines with a high elevation, a lighthouse need not be very tall since topography made the light visible from far out to sea. Where the coastline was low lying, however, as it was along so much of the Great Lakes, it was essential to build tall light towers to ensure that ships could see the light from a considerable distance. In 1810, for example, the British erected the Bell Rock Lighthouse. It was an impressive feat of engineering for the day, not least because it was erected on rocks just below the surface of the North Sea. Since the lighthouse was built at sea level, engineer Robert Stevenson built the tower 115 feet high. This ensured that mariners could see the light from as much as thirty-five miles away. The light tower Winslow Lewis designed at Fort Gratiot was sited only a few feet above water level, but the tower he built was only thirty-two-feet high. America's first two Great Lakes lighthouses were even shorter. These defects all but ensured that early Great Lakes lighthouses were inadequate to meet the needs of lake commerce and would have to be replaced.[23]

Even the short towers built in the 1820s and 1830s were an engineering challenge. Most early lights marked immediate navigational concerns like harbor entrances and reefs.[24] Most of the early light towers were masonry, constructed of rubble or coursed stone and, later, brick.[25] The use of such a heavy material for a tall, narrow structure required two essential design features. The first was a firm foundation. This was essential for supporting the massive weight of the tower. Pleasonton usually issued specifications that called for a firm foundation; however, too often unsupervised contractors chose sites that were close to the water on ground that was soft. The 1818 lighthouse at Erie was built on a four-feet-thick elliptical foundation of crushed stone, mortar, and lime. The foundation proved totally inadequate because quicksand lay beneath it. As a result, the structure began to settle at a dangerous angle, which necessitated the construction of a new tower. The Fort Gratiot lighthouse was built on soft ground, with only a log foundation. The foundation was highly important because of the second requirement of early lighthouse design: thick walls. These early masonry towers were typically built in the form of a frustum, a shape created by cutting off the top portion of a cone shaped structure.[26] This addressed the structural issue of increased weight pressing down on the lower walls as height increased. Therefore, the lower walls had to be thicker in order to bear the burden. The Marblehead Lighthouse on Lake Erie, the oldest remaining such structure on the lakes and one of the few from the 1820s that was well built, is twenty-five feet in diameter at its base with walls five feet thick. The foundation stands upon solid limestone. The tower tapers upward to a diameter of twelve feet with walls two feet thick. As the federal government took the first halting steps toward creating a maritime infrastructure on the lakes, it was betrayed by cronyism and absence of engineering expertise.[27]

Life at Frontier Lighthouses

The first lighthouse keepers on the Great Lakes often manned stations on the nation's far frontier fringe. Of course, from the eighteenth century into the twentieth, a remote and isolated location has fed the romantic image of life at a light station. Yet some of the first Great Lakes lighthouses were not only set in topographically remote locations but in borderland situations where even national sovereignty was in question. The Fort Gratiot Lighthouse was erected only a decade after the War of 1812 in a region solely inhabited by Canadians of dubious loyalty to the republic and Anishinaabe (Ojibwe and Odawa) who had fought fiercely to protect their homelands from U.S. control. The Bois Blanc Lighthouse at the northern extremity of Lake Huron was built in 1829, and it was the only evidence of U.S. sovereignty in the region between Mackinac Island and Fort Gratiot, a distance of more than two hundred miles. Lighthouse keepers had to be exceptionally resourceful and independent.

Eber Ward, the brother of the shipping entrepreneur discussed at the start of this chapter, was named the first keeper of the Bois Blanc Lighthouse. For three years he lived there with his son, who helped him tend the light. Every month or so, a ship would stop by the lighthouse with their mail and occasionally a resupply of lamp oil. Most of their time was spent harvesting wood for heating and cooking, which they brought to the site by dog sled. In summer and fall they ensured their food source by catching and salting barrels of whitefish and trout. A small library of historical and scientific books allowed Ward to tutor his son. Ward tended the Bois Blanc beacon for eight years without ever being absent from his post for a night. When his son left the island to begin a life as a mariner, Ward was joined by a daughter. It was Emily Ward who in 1837 rescued the station's lamps and reflectors when a storm battered the poorly built and positioned tower. As cracks formed in the structure, she risked her life making several trips up to the top and came down with the lamp only moments before the structure toppled into the lake.[28]

Typical of the image of dreary isolation endured by early Great Lakes lightkeepers is an 1840 account of the Thunder Bay Lighthouse. That year the businessman Frederick J. Starin of Montgomery County, New York, went west on the steamboat *Constellation*. One spring evening as the shadows began to fall on the lighthouse at Thunder Bay Island, Starin disembarked long enough to inspect it. Ten years before, Congress had authorized a light to be placed here. The rubble stone tower was poorly constructed, and the keeper had to fight a solitary battle using his own funds to keep it upright. Starin appraised the stark, windswept scene. The station included only a conical tower, a dwelling, and a few acres of cleared ground, presumably a garden. "The rest of it," he wrote, "is one dense forest, and really a bleak, lonely, desolate place." For the next twenty years the same could be said for the entire coast of Lake Huron north of Saginaw Bay.[29]

The first lighthouse keepers on the Great Lakes came from a wide range of backgrounds. Ward had been a farmer, a logger, and an Indian trader and was experienced in small boat navigation. His experience in coping with frontier conditions was in stark contrast to George McDougall, the first official keeper at Fort Gratiot. McDougall was an attorney whose only qualification for the job were his political connections. Overweight and in poor health, he seems to have thought the posting would be an easy, secure salary sinecure. When he found that the job would entail repeated trips up to the top of the tower to trim the lamps, refill the oil, and clean the reflectors, he hired a man to do that part of the job, while he used his connections to supplement his income with an additional federal office, customs collector. Other early keepers won their positions by their past services to the government. The first keeper at the Marblehead Lighthouse on Lake Erie was a Revolutionary War veteran who had settled nearby. After nine years on the job, he died in the cholera epidemic that swept the West in 1832. His wife, Rachel Miller Walcott, who had already been helping with the duties of keeper, was awarded the post in her own right. She became the first female keeper on the Great Lakes. The Barcelona Lighthouse on Lake Erie was originally staffed by a local minister. Sometimes even men with actual maritime experience were named to the post, such as Captain John Bone at Erie Lighthouse.[30]

The Erie Canal

No single event, no invention or innovation, had as significant an impact on the Great Lakes region as the building of the Erie Canal. At the start of the decade of the 1820s the Great Lakes were part of a far northwest frontier. They were important to the nation because they were an area vulnerable to foreign or American Indian threat, but they were peripheral to the main thrust of the U.S. economy. Westward settlement, save for Ohio's Western Reserve lands that lured Connecticut Yankees to Lake Erie, largely accelerated into the Ohio and Mississippi valleys and lands drained by their tributary waters. Emigrants crossed over the Appalachian Mountains in Conestoga wagons to Pittsburgh, where they could purchase a flatboat to float down the Ohio River to new lands in the southern portions of Ohio, Indiana, Illinois, and the newly admitted state of Missouri. In each of these states, settlement was concentrated along the rivers. Families from the upland South followed the Tennessee and Cumberland Rivers into the western country. They brought to the new states of the West the individualism, cultural attitudes, political orientation, and in some cases the social institutions of the South. Northern Illinois and Indiana, far Michigan, and Wisconsin were the domain of American Indians and fur traders. These areas had the image of being remote and were unappealing to a people eager to get ahead economically. Folklore tells of what happened when the town of Chicago on Lake Michigan's cold shores tried to sell bonds to the Shawnee Town Bank, Illinois's first chartered bank housed in an imposing Greek revival stone edifice in far southern Illinois. The bank's officers sent their northern brothers packing with the taunt that no place so far removed from the Ohio River could ever amount to anything.[31]

The Ohio and Mississippi valleys were the loci of western expansion because their waters provided the means to receive manufactured goods and to ship agricultural harvests. Euro-American pioneers may have been willing to abandon settled homes and endure the trials of building new farms and businesses in the West, but most wanted more than a subsistence life style. They sought a chance to prosper. To do so they had to be able to market the products of their labor. For western farmers that meant having an affordable means of shipping agricultural produce to markets that would pay a good price. In 1800 it cost one hundred dollars to ship a ton of grain by wagon overland for three hundred miles. A single barrel of flour cost two dollars to ship one hundred miles overland, while the cost on water transport was a mere twenty-five cents. At best a loaded wagon could make a mere twenty miles a day. This meant that the time and costs for overland transportation were prohibitive, particularly for such high-volume products as corn or wheat. The development of steamboats on western waters made the rivers all the more vital as the conduit of commerce, and soon the decks of these vessels were stacked high with sacks of grain. Pittsburgh, Cincinnati, and Louisville became the great ports on the Ohio River, while St. Louis, where the Missouri, Mississippi, and Ohio Rivers join together, became a major trans-shipment center. New Orleans, at the great river's mouth, thrived as the outlet to the sea. The primacy of river navigation economically tied the growing West to the South.[32]

In 1817 construction began on a canal that would unite the Hudson River with Lake Erie. The goal was to force a water route west from New York City where nature had never intended. Yet if the Empire State and city were to grow with the nation, a connection with the West was required. Thomas Jefferson, the inventor and spinner of western dreams, pronounced the idea of building the world's longest artificial waterway "little short of madness." His successor, James Madison, vetoed a bill that would have provided partial federal funding for the canal. The mammoth project became New York's and New York's alone. Although the cost was estimated to be more than $20,000 per mile, the state raised the $7 million necessary to begin construction. The undertaking was by far the New World's most ambitious engineering project. A difference of five hundred feet of elevation separated the Hudson River and Lake Erie. This meant building eighty-three separate locks to lift the boats up and down as needed. Nonetheless, the work was conducted expeditiously and the canal was finished in 1825, with its official opening in 1826.[33]

Within two years of the canal's completion, a revolution in western settlement was underway. Hundreds of families from New England and New York took passage on the canal boats to Buffalo and from there on schooners and steamboats headed for the upper lakes. Unlike the solitary movement of a family from the southern backcountry to the Ohio River frontier, the Yankee emigrants came in large groups, often settling as a community on the Illinois prairie or in the valleys of Michigan. They brought with them a way of life centered on Congregational churches, wheat farming, township government, and public education. On the canals and ships, they often encountered European

Figure 3. Erie Canal at Little Falls.
Source: Library of Congress.

immigrants from the Low Countries, the German states, or Scandinavia, many of whom also traveled in multifamily groups that helped the newcomers overcome the intimidation of an alien geography and language. These large parties of pioneers usually had a specific destination already scouted out by an advance guard. Timothy Flint, the roving New England minister, observed this migration. In the wake of the canal, "more than half of the whole number of immigrants now arrive in the West by water. This remark applies to nine-tenths of those that come from Europe and the northern states." A federal official traveling the canal in 1827 was amazed by the surge of people and economic activity along the waterway. "It is not possible for me to convey any adequate idea of the wealth which floats upon the canal; nor the advantages which are experienced from it by the people who live upon its borders, and those more remote settlements throughout the entire region of the north-west."[34]

The opening of the Erie Canal was followed by a boom in lake shipping. Prior to the canal, Lake Michigan commerce was estimated "not to exceed the cargo of five or six schooners." Lake Erie was only slightly busier with just forty commercial vessels.

By 1833 a traveler noted that Lake Erie was a "sea of busy commerce." The amount of tonnage devoted to shipping increased from a few thousand tons before the canal to 24,045 tons in 1836 and 29,995 tons just a year later. Ships that carried the migrating farmers devoted their return trips to bringing the golden grain harvest of the West to Buffalo. A skeptical Scottish traveler in 1833 was shocked by the way vessels were "literally crammed" with people and possessions. "Steers, cows, horses, wagons—in short we were like the followers of an invading army, and every one building castles in the air." The uncomfortable Scot did not appreciate that a new waterborne frontier was created, with schooners playing the part of the storied covered wagon of western myth. Throughout the 1830s, sailing ships dropped anchor at river mouths all along the Michigan and Wisconsin shores. Livestock was thrown overboard to swim ashore while husbands and crew members waded to land with wives or children carefully balanced upon their shoulders. If the vessel had a small boat or captain's yawl, a more dignified landing could be afforded the women. Ships were fundamental to the founding and growth of towns like Racine and Milwaukee in Wisconsin or St. Joseph and Grand Haven in Michigan. It was ships that carried the settlers hundreds of miles into the wilderness, and it was ships that gave them the commercial connection to the outside world that allowed them first to survive and then to thrive.[35]

The Yankee and northern European settlers who flocked to the West via the Erie Canal brought with them what some historians have called "a culture of progress." This notion was a fusion of the republicanism of the American Revolution, the religious legacy of Puritan New England, and the personal ambition of a people unfettered by Old World traditions. This vision manifested itself in the belief that they had a responsibility to improve the world—that could mean attacking social problems or reshaping the physical world. "Where God left gaps in the Appalachian Mountains," historian Carol Sheriff has written, "he intended humans to create their own rivers." Making the world a more prosperous place for themselves and their fellow citizens was the responsibility of virtuous republicans. Where the task was too great for an individual, then it should fall to the government for the commonweal. These ideals, validated by the fantastic success of the Erie Canal, became deeply rooted in the political attitudes of the people taking ships to new homes in the Great Lakes states. It was the root of a conflict that would grow between the South and the new Northwest over the proper role of government in American economic development.[36]

What some people regarded as a "culture of progress" could look to others as crass avarice. Margaret Fuller, a gifted writer and literary critic, was herself a daughter of New England, yet she lamented the spirit of acquisitiveness that dominated her fellow citizens. In 1843 she took passage on a steamer from Buffalo to Chicago. "The people on the boat were almost all New Englanders, seeking their fortunes." As she got to know her fellow passengers, she was struck by the degree to which they were motivated by material gain and seemed not to appreciate the history-making adventure before them. "It grieved me to hear these immigrants, who were to be fathers of a new race, all, from the old man down to the little girl, talking not of what they should do, but of what they should get in the new scene." She lamented: "It was to them a prospect, not of unfolding nobler energies, but of more ease and larger accumulation." This was the negative stereotype of the "Yankee" and one that would later loom large in the sectional conflict.[37]

The Yankee wave also broke uncomfortably over the centuries-old multicultural world of the Great Lakes fur trade. Trade in furs continued, and in some cases actually increased, but the communities of American Indians, mixed-blood, French, or Scottish traders were gradually swamped by the noisy new arrivals. Towns like Detroit, Green Bay, St. Joseph, and Chicago had all been founded on an acceptance of cultural difference, a blend of Indigenous values and mercantile self-interest. Less than a decade after the opening of the canal, a large percentage of the Indians south of the lakes had been forced onto a "trail of tears," and in many cases the French Creole traders who had helped found the nascent cities of the region joined them in exile.[38]

A Safe Harbor:
Federal Support for Great Lakes Settlement

The Erie Canal was an outstanding example of what government action, in that case state government action, could do to stimulate economic activity in the largely undeveloped interior of the new U.S. It was, however, by no means the first such intervention. More than perhaps any other region of the country, the Great Lakes region had been the beneficiary of publicly supported, particularly federally supported, development. These actions took the form of critical interventions in the realm of military, diplomatic, economic, and navigational affairs.

When George Washington was sworn in as the first president under the 1789 constitution, the most daunting of his many challenges lay along the Great Lakes frontier. Not only was this area illegally occupied by the military forces of Great Britain, but those foreign troops supported the independence of a powerful alliance of Great Lakes American and Canadian tribes determined to oppose U.S. sovereignty in the region. It was only after a series of humiliating setbacks that U.S. sovereignty was established. Early forts were established at Detroit and Michilimackinac in 1796 and Chicago in 1803—only to be swept away with the comeback of British and American Indian forces at the start of the War of 1812. The end of that conflict led to the reopening of those forts and the establishment of new garrisons at Saginaw Bay (Fort Gratiot, 1814), Green Bay (Fort Howard, 1816), and Sault Ste. Marie on Lake Superior (Fort Brady, 1822). The primary function of these forts was to provide security for American merchants and settlers, but the garrisons did much more. They were a critical instrument of state formation. As historian Francis Paul Prucha, SJ, demonstrated, they brought U.S. law into the region, stimulated the frontier economy by supporting local business, functioned as the first post offices, and undertook critical improvements to roads and communication. An example of the role that military posts played in helping stimulate economic development can be seen in the actions of the Fort Dearborn garrison. In 1828 Major J. Fowle made the first attempt to build a harbor at the head of Lake Michigan when he ordered his men to dig a channel through the sandbar that blocked the mouth of the Chicago River. The effort led to a fifteen-foot-deep passage from the lake into the protected waters of the river. Unfortunately, in this case, the improvement was only temporary as wave action shortly clogged the opening with sand once more.[39]

The presence of military garrisons was a security blanket for the settler colonialists who threatened the sovereignty and survival of the Indigenous people of the Great Lakes region. After 1815 federal officials, urged on by Euro-American settlers, forced repeated land cession treaties on the American Indians. The passage of the Indian Removal Act in 1830 by the Andrew Jackson administration made the ethnic cleansing of the area east of the Mississippi River national policy. At bayonet point the prairies and oak openings of Illinois, Indiana, and southern Michigan were cleared of American Indian peoples. This action, coming in tandem with the opening of the Erie Canal, was a powerful stimulus to the rapid spread of Euro-American farms in the region. Commerce and navigation on the lakes expanded in response to opportunities afforded to Euro-Americans by the federal government's erasure of most American Indian tribes in the region. Only the Anishinaabeg (Odawa and Ojibwe) tribes located along the northern fringe of the lakes and away from the mainstream of settlement were able to adopt strategies that allowed them to avoid removal.[40]

The rapid occupation and commodification of the lands lost by the Indigenous people was facilitated by another critical federal government action—the rectangular system for the survey and sale of the public domain. Authorized by the Ordinance of 1785, the public land survey system cast a precise geometric grid over all the nation's western lands. This was originally conceived by Thomas Jefferson to overcome the chaos of the metes and bounds system of erratic land survey and sale. That system had left land titles compromised by overlapping claims and lengthy lawsuits. Jefferson wanted a system that would lay the foundation for a West inhabited by yeoman farmers who could develop their land secure from competing claims. The sale of land surveyed by the federal government would become an important source of revenue to support the government. The federal surveys started from a baseline laid down in eastern Ohio and proceeded West across all the Great Lakes states. When the system expanded into southern Illinois and Indiana, it was no small inducement for Kentucky famers, such as Abraham Lincoln's family, for example, to leave the uncertain land tenure of the Bluegrass State and purchase secure federal land titles. Both small farmers and rich eastern land speculators liked the new system. The latter also appreciated the orderliness of a system that allowed them to know what land they were buying, where it was, and at what price.[41]

Military garrisons, American Indian removal, and an efficient land survey system all combined with the Erie Canal to stimulate an immigrant flood into the Great Lakes region. Navigational aids were a constituent part of a federal commitment to state formation in the region. The pioneer lighthouses of the 1820s and 1830s were the first phase of the federal commitment to improve the safety and efficacy of shipping. In the wake of their construction came a chorus of requests for the construction of harbor facilities on the lakes. There are only a handful of natural harbors on the Great Lakes, and those were often far removed from the growing towns of the region. The would-be port cities of the Great Lakes tended to be founded where rivers entered the lakes. Buffalo lies on the Buffalo River. Cleveland was born at the mouth of the Cuyahoga River. Toledo was founded at the mouth of the Maumee River. Chicago is at the mouth of the Chicago River, and to the north, Milwaukee is at the mouth of the Milwaukee River. The trouble with these locations as ports were the sandbars that blocked the entrance to the rivers where they met the lake. If the sandbars could be cleared, the river mouths would make excellent harbors and the commercial prospects of each of those locations would be secured. The issue of sandbars was prevalent at scores of other smaller towns along the lakes. Communities tried numerous ways to overcome the problem. Temporary solutions could be achieved, as the Fort Dearborn garrison had done during high-water conditions by simply digging a channel through the bar. However, the natural movement of sand borne by lake waves would soon rebuild the barrier. Where several feet of water flowed over the bar, other expedients were possible. One was to hitch a vessel to several teams of oxen on the shore and have them pull the ship over the bar. Similarly, a ship could have its anchor carried over the bar in a small boat and deposited in the harbor. The crew would then use the capstan to pull the vessel toward the anchor and over the bar. Frontier self-sufficiency, however, could only do so much. None of these methods were practical for regular commercial purposes and all were dependent on special and fleeting environmental conditions.[42]

What was needed was engineering expertise and a considerable amount of money to fund construction, both of which were in short supply at frontier ports. Buffalo, New York, the furthest east of the nascent lake ports and closest to eastern financing, led the way in harbor development. The town was locked in rivalry with Black Rock, New York, for selection as the western terminus of the Erie Canal. To beat out their rival, Buffalo citizens demonstrated considerable initiative and planned to build a pier that would prevent sand from blocking the mouth of the Buffalo River. In 1819, they were helped greatly by a loan from the State of New York. The project was completed by 1821, and Buffalo was made the canal terminus. Buffalo's bootstrap effort went forward because they could secure a loan from the state, which had a vested interest in making the Erie Canal a success. Other would-be lake ports lacked that kind of leverage and instead were reduced to sending appeals to the federal government.[43]

By the early 1820s Congress was beset with appeals for help from across the country to build roads, harbors, and canals and to clear rivers of obstacles. As the Erie Canal neared completion, the idea that Thomas Jefferson had thought was "madness" began to look inspired, and boosters scrambled to secure federal support for similar endeavors. Politicians argued over the constitutionality of lending federal assistance to such requests. Heirs to Thomas Jefferson's vision of a national government of narrowly constrained powers felt that such projects were unfair and unconstitutional because they took money from one state and used it to benefit another. Another faction took the opposite view. Led by Henry Clay of Kentucky, they argued that a series of transportation projects across the country helped draw the nation together and improved the general prosperity. This latter position won out in 1824 when Congress passed the General Survey Act. This legislation authorized the president to order studies to be made of roads and canals "of national importance, in commercial or military point of view, or necessary for the transportation of the public mail." The wording was important, as the reference to military necessity and the public mail tied the measure to powers granted to the federal government under the Constitution's defense and commerce clauses. While nothing was said about harbor improvements in the bill, President James Monroe went ahead and used the bill to authorize U.S. Army engineers to conduct surveys of harbor improvements that were needed on the Great Lakes. Erie, Pennsylvania, was one of the first sites selected, and on the engineer's recommendation Congress allocated funds to build structures to open a deep passage into Presque Isle Bay.[44]

When John Quincy Adams was sworn in as the new president in March 1825, he intended to use the General Survey Act as a springboard for a broad program of wise investments in the nation's transportation infrastructure. In his annual address to Congress, he called for a broad systematic plan. What he got instead was an omnibus bill allotting $86,000 to twenty road, canal, river, and harbor projects. It was not all that Adams wanted, but it temporarily broke the congressional logjam, and funding flowed to Great Lakes harbors, including Buffalo, Cleveland, and St. Joseph on far Lake Michigan. The need was acute on all the lakes, but it was particularly frustrating on Lake Erie since that body of water had the most upper lakes traffic. A traveler on the steamboat *Niagara* from Buffalo to Detroit in 1828 was dismayed to find that the only way for passengers to get ashore on Lake Erie was for them to disembark from the steamer onto small boats or scows that could get over sandbars that obstructed harbor mouths. Passengers were "thus landed from the *Niagara* at Dunkirk, Erie, and Ashtabula"; but when the steamer reached the mouth of the Cuyahoga River, where there was no Cleveland harbor, it was impossible to make a landing. Strong winds had kicked up the water, making it too rough to attempt a disembarkation via small boats. When the steamer reached its next stops at Huron and Black River the same thing happened. Passengers for those destinations "were obliged to remain on board, trusting to have better luck on the downward voyage." At Cleveland, the swampy entrance to the Cuyahoga River was both difficult to locate and beset by a sandbar that prevented entrance to a vessel drawing even as little as thirty inches in the water. As early as 1816, settlers there tried and failed to construct works that would keep sand away from the river mouth. In 1825 the U.S. Congress authorized a $5,000 appropriation to build a pier six hundred feet out into Lake Erie. The pier was supposed to block the flow of sand along the shore and keep a deepened channel open. The project failed and a second pier parallel to the first was built. The problem persisted until 1828 when the piers, combined with channel work, opened the river mouth.[45]

Lake Ontario had a fine natural port at its eastern end in Sacket's Harbor. Along the southern shore of the lake in New York State, there were few other locations so blessed. Army engineers were called in to help lakeside towns reach their maritime potential. Where lighthouses had earlier been built, piers and dredges were added. In 1828 a comprehensive survey of the lakeshore was made with a view to determining the most promising harbor sites. Oswego, Genesee, and Sodus all received early attention. Lake Ontario, however, had lost its lead in inland seas' commerce following the opening of the Erie Canal. Even the Welland Canal around Niagara Falls only partially integrated Lake Ontario ports with the stream of east-west commerce. More important in this regard was the 1828 completion of a canal that linked Oswego with the Erie Canal and federal improvements to the town's harbor. Lake Ontario ports such as Sacket's Harbor and Oswego were able to lobby successfully for more than their share of internal improvement funds because they could play the national security card and remind Washington how important the lake marine was in the War of 1812.[46]

Requests for federal harbor improvements were motivated by more than economic development or national security. The safety of crews and cargoes was the reason for navigational aids. Lighthouses were useful in helping mariners accurately assess their position on the lake and for warning them of some of the hazards lurking beneath the waves. Just as important, if not more so, was the safety issue: the lighthouse showed the way to a place of refuge. Safety was a particular problem on Lake Michigan. The northern third of the lake is filled with islands and peninsulas. These land formations presented many navigational challenges, but in a storm it was theoretically possible to find a sheltered anchorage in which to ride out the weather. The southern portion and larger area of the lake, however, is devoid of islands and the shoreline offers a largely uniform and low relief appearance. The normal wind pattern is from the north or west. When a gale strikes, it has two hundred miles of open water in which to build ship-shattering waves. "The total absence of harbors round this southern extremity of the lake has caused the wreck of many a vessel," observed Charles Latrobe in 1833. He was an English traveler who noted with unease the remains of wrecked ships along the dune-covered shore of the lake. He recognized the cause, that "the action of the storm from the northward upon such an expanse of fresh water is tremendous; and from the base of the sand hills, and the utter solitude of this coast, lives are seldom if ever saved."[47]

In 1826 St. Joseph, Michigan, one of the oldest settlements along the dangerous southern shore of Lake Michigan, received a congressional appropriation, but it was too meager to do more than effect a temporary harbor. By 1828 General Charles Gratiot of the Army Engineers reported to Congress that there were forty-four river and harbor improvement projects underway on the Great Lakes. None of these projects, however, included Chicago, where makeshift efforts to create a harbor had floundered. For the hundreds of pioneers brought by ship to the town each day, it meant the necessity of keeping an eye on the western horizon for any sign of dark clouds. A sudden lake storm might destroy their vessel as they awaited the small row boats and skiffs that would bring passengers and cargo across the sandbar and into the shelter of the Chicago River. It was not until the spring of 1833 that Congress finally approved a $25,000 appropriation to clear the sandbar and create a true harbor. That summer the schooner *Austerlitz* arrived with supplies and workmen, and construction began on works that would make it possible for ships to enter the Chicago River.[48]

The saga of trying to make a port out of the Chicago River reveals the tremendous challenge faced by the government as it tried to improve navigation on the Great Lakes. In 1823 U.S. Army Major William H. Keating warned the government that "the extent of the sand banks, which are formed on the eastern and southern shore, by the prevailing north and northwesterly winds, will . . . prevent any important work being undertaken to improve the port of Chicago." Nonetheless, Congress had authorized a generous land grant to the State of Illinois to stimulate the construction of a canal that would unite Lake Michigan at Chicago with the Mississippi River system. A harbor at the terminus of lake navigation was essential, and so the army went to war with nature. Unfortunately, it could only command a very feeble force. Laborers were scarce in the West, and those who were available demanded double the wages paid in the East. Men skilled in the use of the forges and pile drivers needed to construct piers were unavailable altogether. Once men were retained they had to be housed and even provided with bedding in this frontier location. Lumber needed for the piers was available but only at exorbitant prices that forced the army to detail teams of men into the hinterland to harvest and transport oak logs. Money was in short supply because the government deposited funds in banks that were hundreds of miles away from the work site. Hence the project barely began before the $25,000 appropriation was exhausted. Committed to the project, Congress sent Chicago another $70,000 over the next two years. The work continued at a snail's pace, and the project managers requested and received $40,000 more in March 1837. The two piers jutting out from the mouth of the Chicago River and the dredged channel to Lake Michigan were finally completed in 1838 after a final infusion of $30,000. By that time hundreds of vessels were making regular use of the new harbor. Captain James Allen, who supervised the project, warned Washington that despite all that was done sand was accumulating against the north pier at an alarming rate: "This being the only shelter for a distance of more than 300 miles, . . . the greatest solicitation is felt for its continued improvements and permanent security by all interested in extensive navigation on this lake." The federal government had just invested more than $165,000 to create the first harbor on Lake Michigan, and it was warned that more costly work would be required to keep it open. In the wake of the Chicago experience, the federal government moved slowly to improve other harbors on Lakes Michigan and Huron.[49]

Projects on Lake Erie also drove home the point that harbor improvements absorbed cash like a sponge. In 1829 an army engineer's survey floated the possibility of creating a much-needed harbor as a refuge at the western end of the lake. In 1830 a wooden breakwater was constructed to create a sheltered anchorage in La Plaisance Bay. Within a year, autumnal storms wrecked the structure. A larger, stronger breakwater replaced it in 1835. Within two years it was so battered by ice and waves that it was, in the words of one army engineer, in "a progressive state of dilapidation."[50]

As the federal government took its first steps to build a maritime infrastructure for the Great Lakes frontier, it also took several important diplomatic initiatives that would have a far-reaching impact on inland seas navigation. The Great Lakes had been the

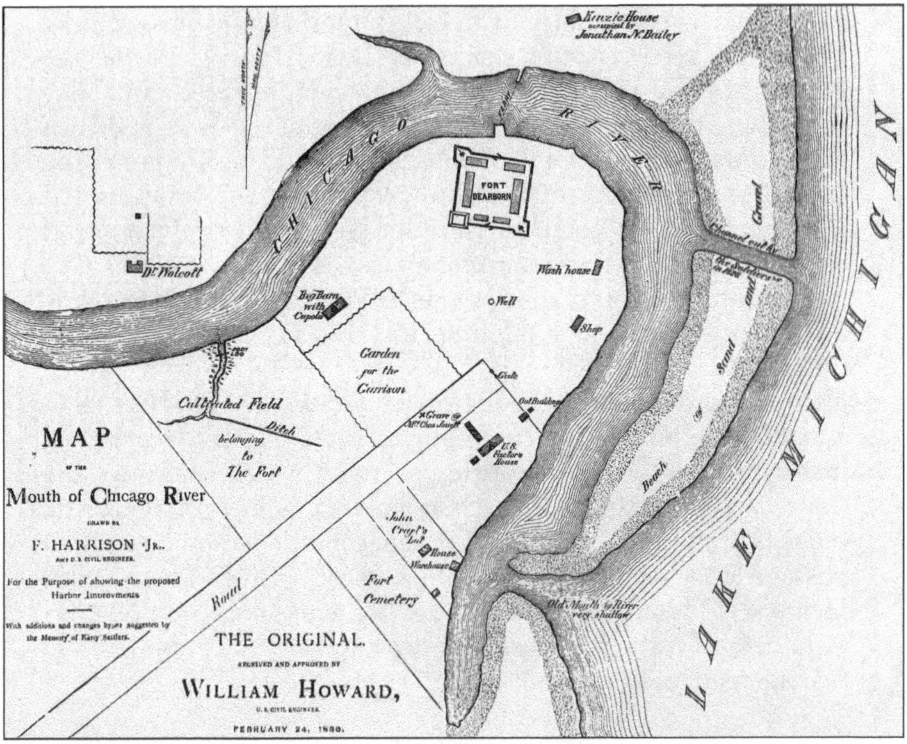

Figure 4. Early attempts to force a harbor entrance through the sandbar at Chicago.
Source: Chicago Maritime Museum.

principal seat of war when Great Britain and the U.S. clashed in
1812. America's goal at that time was to conquer Canada and
add it to their expanding territory. That ambition was easily frustrated by the British, and the new republic was fortunate not to
lose its share of the Great Lakes. It had been the naval victory on
Lake Erie in 1813 that allowed the Americans to snatch stalemate
from the jaws of defeat. Yet it was a fool's game in the long run to
challenge the might of the Royal Navy, even on inland waters, in
the nineteenth century. Hence it was a wise move for Secretary
of State James Monroe to secure an agreement with the British in
1817 to severely limit the number of warships each nation could
operate on the Great Lakes. This created parity, prevented a
costly arms race, and freed U.S. funds for infrastructure development. Nagging issues, however, still lingered between the two
powers sharing the lakes. Among these was the exact location of

the border. The boundary from Lake Ontario to the head of Lake Huron had been carefully delineated by joint survey parties between 1819 and 1821. Uncertainty, however, lingered until 1842 concerning the boundary in the Lake Superior region. The British claimed that the international boundary should pass along the St. Louis River at what is now Duluth, while the Americans argued for a border as far north as Thunder Bay. Fortunately, a broad compromise was reached on many issues that divided the two nations, and the boundary line was fixed north of Grand Portage. For reasons unknown at the time, this was a boon for the U.S. as the generous settlement of the Lake Superior line ensured that the great iron ore ranges in the region fell on its side of the border— a fact that would have a huge impact on Great Lakes maritime history. In the spirit of compromise, the Americans granted the Canadians the right to use the navigation channels on their side of the Detroit River while Great Britain conceded a similar right of passage to the Americans on the St. Lawrence River. These agreements were bundled into what became known as the Webster-Ashburton Treaty, an important step on the road to cooperative management of the inland seas.[51]

The Canal Craze

The example of the wildly successful Erie Canal and the boosterism of President John Quincy Adams inspired Americans to envision a broad network of interlocking waterways. Virginians called for a canal from the Potomac to the Ohio River, while Philadelphians planned a waterway from their city to Pittsburgh. The fact that the Appalachian Mountains stood in the way of both projects dampened neither enthusiasm or fund-raising, and construction began on each. The economic calculations behind these schemes were blinded by the dazzling chimera of the Erie Canal's finances. The $7 million cost of the canal was paid off with toll fees by 1832, and canal revenues went on for many years to fund almost the entire budget of the State of New York. Canals appeared to be surefire economic development engines and potential money-making machines. Between 1816 and 1850 the number of canal miles in the U.S. increased from about one hundred miles to close to thirty-eight hundred. Britain's Canadian colonies, dismayed by how New York's artificial river had diverted the commerce of the Great Lakes from their natural channel on the St. Lawrence River, hastily built a series of canals around the Lachine Rapids near Montreal and undertook the even more daunting task of building a canal around Niagara Falls. The Welland Canal connecting Lake Ontario with Lake Erie opened in 1829. Yet even this waterway acted to siphon trade away from Canada. Many grain ships that used the Welland to bypass Buffalo and the Erie Canal headed for Oswego, New York, not Canadian ports. From Oswego, they could use an extension of the Erie Canal to ship wheat to New York City.[52]

Great Lakes states were particularly swept up in the current of canal mania. Ohio led the way with two major canals. As early as 1816 Ohio's governor Thomas Worthington proposed a waterway linking Lake Erie and the Ohio River. However, it was not until the Erie Canal was a reality that Ohio legislators approved construction. The first canal was to follow the Scioto and Muskingum River valleys to link Cleveland with the Ohio River. The second waterway was to connect Toledo with Cincinnati. By 1825 more than two thousand workmen labored on these ambitious schemes. When cost escalated and threatened to stop construction, the federal government stepped in with a generous land grant that provided the revenue to complete the waterways. The canals proved particularly important to Cleveland and Toledo, which gained sizeable hinterlands in the interior of the state because of their access to water transportation with the East Coast via the Erie Canal. The system was very much a work in progress for many years, with feeder canals added over time, until the state could boast more than one thousand miles of artificial waterways.[53]

Indiana would not be outdone. It had barely achieved statehood before it dreamed up what would become the longest canal of the era—the 468-mile Wabash and Erie Canal. The upper portion of the waterway required the cooperation of the State of Ohio, for Indiana intended to use Toledo as its Lake Erie terminus. Out of fear of competition from its neighbor's project, Ohio dragged its feet on approving the easiest portion of the right-of-way until 1843. The hard part of the project began in northeastern Indiana, where a channel had to be grubbed out and excavated through the hardwood forest to the headwaters of the Wabash

River. As many as five thousand men labored on the canal at one time. Yet progress was slow, as the work stopped and started. The financing of the endeavor was eccentric, if not fraudulent. Segments of the waterway were opened gradually, but completion was elusive despite three generous federal land grants. The waterway was not fully functional between the Ohio River and Lake Erie until 1853. The canal never yielded anywhere near enough in tolls to pay for its cost, but it did provide important commercial stimulus to much of the interior of Indiana.[54]

Illinois's venture into canal speculations had nearly as checkered a history as that of the Hoosier State. In 1818 when Illinois applied for statehood, it successfully had its boundary adjusted thirty-one miles to the north to ensure that a canal connecting Lake Michigan with the Mississippi valley would be entirely within its boundaries. An Illinois and Michigan Canal was a dream older than the state itself. Boosting the state's efforts to build the canal was Abraham Lincoln, then just a young state legislator. He helped craft the bill that got construction started in 1836. When the national economy crashed in 1837 and the state teetered on the edge of bankruptcy, Lincoln struggled to keep the project alive. Construction stopped and restarted, and its planned deep cut was dropped in favor of a more modest excavation. Finally, in 1848 the project was completed, but by that time a railroad paralleled its right-of-way. Nonetheless, the waterway was an important conduit for the great harvests of grain and lumber that made Chicago the metropolis of the West.[55]

The building of these extensions of navigation had a major impact on the economy of the Great Lakes region. While many canal projects such as the Erie and Wabash failed to meet the unrealistic expectations of their boosters, all the canal projects contributed to the growth of the region. The mere promise of a canal attracted settlement and local investment that otherwise would have gone elsewhere. Construction brought a flurry of economic activity and a wave of workers to the canal areas. The federal land grants further stimulated the movement of people to the region. Finally, the completed waterways reduced shipping costs for commercial activity and increased the value of property that lay within a day's travel of the right-of-way. The canals were a powerful example of the spirit of progress that flowed west from the Erie Canal. Along with the lighthouses and harbors that were constructed along the Great Lakes, the canals were the embodiment of a commitment by the people of the region to join in commercial union with the developed states of the East Coast. They had moved to a frontier region, but they had no intention of remaining peripheral in economic, political, or cultural life. The region of the country known as the remote "Northwest" was making the first steps toward becoming the nation's "heartland."

3

The Era of Bad Feelings

1839–1860

May 1840 came in like a lion, whipping up the waters of frigid Lake Michigan and devouring vessels caught on its broad unbroken expanse. On May 1, a northeast gale drove the stout steamer *Champlain* to her doom. Neither anchor cable nor engines pumping for all they were worth could prevent her from being driven ashore and smashed to pieces by the heavy surf. The daring intervention of the schooner *Minerva Smith* saved all aboard the doomed steamer, although the cargo, worth $10,000, was a total loss. Elsewhere out on the lake the spring storms took a heavy toll. The steamer *Governor Mason*, on her maiden voyage, was driven onto a sandbar at the mouth of the Muskegon River and caught fire. Between the flames and the pounding waves, she was a total loss, with an unknown number of lives lost. The schooners *Memee*, *Drift*, and *Victory* all suffered severe damage but managed to stay afloat. A Milwaukee businessman, disgusted at the losses, wrote to Congress, "There has been enough property lost within the last ten days on Lake Michigan, to have built three good harbors." He bitterly added "what a pity" the lost ships were not "loaded with Senators and members of Congress."[1]

By 1840 people living along the Great Lakes were disgusted with the federal government. No funds had been allocated for harbor improvements since 1838. Merchants in burgeoning lake towns like Milwaukee, Racine, and Kenosha in Wisconsin and Muskegon and St. Joseph in Michigan were being economically stymied by the lack of safe harbors. In 1840 there were forty-eight steamboats on the Upper Great Lakes, representing an investment of $2.2 million. Mariners who made their living on those steamboats as well as on the 250 sail vessels were particularly and colorfully vocal. One sailor later recalled a master "who had achieved notoriety in these waters in the early days for his profanity, . . . expressing his fervent hope, when he had a U.S. Senator aboard as a passenger, that he might run into a gale to convince the legislator of the hazards of inland navigation." There was only one fully developed harbor on the lower part of Lake Michigan. Even that harbor, at Chicago, was regarded by sailors to be "in wretched condition," with little in the way of "lights and Buoys to guide the mariner."[2]

The "wretched condition" all across the broad northern lakes was the result of sectional politics and antifederalist ideology. The U.S. government, born in 1789, began life riven by competing political philosophies. Federalists advocated a strong national government exercising all powers not specifically delegated to the states of the republic. The antifederalists opposed the idea of a national government that dominated the states and demanded an interpretation of the Constitution that limited the federal administration to only those powers specifically enumerated. These differences led to the nation's first party system, the Federalists versus the Republicans. This lasted until James Madison left the presidency. Madison and Thomas Jefferson had been leaders of the Republican Party. But Madison's retirement and a weakening of the Federalist Party organization created an opportunity for a period of political rapprochement. From 1817 to 1825 President James Monroe presided over what people at the time called the "Era of Good Feelings" as party divisions all but disappeared and a new spirit of nationalism animated the federal government. The initial expansion of Great Lakes lighthouses, navigational aids, and harbor improvements took place in this cooperative atmosphere. The administration of John Quincy Adams continued and boldly expanded the commitment to national prosperity stimulated by federal investments in internal improvements. Unfortunately for Adams, however, "good feelings" among the nation's leaders—at this point all members of the Republican Party—evaporated due to the heated opposition of Andrew Jackson and his supporters. Jackson felt he had been cheated of the presidency in the disputed election of 1824, and he did everything he could to undermine Adams. He rallied support to his cause by espousing the antifederalist rhetoric of Jefferson and Madison and opposing Adams's internal improvement programs.[3]

As president, however, Andrew Jackson loved executive power too much to fully follow the antifederalist rhetoric he espoused in opposition. He used his executive authority to build his base of support through patronage and the careful support of internal improvements. In 1830 he made a great show of vetoing an extension of the National Road, known as the Maysville Road, claiming such improvements were the province of state and local governments. Yet at the same time, he repeatedly signed legislation that authorized harbor improvements on the Great Lakes and river-clearing projects on the Mississippi. Jackson did this on a selective basis because the development of those regions appealed to his nationalist sentiments while at the same time built allegiance to his newly formed Democratic Party. Jackson focused his antifederalism on the Bank of the U.S., which he set about systematically destroying. Unfortunately, that action and his ill-advised handling of federal financial resources caused a major national banking crisis and widespread depression. Known as the Panic of 1837, it hit just after Jackson left office. Martin Van Buren inherited the mess Jackson had created, although as vice president during "Old Hickory's" second term, he had helped create the conditions for the five-year depression. The public certainly blamed Van Buren for the nation's woes, which made him desperate to bolster his position. To do so, the native New Yorker courted the support of southerners. He did this through tariff policy and by slashing spending on internal improvements. Van Buren had always treated internal improvements inconsistently, motivated by political expediency. But during his presidency, it became an article of faith of the Democratic Party that federal support of harbor or canal projects was unconstitutional. From 1840 until the Civil War, every national Democratic Party platform included the following language: "Resolved, That the constitution does not confer upon the general government the power to commence and carry on, a general system of internal improvements."[4] Southern support for this was solid because a government that could aggressively develop the country's economy might gain the power to attack slavery in the states.

Martin Van Buren was booted from the White House in the 1840 election that featured the famous "Log Cabin and Hard Cider" campaign. The Whig Party, which had formed in reaction to the antifederalism of Jackson and Van Buren, nominated the victor in the 1811 Battle of Tippecanoe, William Henry Harrison. Such was the enthusiasm for the Whig's proimprovement candidate that Oliver Newberry, the so-called Admiral of the Lakes who owned the largest fleet of lake vessels, had each one of his boats fly a banner with the party's slogan, "Tippecanoe and Tyler Too." Unfortunately for the Whigs, Harrison caught a serious cold at his inauguration, and with a little help from his doctors, he was dead less than a month after taking office. Worse still, his vice president, John Tyler of Virginia, was a former Democrat who held strong states' rights views and who soon turned his back on the Whigs. Only in June 1844, when Tyler was struggling to create a third-party candidacy for himself, did he sign several small harbor improvement bills in a vain effort to win the support of lake states. Thereafter, presidential opposition to improved navigation continued.

Fighting the Political Current

During the 1840s congressmen from Great Lakes states were inundated with testimonials from constituents desperate to secure aids to navigation. At the close of the 1842 shipping season, Eber Brock Ward, who as a boy helped his father operate the Bois Blanc Lighthouse on Lake Huron, wrote to Michigan senator William Woodbridge "on behalf of our suffering commerce." Ward first went before the mast as a cabin boy, and he matured into a successful mariner. He was master of the steamer *Huron*, a vessel owned by his uncle, Sam Ward, which he sailed between

Buffalo and Chicago carrying large numbers of immigrants bound for the prairies of the West. Writing on behalf of the "over 4,000 men employed in navigation," he complained about the "frequent distressing shipwrecks on Lake Michigan" and the "want of a few good harbors on that lake." Ward regarded as "indispensably necessary" improvement at three harbors in particular: Chicago, Milwaukee, and St. Joseph. In addition to dredging, these harbors required beacon lights on their piers. "The arrivals and departures of steamboats at Chicago the past year are upward of 480, and St. Joseph 260, besides a great number of ships, brigs, and schooners, arriving and departing daily freighted with the agricultural products of the most fertile portion of the United States."[5]

In referring to the agricultural products of the West, Ward was attempting to demonstrate that the request for navigation improvements on the Great Lakes was not a local issue but one of national significance. In the past, national leaders such as George Washington and, later, John Quincy Adams and Henry Clay had argued that citizens deserved a government that was responsive to their needs. What they got instead under Jackson and the Democratic Party was a government that was beholden to wealthy planters and that rejected the pursuit of the public good in favor of unleashing the pursuit of private gain. But what ideologues in the East did not understand was that in the Great Lakes region, private interests required public expenditure to thrive. Eber Brock Ward, for example, was as much of a capitalist as any man. In later years, he would own the largest fleet of ships on the lakes, and become a prominent real estate investor and one of the founders of the modern steel industry in the U.S. Yet in 1842 he was only a young man on the make. He could build and master a ship. He could attract large numbers of immigrant passengers to embark with him. What he could not do, however—what no individual businessman could do—was construct a harbor, build a lighthouse, or chart shoals and reefs. Such improvements would increase the profitability of his shipping investments and make travel safer for his passengers. Absent those improvements, he did the Jacksonian thing and pursued his private self-interest. He operated less profitably and less safely, all the while looking to change the political dynamic that turned a blind eye to the broader public good.[6]

In the wake of the ascendency of the anti-improvement Democrats, Great Lakes area people and politicians tried to make do as best they could. In 1839 Captain Thomas Jefferson Cram was appointed as the U.S. Army engineer's "head of harbor improvements on Lake Michigan." He and his assistants surveyed harbors for Milwaukee, Kenosha, Manitowoc, Sheboygan, and Kewanee in the Wisconsin Territory and Calumet in Illinois. President Van Buren, however, ensured that funding was reduced to a rare trickle, a policy followed by John Tyler as well. In April 1840 two schooners attempting to load cargoes at Milwaukee were driven ashore by a gale. "They now lay high upon the beach," editorialized the *Milwaukee Sentinel*, "a striking and forceful illustration of the necessity of an appropriation for the improvement of our harbor." Just a year earlier four people drowned trying to row out to an anchored vessel because there was no harbor. An attempt to fund improvements by private subscriptions among Milwaukee citizens fell short of what was needed. In 1842 the town's newspaper, in an effort to shame the government, offered to loan the federal government the money to begin harbor improvements. Finally, in 1843 Wisconsin's territorial representative in Congress, backed by editorials and petitions from Chicago to Buffalo, managed to wrangle a modest $30,000 appropriation. The town's joy, however, was short lived. Captain Cram insisted the best he could do with the money was improve the natural mouth of the Milwaukee River. The work allowed a ship to enter the river, but it then had a mile of narrow, sinuous river to navigate before it could reach the town. Such a passage was difficult for steamboats but impossible for schooners, which made up the bulk of the lake marine. In disgust, Milwaukee businessmen built a pier from the sandbar downtown a quarter of a mile out into the lake. It allowed ships to dock near the town, but only in fair weather conditions. Kenosha and Racine also received a modest appropriation when Milwaukee did, but little could be accomplished in a single season of work.[7]

Communities along the Upper Great Lakes resigned themselves to having to bootstrap a path to safe navigation. Milwaukee, Racine, and Chicago all undertook independently funded and executed projects. Between 1843 and 1851, Racine used taxes and private donations to invest $43,000 to improve its harbor although it was only a town of six thousand residents. Milwaukee wrangled a modest $15,000 appropriation in 1851. The project was budgeted at $90,000, so the town raised an additional $50,000 on its own to get the job started. Chicago was outraged in 1854 when four ships sank after trying and failing to enter its "improved" harbor. The army engineers were without funds or authority to address the problem. The Chicago Board of Trade understood that unless the harbor was opened, their grain exchange would soon be shuttered. They appealed to Secretary of War Jefferson Davis to allow the city to borrow the army engineers' steam dredge to clear the river mouth of sand. Davis refused. In an act of rebellion that rankled the future Confederate leader, the Chicagoans seized the machine anyway and opened their harbor. Far to the east on Lake Ontario the same problems prevailed. Oswego's harbor, which had only been partially improved in the 1830s, remained marginally functional only because private enterprise stepped up to fund necessary work. Vermillion, Ohio, long sought a lighthouse to mark its harbor entrance. Before one was finally authorized in 1847, the town's mariners drove posts into the water from which they hung oil lamps. Smaller towns on the Lake Michigan frontier despaired of ever getting federal aid. At Manitowoc, Two Rivers, and Sheboygan in Wisconsin private piers were built out into the lake. These were commercial endeavors and both farmers and vessel masters had to pay a hefty premium to make use of their facilities. They were useful only in good weather, and any skipper tied up there kept a wary eye on the horizon if he wanted to keep his ship from ruin.[8]

The collapse of federal support for internal improvements hit the development of Lake Superior commerce particularly hard. The St. Mary's Falls blocked the passage of vessels from Lake Huron to the northernmost lake. A handful of ships had been moved around the falls by means of log rollers, but this was hardly the way to unlock the region's mineral wealth. Almost as soon as Michigan became a state, it had attempted to set in motion the building of a canal that would open Lake Superior to navigation by lake vessels. In March 1837 the new state legislature funded an engineering study. With that in hand they went to Congress the following year but failed to win legislative support. Undaunted, the state committed $25,000 to begin the canal. It also tried a new approach to Congress, this time asking not for money but for a land grant of one hundred thousand acres. The

Figure 5. The original lock of the Sault Ste. Marie Canal, 1855.
Source: Library of Congress.

Congress had earlier made such grants to the Illinois and Michigan Canal and to the Erie and Wabash Canal, so Michigan had reason to be optimistic. It was, however, summarily rejected. Even the Senate's great supporter of internal improvements, Henry Clay, rejected the proposal, referring to the Lake Superior canal as "a work beyond the remotest settlements of the U.S., if not in the moon." It was not until the 1850s that Congress could be persuaded to act. Ship owner Eber Brock Ward and other businessmen spent the winter of 1850–51 in Washington, D.C., lobbying for federal support. The Michigan delegation floated a bill for a $500,000 federal appropriation only to see it scuttled by southern opposition. Only when Congress had before it specimens of copper and iron ore from the Upper Peninsula of Michigan were legislators persuaded to make a 750,000-acre land grant to support construction.[9]

While the federal land grant stimulated the Sault Ste. Marie Canal project, it was carried to completion in keeping with the Jacksonian commitment to private enterprise. The State of Michigan hired a company made up of some of the largest New York financiers and Democratic Party insiders to manage the excavation. In return, they would receive the entirety of the vast 750,000-acre land grant. The effect was to turn over huge portions of the public domain to a private corporation. The investors were able to choose whatever acres they wanted from public lands anywhere in the state. They chose very wisely and secured most of the best pine lumber and mineral lands in the state, eventually reaping millions of dollars as their reward. Fortunately, within two years, the canal was completed. The first ship passed through the locks in June 1855 and Lake Superior became an integral part of the Great Lakes commercial system.[10]

Evolution of Great Lakes Ships

The unimproved and frontier conditions that prevailed on the Great Lakes shaped the way ship technology developed along the inland seas. This was particularly true of sailing ships. Early vessels on the Great Lakes were merely copies of designs perfected on saltwater. Shipbuilders on the inland seas adopted sloops and schooners, both fore-and-aft rigged ships, the former with a single mast and schooners with two or more masts. Both types of vessels were popular for coastal trading along the Atlantic Seaboard. Also put into use were brigs (a two-master rigged with square sails) and brigantines (a two-master with the fore sail square-rigged and the aft sail fore-and-aft). The *Niagara* that Oliver Hazzard Perry sailed to victory on Lake Erie was a brig. Over time, vessels rigged with the fore-and-aft sail proved the most popular. The reason for this was twofold. First, fore-and-aft sails were set from a stout wooden gaff that projected from the mast parallel to the hull. Such a sail could be raised from the deck by hauling on lines. This meant that fewer people could set this sail in a shorter amount of time than it would take to deploy a square sail, which hung from a spar high on the mast and could only be set by sending several men aloft to work in concert. Setting a sail or taking it in quickly was an advantage on the enclosed waters of the Great Lakes. Second, sails set from the deck required fewer crew members, an obvious advantage from a business point of view.[11]

As schooners were coming to dominate the lake, marine shipbuilders along the lakes began to tinker with their design to best meet the needs of these dangerous frontier waters. One of the most important of these adaptations was the use of a retractable keel or drop centerboard. Keels help a vessel stay on course. A centerboard was a portion of the keel that extended several feet into the water, giving a vessel much greater stability. With a centerboard, a small sailing vessel could confidently set more canvas and lean with the wind yet not risk capsizing, because the extension under the keel balanced the weight of tall masts. A vessel with a centerboard was likely to sail much faster than one with just a regular keel. Large cargo vessels enhanced their stability with ballast or by carefully loading a heavy cargo. Centerboards improved their handling by stiffening their resistance to the wind. Vessels tacking their way up the lake would inevitably drift sideways. Centerboards substantially reduced the amount of drift, allowing a master to keep true to his intended course. Unfortunately, what made the centerboard so effective in the open sea became a liability when in shallow waters of shoals, rivers, and especially unimproved harbors. Centerboards drastically increased the draft or the depth drawn by a loaded vessel. On the eve of the American Revolution, John Schank, a Royal Navy captain, began to experiment with a retractable centerboard that could be deployed in deep water when at sea and then pulled up as a vessel entered a harbor. Some of his early prototypes were tested on the Great Lakes, and by the War of 1812 the device had been perfected.[12]

In the early 1850s, a shipbuilder in Manitowoc, Wisconsin, used the retractable centerboard as a key element in his clipper schooners. William Wallace Bates was among the most influential shipbuilders in nineteenth-century America. Born in Nova Scotia and raised in Maine, he learned the art of shipbuilding from a master of the craft, his father. He moved to the Great Lakes in 1845 and four years later started a shipyard in Manitowoc. The town was well positioned to tap fine stands of oak to make stout hulls and towering pines for durable masts capable of carrying a large spread of canvas. His clipper schooner was inspired by the

Figure 6. The schooner *Hattie Hutt*, built in Saugatuck, Michigan, 1873, wrecked in 1929.
Source: Library of Congress.

famed Baltimore clippers that sailed rings around British frigates in the War of 1812. Bates modified these ships by giving them a shallower draft and an almost flat bottom. He kept the clipper's sharp, sleek ends and, with the drop centerboard, had a vessel that could swim in only a few feet of water but also sail close to a stiff breeze. His first design, *Challenge*, slid off the stocks in 1852. A year later *Clipper City* joined her. Both proved fast and reliable, and their ample holds with wide hatches made them well adapted for carrying bulk cargoes. Thus was born the classic Great Lakes schooner that would crisscross the lakes for a half century. It was finely tuned to its environment and economic niche. The flat bottom was well suited to carrying large cargoes into shallow harbors while the centerboard, paired with the fore-and-aft rigging, allowed for fast, efficient operation. Bates's design received the highest possible praise from other ship-builders on the lakes. They copied it shamelessly.[13]

There was another type of sailing ship that was common on the lakes, although it was pretty rough-hewn in comparison to Bates's clippers. The scow schooner was little more than a scow equipped with a schooner rig. Flat bottomed, boxy, with a blunt bow and stern and vertically planked sides, these were vessels that did not require a skilled shipwright to construct. Carpenters or coopers in new settlements could knock one together in a few weeks. Built at Erie, Pennsylvania, the first one cast off in 1825, and after that the style spread throughout the region. Often, they were a new lakeshore community's first venture into commerce and a critical link to the outside world. Their flat bottoms made them easy to load with heavy bulk cargoes. That feature also made them easier to pull over a sandbar blocking a potential harbor or off a shoal on which they had become grounded. Insurance underwriters were leery of them because of their poor sailing qualities in the face of a gale on the open lake, but they served an important niche in the Great Lakes economy into the start of the twentieth century.[14]

Between the sleek clipper schooners and the homely scows were the "canalers." These were schooners adapted to fit the re-quirements of the Welland Canal that bypassed Niagara Falls through Upper Canada's Niagara Peninsula. The locks on the original canal were only 110 feet long, and the 1848 expansion was still limited to 150 feet. Hence ships designed to pass from Lake Erie to Lake Ontario had a stunted appearance, with small bowsprit and a snubbed taper to the stern. Canalers had a bad reputation among men who worked lake schooners. They had a nasty habit of slipping when sailing before the wind. It was a habit that, under the wrong conditions, could get a sailor killed.[15]

Although steamboats made wakes on Lake Ontario as early as 1816, it was not until the 1830s that they began to have a major impact on the region's burgeoning trade. By 1833 there were eleven paddle-wheel vessels serving the lakes. In short order, they took over the passenger trade. The ability of these vessels to run on something like a schedule, not being dependent on the whims of the wind, made them popular with families migrating west. Compared with the cramped below-decks quarters offered on sailing vessels, the steamers often had main deck cabins, and after 1839, second-tier cabins that offered fresh air, light, and easy access to the deck. In time, so-called palace steamers joined the vessels serving the eight-day Buffalo to Chicago route. Opulent salons for men as well as separate spaces for women and children to relax, cabins attended by dutiful stewards and stewardesses, and handsome dining facilities made these boats the match for the best hotels of the day. More common were the working boats that mixed passenger service with cargo and catered to immigrant travelers. One traveler described his fellow passengers as a cliched "Congress of Nations." Looking about the upper deck he saw "hardy country-loving Swiss; the drawling, drudging Dutchman; the persevering, opinionated Scotchman; and the reckless, roistering Irishman, as well as the shrewd and penetrating Yankee . . . tumbled in admirable confusion, person and effects."[16]

Unlike the familiar steamboats in service on rivers, the lake vessels had their engines amidships and the giant paddle wheels were positioned one each on the starboard and port sides. After 1841 a better propulsion method, the screw propeller, was gradually adopted. Perfected by the Swedish inventor John Ericsson, who would later win fame as the inventor of the ironclad warship the *Monitor*, the development of propeller propulsion was one of the great maritime innovations. Paddle wheels would continue to be built and used for many years, though the propeller would eventually dominate all the oceans of the world. This innovation was first perfected on the Great Lakes, nearly two years before the first North American propeller debuted on saltwater. In November 1841 a ninety-foot-long, sloop-rigged steamer named the *Vandalia* powered its way out of Oswego harbor. The new design moved the engine to the stern of the vessel and a smoke stack projected from the deckhouse. *Vandalia* was well tested on her maiden voyage by both calm and heavy seas, and she performed admirably. Within two years the first propellers made their appearance on the upper lakes when *Samson* and *Hercules* were launched from Lake Erie shipyards.[17]

Steamers shaped both the early settlement pattern of the Great Lakes region and its environment. The vessels' fire boxes devoured a tremendous quantity of wood. A steamer voyaging from Buffalo to Chicago would consume six hundred cords of

022708 STR. "EMPIRE" 1844. FIRST STEAMER IN U. S. EXCEEDING 1000 TONS. 260X30X15 FT

Figure 7. A Great Lakes paddle steamer, *Empire*, 1844.
Source: Library of Congress.

wood. That amount of fuel was the equivalent of ten acres of
dense forest. Every other day a vessel would be required to stop
and refuel. Established ports of call such as Cleveland, Detroit,
and Mackinac Island had only limited access to the vast amount
of cordwood required by the numerous steamers. Special fuel
stations were established all along the waterways. These were
sites situated so vessels could easily and safely access them, and
they had to be adjacent to large stands of timber. This led to en-
trepreneurs establishing isolated settlements on the peninsulas
and islands along steamship routes. In the twenty-first century,
islands like Beaver Island and South Manitou Island are among
the most remote places on the Great Lakes, but in the nineteenth
century, the needs of lake commerce made them some of the first
areas to be settled.[18]

The proliferation of steamers on the inland seas by no means diminished the importance of sailing vessels. Throughout the nineteenth century, sail maintained a critical place in marine commerce. In 1872, for example, there were 682 steamboats plying the lakes, yet 1,654 sailing ships, mostly schooners, remained in service. The niche occupied by schooners was in transporting bulk cargo. The overwhelming majority of the immigrants taking steamships west were destined to be prairie farmers. They left their homes in rocky-soiled New England or the socially static Old World determined to improve themselves economically by becoming market farmers. A golden stream of grain, beginning as a trickle in the late 1830s and building to a flood, thereafter, flowed from their homesteads and into the holds of Great Lakes schooners. Canals such as the Ohio and Erie, the Wabash and Erie, and the Illinois and Michigan played a critical role in diverting this flow from river towns such as St. Louis toward the Great Lakes–Erie Canal route.[19]

Another key innovation along with these artificial rivers was the grain elevator. Today there are few more prosaic and ignored structures than the humble grain elevator. But in the nineteenth century, they were technological marvels and the tallest, proudest edifices in Chicago and Buffalo. The honor for inventing these commodity towers goes to Buffalo. The city was the terminus of lake navigation, and in 1842 Joseph Dart, a warehouse operator there, was being buried with sacks of grain. He needed more storage space, but harbor frontage was expensive. Moving the sacks from ship to warehouse to canal boat was labor intensive and wasteful. Grain sacks would break and their contents would litter the warehouse and docks. Dart devised a vertical storage system in which the grain was liberated from the cloth bags and moved in a massive stream of individual kernels of corn or wheat. Instead of a procession of stevedores with sacks of cereal, steam-powered conveyor belts brought the grain into and out of the elevator. Chicago's Board of Trade refined the system further by introducing a standardized grading system that established the quality of grain and opened a market in current as well as future grain prices, which was the basis for today's commodity markets. This new Great Lakes system for marketing and transporting grain easily bested the slow, laborious approach to commodities in the old river-centered grain ports of St. Louis and New Orleans.

Illinois, Indiana, and Ohio grain that once made its way to market via the Mississippi River was now directed to the harbors on the inland seas.[20]

Hazards of Antebellum Lake Navigation

Great Lakes shipbuilders such as William Wallace Bates designed vessels that were well suited to shallow, sometimes unimproved harbors while at the same time capable of moving large amounts of grain from west to east. During the shipping season, fleets of these white-winged craft were constantly in motion from Lakes Michigan or Erie ports to Buffalo. Their return cargoes varied from manufactured goods to bulk items such as coal. Lake Superior ports shipped copper and iron ore. The latter was loaded directly into the holds of schooners from large ore docks that projected into the lake. The building of the first of these ore docks at Marquette in 1859 pretty much assured schooners of the iron ore trade because the deck cabins on steamers prevented direct access to their holds. It would not be for another decade before new specialized steamers were designed to secure their share of the trade in bulk cargoes.

The fleets of schooners and steamboats on the Great Lakes effected a revolution in commerce. Between 1816 and 1853 the cost of shipping products from east to west via the inland seas dropped between 70 and 80 percent. The importance and financial success of lake shipping, however, did not mean the trade was not dangerous. Too few lighthouses, the lack of effective charts, and the stoppage of harbor improvements all contributed to numerous shipwrecks on the inland seas. Isaac Stephenson, a ship master and later a major lumberman, argued: "Sailing a ship was not unlike blazing a way through the forest. With conditions wretched as they were the navigator was practically without charts and the master figured his course as nearly as he could, estimating the leeway and varying influence of the winds." The fate of steamboats, the most technologically advanced branch of the lake marine, illustrates the risks involved. Between 1816 and 1871, 216 side-wheel steamboats were built and operated on the Great Lakes. More than half of these vessels were lost to mishaps. Sixty-nine of the steamers were lost in storms or groundings, taking with them at least 136 lives. Thirty-four of the ships burned, killing more than 700 passengers and crew. One of the worst of these was the 1847 disaster that destroyed the ill-named *Phoenix*. The 155-foot vessel was loaded with 275 Dutch immigrants as well as other passengers and crew. Overheated boilers set the vessel afire, and the panicked people had the awful choice of dying from the smoke and flames or the ice-cold waters of Lake Michigan. Two small lifeboats saved a handful, while 258 souls perished. Collisions accounted for the sinking of only 12 steamers but the loss of 601 lives.[21]

The Jacksonian laissez-faire approach to the economy accounted for some of these losses. There was an almost complete lack of regulation of the lake marine. Steamboat explosions on the Great Lakes as well as on the Mississippi River were all too common, with boiler explosions accounting for hundreds of deaths or hideous scaldings every year. An attempt by Congress to address the issue in 1838 was feeble and totally ineffective. In 1852 Congress finally took action with "An Act to Provide for Better Security of the Lives of Passengers on Board of Vessels Propelled in Whole or in Part by Steam." The legislation set up a system by which boilers were inspected every other year and engineers were to be licensed. Less effective were its guidelines for lifeboats, life preservers, and fire-fighting equipment. Prior to this legislation an estimated seven thousand people had died on unregulated steamboats. The inspection service was divided into a series of regional districts, each with an inspector and assistants. There was little central control, and the effectiveness and vigilance of the inspectors varied considerably from port to port. Nonetheless, the federal Steamboat Inspection Service made a healthy inroad into the litany of disasters on inland waterways. It did not, of course, stop all boiler explosions. In 1860 the steamer *Globe*, securely berthed in the Chicago River, blew up with the loss of fifteen lives. It was not until after the Civil War that a properly staffed steamboat inspection service was authorized.[22]

Storms were the greatest threat to shipping. The power of wind and waves magnified exponentially the dangers posed by unimproved navigation on the lakes. In fair weather, a schooner or steamer could manage without harbors of refuge, make port without the aid of pier-head lights, and even overcome grounding on hidden shoals. In heavy seas, these issues became lethal. In

1838 a severe November gale seriously damaged twenty-five ships, mostly schooners. A worse storm struck in November 1842. It raged across Lakes Michigan, Erie, and Ontario with winds estimated at over seventy miles per hour. In its wake more than fifty ships were wrecked and better than 100 lives lost. Worse came in 1860 when 578 people died in shipping-related accidents. The fact that lake shipping was a seasonal affair from early May to mid-November made the number of these losses all the more noteworthy.[23]

Navigation of early Great Lakes vessels was not a science but an art perfected by experience. Accurate charts were slow to become available and were not readily in use until the mid-1850s. Sailing as a passenger in 1836, the British social reformer Harriet Martineau commented: "The navigation of these lakes is, at present, a mystery. They have not yet been properly surveyed. Our captain had gone to and fro on Lake Huron, but had never before been on Lake Michigan; and this was rather an anxious voyage to him." In unknown waters, he had not traveled eighty miles before he ran his ship onto a sandbar that took the better part of a day to get off. Fortunately, the weather was calm. In a gale, the grounding could have meant death for his passengers and crew.[24]

As early as the late eighteenth century, the British government funded surveys of key points along the Great Lakes, but functional charts were not developed. Captain George Mann, a military engineer charged with conducting the surveys, observed that most vessels remained within sight of land: "The Navigation must be considered chiefly as Pilotage, to which the use of good Navigational Charts are essential, and are therefore much wanted." A generation later His Majesty's officials still only had a sketchy knowledge of large portions of the lakes. In 1816 William Owen reported to the Royal Navy: "Of navigation of Lake Huron scarcely anything is known. To the southward of the Manitoulin Islands, it is said to be clear of dangers, and to the northward to be intricate and full of them." Armed only with word of mouth or hard-won experience, vessels had to feel their way down the lakes with considerable caution, using the navigation technique known as dead reckoning. Captains set their course on compass bearings from one familiar headland to the next and estimated their sailing time by using a patent log or taffrail log to measure the ship's speed. A taffrail log was a small brass device with blades that turned in the water. A sailor would throw it over the stern, and as the attached line played out, he would count the knots in the cord and thereby calculate how fast the vessel was going. Each knot was estimated to be a little less than a mile per hour. The frustrations of this type of navigation are illustrated by the log of Captain S. G. Gibbs. In 1856 he was taking the schooner *Augusta* east across Lake Erie when he encountered thick fog. The sailing ship was bound for the Welland Canal. The night before the captain had taken a bearing from Point Rondeau on the north shore of the lake. At dawn, he peered anxiously through the fog for a new landmark. "We saw land but could not tell how far down we got," he wrote in the log. All day long he proceeded cautiously. As evening approached, he became concerned about how close he was to shore, and he began to take depth soundings. His last bearing had been about 140 miles from the canal and somewhere between him and the canal was a long narrow peninsula known as Long Point that reached far out into the lake. When his soundings revealed the depth had decreased to only five fathoms, he changed to a course that would take him parallel to the peninsula, if indeed that point was ahead of him in the fog. The next morning the skies were clear, visibility excellent, and he was able to recognize his position from the features of the shore. Before noon he safely reached the first Welland lock.[25]

Even after charts were readily available, dead reckoning was important to navigation. In May 1876 Captain Timothy Kelly piloted the schooner *Thomas Howland* down a foggy Lake Huron. He noted: "At 5 a.m. thought was about abreast of Point Aux Barks, at 6 a.m. hauled in the log [he had set it when abreast of Thunder Bay] at 6 a.m. ran 67 miles by logs miles." By these calculations and occasional depth measurements, he could estimate that he was approaching the end of the lake and by eleven he was able to "pick-up" a St. Clair River tugboat for a tow. Lighthouses were important to this type of navigation as they were fixed reference points on which navigators could take bearings or locate their position. Ship's log books were filled with notations such as "fog cleared up a little and made Chicago Light right ahead," or "took bearings on ducks light [Duck Island Light]," or "left Cheboygan could hear Spectacle Reef fog whistle all the p.m." Schooner Captain Timothy Kelly was very familiar with the shores of Lake Michigan, on whose waters he had first shipped before the mast, but to him Lake Ontario was unknown water. Before casting off on a trip that would take him through the Welland Canal into that lake and to the Canadian port of Kingston, he sat down with a list of lighthouses and noted the flash signatures of every navigation aid along the northern shore. Also noted were the appropriate compass bearings that would ensure a safe course of travel between each. It was not until the 1850s that U.S. Lake Survey charts became available. These contained sailing directions, which may have been where Kelly got the information. Eventually, the survey produced detailed pamphlets containing sailing directions for all the lakes. These indicated the proper compass bearings to guide vessels from headlands to lighthouses to buoys and hence to their desired port of call. Of course, for a sailing ship skipper to maintain a fixed compass heading was extremely difficult when the wind was variable and shifting, as it often was on the Great Lakes. Monitoring how much the vessel strayed on each tack was part of the art of lake navigation.[26]

Vessel masters operating in familiar waters on regular runs, such as the lumber schooners that crisscrossed Lake Ontario and Lake Michigan, did not make use of anything more elaborate than a compass and a chart. Masters less familiar with the waters they sailed on, bound on journeys that would last multiple days, took other precautions. John Kenlon was made the master of the three-masted schooner *Resumption* because of his decade of saltwater experience, including a passage of Cape Horn. Before setting out on his first lake voyage from Chicago to the head of Green Bay, he went to a pawnshop and purchased a "very fine set of charts of the Lakes" and "an old sextant." The vessel owners who agreed to cover the cost of navigational tools did not give him enough money to buy a good chronometer so he resolved to simply use his pocket watch. After a day and a night sailing, which included a gale, Kenlon used his "crude instruments" to "take a sight and ascertain our position." This gave him a good idea that he was near the entrance to the bay. However, he was not certain until he could verify his position "by bearings on shore." It is safe to say that most schooner captains trusted visual bearings more than navigational instruments.[27]

More commonly, lake mariners employed few instruments and relied on deep experience with the unique character of each of the lakes. Daniel Wilkeson mastered a schooner on Lake Erie for three decades. He knew the way wind and waves were affected by the time of day and location on the lake. A protégé of his observed that Wilkeson was "a practical sailor. . . . He was self-reliant but not to obstinacy, venturesome but not to foolhardiness; possessing in fact all the qualities which together make up the true sailor and man." Wilkeson, for example, knew when sailing Lake Erie at night to hug the south shore and thereby catch a "land breeze." When faced with a westerly gale while beating his way across Erie, he could quickly surmise how far he was from Cleveland and then estimate how long it would take his vessel to make the lee of Kelley's Island and calm water. He made his fortune and reputation by using experience to balance risk. He did, however, take risks. Frequently, when other vessels were in port he would push into the open lake. Wilkeson boasted that his ninety-ton schooner *Eagle* once made three trips across Lake Erie in eight days, each time with a full cargo that had to be loaded and unloaded by hand. There were few things skippers like Wilkeson liked better than setting every inch of canvas and scudding past another ship.[28]

In the early 1840s Great Britain's Canadian colonies received a loan of £1.5 million to improve roads, expand the Welland Canal around Niagara Falls, and make the St. Lawrence River navigable for lake shipping. Not only would these improvements open the Great Lakes to Royal Navy vessels in time of war—a major consideration at the time—but they would open up the possibility of Montreal becoming the logical destination of the trade of the American West. An 1843 Congressional investigation warned that British support for navigation improvements threatened to make the western states "colonies" of the crown in all but name. Yet even such a prospect did little to stir U.S. investment in lake infrastructure. President Tyler signed a modest improvement bill that year, but it only included minor work for three Lake Michigan ports.[29]

Lake sailors and their families had little choice but to accept and deal with the dangerous conditions under which the necessary and lucrative trade took place. In 1842 famed novelist Charles Dickens noted that river steamboats seemed to explode at least once a week, but it did not stop him from touring the Ohio valley from the deck of a paddle wheeler. Similarly, on the lakes, immigrants bound for the West were happy to be able to get their families six hundred miles into the interior of the continent in as little as a week of travel. People who lived in isolated settlements deeply appreciated the regularity of steamboat arrivals and departures. "No one but those who reside on an island can appreciate the steamboat service or what it means to people," wrote a Beaver Island resident. "We learn to love the boats, the sound of the whistle even in the midnight hours was music in our ears and brought cheer and comfort to our hearts." Yet a life before the mast was a life of risk. Elizabeth Whitney Williams, who helped keep the lighthouse at Beaver Island and later at Harbor Springs—both on Lake Michigan—was the daughter of a lake mariner. Her three brothers became sailors. Two of them and three nephews "found graves beneath the deep waters, but mine was not the only sorrow," she wrote in her memoir. "Others around me were losing their loved ones on the stormy deep and it seemed to me there was all the more need that the lamps in our light-house towers should be kept brightly burning."[30]

The River and Harbor Convention of 1847

In July 1847 the infant city of Chicago held its largest Independence Day celebration yet. The city of sixteen thousand people was at a critical juncture in its history. The long-delayed Illinois and Michigan Canal connecting Lake Michigan to the Mississippi River system was finally on the brink of opening. Economic hopes were high. The town was jammed with visitors, somewhere between four thousand and ten thousand. To impress them, the City Council had approved spending $5,000 on patriotic floats for a parade. The most impressive by far was of a fully rigged sailing ship, with jack tars aloft in the rigging, set on wheels and pulled by a heavily labored team of horses. From the ship flew a banner depicting a storm-tossed sea and a "lighthouse lifting its star of joy and hope" marking a safe harbor for the beleaguered sailor. Emblazoned on the banner were the words "What we Want!" The sentiment was greeted with great cheers, for it perfectly captured the reason so many people from across the U.S. had come to Chicago. The next day the largest political gathering up to that point in U.S. history began its formal sessions to demonstrate support for improved navigation on the Great Lakes.[31]

Throughout the 1840s northwestern congressmen pressed their colleagues in the House and Senate to invest in more lighthouses, to chart the lakes, and to improve the region's harbors. The latter issue was by far the most expensive and controversial. Nonetheless, careful fence-mending between legislators, who wanted federal aid to navigation on the Great Lakes, and those who wanted help with a variety of river projects led to a coalition that successfully pushed through Congress the Rivers and Harbors Bill of 1846. It authorized the federal government to spend $500,000 on needed projects. It embraced appropriations along the entire Great Lakes–Erie Canal east-west transportation corridor, including $75,000 for the Hudson River, $72,000 for Lake Ontario harbors, more than $170,000 for Lake Erie improvements, and $160,000 for Lake Michigan projects. Democratic and Whig legislators worked together to craft the bill, and many a congratulatory toast was shared when it was approved by both houses of Congress.[32]

Celebrations, however, proved premature. On August 3, 1846, President James K. Polk vetoed the bill. Polk fancied himself the successor to the mantle of Andrew Jackson. They both hailed from Tennessee, both were Democrats, both were highly partisan. Jackson was known as "Old Hickory." Polk was dubbed "Young Hickory." Jackson had used the presidential veto power more times than any previous president—often to block internal improvement projects. Polk modeled his veto of the River and Harbors Act on Jackson's earlier veto of the Maysville Road. Polk decried the appropriations as "local in character." He complained that Great Lakes harbors hardly deserved the name as they were not "connected with foreign commerce, nor are they places of refuge or of shelter for our navy or commercial marine on the ocean or lake shores." He dismissed the inland projects as "unimportant" and the appropriations as both unconstitutional and subversive of public virtue. Polk also demonstrated a slaveholder's fear of a strong activist federal government. Congressional support for navigation improvements would lead "to a consolidation of power in the Federal Government at the expense of rightful authority of the States. . . . It will engender sectional feelings and prejudices calculated to disturb the harmony of the Union." His veto, however, is what exasperated sectional disharmony.[33]

In Congress, dismayed legislators scrambled to build support to override the veto. Party discipline forced some Democrats initially in favor of the bill to sustain President Polk. The core of opposition, however, came from southern representatives. William L. Yancey of Alabama organized support for Polk in the House of Representatives. In later decades, he would be one of the leading firebrands that stampeded the South into secession and a Civil War. George Houston, another Alabama congressman, expressed a parochial view of the issue. "What interest have my constituents in improvements of the Hudson River; the canals and harbors of Illinois, Indiana, or Michigan?" he asked. Northwestern congressmen warned their southern colleagues that this issue would alienate people in the West and destroy the informal political alliance that had long prevailed between the sections. Yancey blustered that such threats "can have no influence over a single vote I have to give. . . . I fear not the West." The press accentuated the growing sectional divide. A Chicago newspaper saw the issue in the same stark terms: "This harbor question is not a political one, it is a sectional one. It is one between North and South." Polk's veto came at a time when he had requested more funds to sustain the war against Mexico—a conflict many northerners saw as being waged to expand slavery. The *Chicago Daily Journal* scoffed at Polk's claims of fiscal restraint and limited government: "Are not millions being squandered by the same James K. Polk for the invasion of Mexico and the extension of slavery? Are not the Treasury doors unbarred whenever the *'open sessme'* is whispered by the slave driver?" Yet nothing solidified the southern congressional block like a mention of the word "slavery." When put to a vote, the override failed by a 96–91 margin. Southern congressmen were nearly unanimous in support of Polk's veto, voting 43–1 to sustain the president. The sectionalism of the issue was obvious to all.[34]

Polk's veto came at a time when Great Lakes commerce was accelerating like a schooner in a stiff breeze. The veto seemed to many in the region like an anchor suddenly thrown overboard. James Belich, a historian of global settlement patterns, has argued that between 1810 and 1860 the Old Northwest region experienced the "highest rate of growth in human history." The period between the economic panics of 1837 and 1857 was the real "take-off" for the region's trade, although it was not till the early 1840s that settlement in the region had advanced enough to produce sizable grain surpluses for export to the East Coast and Europe. Up to that time much of the food grown in the region was needed to feed the hundreds of thousands who were settling the hinterland. The grain export trade of Chicago, for example, had only been forty thousand bushels in 1841, but it grew rapidly thereafter and by 1847 surpassed two million bushels. The nascent grain trade of the region was greatly aided by the huge investment the individual states, especially Illinois, Indiana, and Ohio, had made in canal networks that linked the interior to the lakeshore. These investments in some cases were so large as to bankrupt the states, leaving them no recourse for harbor improvements. At the same time, private investment in the grain trade built up fleets of ships and constructed steam-powered elevators that brought new efficiency and speed to the loading and unloading process. Yet the lack of harbor and channel work remained a drag on a trade ready to explode. Insurance rates on a cargo from Chicago to Buffalo were greater than on a shipment sent from New York across the Atlantic to Liverpool. One traveler lamented: "With here and there a lighthouse above Detroit everything remains almost in the same state it was found by the commercial pioneers when they first broke their way through Lake Michigan." Southern statesmen countered by pointing out that the states of the Old Northwest were the largest receivers of federal internal improvement funds, a full 27 percent in one recent study. Of course, the region was also by far the most rapidly developing area of the country. Most of the funds spent in the region went to a few very expensive roads to simply give settlers access to farms and towns. When it came to money committed for harbors, the Great Lakes area lagged far behind the federal investment that was routinely made along the entire Atlantic coast from Maine to Georgia.[35]

Lake harbors should have been a national priority because the boom in wheat production along the inland seas coincided with the 1846 repeal of the British corn laws. Those laws had long limited the export of American grain to Great Britain, and their repeal opened a huge new market to American farmers. Ports on the American side of the Great Lakes were also capturing a large share of the Canadian colonies' grain exports. Oswego, New

York, was the major beneficiary of that development as it received most of the wheat grown in the region of modern Ontario. In return, Oswego sent north 79 percent of what that British colony received from abroad. The amount of gross trade on the lakes grew every year in the 1840s, despite the rising tide of marine casualties. In 1841 that trade was valued by the U.S. Treasury at $65 million; by 1851 it exceeded $300 million. Trade across the lakes was becoming increasingly integrated in a way that greatly favored the U.S. Polk's unexpected veto seemed to frustrate the possibilities of a moment and region pregnant with promise.[36]

The solid wall of southern support for Polk's veto appeared to some residents of the Midwest as a betrayal. That it came on the heels of Polk's settlement of the Oregon question rubbed salt in an open wound. While a candidate for office, Polk had trumpeted the popular slogan "fifty-four forty or fight," but as president he agreed to a treaty with Great Britain that set the boundary much further south at the 49th parallel. The Great Lake states had a stronger interest in the Oregon question than the conflict with Mexico over the Texas boundary. Nonetheless, Ohio, Indiana, Illinois, and Michigan supported the war despite fears of slavery expansion. Their commitment of thousands of young men to that war effort and their votes for the massive congressional appropriations necessary to wage a war that was dragging on much longer than expected seemed to earn the region no compensatory consideration. To the men of the inland sea, the creation of a maritime infrastructure on the lakes was as much a part of the process of nation building as expanding its territorial boundaries at Mexico's expense. To foreclose the future of one for the sake of the other seemed self-serving and hardly in keeping with the spread-eagle nationalism of Manifest Destiny. The *Chicago Daily Journal* angrily charged that lake mariners were being denied shelter from the "strife of the natural elements" because Polk wanted "money for the Mexican War."[37]

These factors set the stage for the unprecedented political gathering in Chicago in the summer of 1847. The goal of the River and Harbor Convention was to bring together politicians, opinion makers in the press, and representatives of the many commercial interests engaged in inland trade to express their "indignation" over Polk's actions and to build an alliance to force federal support for internal improvements. The gathering was so big that there was no building large enough in the city to hold the convention, and a giant tent had to be erected. Under its canvas cover, delegates from eighteen states vied with themselves to refute Polk's contention that while there was a national interest in navigational improvements along the Atlantic and Gulf Coasts, such improvements in the interior were purely "local" in character. Young Abraham Lincoln made his first foray onto the national political scene when the lanky lawyer, in an ill-fitted suit, attacked the notion that federal support for harbors was somehow unconstitutional. He called for Democrats and Whigs "to unite, like a band of brothers, for the welfare of the common country." Other future leaders of the Republican Party were also present, including Thurlow Weed, Edmund Bates, and Horace Greeley. Few southern delegates were present, and none of any reputation. Duff Green, a Missouri entrepreneur and Democratic Party insider, urged John C. Calhoun, the champion of the South and slavery, to attend. Calhoun still nursed the ambition to be elected president. Green warned Calhoun that the Chicago Convention would "do much to control the future destiny of this country." Green predicted, "If the South opposes all appropriations for Harbors and Internal Improvements, the Great West will unite with the East, and carry measures against the South. In that case Abolition and Internal Improvements go together & strengthen each other." Calhoun rejected this advice. Typical of the South's reaction to the convention was a Jackson, Mississippi, newspaper's dismissal of the proceedings as "humbuggery." Time would prove such a reaction costly, as an antislavery–internal improvements alliance came to be just as Duff Green predicted.[38]

The 1847 convention was the beginning of a political revolution. Polk's veto of the River and Harbor Bill awoke the nascent political consciousness of the Old Northwest region, solidified the region's political-economic relationship with the Northeast, and sundered much of the goodwill and cooperation that had existed between the West and the South. Although Polk's veto was sustained, the Chicago Convention spurred Congress to draft and the House to approve an even larger river and harbor bill in 1847. The House Committee on Commerce clearly mirrored the convention when it openly challenged the logic of the president's veto message as "casuistry . . . [that] can distinguish between the power to erect and maintain a light-house to guide the mariner by or around an obstruction, and the power to re-move the obstruction itself." Congressman Abraham Lincoln, ever the supporter of internal improvements, laid out his own plan for systematic federal support for harbor projects through a government bureau that would study and evaluate the potential of each project to enhance economic productivity. With this pro-posal Lincoln aligned himself with Albert Gallatin and John Quincy Adams, who each had earlier proposed a systematic and national approach to internal improvements. Predictably, Lin-coln's idea was immediately mocked by South Carolina's Robert Barnwell Rhett, who complained the Illinoisan advocated for an agency "counting all the pigs and chickens in the land." South Carolina had long been the state most opposed to inland naviga-tion enhancement. The Polk administration followed Rhett's lead and ignored both the young Illinois congressman's plan and the new river and harbor bill, which the president killed with a pocket veto. Meanwhile at Chicago, in Lincoln's home state, relentless Lake Michigan wave action built up a new sand-bar, partially restricting entrance to the port city. Sailors dubbed the obstruction "Mount Polk" after the man they held responsible for the barrier.[39]

Polk's focus was on his war in Mexico, yet he and his south-ern Democratic partisans seriously underestimated the long-term political damage of his vetoes. From the perspective of the White House, river and harbor bills seemed a partisan issue. Only 27 percent of Democrats in the House of Representatives supported the 1846 bill while across the aisle 87 percent of the rival Whigs were in favor. Polk saw the issue as a Whig hobby horse he could safely ignore, but the minority of Democrats who supported harbor appropriations were from the Northwest. His vetoes left them vulnerable to disappointed constituents and pushed many into opposition. John Wentworth, congressman from Chicago, had been an enthusiastic Jacksonian. His news-paper, the first in the city, was titled *The Chicago Democrat*, but Polk's vetoes drove him out of the party and eventually into the arms of the Republican Party. Bitterly, he saw Polk's action not in partisan terms but as a sectional issue that laid bare differences "between North and South." The Whig *Evening Journal* in the city supported this interpretation. "The objects of improvement lie north of Mason and Dixon's line, and would benefit the North and the West, whose growing prosperity is hateful to the slave-owners of the South." The editorial closed on an ominous but prophetic note: "If we are to be downtrodden, and all our cherished interests crushed by them, a signal revolution will inevitably ensue."[40]

State government action was Polk's answer to the cries for infrastructure investment. He regarded the individual states as strong enough to make their own investment in transportation. Unfortunately, this advice arrived in the Great Lakes states at a time when those commonwealths were only beginning to recover from the massive expenditures they had made on canals and roads during the 1830s. The ambitious navigation schemes they developed in imitation of New York's Erie Canal had been undone by inadequate finance and the devastating Panic of 1837. Ohio, Indiana, Michigan, and Illinois had borrowed a combined $37 million for their projects, and by the early 1840s all save Ohio had been forced to default. The result was a series of constitutional provisions that forbade future state investment in large-scale transportation. Polk's notion of a solution to internal improvements had already been tried, and it had failed.[41]

Harbor appropriations were a significant issue in the 1848 presidential election. The Democratic candidate should have been enthusiastically embraced by western voters. Lewis Cass was the former governor and senator from Michigan. He voted in favor of the River and Harbor Bill of 1846. He knew the lakes as well as any man in American politics, having crossed them many times via canoe, schooner, and steamboat. Yet his popularity in the West was compromised by his failure to accept an invitation to the River and Harbor Convention and his support for the Democratic platform plank that declared federal support for such improvements unconstitutional. The Free-Soil Party, a third-party upstart that focused on restricting the spread of slavery, and the Whigs both endorsed improvements. The victorious Whig candidate was war hero Zachary Taylor and his vice president Millard Fillmore. The latter was a lawyer from Buffalo, New York, who had been active in the promotion of the Chicago convention and was a strong supporter of internal improvements. In fact, it had been Polk's veto that prompted Fillmore, who had previously been a member of Congress, to reenter politics. When President Taylor died suddenly in the summer of 1850, supporters of federal navigational aids and harbors finally had a spokesman in the nation's highest executive office.

Fillmore came into his high office with the nation in political crisis over the issue of slavery in the territories won in the recent war with Mexico. Only the Compromise of 1850, which was ushered through Congress just after Fillmore took office, headed off secession by slaveholding states. Implementing the carefully balanced set of policies bundled into the compromise was Fillmore's first order of business. Internal improvements, however, were never far from his mind. In his first annual address to Congress in 1850, he went out of his way to make it clear that he did not regard the Constitution as an impediment to safe navigation. He based his case on the so-called commerce clause of the Constitution, under which all "light-houses, buoys, and beacons" along the nation's seacoast had been "established and floating lights maintained" and "harbors have been cleared and improved, piers constructed, and even breakwaters for the safety of shipping and sea walls to protect harbors . . . have been erected at very great expense. . . . Nor do I perceive any difference between the power of Congress to make appropriations for objects of this kind on the ocean and the power to make appropriations for similar objects on lakes and rivers, wherever they are large enough to bear on their waters an extensive traffic." Unfortunately for Fillmore and his internal improvements agenda, moving from words to action was difficult, as the Democrats controlled both the Senate and the House of Representatives.[42]

While sectional conflict consumed Congress's attention in 1850, maritime commerce on the Great Lakes had its most disastrous year yet. The greatest tragedy in the calamitous year was the June sinking of the steamer *Griffith*. She was out of Buffalo coasting the south shore of Lake Erie on her way to Toledo with a large number of passengers, including 256 immigrants in steerage, when the vessel caught fire. Captain C. C. Roby immediately steered the ship toward shore and nearby Cleveland harbor. The four-hundred-ton vessel unfortunately struck a hidden sandbar and became hard stuck just as the flames began to spread. There was no hope for the passengers but to plunge into the cold lake. It was estimated that at least 300 persons perished. The *Griffith* was only one of the eleven steamboats lost that year. Losses were heavier among the sailing vessels. Twenty-one were lost during the navigation season. The total property loss on the lakes that sad season was $558,926. More importantly, 431 sailors and passengers lost their lives. The 1851 season continued the mounting toll. Only seventy-nine lives were lost, but property damage exceeded $730,000. That increase was part of a steady escalation of the loss of property on the lakes. Between 1848 and 1855 total financial losses to Great Lakes ships increased from $404,830 to $2,797,839.[43]

As the 1851 shipping season ended, Fillmore again addressed Congress on the issue of Great Lakes navigation. He reminded them that "great numbers of lives and vast amounts of property are annually lost for want of safe and convenient harbors on the Lakes. None but those who have been exposed to that dangerous navigation can fully appreciate the importance of this subject." Not only did inaction increase the number of lives at risk but lack of maintenance also meant that works already constructed were being lost. "The whole Northwest appeals to you for relief, and I trust their appeal will receive due consideration at your hands." He also reminded catchpenny legislators that for a rare moment in U.S. history the federal government was running a revenue surplus.[44]

At the heart of the controversy over Great Lakes navigation improvements was the perception of those waters in the public mind, what might be called the social construction of the lakes. Were these mere lakes or should they be regarded and funded as genuine inland seas? There was a history of depreciating or diminishing the lakes among those who had limited familiarity with them. In Congress they were frequently referred to as "interior waters" or "the Northern Lakes," which tended to suggest their isolation and sectional character and lessen their potential and significance. At the same time there were southerners, such as John C. Calhoun, who floated the idea that the cotton South's Mississippi River should be regarded as an "inland sea." While westerners did not oppose federal funds to clear snags from the great river's channels, they were at pains to convey the size and potential danger faced by ships on the Great Lakes. Travelers needed only a brief exposure to gain a healthy respect. In 1840 the French naturalist Francis Count de Castelnau wrote after enduring a Lake Michigan gale: "I have seen the storms of the

Channel, those of the Ocean, the squalls off the banks of New-foundland, those on the coasts of America and the hurricanes of the Gulf of Mexico. Nowhere have I witnessed the fury of the elements comparable to that found on this fresh water sea." Herman Melville, who crossed the lakes in 1840, appreciated their beauty and dreaded their ability to quickly turn deadly. In *Moby-Dick*, his character Ishmael states that the lakes "possess an ocean-like expansiveness, with many of the ocean's noblest traits," but that "they are swept by Borean and dismasting blasts, as direful as any that lash the salted wave, they know what ship-wrecks are, for out of the sight of land, however inland, they have drowned full many a ship with all its shrieking crew." When President John Tyler requested funding for lighthouse construction on the lakes, something strict constructionists did not challenge, he referred to "our inland seas." Yet when it came to harbor or channel improvements, he dismissed the issue as pertaining to "far points in the interior." The challenge for lake harbor and channel improvement advocates was to have the Great Lakes accepted as genuine inland seas.[45]

In 1851 Great Lakes supporters received help from an unexpected quarter—the U.S. Supreme Court. In the case of *Genesee Chief v. Fitzhugh*, the court established that federal jurisdiction extended not simply to coastal waters as James K. Polk had argued but to all waters where interstate and international commerce take place. The case was based on an 1846 collision on Lake Ontario between the propeller steamer *Genesee Chief* and the grain schooner *Cuba*. The latter vessel was bound from Lake Erie with a cargo of grain when she encountered heavy seas. She took in most of her canvas and was running with the wind. The steamer, being a powered vessel, had much more control over her movements, but the master did not maintain a proper lookout and collided with the *Cuba* and sent her to the bottom. The Federal District Court heard the case in accordance with a law passed by Congress in 1845 that extended U.S. Admiralty law to inland waters. There had been much doubt about the constitutionality of the law, and many Democrats assumed it could not survive review by the high court. Yet when the owners of the *Genesee Chief* challenged federal jurisdiction, Chief Justice Roger B. Taney overturned previous precedence and upheld the law. In doing so he left no doubt that the Great Lakes were as much a legitimate sphere for federal responsibility as the Atlantic Coast. "These lakes are in truth inland seas," he wrote for the majority. "Different States border on them on one side, and a foreign nation on the other. A great and growing commerce is carried on upon them between different states and a foreign nation, which is subject to all the incidents and hazards that attend commerce on the ocean. Hostile fleets have encountered on them, prizes have been made and every reason which existed for the grant of admiralty jurisdiction to the general government on the Atlantic seas, applies with equal force to the lakes."[46]

Empowered by the Supreme Court and entreated by the president, Congress finally acted on navigational improvements in 1852. It was this Congress that enabled the building of the Sault Ste. Marie Canal by making a huge federal land grant to the State of Michigan to pay for that project. With the disputes over Mexican War territories temporarily shelved, the House of Representatives also responded with a massive harbor appropriations bill. The legislation was a pragmatic alliance of Democrats from the Great Lake states with northern Whigs. The River and Harbor Bill of 1852 was bigger than any that came before. It called for more than $2 million to be devoted to the Great Lakes and inland rivers.

The bill did not, however, enjoy smooth sailing in the Senate. Stephen A. Douglas of Illinois tried to restore the old political alliance between the West and the South by offering an amendment. His plan called for internal improvements to be paid for not by congressional appropriation but by local levies on shipping. This was an old and long discredited idea that was a favorite of strict constructionists. It was also a provision that likely was contrary to the 1787 Northwest Ordinance, which forbade restriction on the use of inland waterways. Douglas even went so far as to depreciate the competence of army engineers to plan and construct proper harbor works. An army engineer's "knowledge and science" was "only equaled by his profound ignorance of all those local and practical questions which ought to determine the site and plan of the proposed improvement." Rather, he proposed, let local people familiar with local conditions raise the necessary money and handle such works. Drawing on what was even then a timeworn conservative dogma, Douglas dismissed federal funding for navigation improvements as a waste of money and an invitation to "failures and extravagance." Instead, let local communities level duties to pay for harbors, and consumers of shipping products would in the end bear the cost. His plan left unstated that even if unimproved sites could generate enough revenue to make improvements, there still was a need for federal expenditures for items that were nonetheless "in the general welfare." Emergency harbors of refuge that would have limited commercial viability were still needed, and there was a desperate necessity to improve the various connecting channels between the lakes, such as the St. Clair Flats or St. Mary's River that were controlled by no port authority.[47]

Douglas was at heart a nationalist, but he floated this unseaworthy idea out of ambition for the presidency, which could come his way only if he could win the support of southern colleagues in Congress. Dixie state colleagues eagerly followed his lead. South Carolina's Andrew Butler, who was given to emotional outbursts, claimed the House River and Harbor Bill was so sectionally biased it was the equivalent to "burning the cotton of the South," and he threatened to filibuster if Douglas's amendment was not accepted. Jefferson Davis was only slightly more measured when he said the massive River and Harbor Bill threatened the nation with "dissolution." Henry Clay, the Whig leader on internal improvements, responded with a warning. How long would it be, he argued, "before the people would rise up on mass and trample down your little hairsplitting distinctions about what is national and state and demand what is fair and just." Despite Douglas's attempt at political log rolling and the overheated outbursts of southern senators, the House bill was accepted by the majority of the Senate, and it was signed into law by President Fillmore in August. The bill was a much-needed and much-appreciated infusion of federal funds for lake ports struggling to maintain commerce with private and municipal investments. Yet even with this $2 million investment, the "northwestern lakes," with their annual trade topping $300 million, had received only one-eighth of all federal river and harbor appropriations, and the political position of the region was about to go from bad to worse.[48]

In the ever-escalating battle between the North and the South, the issue of internal improvements was second only to slavery in deepening the political divide. It would be a mistake, however, to downplay the importance of navigational improvements in creating the momentum that led to the eventual formation of a purely sectional party. Isaac Stephenson, a sailor, vessel owner, lumberman, and eventually a U.S. Senator, was disgusted by the Democratic Party's antifederalism. "The idea that the lakes were little more than a 'goose pond' prevailed in Congress with the result every sailor on the lakes became a Whig and afterwards a Republican." Even loyal Democratic legislators were dismayed by their inability to help constituents on the lakes. In 1854 Indiana Senator John Petitt complained that when he visited the would-be port of Michigan City, Indiana, "standing upon the pier, as far as the eye can reach, you can see wrecks on either beach. . . . A small amount of money . . . would have saved all that wreck and ruin, would have prevented the loss of thousands of lives, and perhaps millions of property." Even Petitt's support of the unpopular slavery-expanding Kansas-Nebraska Act could not leverage support for a harbor appropriation from his southern colleagues. Instead, when a $2.5 million river and harbor bill was passed in 1854, the cotton states legislators supported Democratic President Franklin Pierce's veto. Pierce was unfazed by the fact that during the year there had been 384 "disasters" on the lakes, with a valuation of property lost amounting to $2,187,825. To be fair, not all marine losses were caused by a lack of harbors. There were so many vessels on the Great Lakes that collisions were not infrequent. It is fitting, however, that one of those vessels lost on the lakes was the schooner *Franklin Pierce*. On hearing news of the veto, all ships in Chicago harbor lowered their colors to half-mast. The president was clearly a foe of the lake marine. In 1856 Pierce once again wielded his veto pen to try to stop a Great Lakes appropriation. He relied on southern senators to uphold his action. Robert Toombs, senator from Georgia who earlier in his career had been a Whig sympathetic to a national program of improvements, rose in defense of Pierce's constitutional hair-splitting. In his opinion, congressional appropriations for Atlantic coast harbors were appropriate because they provided shelter for U.S. Navy vessels and therefore served a national purpose. But constitutional arguments were less persuasive on this occasion because funding for clearing Great Lakes connecting channels was paired with funding for dredging at the mouth of the Mississippi River, and hence the solid South in the Senate was breached and Pierce's veto was washed away.[49]

Both Pierce and his successor in the White House, James Buchanan, were northern men, but they understood that the unity of the Democratic Party depended on acceding to the South's strict interpretation of the Constitution. When the Whig Party disintegrated following the 1852 election, the issue of inland seas improvements became a cornerstone of the new Republican Party—an organization founded in 1854 in the Great Lakes states. In their haste to demonstrate the central role of slavery in the coming of the Civil War, most historians have downplayed the important economic issues, particularly navigation improvements. Yet it is clear that they were a factor in the emergence of a purely sectional political party, the Republicans. Undoubtedly it was the sundering of the Missouri Compromise by the 1854 Kansas-Nebraska Bill that triggered the party's birth. But navigation issues were always a supporting issue in bringing diverse political factions together in the northwestern states. At both the 1856 and 1860 Republican National Conventions, navigation issues were a vital unifying issue. The 1856 convention meeting at Philadelphia enthusiastically "resolved, That appropriations by Congress for the improvement of rivers and harbors, of a national character, required for the accommodation and security of our existing commerce, are authorized by the Constitution, and justified by the obligation of the Government to protect the lives and property of its citizens."[50]

While harbor improvements were clearly in the economic interest of the Great Lakes states, their mounting frustration with southern antifederalists also reflected a growing cultural gap between the sections. Settlers flocking to the region took pride in the spirit of progress that animated the region. Alexis de Tocqueville, who traveled the region as far as Lake Huron, noted this and commented that save for the people of the South, Americans were infused with a "spirit of public-mindedness." He was impressed by their commitment to community, which was broadly evident in their support for schools, libraries, hospitals, and churches as well as in their desire to support infrastructure projects such as canals, harbors, wharves, water companies, and roads. The more that southern politicians frustrated the improvement schemes of the Old Northwest region, the more they fostered the notion that the slaveholding states had strayed from the values on which American progress had been based. In 1860, on the eve of the convention that would eventually nominate Abraham Lincoln, *New York Tribune* editor Horace Greeley captured the relationship between economic issues and antislavery when he observed: "I know the country is not Anti-Slavery. It will only swallow a little Anti-Slavery in a great deal of sweetening. An Anti-Slavery man per se cannot be elected; but a tariff, river and harbor, Pacific railroad, free-homestead man may succeed although he is Anti-Slavery."[51]

Only a handful of historians have recognized the important role navigation issues played in fueling the rise of the Republican Party and the coming of the Civil War. The Republican Party was a fusion of diverse elements. A key portion of the post-1854 coalition were northern Democrats who had become frustrated with the strict constitutionalism imposed by the southern wing of the party. They understood the needs of their region and were willing to make common cause with Whigs to secure needed navigation improvements. In 1856, in the wake of President Pierce's veto of a river and harbor bill, a number of Democrats from the Northwest crossed the aisle to vote with the Whigs to override. This prompted Congressman William Barksdale of Mississippi to complain that he was "astonished" to find "fusion between Democrats and Whigs, Free-Soilers and Abolitionists." Barksdale, who would later die at Gettysburg, should not have been surprised, since southern inflexibility drove many northern Democrats into the emerging Republican fusion. Navigation improvements were a key common ground on which former Democrats and former Whigs could unite. Fear of slavery's expansion was the prime mover behind the creation of the Republican Party. Yet its economic agenda insured that it was not a one-issue, flash in the pan like the recent Liberty, Free-Soilers, or Know-Nothings. The economic agenda of homesteads, a Pacific railroad, and navigation improvements joined with restricting slavery to give the new party a powerful progressive message that looked beyond the anxieties of the age and toward a prosperous future.[52]

More than a political issue, lake shipping was, on a daily basis, on the front lines of northern resistance to slavery through the Underground Railroad. Enslaved people who escaped from bondage in the South settled in northern lake ports such as Buffalo, Cleveland, Detroit, and Chicago. After the 1850 Fugitive Slave Act, however, legal freedom for runaways could only be found on the Canadian side of the Great Lakes. Passage on a lake ship was often the final phase of a successful transit of the Underground Railroad. The earliest known escape via Great Lakes shipping occurred in 1820 when a male slave managed to elude pursuers all the way from the Ohio River to Sandusky. There he was smuggled aboard the steamer *Walk-on-the-Water* on Lake Erie. After arriving in Detroit, the fugitive was then smuggled across the river in a small sailboat to Canada. A decade later Josiah Henson and his family staggered exhausted to the shore of Lake Erie. There he saw a small schooner being loaded with corn. Taking a chance, he approached the vessel's captain, who immediately employed Henson as a stevedore and made secret plans to embark that night with the runaway and his wife and children. When Henson and his family were rowed out to the schooner he was surprised at their warm reception. To "my astonishment," he later wrote, "we were welcomed on board, with three hearty cheers; for the crew were as much pleased as the captain, with the help they were giving us to escape."[53]

In the influential antislavery novel *Uncle Tom's Cabin*, Harriet Beecher Stowe has her protagonists George and Eliza complete their harrowing escape via a Lake Erie steamship. A real-life drama played out in Wisconsin in 1854 when fugitive slave Joshua Glover was recaptured by a federal marshal and locked in a Milwaukee jail. A mob of black and white abolitionists broke down the door to the lockup and spirited Glover to the lake port of Racine. There he was hidden for several weeks while they waited for the ice to break up on Lake Michigan. When the shipping season opened, Glover was put aboard the vessel that took him to freedom.[54]

It is likely that no one in the lakes played a more important role in the Underground Railroad than Eber Brock Ward. As owner of the largest fleet of vessels on the lakes he had the opportunity, and as a firm abolitionist he had the motivation, to defy what he regarded as the immoral fugitive slave law. Ward was thought to be one of the secret funders of John Brown's terror campaign against slavery in Kansas and Virginia. As owner of the arch-Republican *Detroit Tribune,* he actively promoted the careers of two of the Midwest's leading antislavery politicians, Zachariah Chandler and Benjamin Wade. His steamships were a reliable last link in the escape route to Canada. The regular service from Cleveland to Detroit was particularly active in this regard. As many as thirty runaways at a time might be smuggled aboard. Federal marshals regularly staked out his vessels, but Ward's crew usually found ways to secret the escapees into steerage. Once in Detroit they would be quickly ferried across the river to freedom. In 1856 the shipping magnet personally participated in an escape. After three fugitives had been smuggled aboard a steamer, their Kentucky owner boarded the vessel and during the passage to Detroit discovered where they had been hidden. Confident they were again in his power, he took "great pleasure in telling them that he now had them as surely as though they were back on their native soil; that he telegraphed the U.S. Marshal at Detroit before leaving Cleveland to be at the dock on the arrival of the boat." When Ward was informed of the situation, he took to the pilothouse, turned the ship's wheel hard over, and directed the boat to the Canadian shore, where he deposited the runaways. The Kentuckian scrambled to the deck just in time to hear one of his former bondsmen shout out, "Good by Massa, when yous gets back to Lexington tells them all we is safe in Canada."[55]

The Survey of the Northern and Northwestern Lakes

In the winter of 1838–39, army engineer William G. Williams put the finishing touches on an extensive survey he had made on the waters around Buffalo, New York. He saw this survey as a useful extension of his work on harbor improvements at the mouth of the Buffalo River. The town, which only had a few hundred residents when it received its first lighthouse in 1819, had grown close to sixteen thousand people. Many more thousands passed through every year when they transferred from canal boats to lake steamers on their migration west. A chart indicating the depth of the channels and fully articulating the shore would add to the safety of vessels entering and leaving Buffalo's port. Great Lakes shipowners and merchants had lobbied for accurate charts of the inland seas for a decade. Captain Williams's Buffalo chart was the beginning of a long process by which scientific methods would win from the wilderness waters the true shape, depth, and size of the Great Lakes.

The U.S. first turned its attention to charting its national shorelines in 1807 when Thomas Jefferson signed legislation authorizing the production of nautical charts of the Atlantic Coast. As commerce on the Great Lakes skyrocketed in the wake of the 1826 opening of the Erie Canal, petitions made their way to Congress to extend chart making to the lakes. An October 1831 petition complained that there were now so many vessels on the lakes that it was no longer possible "that knowledge of the Lake dangers should be in the minds of a few able navigators, and by them handed down, with more or less certainty, to their successors." What the lake marine needed were charts locating the dangerous shoals and accurately depicting the size of channels and the location of lighthouses and harbors. The Royal Navy, largely through the efforts of Henry W. Bayfield created a series of charts of the Great Lakes shoreline, but these were not generally available to sailors on the U.S. side of the lake, and Bayfield's charts were based on very limited depth soundings. In 1841 Congress responded to this need by making a $15,000 appropriation for the Army Corps of Topographical Engineers to inaugurate "a hydrographic survey of the . . . northern and northwestern lakes of the United States." The task was assigned to army engineers and not the navy, which might seem the logical branch to undertake chart making. However, the navy had a very limited presence on the Great Lakes owing to the Rush-Bagot agreement, which restricted warships on the lakes, and army engineers were already at work on the lakes undertaking limited harbor surveys and improvements. It was the beginning of a long process of charting and recharting that would extend into the second half of the twentieth century.[56]

The task was extremely daunting, and the paltry appropriation made by Congress to begin the process reflected the legislators' lack of appreciation for the size and complexity of the Great Lakes waterway. Even a glance at the imperfect maps of the region that were available in the capital would have revealed over 3,000 miles of shoreline stretching from east to west. Charting these waters, of course, meant properly mapping every bay, inlet, peninsula, and shoreline meander. This would entail 4,700 miles of lakefront. Because the lakes narrowed at key points on Lakes Ontario, Erie, Huron, and Superior, and especially the Detroit River and Lake St. Clair, it was also necessary to map a corresponding portion of the shoreline of British North America. This would require that better than 6,000 miles of Great Lakes waterways be mapped and charted. In comparison, the combined U.S. shoreline of the Atlantic, Gulf, and Pacific Coasts was only 5,705 miles.[57]

Many of the engineers who helped to begin the survey had earlier worked on harbor improvements, and although those projects were slowed by political infighting in the 1840s and 1850s, the work of charting was carried on. There were two phases to the fieldwork of the U.S. Lake Survey. The survey party undertook topographic mapping, and the shore party made hydrographic measurements. The survey party faced a challenging task. They had to establish baselines from which a series of triangles could then be projected. The advantage of this method was pinpoint accuracy and the fact that many lines did not have to be actually traced out but could be calculated on the basis of the coordinates of previously fixed points. The hard part was establishing the baselines in the heavily forested Great Lakes region. Work started on Mackinac Island and in laying out a baseline at the head of Green Bay. The Green Bay site was chosen for the baseline because its complex web of islands and channels were a navigational gauntlet. The peninsulas and islands of the region also created a means of laying out a series of triangles from the western shore of Lake Michigan to the eastern shore. Army engineers were also cognizant of the relationship of what they were doing to national defense. The area between Mackinac Island and Green Bay would inevitably become a seat of war if conflict between Great Britain and the United States was resumed.[58]

The survey party tried to make use of hills and promontories from which to take measurements, but along the heavily timbered, topographically flat shoreline typical of Lake Michigan, they were forced to build wooden towers. To get over the towering white pine trees these towers sometimes had to be 120 feet in height. They also had to be very stable so that transits could be brought to a platform at the top and used to determine the coordinates of another station ten to twenty-five miles away. John H. Foster worked as a surveyor in 1844 establishing a baseline at the northern tip of Lower Michigan. His day began at four in the morning with a breakfast of hardtack and fried pork washed down with coffee. The men then left camp for the place they had finished clearing for the baseline. "The mosquitoes and black flies fairly swarmed in that close, hot, forest-lined avenue, termed the base line, base in more senses than one. Without the protection of shields over the face, buckskin gloves, and top boots, it would have been impossible to work in such a place." They chopped down trees and cleared brush along the baseline, and other than a lunch break, they worked as long as light allowed, which in the summer months meant a fifteen-hour day. Arriving back at camp, the men supped on the same monotonous fare as breakfast before retiring to their white canvas tents and sleep— all save one. The chief engineer had to sit down and then transfer from his field notebook all the measurements recorded during the day. Foster described using a barrel head as a writing desk, and many times he would find himself stiffly sitting with the makeshift desk in his lap when he awoke to the morning call "turn out." In later years, he thought of these long, hard days whenever he heard people scoff at loafing government workers. To hack out a baseline and build the transit tower required a large crew of experienced woodsmen. French-Canadians and American Indians, often as many as sixty in number, did the axe work and manned the oars when it was necessary to move the camp. The experienced boatmen were particularly helpful when the surveyors measured the depth of the inshore waters.[59]

While work at the head of Lake Michigan went on, other topographical engineers had begun surveys of Lake Erie's busy harbors. To survey the difficult waters around the Lake Erie Islands the engineers laid out a baseline on South Bass Island from which triangulation could capture the rest of the archipelago. In 1852 charts of this section of the waterway were released. Any vessel master who presented a certificate from a customs collector could receive this chart free of charge. This was also true of charts issued in subsequent years. In the 1850s the survey proceeded to chart the approach to the St. Mary's River and Saginaw Bay on Lake Huron, and their work on northern Lake Michigan was extended into the busy Manitou Passage.[60]

The early years of the lake survey were beset by the same antebellum penny-pinching policies that hurt all aspects of federal administration from national defense to lighthouse administration. The topographical engineers had few and inferior technical tools to work with. Their budgets were small and doled out in small annual appropriations that inhibited comprehensive planning. Just as the survey began to build some momentum in 1846, the Mexican War hit staffing and funding. Fortunately, in the wake of the conflict healthy appropriations followed. By this time the lake survey's engineers and crews developed an intimate knowledge of the topography and hydrology of the areas in which they worked. They promoted safer navigation not simply by preparing charts of the inland seas. When they came across exposed reefs, they erected wooden tripods so that the danger could be more readily identified from the deck of an approaching ship. Wherever their measurements of water depth revealed dangerous shoals, they attempted to place buoys. Working one season in the Mackinac Straits area, the engineers made more than ninety-seven hundred separate depth soundings, placed wooden tripods on two exposed reefs, and placed eighty-two marker buoys. In this way, the hardworking engineers made an immediate impact on the safety of Great Lakes navigation. Engineer W. H. Hearding recalled that "during the year 1859 more than five thousand charts were issued by the lake survey office in Detroit and there is scarce a vessel of any consideration on the lakes which has not a full set of them on board."[61]

Communication between the army officers working on the Lake Survey and mariners worked to improve safe shipping on the inland seas. In 1854 a schooner belonging to George Tifft, one of Buffalo's most important capitalists, was caught in a Lake Michigan gale. The vessel's rudder was carried off and only an improvised mechanism and skilled seamanship allowed the captain to guide his vessel into a narrow channel that broke the sandy shoreline. To their relief, they found more than four feet of water in the Betsie River and followed it to a small lake where they were sheltered from the gale. Tifft operated a fleet of sailing ships called the Troy and Michigan Six-Day Line. He knew the importance of harbor of refuge along the broad undeveloped shore of Lake Michigan and immediately bought up the land around the small sheltered lake. He then used his influence in the Congress to secure funding for a special survey of the Betsie River and Lake. In 1859 Captain George G. Meade ordered

Lieutenant Orlando Poe to sound the depth of the water in the vicinity and to assess its potential as a harbor. Poe reported favorably on the site but recommended dredging to make the Betsie River navigable during all seasons. Rather than wait vainly for Congress to make an appropriation, lumbermen who were building a sawmill on Lake Betsie's shore undertook the work themselves. The survey and the dredging led to the founding of the city of Frankfurt, Michigan.[62]

By the 1870s the mapping of the Canadian side of the lakes had fallen behind the high standard set by U.S. Army engineers. Officials in British North America relied on the marvelous charts made by the Royal Navy's Henry W. Bayfield between 1817 and 1825. Bayfield had been both diligent and careful. He spent four years on Lake Huron and Georgian Bay, where he reported that "we have ascertained the Shape, size & situation of upwards of six thousand islands, flats and Rocks." But Bayfield operated under the most primitive of circumstances and tailored his charts to the navigation needs of the day, in which most vessels were shallow draft sailing ships and Georgian Bay was remote from the main lines of commerce. This changed in the 1870s and 1880s when ship size grew, and Bayfield's charts were inadequate to the needs of navigation. Requests for new charts were ignored until tragedy struck in September 1882. The steamer *Asia* was one of a fleet of vessels that carried passengers between two sections of the Canadian Pacific Railroad—from Georgian Bay to the western end of Lake Superior. When the *Asia* foundered, 123 people died; only 2 hardy survivors lived to tell the tale. Poor charts were not the direct blame for the disaster, but it awoke Canadian officials to the need for greater vigilance. In 1883 the Royal Navy answered the Dominion of Canada's request for a new survey of Georgian Bay, which eventually led to a resurvey of all their Great Lakes waters.[63]

The publicly sponsored work of charting the lakes and siting lighthouses and buoys spawned private initiatives that pulled together navigational information into a single source. James Barnet, a Chicago publisher, for many years produced an annual volume titled *Barnet's Coast Pilot for the Lakes, on Both Shores: Michigan, Superior, Huron, St. Clair, Erie, and Ontario*. In its pages were sailing directions from one port to the next and minute descriptions of navigational aids and hazards, including thumbnail sketches of each lake lighthouse. It was an invaluable aid to the master taking his vessel into an unfamiliar harbor or channel.[64]

Free Trade on the Great Lakes: The 1854 Reciprocity Treaty

One hundred and forty years before the North American Free Trade Agreement (NAFTA) of 1994, the people and business of the Great Lakes basin enjoyed an experiment in duty-free commerce. In 1854 U.S. Secretary of State William Marcy and Lord Elgin, governor-general of Canada, signed the Reciprocity Treaty, an agreement to unfettered trade across the lakes. Following the 1846 repeal of Great Britain's corn laws, which had given preference to imports from her colonies, Canadian merchants were forced to look south to the U.S. as their natural market. There was strong interest on both sides of the lakes to facilitate more trade. However, while the Canadians would gain access to a market of thirty-four million people, all they had to offer the Americans was access to a market of just three million. The agreement only became attractive to the U.S. when Great Britain offered the right to fish in British North America's offshore Atlantic waters. With Atlantic cod as the unlikely sweetener, a deal on trade and navigation was concluded. Oddly, the Pierce administration left the lobbying necessary to get the deal ratified by the U.S. Senate to Lord Elgin and a large British delegation in Washington. A week of well-lubricated levées and receptions washed away the reservations of Democratic senators, and in the words of one participant, the treaty "floated through on champagne." The agreement called for the duty-free movement of a wide range of agricultural produce and raw materials. For the Great Lakes, there were important navigational concessions. American vessels secured the right to use the Welland Canal and the St. Lawrence River, while the Canadians won the right to sail on Lake Michigan, the only Great Lake wholly within U.S. territory, as well as access to all American canals connected to the inland seas.[65]

The treaty had an immediate and salutary impact on trade between the two countries and across the lakes. Between 1851 and 1861 total trade between the U.S. and the British North American colonies grew from just under $11 million to well over

$31 million. Some of the increase undoubtedly included trade that in the past had been illegal smuggling, and some was the result of the surging population of the region. Nonetheless, it is clear the treaty enhanced a growing integration of the lake economy across boundary lines that was already underway. Grain and lumber were the main cargoes carried across the lakes, with the latter remaining a staple of transnational lake traffic for the remainder of the century. Oswego on Lake Ontario was a particular beneficiary of the treaty, as vessels from Canada kept its harbor and elevators busy. Chicago received its share of the Canadian market after a railroad was completed in 1854 from Toronto to the Georgian Bay port of Collingwood. The railroad company quickly put five new steamers into service between Chicago and Collingwood. Not just goods but people moved across the border. The Ontario peninsula became a considerable source of immigration into the more socially and economically dynamic American states. Michigan was the prime beneficiary, and for much of the nineteenth century Canadians would be the most numerous immigrants to the Great Lake state.[66]

By granting Americans on the Great Lakes access to the locks on the St. Lawrence River, the Reciprocity Treaty stimulated direct trade between the Upper Great Lakes and Europe. A handful of lake vessels had earlier transited from the inland seas to the ocean, mostly Canadian barks from Kingston, although in 1850 the propeller *Ontario* sailed from Buffalo for California. The sleek two-masted schooner *Dean Richmond* was the first vessel built on the Upper Great Lakes for trade with Europe. In July 1856 she was loaded with four hundred tons of grain and set sail from Lake Michigan for Liverpool. Her successful arrival in the British port was hailed by the *Liverpool Daily Post* as "opening a new field for commercial enterprize [*sic*], marking an epoch in the annals of the far west." The trip was organized by Chicago businessmen very much as an experiment, and after selling off the cargo of wheat, the *Dean Richmond* was sold in Liverpool. The vessel then served out her life on the salted wave. The following year Liverpool returned the favor by sending the schooner *Madeira Pet* with a general cargo across the ocean and through the lakes to Chicago. The Chicago Board of Trade enthused that the event was "one of the most important and significant events in the commercial history of our city" and hailed the *Pet* as "the pioneer of an immense foreign trade soon to be opened between Chicago and Europe." Despite the excited predictions made in Liverpool and Chicago over beginning direct trade, the numbers did not quite add up. Both the *Dean Richmond* venture and the voyage of the *Madeira Pet* were financial losers. The latter ship had trouble disposing of its cargo as well as taking on another for her return trip. Lake vessels continued to make trips to Europe or the West Indies throughout the 1850s and into the 1860s, sometimes a dozen in a single year, but they were generally only marginally profitable. Even for the commerce of the mid-nineteenth century, the St. Lawrence locks and the navigation channels of the Great Lakes were inadequate for vessels large enough to make oceanic trade successful. It would take more than a century for engineers to make a serious attempt to open the natural outlet of the Great Lakes to the commerce of the world.[67]

Lighthouses in the Era of Bad Feelings

Lighthouses, like harbors and accurate charts, were part of the web of navigation aids that were desperately sought in the antebellum Great Lakes region. Unlike harbors, lighthouses were not opposed in principle by strict constitutional constructionists or sectional partisans. The early embrace of lighthouses by the "founding fathers" in the first Congress under the Constitution and in the administrations of Washington, Adams, Jefferson, and Madison went far to inoculate these types of navigational aids from partisan wrangles. For example, in 1847, while the issue of harbor and channel improvements was sparking sectional tensions between the West and the South, Congress approved a massive expansion of the lighthouse system, including seventeen lighthouses or beacons on the Great Lakes.[68]

Although lighthouses and related navigational aids such as buoys were not challenged in principle, as the system grew, they began to occupy a larger and larger role in federal appropriations. In 1822 there were 70 lighthouses in the U.S. By 1842 this number had grown to 256 lighthouses and 30 lightships. The Great Lakes were included in this growth with 34 new lighthouses constructed in the 1830s, but only 20 new lights in the 1840s. Individual lighthouse keepers received little in the way of supervision or assistance. Each spring Stephen Pleasonton, the Treasury auditor who oversaw the lighthouse system, chartered a vessel for a general inspector of lights to visit the upper lakes. This ship would then deliver to each lighthouse its annual supply of oil. Accompanying the inspector was a lamp maker who could make any necessary repairs to the apparatus. After this brief visitation, the lightkeepers were generally left to their own devices for the rest of the season. The set orders for keepers only specified when their lights were to be lit at the start of a season, when they could be extinguished, and that the reflectors should be kept clean and the lamps trimmed.[69]

As the system grew and complaints about the quality of lights increased, it was inevitable that Congress would begin to scrutinize lighthouse management. In March 1837 Congress approved the Lighthouse Act, a bill authorizing the construction of a large number of new lighthouses from Maine to the mouth of the Mississippi, including new structures on Lakes Erie, Huron, and Michigan. Some of these new lighthouses, such as ones at Manitowoc and Racine in the Wisconsin Territory and at the mouths of the Kalamazoo and Grand Rivers in Michigan, were at sites where Congress had not made any provisions for constructing a harbor. With one hand, the government recognized these locations as places of marine activity and, with the other, dismissed the need for navigational improvements. Perhaps it was this anomaly that prompted legislators to add a provision to their authorization bill. A temporary Board of Navy Commissioners was created to examine each proposed project to determine if at some sites "navigation is so inconsiderable as not to justify the proposed works." Twenty-two naval officers were assigned to the inspections, and their recommendations revealed something was amiss in the way lighthouse decisions were being made. The navy determined that thirty-one of the proposed lighthouses were not needed.[70]

The navy's involvement was not continued beyond the 1837 Lighthouse Act, but it was an indication that Congress was beginning to pay closer attention to the nation's growing lighthouse establishment. An important critic was Edmund March Blunt, author of the most widely used mariner's guide to the American coast. He complained to the secretary of the treasury that "the whole lighthouse system needs revision, a strict superintendence

and an entirely different plan of operation." The House Committee on Commerce, after reviewing the report from the naval inspectors, concluded that Blunt was right. The committee admitted
that in the past Congress had simply responded to the requests
of petitioners for a lighthouse without investigating how legitimate the need was for a beacon. To address this issue, in 1838
Congress ordered the creation of regional lighthouse districts.
Each of these districts was then assigned a naval officer to inspect
all navigational aids therein. The inspectors were also expected
to make reports regarding the condition of each and make recommendations for any future lighthouses.[71]

The Great Lakes were divided into two districts. Lieutenant
James T. Homans was given the task of inspecting the lakes west
of Detroit. During the course of the summer, he covered 1,825
miles. He was not pleased with most of what he found. At the
shallow and difficult to navigate St. Clair Flats he found a channel
marked by a "public spirited ship captain" when it clearly should
have had government buoys showing the way in day and night.
He sited a new lighthouse at the entrance to Saginaw Bay. At the
northern end of Lake Huron, he found the tower at Bois Blanc
Island collapsed, and he had to locate a new spot for reconstruction. He noted that the Straits of Mackinac where Lakes Michigan
and Huron came together were not properly covered. A lightship assigned to duty there in 1836 was almost never on station.
The vessel had been repeatedly driven from its moorings, storm
battered, and beached. Mackinac lacked the ability to dry dock
the vessel and properly patch her, so each time she was beached,
the lightship had to be sent to Detroit for repairs. Homans recommended the lightship be sent to the more protected waters of
Lake St. Clair and a new, more durable vessel or a permanent
lighthouse be assigned to the dangerous Waugoshance Shoal
that stuck like a bone in the throat of the strait's western entrance.
He also recommended that a new lighthouse be placed at Mackinac Island. At South Manitou Island Homans recognized Crescent Bay as one of the best natural anchorages on the Great Lakes,
and he selected an advantageous site for a lighthouse. He arrived
at Grand River as a new lighthouse there was being constructed.
He found the materials and methods decidedly flawed. This disturbing finding and his other recommendations were reported to

Stephen Pleasonton, the Treasury Department auditor who supervised the U.S. lighthouse system. The auditor's response was predictably defensive. He claimed Homans's critique of the Grand River work was unfounded. The overmatched lightship at the Straits remained in duty until 1844, and the recommended lighthouse at Mackinac was put off even longer.[72]

The naval officers pulled no punches in their report. They were independent of the Treasury Department that administered lighthouses as well as the army whose engineers developed harbors. They looked at Great Lakes navigation and navigational aids with the eye of experienced seamen. They unhesitatingly stated that "the formation of harbors at convenient distances along the entire lake shore is a matter of the first importance" and that it was the only way to secure lives and property in the region. They also were critical of the way harbor improvements and lighthouse construction had been carried out via small annual appropriations that prevented effective management of multiyear projects. Much money was wasted because incomplete works were destroyed by winter storms while they were waiting for funding for completion. Congress was generous in funding lighthouses, but again wasted money because the lights were not part of comprehensive harbor plans. Congress would fund, and Pleasonton's office would site, a lighthouse with no regard for how harbor improvements might change navigation requirements. For example, most Great Lakes harbors required piers to be built at the mouth of rivers to block the formation of sandbars. Those piers jutting out into the lake needed pier-head lights, while light towers built farther inland might no longer be needed. The naval officers went so far as to say that "nearly all light-house appropriations would have been much more advantageously employed in constructing harbors." Perhaps most alarming of all, the naval officers found that many lighthouses in the western Great Lakes often ran short of oil with which to light their lamps and that they had no way of securing additional oil.[73]

Pleasonton's response to the naval critique was balky and defensive. Navy inspectors determined that 40 percent of American lighthouses had serious defects, yet Congress took no formal action to improve the management of the system. In 1842 Pleasonton's administration of U.S. lighthouses was again brought under direct scrutiny when Congress authorized the House Commerce Committee to determine if the Lighthouse Establishment should be completely reorganized. The auditor's relationship with Winslow Lewis, and the numerous times his lighthouses had to be rebuilt, was finally broached in an open hearing. Yet Pleasanton managed to deflect these attacks as well as complaints from mariners that U.S. lighthouses were totally inferior to those operating in Europe. The committee seems to have been more concerned with seeing if expenses could be reduced. Penny-pinching was the one thing that Pleasonton did well, so it was no surprise that the committee endorsed his administration. Yet complaints from the marine establishment did not cease, and in 1843 Congress acted to provide more professional management for lighthouse construction. It specifically ordered that an army engineer be detailed to oversee the building of a Lake Michigan lighthouse. In the years that followed, this became increasingly common.[74]

The mediocre state of navigation aids along America's sea and lake shores gradually became an embarrassment to the nation's pride. America was becoming a country that reveled in invention, with the production of new and improved ways of doing things. At the Crystal Palace Exhibition in London in 1851 it was the products of American workshops that had excited the admiration of the world, including Cyrus McCormick's reaper, Samuel Colt's revolvers, and Charles Goodyear's rubberized waterproof clothing. Even the stuffy *Times* of London was forced to admit: "Great Britain has received more useful ideas, and more ingenious inventions, from the United States, through the exhibition, than from all other sources." Yet the quality of American lighthouses, due to shabby construction of the towers and their dim illumination, lagged behind the nations of the Old World.[75]

Comprehensive reform finally came in 1851. As part of its normal lighthouse appropriation bill, Congress ordered the formation of a board to undertake a complete review of the management of American lighthouses "and to make a general detailed report and programme to guide legislation in extending and improving our present system of construction, illumination, inspection, and superintendence." The bill specified that the composition of the board include two high-ranking naval officers, two army engineers, and a civilian of "high scientific attainment."

Under the direction of Commodore William B. Shubrick, this board undertook a wide-ranging investigation, visited many lighthouses, interviewed mariners, and examined the new technology that was being deployed by other nations. Their 760-page report was the final torpedo into Stephen Pleasonton's leaky administration of U.S. navigational aids. In every aspect of the program, they found problems. Pleasonton's lighthouses were poorly lit, had inferior lenses, were constructed too low and of inferior materials; buoys were too small; lightships were all but useless because of poor illumination; lightkeepers were without instruction and in need of assistants; many lighthouses were in desperate need of repair; and even colonial-era lighthouses were in better shape than those constructed since 1789. A final damning shot at Pleasonton was the contention that with competent professional management, the U.S. would operate with greater effectiveness and less expense. Congress wasted no time implementing the report. In October 1852, all administrative duties for lighthouses were transferred from Pleasonton to the Lighthouse Board, which became a permanent administrative body. The Lighthouse Service would remain in the Treasury Department with its secretary acting as ex officio president of the board, but all management would be in the hands of the board. Twelve local administrative districts were created, with the eleventh and twelfth in the Great Lakes. Each district would have a full-time inspector appointed by the president. This new, much-improved management system would remain in place until 1910. The demise of Pleasonton's control of American navigation aids was spurred by two factors: his age and the spirit of the age. A close friend remarked that Pleasonton's "advancing age unfitted him to contend with the many who sought to dispose him from office." His prior "impregnable" position became more vulnerable when the seventy-five-year-old man's congressional clout waned as old supporters retired. Perhaps more important, there was a growing recognition of the need for science and expertise in managing the ongoing communication revolution. The trained engineers of the U.S. Army were already surveying routes for interstate railroads, charting the inland seas, and now would take charge of lighthouse construction and management.[76]

Just as important as this administrative change to Great Lakes lighthouses was the technical change ordered by Congress as

Figure 8. Fresnel lens, Split Rock Lighthouse, Lake Superior.
Source: Library of Congress.

part of the March 3, 1851, act. Without even waiting for the recommendations of the Lighthouse Board, the Congress authorized the adoption of the Fresnel lens for all U.S. stations. This was a change long overdue and needlessly delayed by Stephen Pleasonton because of his misguided loyalty and questionable association with Winslow Lewis. While American lighthouses were outfitted with Lewis's flawed parabolic reflectors, every advanced maritime nation had adopted the Fresnel lens. Invented in 1822 by the French scientist Augustin Fresnel, the new lens was a series of concentric rings of glass prisms looking rather like a bee hive. The effect was to bend the light into a powerful, narrow beam that could be seen from between twenty and forty miles away.

Fresnel lenses were produced in a variety of sizes or "orders." The largest size was the giant first-order lenses that stood twelve feet high and six feet in diameter. These lenses were designed for coastal navigation and could project their beam far out into the ocean to notify vessels they were approaching a continental coast. In contrast, a sixth-order light was only a foot wide but did the job of marking the entrance to a harbor. There were no first-order lights deployed on the Great Lakes; the enclosed nature of the waterway made their size and range unnecessary. Only five of the next largest second-order Fresnel lenses were deployed on the Great Lakes. The first was at Grosse Point just north of Chicago. These six-foot-high lights were only deployed at stations designed to be, in the Lighthouse Board's words, "the largest and most important lighthouse in the district." The vast majority of lenses deployed on the inland seas were third-order and fourth-order lights, with even smaller ones set on pier heads.[77]

On the Canadian side of the lakes, lighthouse construction was the charge of the colony of Canada West (Ontario) and its Board of Works. While not as irresponsible as the Pleasonton administration in the states, the board was just as frugal. Navigational aids were funded but largely on the well-traveled waters of Lakes Ontario and Erie. In general, the lack of transportation improvements slowed the development of the colony. Canada West did not receive its first railroad until 1853. Two years later, track was extended to Collingwood on Georgian Bay. The effect of this connection was to spur the rapid settlement of the area, and Collingwood became one of the busiest Canadian lake ports owing to dense stands of merchantable timber and its proximity to the growing U.S. ports of Chicago and Milwaukee. The opening of the Sault Ste. Marie Canal and the signing of the free-trade agreement between the U.S. and the Canadian colonies in 1854 further increased lake traffic on Georgian Bay and Lake Huron. Despite this, there were no navigational aids on Georgian Bay. In 1855 John Brown, a successful masonry contractor, was given a commission to bring lighthouses to Canada's Huron shore. Unfortunately, the task of building the towers at remote locations exceeded colonial appropriations, and Brown nearly went bankrupt trying to complete six of the projected eleven. However, those six were stout, strong, and tall (five of the six were eighty feet in height) and outfitted with Fresnel lenses. Known as the "Imperial Towers," they remain some of the most picturesque lights on the entire Great Lakes.[78]

The establishment of the Lighthouse Board brought professionalism to the management of U.S. Great Lakes lighthouses. Between 1854 and 1857 scores of new lighthouses were built, and the rest were enhanced with the new, more efficient Fresnel lenses. An even bigger job was the rebuilding of the many lighthouses that, under Pleasonton, had been built too short or of inferior materials. Between 1857 and 1859 the board rebuilt or refitted forty-five Great Lakes lighthouses. The new towers and their beacons, piercing a murky midnight, were a powerful signal to both mariners on the somber seas and the farmers and merchants who depended on lake commerce that a change for the better was at hand. Scientific mapping and lighting reduced the dangers to inland seas navigation. Only the growing sectional and partisan divide that inhibited investment in clear channels and safe harbors continued to darken the dawn of a new day.[79]

4

The Construction Era

1860–1880

The Crisis Comes

As the snow fluttered past his window in the Detroit office of the U.S. Lake Survey, Captain George Gordon Meade contemplated the future of his country, his service, and the daunting mapping project that was under his command. He had headed the Lake Survey since 1856. During that time, he had done much to increase its scope and to improve the scientific footing of its operations. Meade began the first systematic collection of meteorological data in the Great Lakes region by setting up nineteen formal collection stations from northern Minnesota to the head of the St. Lawrence River. Although embryonic in 1861, it was the basis for the future study of regional climate patterns and important for the eventual production of the first marine weather forecasts. He also began the systematic collection of data on Great Lakes water levels, of no small concern to the mariners. Meade dramatically

Figure 9. George Gordon Meade, 1864. Photograph by Matthew Brady.
Source: Library of Congress.

improved the accuracy of the survey's longitudinal measurements through the ingenious use of the telegraph to make simultaneous readings of the meridian passage of stars at two separate points. To do this Meade collaborated with civilian scientists at Western Reserve College in Cleveland and at the University of Michigan. He also established an astronomical observatory in Detroit to improve the survey's calculation of longitude. Joseph

Henry of the Smithsonian Institution and the Lighthouse Board regarded Meade as the nation's most gifted marine engineer and a budding man of science. Meade was an example of someone who would become of increasing importance in Great Lakes history. He was a skilled and dedicated professional attuned to the application of science to marine safety.[1]

Meade came to his scientific approach to navigational improvements through long exposure to marine infrastructure engineering. Although he was a West Point graduate, Meade had never sought a military career, and he went to the academy because he was too poor for any other school. He stayed in the service only because it allowed him to support his family and develop his skill as an engineer. He had nonetheless proved a bulldog in combat during the Mexican War, and after the Battle of Monterey he was brevetted to first lieutenant. It was in lighthouse work, however, that he really distinguished himself. From 1851 to 1856 he worked on a wide variety of lighthouse projects from the Delaware River to the Florida Keys. He pioneered the American application of new designs such as the screw-pile lighthouse that could be secured on soft alluvial soil. He also experimented with the use of iron in lighthouse foundations and superstructure. So keen was his interest in the technical workings of navigational beacons that in 1853 he designed a new type of lamp to be used with Fresnel lenses. Its operation was based on hydraulic pressure and was well suited to the Florida coast—although it was not used on the much colder northern lakes.[2]

While Captain Meade could look with satisfaction on the innovations and energy he brought to his five years of work on the Lake Survey, he was greatly distressed by the political drift of the nation whose uniform he wore. Like most Euro-Americans, Meade neither practiced nor supported the institution of slavery, but also like most of his countrymen he did not favor disturbing the national harmony with discussions of the morality of human bondage. He was disturbed equally by the evangelical fervor of antislavery activists and by southern rights fire-eaters, who argued slavery was a necessary and positive social good. He was a man of science who distrusted emotion-driven politics and the application of moral sentiment over rational calculation. Antebellum America, both North and South, was heavily influenced by the emotional appeals of evangelical Christianity. Moral outrage over slavery and the opposite reaction it elicited from southerners excited the passions that pushed the country toward civil war. Meade distrusted what he regarded as the Republican Party's overemphasis on slavery, but he had no appetite for the Democratic Party, which seemed determined at all costs to placate the southern slave interest. In the 1860 election, he cast his vote for John Bell, the candidate of the short-lived Constitutional Union Party that sought to defuse growing sectional tensions by the somewhat vague prescription of staying true to the Constitution.[3]

Meade's son and biographer remembered that his father "depreciated all violent language, as subordinating reason to passion, as productive of no possible good, and certain to entail evil." This dispassionate approach to politics in the most passionate era of American civilization led some Detroit partisans to doubt the loyalty of the officers serving in the U.S. Lake Survey. At a mass meeting in the spring of 1861, resolutions were enthusiastically passed calling on the men of the survey to swear an oath of allegiance to the U.S. This demand came at a time when a Confederacy of seceded states was being organized and many veteran serving officers had resigned their commissions and treasonously accepted high rank in the rebel military. Meade gathered his subordinates in his office. The majority found the demand that they swear an additional oath offensive. Lieutenant J. L. Kirby Smith was especially aggrieved because his uncle, a regular army officer, had quit U.S. service and become a Confederate general. Meade and his officers responded by ignoring the patriotic mob and communicated to Washington, D.C., their willingness to stand by the government. In a matter of months, most of them were seeing active service in America's bloodiest war. Lieutenant Kirby Smith removed any question of his allegiance when he fell mortally wounded while leading his regiment in the Battle of Corinth. Lieutenant Orlando Poe led troops in the Peninsula Campaign and later served as William T. Sherman's chief engineer during the March to the Sea. In 1863 George Gordon Meade, by then a Major General in command of the Army of the Potomac, turned back Robert E. Lee's Confederate tide on the field of Gettysburg. The former Lake Survey officers had more than proven their loyalty to the nation.[4]

While it was the clash over slavery and its right to expand west within the U.S. that triggered the awful Civil War of 1861–65, economic differences between the North, South, and the West were critical in helping cut away the middle ground on which that issue might have been solved by compromise. A good example was the fate of an 1859 congressional appropriation to clear and mark the so-called St. Clair Flats, a notorious choke point for inland seas shipping. Lake Huron is joined to Lake Erie by the St. Clair River, Lake St. Clair, and the Detroit River. These narrow and shallow waters were a challenge to all vessels but especially so for the more than twelve hundred sailing ships trying to fight river currents. All types of vessels risked running aground on sandbars in Lake St. Clair or in the St. Clair River's marshy delta, known as the "flats." So frequently did ships run aground in the flats that there were by the mid-1850s more than a dozen tugs constantly employed in pulling free the stranded vessels. A storm could drive as many as a hundred ships out of the narrow channel and onto the muddy shallows. Yet after the bill was passed, President James Buchanan deployed his presidential veto, complaining that this waterway, through which ships from eight states and several nations passed, was a local, not a federal, responsibility. This type of obtuse executive action and the southern congressional support that upheld it helped to push voters in the Great Lakes states away from the sole national political party, the Democrats, and into the arms of the purely sectional Republican Party.[5]

The rise of the Republican Party in the Great Lakes region was, in the words of one historian, "nearly instantaneous and overwhelming." The Kansas-Nebraska Act of 1854, which erased the Missouri Compromise line restricting slavery in the West, triggered the party's birth. The actual birthplace of the party—either Ripon, Wisconsin, or Jackson, Michigan—has been hotly debated, but historians are very clear that the Midwest's antislavery stance was driven as much, if not more, by economics as moral outrage. The bitter racism of the Black Laws that denied basic civil rights to African Americans in Iowa, Illinois, Indiana, and Ohio were popular legislative actions. Restricting slavery reflected a regional determination to avoid economic competition with the potential of black labor in the West and the reality of southern political clout in Washington. The Republicans espoused an economic agenda that was in harmony with the "culture of progress" that had been planted in the region since the opening of the Erie Canal. At its core was the notion that government had the job of removing obstacles to collective economic progress.[6]

Some of the strongest sectional appeals made by the Republican Party in their 1860 platform had nothing to do with the issue of slavery. The platform appealed to farmers interested in expanding their acreage or moving to new territories in the West by the promise of a free homestead policy. A bill to authorize this had passed in the last Congress with only a single vote from a slave state representative, only to be blocked by a James Buchanan veto. The platform promised federal support for building a railroad to the Pacific Coast. This measure had also been the subject of a bill in the recent Congress, but it failed to pass largely because it received not a single vote from a slave state representative. The most obvious sectional appeal was a platform plank that called for navigational improvements on the grounds of marine safety: "That the appropriation by Congress for river and harbor improvements of a National character, required for the accommodation and security of an existing commerce, are authorized by the constitution and justified by the obligation of Government to protect the lives and property of its citizens." Abraham Lincoln, the party's nominee for president, would no longer block congressional support for Great Lakes navigation with the threat of a veto. Lincoln had defended the constitutionality of such appropriations at the 1847 River and Harbor Convention. As a lawyer, he had specialized in transportation cases. As a legislator, he had been a champion of the Illinois and Michigan Canal. As a youth, he had piloted flatboats and river steamers, and he even held a federal patent for a device to lift vessels over sandbars. In 1860 the Republican Party, through its platform and its candidate, promised voters that the national government would be a progressive force in American economic development. The Lincoln administration, although constrained by the need to fight a war to save the Union, nonetheless immediately moved to aid lake navigation. Between 1861 and 1865 funding for the Lake Survey and its critical task of charting the lakes was drastically increased. By the end of the war 40 percent more was devoted to the survey than under the Pierce-Buchanan administrations, and that was a mere down payment on support that would follow Appomattox.[7]

The Great Lakes states were decisive in saving the federal Union. In terms of military enlistments, no area of the country supported the war as enthusiastically. Indiana was first, Illinois second, Ohio fourth, with Michigan and Wisconsin sixth and seventh, respectively, in percentage of population serving in the military. Those troops fighting mainly in the western theater cut the Confederacy in half when they captured Memphis and Vicksburg and kept going till they had burned Atlanta and wreaked a path of destruction all the way to the Atlantic Coast. This was a bitter reckoning for southern politicians like Jefferson Davis, who in the 1840s and 1850s had spurned a political alliance with the west. In 1846 he had scuttled any attempt to reconcile the South and the West over the issue of navigation improvements. In 1862 soldiers from the Great Lakes occupied his plantation in Mississippi, scattered his slaves, ravaged his fields, and turned his Greek revival mansion into their field headquarters. When in 1865 the entire Confederacy was in ashes, those soldiers could go back to their heartland farms, foundries, docks, and ships confident that the reconstructed federal government would meet their economic needs.

The Impact of the Civil War on Great Lakes Navigation

The initial impact of the war on the lake marine was to depress shipping. The economy of the region had slumped in 1857 following a national recession, and the secession crisis continued the economic slowdown. It was not until it was clear to the nation that fighting the Southern rebellion would entail a long, hard struggle that the economy began to revive and then thrive under the stimulus of military procurement.

The grain trade dominated the lake marine in the antebellum period, and the need to feed armies, together with crop failures in Europe, meant that there was a huge demand for the harvest of the prairie. Chicago was by this time the greatest primary grain port in the world. Its shipments jumped from a prewar high of thirty-one million bushels of grain to better than fifty million bushels. Railroads, and to a lesser extent canals, brought a large part of this grain to the port, but 99 percent of wheat and 95 percent of corn left by ship. This surge in grain production required the building of new and larger grain elevators not only in Chicago and Milwaukee, the main collection points on Lake Michigan, but also at Detroit and Erie, which previously had not figured in the grain trade. Buffalo, where most shipments were destined, built nine new massive elevators during the Civil War, doubling its storage capacity.[8]

The tremendous harvests that flowed into the holds of Great Lakes vessels came from a highly productive agricultural sector in the loyal states, which became even more productive under the stimulus of a national emergency. This was enhanced by the still expanding number and size of farms in the northwestern states. Illinois and Wisconsin led the nation in wheat production, the staff of life for the Union Army. During the war Wisconsin alone produced one hundred million bushels of wheat. This production occurred when that state, still in the midst of frontier settlement, had sent eighty thousand men, mostly farm boys, to fight in defense of the republic. One reason for this leap in production was Northern farmers' investment in technology. At the start of the war, the Northern states had almost twice the number of reapers and threshing machines per acre and per farm worker as their Southern counterparts. This difference increased as the war progressed. During the conflict, Northern farmers added 233,000 new pieces of farm machinery. The Union, despite having 20 percent of its farm labor supply away in the military, was able to add 2.7 million acres of new farmland. The South was a largely agricultural region, but its prewar farming sector was both labor intensive because of the slavery system and oriented to nonfood crops such as cotton, hemp, and tobacco. There was some conversion to foodstuffs because of the war, but the Southern military did not benefit from this as much as it needed to because, unlike the North, the South had a weak transportation infrastructure. The combination of the North's Great Lakes shipping, its interstate and intrastate canals, and its railroads facilitated the movement of foodstuffs from where they were grown to where they were needed. Yet as the war went on, expanding agricultural productivity strained the transport system and encouraged schemes to move grain even more efficiently from west to east.[9]

The wartime boom stimulated midwestern boosters to dust off several long-dreamed-of waterways projects. For Chicago, this meant expanding the Illinois and Michigan Canal that linked Lake Michigan to the Illinois River and hence the Mississippi valley. The canal was crowded with grain barges during the Civil War. Yet what many leaders in Chicago had on their minds was not wheat but sewage. By 1862 the Chicago River was choked with the filth of the town's streets and food-processing plants. Just between 1861 and 1863, Chicago's meat-packing business, already substantial, tripled in size as a result of army contracts. Never in the history of the world were so many animals and their filth concentrated in one city. Cattle and swine were delivered by rail and sent to the North Branch of the Chicago River, whose banks were lined with distilleries turning grain into whisky. Rather than waste the leftover mash, the distilleries erected feed lots along the river where they recycled the soggy grain to fatten up the livestock. The filth left by the engorged animals was shoveled into the river. The cattle were then driven through the streets to meat-packing houses along the South Branch of the Chicago River, where they were cut up and packed into cans or barrels for shipment to the army. What was left over from the processing was shoveled into the river. Both branches of the river flowed into the main stream, and hence into Lake Michigan from whence Chicago drew its drinking water. For years city officials knew they had an ever-escalating problem, and they had a solution in mind. If the Illinois and Michigan Canal was cut deeper than the level of Lake Michigan, then the clean water of the lake would naturally flow into the river, reverse its course and flush all the filth downstream. Of course, deepening and widening the canal would also allow a greater volume of grain barge traffic, which would be another boon to the city. Therefore, Chicago proposed the federal government take on the expensive project of expanding the canal.[10]

Chicago's proposal was recognized both in Congress and the press for what it was—local self-interest. New York, in particular, was outraged. Under its own funding it was nearing the end of a major expansion of the Erie Canal to a new width of seventy feet. Undaunted, Chicagoans tried to repeat the success of the River and Harbor Convention of 1847 by organizing a National Ship

Canal Convention to be held in the windy city in 1863. They also sought to make allies of their biggest opponents—the legislators of the State of New York. While the Erie Canal enlargement was completed by 1863, the Empire State, it was thought, could be seduced by the resurrection of one of their long-pondered pipe dreams—a canal around Niagara Falls. Of course, there already existed the Welland Canal, but that was on the British side of the border. In the name of national defense, the Chicago convention called for an all-U.S. route between Lake Erie and Lake Ontario. The Illinois and Michigan Canal enlargement was also refashioned as a military necessity. "The national interest requires that you should have this canal so enlarged as to permit the passage of gunboats from the Mississippi to the Lakes," an Illinois delegate proclaimed.[11]

The national defense argument was strained, but it was not invented out of whole cloth. In 1861 a U.S. naval vessel stopped a British flagged ship carrying Confederate agents bound for Europe. By early 1862 the violation of international law provoked a diplomatic confrontation, and Great Britain dispatched eleven thousand soldiers and a large naval force to its Canadian colonies. Major lake cities such as Buffalo, Cleveland, Detroit, and Chicago had no defense from an attack across the lakes. Hundreds of Union gunboats on the Mississippi and Ohio Rivers could not be brought to bear in the crisis. Wisely, the Lincoln administration offered an apology to England, and the cloud of a foreign war dissipated. That action, however, did not stop Chicagoans and New Yorkers from reanimating the specter of invasion from Canada to strengthen their argument. President Lincoln, who in many ways owed his office to Chicago politicos, played the issue deftly. While he was focused on trying to save the Union, he played along with the boosters. Administration support was made public when Vice President Hannibal Hamlin was dispatched to preside over the Chicago convention. Lincoln then showed he took the deliberations seriously when he commissioned engineer Charles B. Stuart to study its recommendations. That delayed any further action for more than six months. When Stuart delivered his report in March 1864, Lincoln endorsed it and sent it to Congress. A bill was eventually introduced, but with the trauma of the war reaching its climax and a presidential election underway, it did not advance. The war ended without either the Niagara or the Illinois canals receiving national support. After the war, Chicago renewed its efforts to clean sewage from its rivers by using local resources and in a way that would have a controversial effect on Great Lakes navigation.[12]

Rising freight rates were one of the reasons farmers supported Chicago's attempt to improve its canal. The heavy production and demand for grain during the war and the rising mining and manufacturing sectors strained available shipping on the lakes as well as the canals. The best of the Great Lakes schooners were devoted to the grain trade. Water would ruin a grain cargo, so stout, dry ships were tied up on the Lake Michigan to Buffalo route. One effect of this was to retard the rapid development of copper and iron production in the lake states during the Civil War. Mining in Michigan's Upper Peninsula began in the late 1840s and really took off following the 1855 opening of the Sault Ste. Marie Canal. The Keweenaw Peninsula boasted the most productive copper deposits. The industry grew slowly in the 1850s, but when the military placed orders for brass buttons, cannon barrels, and belt buckles, the price of copper jumped from nineteen cents per pound to forty-six cents. The number of companies purporting to operate in the district increased from fourteen to sixty, but actual production fell because of a severe labor shortage. An important impact of the war was to improve mining methods and to introduce technology below ground. The Marquette Range east of the Keweenaw was the center for early iron mining. Despite more than a decade of extensive investment in numerous mines and a railroad, there had been no capital returns on iron district investments. The Civil War changed this. In 1862 the Jackson Mining Company declared its first dividend. The Cleveland-Cliffs Mining Company also declared a profit when it saw output jump from twelve thousand tons of ore per year to a wartime average just under forty-five thousand tons. Investors took notice, and in 1864 alone nine new mining companies were established in the district. At the port of Marquette, schooners could be quickly loaded owing to the large ore dock that dropped the ore directly into the vessels' holds. However, to unload a schooner with a three-hundred-ton cargo could take as long as three days, with the ore laboriously shoveled out of the hold and into wheelbarrows. The first experiments with mechanical unloaders did not begin until 1867. The transportation of

Michigan copper and iron ore to the ports and furnaces of the lower lakes greatly expanded shipping on Lake Superior.[13]

During the Civil War, the cities of the Great Lakes region, particularly Chicago, Detroit, and Cleveland, moved from being mere transshipment hubs for copper and iron ore to developing the means of industrial production. The war stimulated industrialization through the reliance of the Union Army on rail transport to move and supply its armies. The Northwest Manufacturing Company in Chicago illustrates how this happened. In 1855 Richard Teller Crane founded the company as a small brass foundry. He was at first the sole employee and saw church bells as his main market. As Chicago grew to become the rail center of the West, his company began to focus on making brass fittings for rail cars and steam engines. During the war his company more than doubled in size and production. Iron foundries were even more directly influenced by the war. The greatest manufacturing need was for iron rails. By 1865 the production of rails had increased 250 percent over 1850s levels. The intensive use of railroads to answer military needs and the simultaneous construction of the Central Pacific and Union Pacific Railroads exacerbated normal production. This led to critical experiments in manufacturing long-lasting steel rails.[14]

The strong connection between Great Lakes shipping, mining, and manufacturing is illustrated by the role played by Eber Brock Ward in building the steel industry along the lakes. After growing up in a Lake Huron lighthouse and going before the mast as a cabin boy, Ward became a shipbuilder and the owner of the largest fleet of Great Lakes steamboats. His early interest in iron making stemmed naturally from his involvement in shipbuilding. In 1848 he supervised the forging of some of the first iron ore to come out of Michigan, which was used to make the walking beam for his steamer *Ocean*. Thereafter, he expanded his interest in iron. In 1853 he founded the Eureka Iron and Steel Works just north of Detroit. Here he experimented with using several new processes that would blast hot air on molten iron to burn off impurities, resulting in the stronger, lighter, and more durable product—steel. Although he was a man of limited education, he believed in bringing science to bear on business. He was the first American iron maker to use chemists to test the suitability of ore for steelmaking. In 1858 he built a second plant on the North

Branch of the Chicago River. Here the focus was on rolling a steel rail, a critical need yet up to this time only available by import from Great Britain. Stimulated by the heavy wartime demand, Ward's North Chicago Rolling Mill was finally able to produce the first U.S. made steel rail in May 1865. This steel rail became the cornerstone of the Great Lakes steel industry, and Ward's plant eventually grew into the mammoth U.S. Steel Corporation.[15]

The growth of the mining industry and industrial manufacturing and even the expansion of railroads all stimulated lake shipping. The lake marine was not a backward industry pushed aside by the juggernaut of the iron horse. Rather Great Lakes ships, even sailing vessels, continuously adapted to new technologies and changing trade patterns. Rails and sails had missions that were more complementary than competitive. Bulk cargoes such as grain or ore, then as now, could be most cost effectively moved by water. It could cost twice as much to ship grain by rail as by lake schooner. Water transport generally took longer, but the movement of bulk cargoes was not especially time sensitive. The movement of specialized manufactured goods and passengers created situations where speed of transport mattered greatly. Hence, Great Lakes ships retained the edge in bulk transport, while during the 1850s the railroads captured the lion's share of the passenger traffic. By 1861 three separate railroad lines paralleled the New York City to Chicago, Great Lakes–Erie Canal water route. The competition offered by the waterway held down railroad rates and favored the economic development of businesses located in those areas. Chicago, for example, had some of the lowest railroad shipping rates in the nation because its large fleet of ships prevented railroads from monopolizing access to eastern markets. Historian William Cronon has demonstrated that during the April to November Great Lakes shipping season, railroads entering Chicago from the East slashed their shipping rates to secure a portion of the grain trade. When vessels withdrew due to winter gales, the railroads' rates would more than double. This process of radical rate fluctuation was a feature of the eastern railroads entering Chicago. Not just season and shipping affected their rate structure, however, as each of the three railroads had similar beginning (the Atlantic Coast) and end points (Chicago), which meant they had to compete with each other as well as with lake shipping. On the other hand, railroads that radiated out from Chicago to the north, south, and west all brought their hauls to the Lake Michigan port, which greatly enhanced the city's maritime interests. Milwaukee and Toledo, to a lesser extent, also enhanced the importance of their ports by railroad hinterlands to their west. At the other end of the lakes, Buffalo's emergence as a major railroad hub only enhanced the business of its great grain port. By 1887 Buffalo had eleven railroads radiating out from its port tying the harbor to Canadian cities, the Atlantic Coast, and the vast interior south of the lakes.[16]

The degree to which the lake marine and the railroad complemented one another reflects a harmonization of the U.S. economy that began to emerge during the Civil War. This was symbolized by the adoption of a standard rail gauge by the Congress when it offered generous financial support for the Pacific Railroad and by the creation of a national banking system, which triggered the move toward a national paper currency. Historian Peter D. Hall commented on the centralizing impact of the American Civil War on the nation. "The war changed everything," he wrote. "The large scale integration of transportation, communication and credit facilities, and the reorganization of government agencies were . . . at last leading Americans towards the achievement of functional nationality."[17]

"Rules of the Road" for Lake Commerce

On the night of September 8, 1860, a brightly lit steamer surged through a Lake Michigan thunderstorm. Onboard were at least 350 people, exhausted from a day of marching, dancing, and partying. They were about to be involved in an incident that would alter Great Lakes navigation regulations. Most of those onboard were Milwaukee residents who had come down to Chicago for the day to cheer for their candidate for president, the "Little Giant" Stephen A. Douglas. Rather than take the train, they had booked passage on the *Lady Elgin* so they could enjoy dancing and singing on their way home. By two thirty in the morning, however, they likely had had their fill of drink, and the pitching ship made dancing dicey and dinner difficult to keep down. Suddenly out of the dark lake, the steamer's captain saw a heavily laden lumber schooner careening toward his ship. The schooner *Augusta* tried to pass the *Lady Elgin* on her starboard side. The steamer's helmsman may have anticipated the schooner would pass on the more customary port side. In any event, in the darkness and confusion the *Augusta* struck the steamer at her port paddlewheel. The wind and rough seas quickly parted the ships, with both captains initially thinking the schooner had taken the worst of the incident. Then the *Lady Elgin* began to list and in short order began to break up. Though no passenger manifest was taken, perhaps as many as 385 passengers and crew went into the lake that night. Yet only 98 staggered ashore at dawn.

Darius N. Malott, the Captain of the *Augusta*, was brought before a Cook County Coroner's Jury to explain what had happened. The schooner master and his crew were admonished for not keeping a better lookout, yet otherwise were found free of blame. There were no formal rules that guided mariner's actions on the approach of another vessel. It was commonly considered that the steam-powered ship should give way to a sailing ship since mechanical propulsion gave the steamer much more maneuverability. Britain and France had already adopted formal rules to govern maritime encounters, but the U.S. Congress had always been deterred by businessmen and sailors, who sought to avoid government regulation. The terrible loss of life from the *Lady Elgin* collision and the fact that there were then better than seventeen hundred commercial vessels on the Great Lakes—not to mention hundreds of fishing boats and pleasure craft—finally impelled action. Federal rules, passed by Congress in 1864, required all ships to post a white light near the top of the foremast. A green light was to be posted on the starboard side and a red light to port. All vessels were further required to have a fog signal. Clearly spelled out in the rules were clauses detailing how vessels should maneuver when crossing, approaching, or passing one another. The new law, signed by President Abraham Lincoln, was a clear attempt to use legal means to help bring order to the burgeoning maritime frontier of the inland seas. Like most efforts to legalize behavior, it was not a complete success. Confined waters, numerous vessels, and unpredictable weather continued to make collision a real danger. In 1871 alone, there were at least 225 ship-to-ship collisions on the lakes.[18]

Great Lakes Lighthouses
in the Post–Civil War Era

In 1866 Aaron A. Sheridan, late corporal in Company E of the 13th Illinois Infantry, hopped out of a boat and onto the broad beach of South Manitou Island. Perhaps he held out his strong right arm to his wife, Julia, and helped her ashore. It would have made him feel good to be able to do that, perhaps more than other men, because Sheridan's lower left arm had been shattered by a rebel bullet in the November 1863 Battle of Ringgold in northern Georgia. Keeping the arm, getting his health back, and adjusting to his disability had been a long battle. Coming to northern Lake Michigan to be the keeper of the South Manitou Island Lighthouse marked his success in a struggle to live a normal life, to be a provider, a husband, a father, a man.

Aaron Sheridan was just one of many Civil War veterans who became lighthouse keepers in the wake of their military service. Many of these were men like Sheridan who had suffered severe wounds in combat but had proven themselves dedicated to their duty. Barry Litogot was twice wounded before being awarded the keeper's post at Mamajuda Island in the Detroit River. James S. Donahue, like Sheridan, had suffered a permanent disability while leading a company in the 8th Michigan Infantry in the 1864 Overland Campaign. Wounded in the thigh, he lost most of one leg. He was assigned to the South Haven lighthouse. All across the Great Lakes—at Cana Island Light, Potawatomi Island Light, Squaw Point Light, Rock Island Light, Fairport Harbor Light, and scores of other stations on the inland seas and the nation's seacoasts—Civil War veterans were given preferential consideration for light-keeper jobs. This comported with an earlier preference given to Revolutionary War and War of 1812 veterans. The Civil War, however, had a much broader and deeper impact on American society. The three million Union Army veterans were much more numerous, and the wounded, many with amputated limbs, were much more visible to the broader society. Through the Grand Army of the Republic and smaller regimental associations, Civil War veterans were organized and pushed the nation to embrace its first genuine social welfare programs. Congress created and gradually broadened a system of pensions for fallen, wounded, and aged veterans as well as their dependents.

It was another manifestation of a more active and engaged federal government.[19]

While the Lighthouse Board was inclined to reward veterans where possible, it would not do so at the expense of the efficient management of vital navigational aids. When the one-legged veteran James Donahue applied for a keeper's position, he was initially rebuffed by the board. "Mr. Donahue, we appreciate your service to our country, but we question your ability to carry out the duties of a lighthouse keeper," the Lighthouse Board secretary wrote. "The position requires strength and coordination, which would be very difficult for a person crippled like yourself." Donahue, however, did not see himself as an invalid, as he made clear to the Board. "Gentlemen, it is true that I was twice injured in the war, the second time losing a leg in the Battle of the Wilderness, however, I am not crippled, as you assert," he wrote. "I am capable of carrying out any and all duties required of a lighthouse keeper and will gladly prove it to you if you will give me the opportunity to serve my country in this manner." He won his appeal and was given the South Haven Lighthouse. It was a pier-head light. A seventy-five-foot-long catwalk led out across the pier to the light. Every evening regardless of waves, ice, or storm Donahue had to make his way out to the tower and then climb the thirty feet to the top to light the beacon. He unfailingly did this duty with his crutch for thirty-six years. He also performed heroically, rescuing citizens in distress. During his long career, he pulled fifteen people from the Lake Michigan surf, and he was awarded the government's silver lifesaving medal.[20]

Among the Civil War veterans who had the greatest impact on Great Lakes lighthouses and navigation aids was Orlando Poe. When the war began, he was a first lieutenant working on the U.S. Lake Survey. From 1861 to 1865 he saw active service as a combat officer, first leading the 2nd Michigan Infantry in the Peninsula Campaign, then as a brigade commander during the Second Bull Run battle, and finally as a military engineer in the western theater. Eventually, he joined William T. Sherman's staff as chief engineer. It was Orlando Poe who organized the burning of Atlanta, destroying the railroad and manufacturing facilities of the city—although he regretted that some civilian residences were also destroyed by undisciplined troops. At the war's conclusion, Poe was awarded the honorary rank of brevet brigadier general. With a regular army rank of major, his initial postwar job was as chief engineer for the Lighthouse Board. In this capacity, he was in almost constant motion, traveling the country supervising the refitting of lighthouses that had deteriorated during the war and overseeing the construction of new beacons. He held this position for five years, all the while looking for an opportunity to return to the Great Lakes region where he had worked before the war. During his time with the Lighthouse Board, he had a chance to learn and then master the intricacies of lighthouse construction. He visited many poorly built stations and had a chance to inspect some of the recent projects of the Lighthouse Board's best prewar engineers.[21]

In 1870 Poe returned to Detroit as the chief engineer for the 11th Lighthouse District, which included Lakes Michigan, Huron, and Superior. More than any other nineteenth-century engineer, Poe made vital contributions to Great Lakes navigation. His first stint as the lead engineer in the district lasted only three years. He left the region from 1873 to 1883 to serve as aide-de-camp to William Tecumseh Sherman when that general commanded the U.S. Army. He then returned to the Great Lakes and resumed his work with the 11th District. Among his notable accomplishments during this final lakes posting was the expansion of the Sault Ste. Marie locks. He died in 1895 from an infection contracted during a minor accident at the Soo construction site.[22]

Poe supervised numerous navigational aid projects, but he was most famous for his design of a series of lighthouses on the Great Lakes in the post–Civil War era. Only six lighthouses had been built on the lakes during the war, and the expansion of shipping and settlement required the Lighthouse Board to aggressively expand construction of new lights in the 1870s. Poe's eight Great Lakes lights were not hasty, stopgap efforts. The renowned "Poe lights" are distinctive for their ornate style, architectural integrity, and navigational utility. It is likely that Poe's design was influenced by light towers he visited on the Atlantic Coast. During the late 1850s, army engineers working with the Lighthouse Board using modern construction techniques and a knowledge of navigational needs began to construct very tall brick coastal lights. George Gordon Meade pioneered these in 1857 when he designed the Absecon Lighthouse near Atlantic City, New Jersey. His tower was 171 feet tall, more than twice the height of anything built under Stephen Pleasonton's benighted regime. Poe's Great Lakes towers were the tallest on the inland seas, but they did not need to be as high as Atlantic Coast towers. Poe's designs also reflected an architectural refinement and an eye for convenience and efficiency absent in the tall towers of the antebellum era. The first of these distinctive lighthouses was the 1870 Presque Isle Light Station. Poe sited the light on a peninsula near the northern reaches of Lake Huron. He designed a 109-foot tower that could be seen by ships far out on the lake. The graceful structure rested securely on a limestone foundation sunk ten feet into the earth. The conical tower rose from a base a little over nineteen feet in circumference with brick walls five-feet thick, and it tapered to a twelve-foot diameter at the watch room. A 144-step iron spiral staircase led up to the top and a third-order Fresnel lens. A sixteen-foot enclosed passageway connected the one-and-a-half-story brick keeper's house to the tower, a feature no doubt much appreciated by generations of keepers when autumn storms swept down. The station was taller than any other lighthouse on the Great Lakes, and its arched Italianate windows gave it an elegant look seldom found in utilitarian structures. His keeper's house at Presque Isle as well as his other lights were designed with an eye for both comfort and utility. They tended to be two stories, with an attic and a basement where oil could be stored. With slight variation, this design was repeated over the next four years at South Manitou Island, Outer Island Light Station (Apostle Islands), Au Sable near Grand Marais on Lake Superior, Little Sable Point and Seul Choix on Lake Michigan, and Grosse Point just north of Chicago. In 1880 the Wind Point Light near Racine, Wisconsin, also followed the same design.[23]

Poe's other outstanding contribution to Great Lakes navigation aids was his construction of the Spectacle Reef and the Stannard Rock Lighthouses. The Spectacle Reef was a rocky shoal between six and seven feet under the water set in the channel that ultimately connected the Straits of Mackinac with the St. Mary's River and the route to Lake Superior. As vessels on the lakes became larger and had deeper drafts, the shoal became more and more of a threat to navigation. In 1867 two schooners were wrecked on the reef with a total loss. The next year a buoy was placed there as a stopgap measure, and the Lighthouse Board requested Congress to authorize $300,000 for a lighthouse to be

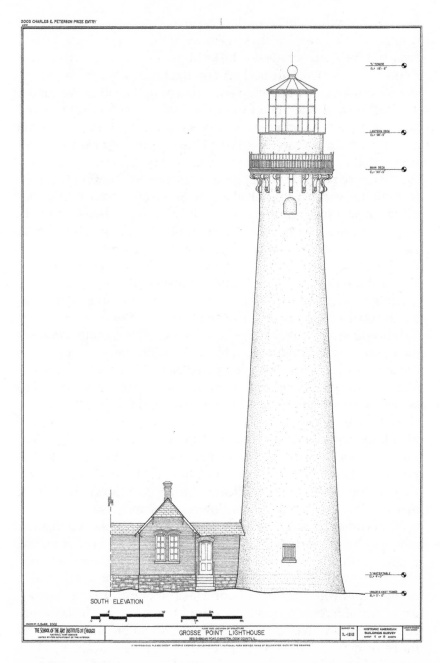

SOUTH ELEVATION

Figure 10. Historic American Building Survey drawing of Orlando Poe's Grosse Point Lighthouse, a National Historic Landmark.
Source: Library of Congress.

placed on the reef, a hazard "more dreaded by navigators than any other danger now unmarked throughout the entire chain of lakes."[24] The massive appropriation was recognition that building a lighthouse above a shoal in the open lake was a major engineering challenge. Poe's design would have to withstand powerful gales in autumn and the relentless assault of thick ice floes in winter. The construction project proceeded like a siege with a small army of workers making incremental progress. First, they cleared the wreckage of the schooner *Nightingale*. They then towed a precisely measured combination wooden crib and coffer dam from its construction site seventeen miles away, sank it on to the shoal, and anchored it with eighteen hundred tons of rock. Next Poe's men laid down a solid base of limestone anchored by iron bolts and Portland cement. By summer 1872 the tower had been raised to a height of better than twenty feet when Lake Huron launched a counterattack. A September storm caused considerable damage and was followed by a severe winter. When Poe and his men returned to the site in the spring, huge blocks of ice were piled pyramidlike around the tower. Days were spent pulling and cutting their way through the white wall just to reveal the lighthouse. That summer they raised the tower to its full ninety-three feet. The stone for the solid base had been barged to the site from Marblehead, Ohio. The upper tower had an exterior stone wall and the interior was lined with brick. The upper five stories of the tower were divided into dwelling quarters and storage areas stacked one atop another. The light was equipped with a powerful second-order Fresnel lens in June 1874. The project cost more than $400,000, making it one of the most expensive lighthouses ever built in the U.S. It was, however, a marvel of engineering in which the Lighthouse Board took great pride. The slipshod ways of the Pleasonton era were clearly in the past, and engineers from around the world took note of Poe's accomplishment. Crib (or submarine) foundations had been in use since 1832, and the integration of a coffer dam to facilitate construction predated Spectacle Reef. However, Spectacle Reef proved to be one of the two most significant crib-foundation type lighthouses ever constructed, and crib foundations would be used extensively on the Great Lakes.[25] As late as the 1893 Columbian Exposition, the Spectacle Reef Lighthouse occupied a place of pride in the board's exhibit.[26]

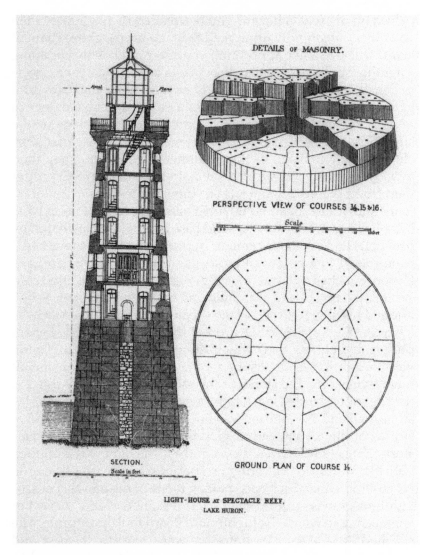

Figure 11. Orlando Poe's design for Spectacle Reef Lighthouse.
Source: Library of Congress

The techniques improvised by Poe at Spectacle Reef were soon put to use on an even more difficult project on Lake Superior, one that became the other most significant crib-foundation type light ever built.[27] An underwater mountain with a summit nearly a mile tall rises from the depth of the lake to within four feet of the surface. This hazard was unfortunately situated within the shipping lane of vessels leaving the western end of the lake and bound for the Sault Ste. Marie locks. An army engineer characterized it as "an object of great concern and terror, especially in dark nights and the almost interminable fog which prevails." By 1866 the Lighthouse Board considered the shoal the most dangerous obstacle to maritime travel on Lake Superior, but it would not be until 1877 that Congress authorized funding to begin lighthouse work at the site.[28] Complicating the task was the fact that Stannard Rock was twenty-three miles from the nearest land and almost fifty miles from the nearest port. During the first two months of work at the site, more than forty days were lost because heavy seas drove away the construction team. Numerous shipments of stone or supplies were lost to Lake Superior's notorious gales. Captain John A. Bailey, who had worked with Poe on Spectacle Reef, headed the Stannard Rock project. Five years of dogged effort were needed to build the lighthouse. The protective pier at the tower's base was anchored with 875 tons of rock. The 102-foot tower with a powerful second-order Fresnel lens was completed for a cost of $305,000.

Following the successful construction of the Stannard Rock Light, keepers there manned the most remote and isolated lighthouse in the U.S. They were completely out of sight of land. In keeping with the hardship nature of the post, no families were allowed there, and even many of the all-male crews had trouble with the posting. The station became known as the "loneliest place in America." A small library on the tower's fifth level was solace for some, but at least one keeper, perhaps not much of a reader, had to be removed from the station in a straitjacket.[29]

Naturally, having a spouse or a family on station could be a great source of comfort and well-being for a lightkeeper. For many of the wounded Civil War veterans, their wives were also practical partners in the operation of the beacons. Not only was Aaron Sheridan, with one good arm, helped by his wife through her domestic duties but she was also the official assistant keeper of the station. This was not at all unusual. Twice-wounded Barney Litogot at Mamajuda Island was aided by his wife, Caroline, the official assistant keeper. Litogot's wounds had been severe, and after several years of duty at the light he died. When the Lighthouse Board made plans to replace Caroline Litogot, Michigan Senator Zachariah Chandler sent an immediate telegraph to the secretary of the treasury, which oversaw the board, to "suspend action on the removal of Mrs. Litogot." In a follow-up letter, he explained that Caroline had really been the de facto keeper for some time. According to Senator Chandler, "The vessel men all say that she keeps an excellent light, and I think it very hard to remove a woman who is faithful and efficient, and throw her upon the world with her children entirely destitute when her husband lost his life in defense of the union."[30]

Having a spouse as an official assistant keeper was a boon to the family economy. While lighthouse keepers did not enjoy a princely salary, they did earn a better than average wage. In the post–Civil War era, a keeper generally earned about $600 a year. Considering the job came with free housing, it was good pay. A lake sailor was happy to make only $1.50 a day. When a keeper's wife became the assistant, another $400 annually was added to the family income. Aaron and Julia Sheridan used their extra income to improve their homestead claim on South Manitou Island. Julius William Warren, the keeper at Cana Island Lighthouse in Wisconsin, and his assistant Sarah Warren also invested in a farm. After only a few years in the lighthouse service, they built the finest home on Cana Island and retired to a life of farming.[31]

Even when women were not officially recognized for their work at the station, they often performed work crucial to its operation. The South Haven pier-head light was kept by James S. Donahue, the disabled Civil War veteran. When he was away from the station to get supplies or to attend to business in town, his wife did his job. On one occasion, she spent a large part of the night in the tower operating the fog horn to help bring a distressed vessel into harbor. More often she kept vigil for her husband. When storms battered the tower, the catwalk back to the house was too dangerous to use and the keeper had to stay there to be sure that the light was not extinguished. His wife sat by her window looking for his silhouette in the watch room making sure he was safe. When Clement Van Riper, the keeper at Beaver Island disappeared in a Lake Michigan gale in a vain attempt to aid a storm-ravaged vessel, his wife, Elizabeth, kept the light operational that night and until the Lighthouse Board could be notified. Although she confessed to being "weak with sorrow," she was animated by the knowledge that the beacon played a crucial role for sailors "out on the dark treacherous waters who needed to catch the rays of the shining light from my lighthouse tower." She knew exactly what had to be done because her husband had often been in poor health, and she had frequently taken the task of climbing the steps to tend to the lamps and clean the lens. So well did she manage the station after her husband's death, the board offered her the official appointment as keeper. She accepted, and at Beaver Island and later at Little Traverse she devoted a total of forty-four years to managing navigation lights.[32]

While the total number of female lighthouse keepers on the Great Lakes was small, their service was notable. Most of these were widows of lighthouse keepers or related to the previous keeper. Anastasia Truckey was married to the Marquette Harbor Lighthouse keeper when the Civil War broke out. Although he was the father of four children, Truckey enlisted in the 27th Michigan Infantry. For the three years he was in the service, Anastasia maintained the lighthouse and looked after her children. While the dual responsibility was no doubt taxing, maintaining the family's income base while he was gone was essential. Georgia Stebbins was the widowed daughter of the keeper of Milwaukee's North Point Lighthouse. She lived with her father at the lighthouse for seven years. As his health declined, she took over more and more of the daily duties of the keeper: trimming the wicks, lighting the lamps, and cleaning the lens and the windows. In 1881 the district inspector removed her father and appointed her the keeper. She held the job for ten years before the light was decommissioned. A typical case was Mary Terry, who became keeper of the Escanaba, Michigan, Sand Point Light after her husband died of tuberculosis. As with Georgia Stebbins, it was possible for Mary Terry to demonstrate her competence as a keeper prior to the appointment because she had gradually taken on the job over the course of several years. Similarly, Katherine Marvin was appointed keeper at Squaw Point Lighthouse on Little Bay De Noc when her Civil War veteran husband passed away. In her case and several others, there seems to have been a compensatory element in the appointment. She was the mother of ten children, with five young ones still at home when her husband died. When the indomitable Mrs. Marvin remarried six years later, she resigned her lighthouse job. All these women who became lightkeepers underwent the same three-month probationary trial period required of their male counterparts and passed a qualifying inspection before receiving their job.[33]

Certain isolated stations were sometimes reserved for married men with the thought that a wife would make the lonely job more bearable. Isle Royale Lighthouse in Lake Superior was one such post. First lit in 1875, the lighthouse was placed on Menagerie Island, a small rocky islet off the southern coast of remote Isle Royale. John H. Malone was made keeper there in 1877 and brought his new bride, nineteen-year-old Julia Shea. The two-story keeper's dwelling there quickly went from a cozy to a crowded home for the Malones. In the couple's thirty-two years on the rock, Julia bore a dozen children; although one died in childbirth, the rest grew up on the tiny island. Over time the children became expert at maneuvering small boats, fishing, and supplementing the family diet with seagull eggs, which they gathered from adjoining islands. With so many mouths to feed, keeping the family larder full was a constant concern. At breakfast, the family would consume up to thirty gull eggs, which they claimed did not have the fishy taste one might expect. Julia used them in all her recipes. In the summer, the children were tasked with picking berries on Isle Royale, while their father and the older boys hunted waterfowl. When gales swept Lake Superior, the entire family huddled in the house while waves washed over the entire island. Remarkably, none of the adventurous children ever drowned. When John and Julia finally left the island for a less remote station, they were replaced by the assistant keeper, their son John Jr.[34]

Having an official assistant keeper on duty at most light stations became more common in the Civil War era and continued until lighthouses were automated. Several factors made it necessary for the Lighthouse Board to take on this added personnel expense. The physical task of maintaining a lighthouse became more arduous as the equipment and design of the structures was upgraded. Under the antebellum regime of Stephen Pleasonton, few lighthouses were taller than thirty feet. This seriously reduced their effectiveness. Under the Lighthouse Board, towers, particularly for coastal lights, became taller. This made tasks such as checking on the light during the night, which sometimes had to be done every four hours, and hauling fuel up to the lamps more difficult. The Fresnel lenses were very expensive, and most were imported from France. The second- and third-order lenses on the Great Lakes cost $4,400 and $1,860, respectively. Hence great attention was paid to the maintenance of these intricate glass devices. Cleaning was a daily task, as was hooding the lens to protect its panels from sunlight. For the large second- or third-order lenses, this was a time-consuming task, and the work could take four to five hours. As the number of lighthouses and navigational aids increased, it was also necessary to alter their beams so sailors out on the lake could differentiate one light from the next. Hence some lights were given a red or green beacon, and many were equipped with a flash rather than a steady beam. Flashes were facilitated after the Fresnel lens had been adopted. The effect was achieved by mounting the lens on a large clockwork mechanism that rotated it in such a way as to systematically interrupt the beam of light. Various types of rotation devices were employed over time. All of these required the vigilance of the keepers to stay in operation. Some rotation mechanisms needed to be wound like a clock every several hours. Every time winding was necessary, someone had to climb to the top of the tower to do so, and winding the device was hard work. The clock mechanisms employed heavy lead weights suspended by cables that hung down into the tower, and winding the clock for the rotation required cranking those lead weights back up to the top of the tower.[35]

Another post–Civil War addition to most light stations was the fog signal. Going back to colonial days, sound had been used at certain coastal lighthouses to help ships locate their position in conditions of poor visibility. This was usually done by means of a cannon that fired a blank charge. The gun would fire in response to an audible signal, usually a cannon shot, from an approaching ship. Bells were also sometimes used, and many Great Lakes lighthouses had brass fog bells. As part of their effort to upgrade U.S. navigational aids, the Lighthouse Board in 1855 began to experiment with steam whistles. The whistles made a very distinct sound, but since whistles were the way steamboats communicated with each other, a lighthouse signal was sometimes confused with an oncoming vessel. The first steam whistles came to the Great Lakes in 1875 when one was installed at South Manitou Island. A small wood-frame structure was built to house the coal- or wood-fired boiler, and a second assistant keeper was retained to handle the extra duty. In the decade that followed, fog signals were installed all across the inland seas.[36]

During the 1860s a new type of navigational aid was added to the system of lights and buoys on the inland seas. The first range lights deployed on the Great Lakes sprang from the practical experience of Dewitt Brawn, the son of the lightkeeper at Saginaw, Michigan. Brawn delighted in taking a small boat out into the bay, and in navigating, he noted the utility of lining up prominent objects on shore to keep his course steady. When not on the bay, he assisted his father, a partial invalid, in the operation of the lighthouse that marked the entrance to the Saginaw River. He understood his observation could be of value to navigation because each morning he would awake to find one or more schooners anchored off the river mouth. The lighthouse had during the night helped guide them to the river's mouth, but they dared not enter the river in darkness. This caused a regrettable delay in reaching the busy sawmills of Bay City. Sometime around 1865 young Brawn proposed erecting two wooden towers from which he could hoist a lantern. The towers would be lined up exactly with one another. The first tower would be shorter than the second, taller tower, which was set back a considerable distance. The helmsmen of an approaching ship could enter the river with confidence when he lined the first light with the second. Subscriptions were collected from the lumber ships that frequented Bay City, and the range lights were installed, with young Brawn lighting the lanterns every evening. In 1876 the Lighthouse Board replaced Brawn's entrepreneurial venture by erecting a thirty-four-foot tower with a sixth-order Fresnel Lens atop a rock crib near the river mouth. Farther back, a new lighthouse with a sixty-one-foot tower with a fourth-order Fresnel Lens was placed in alignment. In the late 1860s the range light concept was put in place by the board at several sites on Lake Superior and Lake Michigan and was soon adopted throughout the service. It was particularly useful on the Great Lakes because of the long piers constructed to keep river harbors clear of sand. Pier-head lights often function as the first of two sets of range lights that helped mariners keep the correct course for entering the narrow harbor. Although Brawn has often been credited with having invented the range light concept, the deployment of such lights began in the British Isles in the eighteenth century, where they were known as leading lights.[37]

By the start of the twentieth century, range lights were in place to guide ships through most confined waters. They were particularly useful on twisting channels of the Detroit River. A vessel would be assured it was on the proper course when it could line up the front and rear range lights at Belle Isle or the St. Clair Flats. Experienced wheelsmen even used range lights when leaving a harbor by standing backward and lining up with the ever-retreating range lights. However, this was a trick only for the veteran helmsman, as he had to remember that when facing to the rear, every action taken had to be done backward from what was usually done. Range lights were especially useful for narrow harbor entrances like that of the Duluth Ship Canal.[38]

The post–Civil War period was one of considerable experimentation with the fuel used in lighthouse lamps. Sperm whale oil had been the most popular fuel in the antebellum period. It had excellent burning characteristics, and at first it was readily available thanks to the large fleet of American whaling vessels. Between 1840 and 1855, however, the price of whale oil kept escalating, eventually increasing fourfold as the great leviathans were slaughtered in all but the most remote polar waters. Many possible replacements were tested, from cabbage seed oil to olive oil. Fortunately, Joseph Henry, one of the nation's leading scientists, was a member of the Lighthouse Board, and his investigations demonstrated that lard worked nearly as well as whale oil, and it was widely adopted. With Chicago's mammoth Union Stock Yards located in the heart of the Great Lakes region, lard was very readily and cheaply available. One problem with it, unfortunately, was that to burn clean it had first to be heated to a high temperature. Harriet Colfax, the keeper of the Michigan City pier-head lighthouse, discovered the drawback of this one storm-tossed night. She heated her oil at the keeper's house, but to reach the beacon she had to row across a creek and then walk through a dune, and finally brave the wave-washed catwalk out to the tower. By the time she climbed the tower stairs to the watch room, her lard had congealed. Going back and repeating the process at the literal hazard of her life did not make her a fan of the new fuel. She was no doubt relieved when in 1878 the Lighthouse Board ordered the transition to mineral oil.[39]

The use of mineral oil or kerosene for lighthouse lamps did not come without its difficulties. In 1864 a Lake Michigan lighthouse keeper decided to experiment with a kerosene lamp. It worked great for several nights. The flame was brighter than the lard oil, and the household kerosene lamp he deployed did not require that he trim the wicks several times during the night. He was about to congratulate himself on a wonderful innovation one morning when an accident occurred. He tried to extinguish the lamp by blowing down its glass chimney. This ignited an explosion that scattered burning oil about the deck of the tower and on the hapless man's clothes. In a panic, he ran down the spiral steps of the tower and struggled to save himself. As he did so, a second, much more powerful explosion caused by accumulated petroleum vapors took place that blew the top off the tower. When the incident was sheepishly reported to the Lighthouse Board, it confirmed them in the use of lard oil. In the early 1870s both the French and British launched further experiments with kerosene with good results. The U.S. Board also undertook experimentation at the Staten Island depot and came up with an appropriate lamp design that could burn kerosene safely. This was known as the incandescent oil vapor lamp and it was first deployed in 1877. Conversion of virtually all lighthouses on the Great Lakes followed, although the process was not completed until 1889.[40]

The post–Civil War era saw the addition of a new structure at almost all Great Lakes lighthouse stations—the oil house. Lard oil had been a rather safe and stable fuel source while it was employed as the main illumination fuel for lamps. That oil could be stored in the basement of a dwelling or in the lower level of the tower. When kerosene was gradually adopted, lighthouses got a much brighter, cleaner source of fuel but one that was much more volatile. To store it under a dwelling or in the tower was to risk a disastrous explosion or fire. Hence, small oil houses were constructed some distance from the dwelling and tower.[41]

The use of kerosene also brought another change to lighthouses, one that made the keeper's job easier. In 1901 the Englishman Arthur Kitson invented the valorized burner. After some modifications by Trinity House, the English lighthouse authority, the device was installed in most lighthouses throughout Europe and the U.S. Kitson's burner replaced the need for wicks and the tiresome task of trimming the wicks to reduce smoking from the lamp. The invention placed the kerosene under pressure, causing it to vaporize, mixing with the air. It burned in an incandescent gauze mantle. Similar to camp lanterns used to this day, the new burner allowed for a light as much as six times brighter than the old oil-wick lights.

The Construction Era:
Safe Harbors at Last

Union victory in the Civil War had an immediate and lasting impact on the navigation of the Great Lakes. After 1865 harbor and channel improvements, long the subject of political controversy, became a normal part of the federal appropriations process. Between 1866 and 1882 harbor improvement bills passed Congress every year with the single exception of 1877. With frequent surpluses in the federal budget, there were few financial checks on internal improvement expenditures. When budget-minded presidents made a rare attempt to slow the flow of construction money, as Chester A. Arthur did in 1882 and Grover Cleveland in 1896, their vetoes were overridden by Congress. Heavy investments in ports and harbors of refuge were a necessity because of the budgetary neglect that occurred under the Pierce and Buchanan administrations and that had by necessity continued during the struggle to save the Union. In 1863 an Army Corps engineer assigned to the lakes complained that virtually all harbors improved in the antebellum period were "more or less dilapidated. . . . We have had eleven years of a deterioration without any means of remedy whatever." Congress approved $250,000 in 1864, which before the war would have been a cause of celebration but was now seen as only a stopgap measure. During the lean years, lake ports did not simply languish. Rather, dredging and breakwater repairs were funded through a variety of local means, from subscriptions to local taxes and state grants. In 1864 Muskegon, Michigan, merchants, lacking the equipment to dredge their harbor, paid a steamer captain to literally bore his way into the port by running his vessel backward so that the propeller excavated a narrow channel through the sandbar. In 1866 such makeshift measures ended and a new era of federal support finally dawned.[42]

The period after the Civil War has been traditionally known in American history as the Reconstruction Era, and its scholarship has focused on the effort to gradually bring the rebellious Confederate states back into the Union and to incorporate formerly enslaved African Americans into the social and political body of the nation. More recently historians have broadened their perspective and incorporated into our understanding of the Reconstruction Era labor struggles in the industrial north and Indian wars in the far West. If this new historiography of the post–Civil War period included the experience of the Great Lakes region, the era might be better known as the "Construction Era" because of the long-delayed but impressive federal investment in navigational improvements on the inland seas that followed Union victory. Between 1865 and 1900 the U.S. Army Corps of Engineers was lavished with river and harbor appropriations to the tune of $333 million. The funding flood started in 1866 when Congress dedicated $3.6 million to survey the navigation needs of not just the Great Lakes but all underfunded waterways, and the construction money soon followed. From 1868 to 1908 the nation elected presidents who hailed from Great Lakes states. Republican senators and congressmen from the region occupied key leadership positions in Congress and incorporated into national policy a partnership between capital and government that provided the canals, harbors, lighthouses, and lifesaving stations that transformed the untamed lakes into an American Mediterranean of industrial and commercial integration.[43]

In the wake of Appomattox, the single most important navigational improvement needed was to clear a broad, deep passage through the St. Clair Flats, the marshy mouth of the St. Clair River that connected Lakes Huron and Erie by way of the Detroit River. Colonel Jefferson Cram of the Army Corps of Engineers contended that "very few channels of the world present such a constant stream of passing vessels. . . . The number of tugs, steamers, propellers, scows, barges, sloops and schooners that passed the St. Clair Flats between April 1 and December 14, 1865, was 22,274, and the number of timber rafts, 90." It was not unusual during the height of the navigation season for there to be as many as one hundred vessels meandering their way through the shallow channel at one time. Often, they would be backed up for days when a grounded vessel blocked their passage. There had been preliminary attempts to create a clear channel between 1852 and 1858 using funds privately raised by the shipping industry when Congress balked at funding the work. James Buchanan's veto of a St. Clair appropriation had been the last shriek of anti-federalism before the Civil War. In 1866 army engineers were given a strong appropriation and instructed to plan a lasting solution. Their plan was basically to build a canal through the marsh. At the cost of $480,000, a one-and-a-half-mile channel three hundred feet wide was cut through the St. Clair Flats, drastically shortening the time and difficulty for ships passing between the lakes. It was not, however, a lasting solution. The Flats were a reoccurring problem in part because the water levels in the Great Lakes fluctuated, sometimes wildly, from year to year and because over time the size of vessels using the waterway increased.[44]

Lake Michigan harbors were the prime beneficiaries of the postwar federal largesse. The funds began as a trickle in 1866 when Congress appropriated $175,000 for harbors on the Wisconsin side of the lake. During the Civil War, Milwaukee shipped fifteen million bushels of wheat per year in addition to millions of dollars' worth of manufactured products. The harbor developed in 1852 under the last Whig administration needed new work to increase its depth from twelve feet to eighteen. Just a few miles south, the town of Racine, Wisconsin, had grown during the war to ten thousand people, and its harbor served 574 ships annually. While wheat was their principal cargo, the town, like Milwaukee and Chicago, had begun to move into manufacturing as well. By the 1870s Racine was producing more than a thousand threshing machines annually. Federal appropriations immediately after the war increased the harbor's depth to sixteen feet and contributed to this growth. While ports like Milwaukee, Kenosha, and Racine enjoyed unprecedented federal support in the wake of Union victory, they also continued to invest local resources into navigation improvements. Milwaukee's investment exceeded a half million dollars. Sheboygan, Wisconsin, used city and county funds to build its first harbor, and by the end of the Civil War better than a thousand ships visited the port each year exporting wheat and bricks. Consistent federal support for improvements in the 1870s increased the port's depth to nineteen feet. Kenosha, Manitowoc, Kewaunee, Port Washington, and Menominee on the Wisconsin shore also blossomed under federal appropriations. While federal funding began modestly, once the money began to flow it was a steady stream, and by 1900 close to $8 million had been spent on Badger State harbors. On the eastern side of Lake Michigan, the same pattern prevailed. Harbors begun by private or municipal investment soon won congressional funding. For example, the lumber port of Manistee had on its own erected a crude set of piers to make a five-foot channel some ships could pass over. In 1867 Congress came to their rescue and built a proper harbor and erected a lighthouse to guide ships into it. In 1874 the port boasted 3,488 vessel clearances in a single year.[45]

Before the Civil War, Lake Superior had been the least developed of the inland seas for navigation purposes. The expansion of the copper- and iron-mining industries under the stimulus of war necessitated aggressive action in the wake of Appomattox. Marquette, Michigan, was the most important iron ore port on the lake. In 1866 the government funded a new lighthouse for the harbor and began work on an extensive breakwater system that included an additional breakwater beacon. In 1867 Ontonagon, Michigan, was given a new system of piers and the inner harbor was dredged to allow the passage of ore and lumber ships. By the end of the Civil War, the copper country of the Keweenaw Peninsula supplied 97 percent of the nation's supply of the ore, which was indispensable for the manufacture of brass implements. The richest mine in the district—the Calumet and Hecla—was discovered in 1865, and its opening greatly accelerated production. By 1874 northern Michigan mines were producing—and Great Lakes schooners were transporting—thirty-four million pounds annually. For years the profitability of the mines had been hurt by the cost of shipping the ore overland or by small boats to the shore of Lake Superior. In 1861 the copper men funded the dredging of the Portage River from its Lake Superior mouth to Portage Lake, an inland body of water near the richest mines. They had bigger dreams, and when the Republicans took over Congress, the mine owners secured a two-hundred-thousand-acre land grant from the federal government to build a canal north from Portage Lake to Lake Superior. This would create a waterway through the heart of the Keweenaw Peninsula. Work was begun in 1868, but it did not proceed well, and the company that was awarded the project by the State of Michigan faced bankruptcy. Congress was persuaded to come to the rescue and offer an additional two-hundred-thousand-acre land grant to reanimate the project. The twenty-one-mile waterway was completed in 1873.[46]

The legal basis for aggressive federal support of Great Lakes navigation improvements was strengthened in 1870 when the U.S. Supreme Court ruled that not only did the Great Lakes have the same status as "high seas" but the navigable streams and rivers flowing into the lakes were also under federal jurisdiction. The ruling stemmed from an 1868 case involving a steamer operating on Michigan's Grand River, whose owners claimed they need not abide by federal navigation regulations. The court ruled that since the Grand River flowed into Lake Michigan and any traffic on the river might continue on to other states or nations, the waterway was clearly under direct control of the national government owing to its right to manage commerce "among the several states." It logically followed that Congress had the right—and indeed, the responsibility—to undertake improvements to navigation not only on the Great Lakes but also their connecting waterways.[47]

Among the initiatives that followed this ruling was the construction of harbors of refuge along the shore of the lakes. Previously, existing lakeshore towns had to scrap, beg, and scramble for harbor funds. Beginning in the 1870s not only were such communities given federally funded navigational improvements but the government also actively sought out other sites where harbors needed to be constructed simply for marine safety. The large, undeveloped shoreline of Lake Huron was one of the first locations where the new program was implemented. There was no safe harbor along an eighty-mile stretch of shore between Port Huron and Saginaw Bay. Yet more than thirty thousand vessels passed that shore annually. Congress, therefore, authorized the U.S. Army Corps of Engineers to study that coast and locate the best site for a man-made harbor. A location known as Sand Beach (later Harbor Beach) was selected, and Congress committed the hefty appropriation of $1.5 million. It took until 1885 for the project to be completed, although vessels began to seek its safe harbor as soon as the breakwaters were installed. The crowning touch of the project was the lighting of a brick-tower lighthouse at the entrance to the new refuge.[48]

The Harbor Beach harbor of refuge was just one of a series of such projects. The Army Corps soon had other projects underway along other isolated stretches of Great Lakes shoreline, such as Grand Marais on Lake Superior. Early attempts to build these harbors relied on long breakwaters that would create a basin of calm water even in the face of lake gales. At first these structures were built by sinking wood cribs loaded with stone rubble, but winter storms and ice shortly took their toll, particularly on the upper part of the structure that was exposed to the air. Concrete construction became the preferred medium of building break-waters after the successful use of that material at Buffalo harbor in 1889. The new concrete breakwaters for harbors of refuge re-quired navigational aids to mark the entrance for ships. Usually these were cast iron and later steel structures. A skeletal tower about thirty feet high supported by four steel-beam legs was typical, although busier harbors often received more elaborate designs, such as the octagonal steel tower that was lit in 1920 at the entrance to the Keweenaw Waterway or the north Duluth breakwater light. These lights were often difficult to reach and were among the first to be automated in the 1910s.[49]

Major ports of the Great Lakes such as Buffalo, whose indus-tries absorbed the cargoes of iron ore and the rivers of grain, all received substantial makeovers in the wake of the Civil War. The core of these ports was a river or a stream, the Buffalo River and the Chicago River in the case of those cities, the Cuyahoga in the case of Cleveland. Even with constant dredging of slips to create additional dockage, these narrow waterways could not contain all the shipping bound for their ports. Cleveland, for example, which had originally built its trade through wheat and corn, be-came a center for iron- and steelmaking as well as oil production after the Civil War. By 1870 there were fourteen rolling mills in the city, and the harbor was handling the delivery of five hun-dred thousand tons of iron ore annually. Supported by generous congressional appropriations, the U.S. Army Corps of Engineers developed outer harbors for each of these cities. A network of breakwaters was positioned several hundred yards out from the river harbor, creating a partially sheltered anchorage for ships waiting for dockage space or new cargoes. The Buffalo outer har-bor eventually entailed a series of breakwaters extending more than four miles. Such was the tenor of the times that million-dollar appropriations for the improvement of a single Great Lakes port sailed through Congress like a scudding schooner with a follow-ing breeze.[50]

Just as important as the harbor improvements was the transformation of the connecting channels between the lakes. In this era of Republican investment in the inland seas, extensive work was done dredging a new and deeper channel through the St. Mary's River that linked Lake Huron to the Soo Canal. In 1881 the canal itself was transformed by the opening of the so-called Weitzel Lock, then the largest in the world at 515 feet with a seventeen-foot depth. The even larger Poe Lock followed in 1896. By this time Great Lakes improvements were so interwoven into the fabric of government that the U.S. Army Corps of Engineers had adopted a comprehensive plan for inland seas navigation that promised shippers twenty-foot channels throughout the system. With every new project and every increase in the scale of lake navigation, the consequences of the Civil War were palpable, from Lake Ontario to Superior's far shore.[51]

Canadian Harbor Improvements

The improvements in navigation on the U.S. side of the Great Lakes were only partially matched by British North America, largely because of the vast difference in population and economic activity. The key development was the July 1867 creation of the Dominion of Canada, a confederation of a number of Great Britain's American colonies. Founders of the new nation believed inland seas navigation was so "valuable to our people" as to be "essential to the national well-being." Prior to confederation, harbor improvements had largely been left to municipalities or private companies, but the new Dominion government established a vigorous public works program under its central administration. Channel dredging and breakwater construction similar to that undertaken by American army engineers took place at the nascent ports along the northern shore of the lakes. Prime Minister John A. McDonald's "National Policy" sought to rapidly develop the Canadian economy through internal improvements and protective tariffs. McDonald was painfully aware that the American economy dwarfed that of the new Dominion's. His policy put an emphasis on public works designed to bind the diverse parts of the new confederation together. He was not interested in strengthening further the already advanced international economic integration that occurred in the Great Lakes region. McDonald's Conservative Party was driven by the fear that if they did not build Canada's internal economy, the Dominion would fall to the aggressive expansion of their American neighbors. The core region of the new Canada would be along the Great Lakes axis between Montreal and Windsor, but for the nation to survive on a transcontinental basis, transportation from east to west had to be improved. A Dominion Board of Lights ensured that the northern margin of the lakes would be properly marked. Just between 1867 and 1871, 93 new lighthouses were built, with 43 more in planning. By the beginning of the twentieth century this number had grown to 220 light stations and 3 lightships.[52]

Great Lakes Maritime Culture

The decades after the Civil War saw the Great Lakes crisscrossed by more ships than at any time before or since. Commerce rushed to take advantage of the new harbors and improved channels. A unique inland seas maritime culture also emerged during these years. In the early nineteenth century, many of the men at the helm and before the mast of lake vessels were bred and born on saltwater. For good and ill they attempted to bring with them the manners and practices of the oceangoing mariner. The often-harsh discipline employed at sea, where captains were a law unto themselves, did not translate to the lakes, where labor was always at a premium. In the heartland, a more egalitarian culture took root. This was especially the case on schooners, the backbone of the lake marine in the nineteenth century. Many vessel masters were men who had worked their way up from the forecastle and were owners or part owners of their ships. Crews were much smaller than found on many big square-rigged ocean clippers. Masters and mates were necessarily on more intimate terms with their crew. Meals, for example, were taken together in the captain's cabin. This social equality surprised observers used to saltwater ways.

> You only have to go below into the cabin and listen to the conversation which passes around the table to hear the sailor and master discuss abstruse questions of politics and religion, science, or social life, and the interjected comments of the remainder of the

company, to know you are in the midst of a good-tempered family. Social distinctions, there are none at the table, but the meal over and the routine business of the vessel is resumed, all is changed.[53]

Atlantic mariners would also have been surprised by the quality of the fare put before a crew of lake sailors. Since vessels were seldom out for more than ten days, and frequently less, fresh produce was enjoyed instead of the tiresome diet of salted meat and sea biscuit gagged down by jack tars at sea. By the early twentieth century when the majority of lake vessels were the large five-hundred-foot steel freighters, the social democracy of the small sailing ships gradually fell away. Officers and crew did not usually eat at the same table, although the quality of the food was the same for both.

Lakemen gradually adopted their own peculiar terminology, and they heaped scorn on salts who came inland uninitiated. A vessel that set sail from Chicago to Buffalo was not on a "voyage" but a "run." Nor was time kept and deck watches determined by "bells." A sailor on the lakes would say his watch ended at twelve o'clock, not "eight bells." Over time lake mariners took to referring to their vessels, even three-hundred-foot schooners, as "boats," not "ships." A favorite trick was to put a new arrival from the ocean on "shark watch." An experienced Atlantic skipper could be easily humbled by their unfamiliarity with the inland seas. Captain John Kenlon, on his first run up Lake Michigan, was alarmed to find that his vessel had no casks of water. He began to make an issue of what would be a life-threatening oversight at sea when he noticed everyone looking at him in an amused manner. The cook eyed him over and declared "By Heavens, fresh from salt water." She bade him to dip a cup into the lake. The entire crew turned to see him take a sip and laughed when Kenlon "was pleasantly surprised to find the water cold and sweet." As he retreated to his cabin Kenlon could literally "feel" the crew's distain.[54]

Lake sailors, however, did share with their saltwater cousins a host of taboos and superstitions that they regarded just as important to safe navigation as a good chart. These were actions or omens that could put a sailor and his ship in grave danger. For example, it was an ominous portent if a hatch cover support was knocked into the hold as a ship prepared to leave port. Mariner

Joseph Hendricks reported that the entire crew of a schooner deserted a ship in the wake of this seemingly minor mishap. Yet if the accident occurred at the end of a run it would not have raised a single eyebrow. An even stronger superstition was the danger of beginning a run on a Friday. It was regarded as even more damning to begin the shipping season on a Friday. In April 1883 word went out that the ice was clear at the Mackinac Straits and the grain fleet, bottled up by winter in Chicago, Milwaukee, and Racine, could set sail. However, it was a Friday and the majority of the vessels stayed in port. This infuriated grain merchants and commission agents, but most ships remained at anchor. A Chicago journalist visiting the harbor noted, "No matter what the orders are there is always something to do, or something out of shape so that it is after midnight when the craft starts." The obstinate mariners pointed to the wreck of the schooner *Van Valkenberg* in 1881.[55] She had violated the taboo and sank with all hands, save one survivor who it was said went mad after the ordeal. On another occasion, the master of a newly launched vessel stayed in port till midnight to avoid the Friday curse and was rewarded with a firm breeze. The next morning his ship came across a schooner that had left port that Friday. The vessel's flag was at half-mast. The willful master of that ship had fallen, hit his head, and died. To the sailors of both ships the incident "proved the point."[56]

Inevitably a large store of sailor lore focused on weather. It was the great unpredictable natural force that shaped their daily lives. Weather-wise mariners knew well the saying, "Red sky at night, sailor's delight," as well as the inverse warning, "Red sky at morning, sailor take warning." A variation on this theme intoned, "Evening gray and morning red, put on your hat or you'll wet your head." Gulls were also thought to be a clue to a change in the weather. When the birds flew low in the sky, it was an indication of continuing fair weather. It was not unusual for sailors to feed scraps of stale bread to them off the stern of the vessel. It was a widespread belief among saltwater men that gulls held the souls of dead sailors. One lake sailor who often fed the gulls claimed he could even recognize former shipmates.[57]

While few sailors left letters or diaries of their life on the lakes, they did give to posterity a rich tradition of songs. Some were work songs or chanties that were sung to help sustain and pace the heavy labor of hoisting an anchor or sail. Many of these were borrowed from the chanties of Atlantic mariners, with freshwater place-names substituted for saltwater seaports. The actual every-day experience of navigating the inland seas during the nineteenth century came alive in songs composed, often on the spur of the moment, in schooner forecastles or harbor dives. The song "Up Anchor" captured the excitement of setting off on a run down the lakes.

> We've got the rusty mud-hook up,
> She's green with Chicago slime;
> We're sailing with a gale of wind.
> No more of city's grime!
> We'll head for the old blue waterways,
> And mates, we'll drink our fill
> Of winds that hail across our bow
> And through the hatches spill.

"The Timber Drogher *Bigler*" recounted and lampooned incidents that occurred during a run from Milwaukee to Buffalo. The song also celebrated the comradeship of shipmates and the relief of reaching port and getting paid off.

> An' now my bully lads, we're in Buffalo port at last,
> Under Rood and Smith's Elevator, the *Bigler* she's made fast.
> An' in Tommy Doyle's saloon we'll let the bottle pass,
> For we are jolly shipmates, and we'll drink a social glass.

There also was a rich tradition of songs that memorialized the ships and crews that never made the safety of harbor or home. "Lost on Lake Michigan" is a song sung for generations among the Irish American sailors of Beaver Island.

> Come all brother sailors, I hope you'll draw nigh,
> For to hear of your shipmates, it will cause you to cry;
> It's of noble Johnny Gallagher, who sailed to and fro,
> He was lost on Lake Michigan where the stormy winds blow!

While songs of disaster were many, those celebrating the mundane navigational aids were few. A notable exception was "Let the Lower Lights Be Burning," popular with evangelist Phillip Bliss, who focused his ministry on lake sailors. The opening lyrics play homage to the lightkeepers of the lakes.

> Brightly beams our Father's mercy,
> From His lighthouse evermore;
> But to us He gives the keeping
> Of the lights along the shore.[58]

5

The Emergence
of the Maritime-Industrial Complex

1880–1910

Summer 1893/Spring 1894

In 1893 the world came to the shores of Lake Michigan, or at least twenty-one million people did. That year the equivalent of one in four Americans braved a nationwide depression and attended the World's Columbian Exhibition. The Chicago World's Fair was intended to honor four hundred years of "progress" since Christopher Columbus bumped into the New World. The glittering White City of classical revival temples showed off the latest accomplishments in technology's growing mastery over nature. Eager to demonstrate the strides the U.S. had made in improving navigational safety, the Lighthouse Board proposed a major exhibit to be housed under the towering dome of the ornate Government Building. Unfortunately, the secretary of the treasury, in view of the hard economic times, significantly scaled back their budget. However, the board did manage to present what

157

one observer dubbed "a brilliant display" when it showed off a new hyperradiant lens and a model of Orlando Poe's still impressive Spectacle Reef Lighthouse. Even more memorable was a new steel skeleton light tower erected on the banks of the lagoon. Visitors could ascend its spiral staircase and were rewarded with a stunning panorama of the fairgrounds, which made the exhibit among the most-frequented attractions.[1]

The Lighthouse Board had reason to be proud of their accomplishments. In the four decades that followed their takeover of responsibility for navigational aids, they had modernized and expanded the American system of lighthouses to become the largest in the world. They managed more than three thousand major lights. Those major lights and ten thousand other navigation markers, together with the charts, harbor, and channel improvements of the U.S. Army Corps of Engineers, had transformed the Great Lakes shoreline from a wilderness waterway to an artery of industrial commerce. From atop their World's Fair lighthouse, visitors looked out over a city that had risen from the swampy prairie to become the nation's second-most-populous metropolis and its busiest port. The board's pride in seeking recognition for their accomplishment was understandable. So, too, was the hubris of the fair organizers, who so stunningly celebrated the victory of civilization over wilderness and technology over nature. In the summer of 1893, the shimmering White City, aglow in the night with the illumination of more than one hundred thousand incandescent lights, was a promise of a well-ordered, safe, bright future.[2]

In less than a half century, electricity, in the form of radio waves as well as illumination, would indeed transform navigation and navigational aids, but in the 1890s nature could still respond to human hubris with nemesis. Seven months after the World's Columbian Exposition closed, nature put on an exposition of her own when a massive spring storm swept the Great Lakes region. On May 16, 1894, unusually warm weather with temperatures in the high eighties was confronted suddenly with a cold front arriving from the west. Tornadoes descended on the heartland. In Ohio, Illinois, and Michigan, towns and farms were ripped apart. For the next three days, a powerful gale with winds in excess of fifty miles an hour ripped the surface of Lakes Huron and Michigan. The storm was what some of the old-time sailors called a "schooner eater." Most of the large modern steamers caught in the gale suffered severe damage but were able to fight their way into harbors of refuge. Less fortunate were the sailing ships. Across the northern reaches of the lake, schooners were driven ashore. At Milwaukee, two schooners failed to make the harbor and were sunk in the shallows. Their crews climbed up the wind-lashed rigging. Rescue attempts managed to reach only one of the five sailors of the *M. J. Cummings*, and the others were either swept away or died frozen to the ratlines.[3]

It was in Chicago, where just the summer before millions from around the world had gathered to celebrate American progress, that the spring gale enacted its most awful drama. Scores of vessels had been driven by the fierce wind to the ports at the south end of the lake. Here the waves were highest as the storm had fully three hundred miles of open water to build its strength. Yet here also the vessels that had run before the gale suddenly ran out of room. Breakwaters built in the 1880s that created an outer harbor provided some protection for those who could chance the passage through the narrow opening. Others cast their anchors outside the refuge and hoped their lines would hold until the storm abated. For most, it was a forlorn hope. One by one eight schooners lost their anchorage or were smashed by other ships careening out of control. As many as one hundred thousand people gathered on the lakeshore to watch as mariners fought to save their vessels and then their own lives as ship after ship was smashed against breakwaters or were washed over them by towering waves. Lifesaving crews and makeshift rescue efforts by police and citizens pulled many storm-tossed sailors to safety. By day's end, however, the spring gale of '94 had severely damaged or sunk thirty-five ships with the loss of twenty-seven lives. Civilization could celebrate the conquest of the New World in splendid fairs, but the Great Lakes remained unpredictable, dangerous, and wild.[4]

Storm Warriors:
The U.S. Life-Saving Service

The 1890s were a storm-tossed decade on the Great Lakes. Between 1891 and 1895, an average of fifty-eight ships were lost annually on the lakes. Many of these were older sailing vessels nearing the end of their useful careers. The loss of life in these incidents was reduced because of the addition of a new agency to the maritime infrastructure of the inland seas. All along the shores of the lakes, fully staffed lifesaving stations were added to that infrastructure, expanding the federal government's commitment to marine safety. In the U.S. the federal government began its formal involvement in lifesaving in 1848 when it established a series of volunteer-manned stations along the Atlantic Coast. Boat stations came to the Great Lakes in 1854. Lake Michigan received the most, with twenty-three positioned along its margins. At best the stations were simply a boathouse with a government-owned lifeboat. In Canada the same haphazard approach was initially followed. In the 1870s the U.S. moved past this volunteer nucleus and developed a network of fully manned and equipped stations under the Treasury Department that was designated the U.S. Life-Saving Service. Up to this time, lifesaving had been restricted to the ad hoc heroism of brave bystanders or the intervention of lighthouse keepers. Following congressional action in June 1874, a series of fully staffed lifesaving stations were established on the Great Lakes.[5]

Under the new scheme, the nation's coastline was divided into a series of lifesaving districts. The Great Lakes were awarded the Ninth (Lake Ontario-Erie), the Tenth (Lake Huron-Superior), and the Eleventh (Lake Michigan) Districts. Lifesaving in the Lake Ontario-Erie district was put under the direction of veteran schooner master David P. Dobbins. He had already won a reputation for heroism through his rescue of distressed mariners in the 1850s and 1860s. In 1876 he set up stations near the major harbors, including Oswego, Buffalo, Erie, and Cleveland. Key to the successful management of this and other lifesaving districts was the appointment of the right man as keeper. Dobbins's experience as a mariner helped him recognize the type of individuals whose steady attention to detail and self-discipline, combined with a cool head and courage, would allow them to excel at the post. For the Fairport station on Lake Erie he selected George F. Babcock, an experienced schoonerman and an assistant lighthouse keeper. For twenty-two years he was in charge of the Fairport station, which was responsible for saving the lives of more than three hundred people. Charles C. Goodwin of the Cleveland station was a state of Maine man and a Civil War veteran. He had been engaged before the mast since the age of fourteen, with long experience at the helm of Great Lakes schooners. His numerous rescues of distressed vessels won him and every member of his crew the Gold Life-Saving Medal First Class.[6]

On Lake Superior lifesaving stations were established mainly along remote isolated stretches of coastline where sailors who survived a shipwreck might easily die of exposure before reaching aid. On Lake Huron, however, all the first lifesaving stations were erected near existing lighthouses, some of which, like Thunder Bay Island, were themselves fairly remote. In the Eleventh District that covered Lake Michigan, nearly all the stations were at port cities. The exceptions were two stations at the north and south ends (North Manitou Island and Point Betsie) of the busy Manitou Passage, the doorway through which most Lake Michigan traffic entered or exited the lake. For the crew that worked these stations between April and the beginning of December, location greatly impacted the nature of their work experience. Crews at isolated stations operated at greater peril, with little support other than their good judgment, strong arms, and stout boats. Even nightly beach patrols were riskier on lonely, wild shores. Crews based at major ports such as Buffalo or Chicago encountered much more action but could count on backup from tugboats. They became accustomed to crowds of citizens watching and cheering on their surf boat drills. Their sweethearts, wives, and children were never far away. Leave from the station could be enjoyed in lively urban communities, while their mates at many Lake Superior or Lake Huron stations literally had nowhere to go.[7]

In Canada a professionalized lifesaving service did not emerge until 1882 when the first manned station was established at Cobourg on Lake Ontario. The next year four more stations followed, with the most important being at the busy harbor of Toronto. Thereafter the number of stations grew to include Lakes Erie and Huron. A reciprocity agreement was developed with the U.S. Life-Saving Service so that each nation would come to the aid of distressed vessels regardless of the flag they flew.[8]

The actual work of lifesaving took three forms. Nightly beach patrols kept a lookout for vessels in distress. The patrollers also kept a lookout for ships heading toward shoals or reefs and would ignite Coston flares to warn them off if they were. If a ship was pushed close to the shore and grounded in the surf, the life-savers had an elaborate set of beach apparatus to deploy to extract the crew from the stranded vessel. Heavy surf and rip currents put sailors in great danger. The icy spring and autumn water temperatures usually precluded any attempt to swim for shore. If the wreck was within six hundred yards of shore, the lifesavers would set up a small smooth bore cannon known as a Lyle gun. Invented by West Point graduate David A. Lyle, the gun shot a lightweight line from the beach to the distressed ship. That line could then be used to pull a stout rope out to the wreck. From this line a breeches buoy could be attached above the waves and one by one crew members could be pulled safely to shore. All these tools were stored on a broad-wheeled beach cart that res-cuers could maneuver from their station to the site of the wreck. The final and most dangerous duty of the lifesavers was when a beleaguered ship was far off the shore. After spotting a distress signal or receiving a telegraph from a lighthouse keeper, the crew of the station would use a flare to signal the ship and then launch a lifeboat and attempt to row out to the sinking vessel. It took courage to launch a small lifeboat, often at night, in cold, heavy seas that had already floundered a much larger craft. It also took great endurance for six oarsmen to force a two- to four-ton wooden boat through storm-tossed waters. It could take hours of effort to reach a ship and great strength and skill to keep a heaving wreck from smashing the lifeboat when they tried to bring the crew aboard. In 1878 David P. Dobbins, the superintendent of the Ontario-Erie district, designed a self-bailing, self-righting lifeboat. With a capacity for thirty people, airtight compartments in the bow and stern, cork ballast, and a stout white oak fame, it quickly became a favorite tool for lifesavers throughout the Great Lakes.[9]

By 1893 there were forty-seven lifesaving stations along the shores of the inland seas. The fortitude and tragedy that marked the infrequent but arduous work of the U.S. Life-Saving Service is exemplified by the October 1880 wreck of the *J. H. Hartzel*. On a storm-tossed sea, the three-masted schooner stranded on a sand-bar near Frankfort, Michigan. The battered vessel broke and sank, with the crew seeking refuge in the crosstrees of the foremast. The men of the Point Betsie Life-Saving Station had to haul their thousand-pound beach apparatus ten miles through pathless dune country to reach the site. By Herculean effort and the occasional use of a horse, the crew made it to the wreck site in an astounding but exhausting two hours' time. All the while, the *Hartzel's* captain and crew of six, lashed by frigid water, were gradually being encased in ice. Three shots from the Lyle gun were required to finally get a secure line out to the wreck. When the first sailor was pulled to safety, he informed the rescuers that among the crew was a woman, the cook, who was very ill and who would not go in the precarious breeches buoy. Hoping to speed the process and safely rescue the woman, station keeper Thomas Matthews ordered his men to attach a "life car" to the line. This small watertight vessel was capable of carrying several passengers. Three times it was pulled out to the wreck bringing two of the crew to safety. Each time the life car hatch was removed the rescuers expected to find the woman. When the final two men were taken off, they announced the woman had been left for dead in the cross trees of the wreck. Her body was recovered seventeen days later. For the men of the Point Betsie station and the group of citizen volunteers who aided their long effort, it was a dispiriting end to their labor. They loaded their gear onto the cart and began the long journey back to the station, which they reached "wearied beyond expression" after nearly twenty-four hours of unceasing effort without food or rest.[10]

The establishment of the Life-Saving Service did not relieve lighthouse keepers from their duty to help distressed mariners. It was not uncommon for light stations and lifesaving stations to be located near one another as they both needed to be placed where ship traffic faced hazards. When an endangered vessel was sighted by a lightkeeper, they would send a report to the lifesavers. Eventually this was done by telegraph or telephone, but when necessary, keepers made the trip in person. Lightkeepers, however, did attempt rescues on their own when required. Martin Knudson, keeper of the Pilot Island Lighthouse in the infamous Death's Door Passage on Lake Michigan, may have set a record for rescues in 1892. That fall a schooner went ashore near his light and he helped the sailors get ashore and into the warm keeper's quarters. Only a week later, while still hosting his castaways, the schooner *A. P. Nichols* ground on a narrow shoal that extended out into the passage. In spite of the heavy surf, the stocky Knudson repeatedly waded out onto the shoal and one by one escorted the crew to the shelter of his lighthouse. By this time the brick keeper's quarters had sixteen guests. Knudson won a silver life-saving medal for his heroism. His wife, Theresa, who had to find a way to feed such a large group of unexpected guests, likely deserved one as well. Joseph Fountain, the keeper of the St. Helena Lighthouse just west of the Strait of Mackinac, knew well the danger of his island station. The keeper he replaced drowned in its vicinity. Twice Fountain saved people from the same fate, once by rowing out to two men whose leaky boat was ready to go under. His other rescue was more unusual. In 1913 early ice had all but closed the straits, and from his tower Fountain spotted two men out on the frozen lake far from shore and wandering to and fro. While it was not uncommon for Michiganders to walk out on the ice, it was also not unusual for people to become disoriented and freeze to death. Fountain's quick action, however, located the men and got them to the safety of the light station.[11]

Origins of Marine Weather Forecasting

The first efforts toward predicting weather along the Great Lakes were made in 1859 by George G. Meade in conjunction with his work leading the Lake Survey. The onset of the Civil War and the strain it placed on the U.S. Army disrupted his system of reporting stations just as it was beginning. The person responsible for prompting the government to return to this responsibility was Increase A. Lapham, a remarkable pioneer of American science. Lapham was the son of an engineer who worked on the building of the Erie, Welland, Miami, and other canals that played a key role in opening the Great Lakes frontier. The son worked at his father's side, learning both manual skills and engineering. Canal work led to one of his first scientific papers on the geology of Ohio. With his relocation to Milwaukee in 1836, Lapham devoted himself to the study and advancement of Wisconsin. He cooperated with Captain Meade in the study of both lunar tides on the Great Lakes and meteorology. Lapham had long pressed shipowners and mariners on the need to establish a weather-reporting system to reduce the loss of vessels to violent storms. As early as 1858 a handful of merchants involved in the lake trade petitioned

Figure 12. Increase Lapham, the Wisconsin scientist behind the creation of Great Lakes marine
weather forecasting.
Source: *Popular Science Monthly* 22 (April 1883).

Congress to give lighthouse keepers meteorological instruments. Nothing came of that, and such forward thinking was not widespread in the industry. When Lapham presented his ideas to one mariner, the fellow rebuffed Lapham by claiming he had "little time to investigate meteorological papers and had never been impressed with the opinion that our changeable and fickle climate could be put under any rules by which mariners might be guided with any certainty or much profit."[12]

When explanations of meteorology failed to win converts, Lapham resorted to something businessmen would understand—dollars and common sense. In 1868 and 1869 he issued a report titled "Disaster on the Lakes," which listed marine losses on the Great Lakes for those years. In 1868 the list included 1,164 vessels damaged (105 of which were sunk), 321 deaths, and $3.1 million in property damage. In 1869 the total number of vessels damaged was 1,914 (126 of which were sunk), 209 lives lost, and $4.1 million in financial losses. These figures got the attention of the leaders of the Milwaukee Board of Trade, and he persuaded them to push for the creation of a national weather service. This was done first as a resolution at the 1869 meeting of the National Board of Trade and then as legislation approved by Congress and signed by President Ulysses S. Grant in 1870. Under the law, the U.S. Army Signal Service was given responsibility "for taking meteorological observations at the military stations in the interior of the continent and at other points in the States and Territories . . . and for giving notice on the northern (Great) lakes and on the seacoast by magnetic telegraph and marine signals, of the approach and force of storms." It was thought that "military discipline" would provide for the "promptness, regularity, and accuracy" required. Twenty-four stations were established, most at existing military posts in the West and along the Great Lakes. Lapham coordinated the early reports, and in November 1870, he had the satisfaction of issuing the first marine forecast for the region.[13]

What the army signal men undertook amounted to synoptic weather observations. They recorded the sky cover, wind velocity, high and low temperatures, and barometer readings. What gave these various readings value was the use of telegraphy to quickly gather data in a central location, and the recognition that in North America weather fronts generally followed a west to east pattern. A system of regular storm warnings was in place by the 1871 shipping season. Major ports received notice from the Army Signal Service when winds twenty-five miles an hour or more were predicted for their vicinity. Signal service personnel would hoist a red flag with a black square in the middle as a storm warning. At smaller ports, mostly in Michigan and Wisconsin, civilian employees were charged with receiving storm warnings and posting signal flags. Great Lakes forecasting was further enhanced in 1871 when the U.S. and the Dominion of Canada agreed to share information, thereby giving notice of the notorious low-pressure systems descending from the sub-Arctic that brewed up the worst storms on the inland seas. The system soon won the respect of shipowners. A striking example is offered by the results of a storm tracked by army signal men beginning in Omaha on November 11, 1871. Over the course of the next five days the storm warning flag was raised at eight major ports on the lakes between five and twenty hours before the front hit. Faced with this warning, no vessels left Milwaukee harbor, and most stayed at their moorings in Chicago and Cleveland. Those that did chance the weather returned damaged, and one sank with loss of life. The same pattern repeated itself at Oswego on Lake Ontario: most vessels stayed in port; those few that insisted on venturing out returned damaged, and one was lost in the storm.[14]

The availability of reliable marine weather forecasts made shipping grain during the dangerous spring and fall seasons more secure. Insurance costs fell, and as a result so too did shipping rates for the long haul from Lake Michigan to Buffalo. The impact marine forecasts had on the safety of Great Lakes navigation can be seen by what happened when the system of reporting was reduced through congressional budget cuts. In 1882 it was discovered that the disbursing officer for the Signal Service had been embezzling as much as $60,000 annually from the weather system budget. Congress reacted by reducing the service's budget for 1883. As a result, the number of storm-warning stations was reduced from more than seventy to a mere forty-three. This was followed in 1883 by an immediate and steep increase in the number of shipping losses. One economic historian has estimated that losses that year were 87 percent greater than the year before or the year following when the stations were reopened. Marine weather forecasts ever since have been regarded as one of the most important ingredients in safe navigation.[15]

Great Lakes Vessels and the Birth of the Maritime-Industrial Complex

In the mid to late 1880s there was a dramatic increase in the percentage of the Great Lakes merchant fleet that was powered by steam. In the 1860s and 1870s the overwhelming number of vessels carrying grain east to Buffalo or iron and copper ore south from Lake Superior were sailing ships, most either barks or three-masted schooners. In part, this was because the basic design of Great Lakes steamers had been set in the 1840s and 1850s when passenger traffic was the high value trade on the lakes. As the railroads expanded into the region, however, steamers lost their passengers to trains, which took a more direct route west and one that was relatively safe and available regardless of the season.

At the same time, there was an expansion in the amounts of grain, ore, and timber moving east and coal headed west, all of which needed ships to carry them to market. These factors combined to bring about a revolution in both ship traffic and vessel design on the Great Lakes.

The first small sign of things to come was evident as early as 1848 when *Petrel* was launched at Port Huron, Michigan. She was a propeller-driven ship, 225 feet in overall length and 32 feet in width, with her engine located aft to allow a large cargo hold at midship. She was initially built to carry lumber, but that trade was still in its infancy before the Civil War so she went on to carry a wide variety of cargoes. The launching of the *R. J. Hackett* at Cleveland in 1869 was a better merger of technology, ship design, and business plan. This was a steamer designed for the carrying of bulk cargoes with no accommodations for passengers, and while she sprouted three schooner-rigged masts, her principal power source was a steam engine located aft that drove a single powerful propeller. A forward pilothouse and cabin kept the midship area available for cargo and began a long tradition of "lakers" having the pilothouse in the bow. Large, open hatches made it easy to load her with either grain or ore. Put on the iron ore route between Marquette's iron ore docks and Cleveland's blast furnaces, the *R. J. Hackett* was such a success that she was given a sister ship, the *Forest City*, in 1871. Numerous other vessels copied their design, which became known, somewhat incongruously, as steam barges.[16]

By 1884 the tonnage of steam-driven vessels, many of which were propellers like the *R. J. Hackett*, was greater than the tonnage of sailing ships on the lakes. Two years later the absolute number of steamers was greater than the number of sailing ships still in service. In 1870 steamships represented only 39 percent of the new ships launched on the inland seas, yet by 1910 that number had grown to 100 percent. An increasing emphasis on efficiency drove this transition. Navigation on the Great Lakes was a seasonal business. With most traffic halted between December and April, merchants needed to maximize the number of trips that could be made during the shipping season. By the 1890s shipping agents estimated that, on account of their greater speed, steamers could carry two and a quarter times the cargo in a season than a sailing ship. Steam-powered vessels were particularly desired for trades that required adherence to a schedule. The iron and steel industry required iron ore, coal, and limestone to operate their blast furnaces. A shortfall in the availability of any of these commodities could force the shutdown of a blast furnace, with both the loss of production time and increased energy costs. Therefore, steamers pushed schooners out of this trade long before the windjammers lost their place in the grain or lumber trade. The switch from wood to coal as the main fuel for lake steamers also improved their efficiency. Although coal from the Midwest region was not readily available until the 1880s, its use instead of wood in firing boilers gave vessels much greater range and did away with the numerous refueling stops of the original steamers.[17]

The next big step in ship design was taken by the Globe Iron Works of Cleveland in 1882 when they launched the *Onoko*. At 282 feet in length, she was dubbed the "Queen of the Lakes." *Onoko* was also one of the first iron-hulled freighters. The design, however, was not popular. Insurance underwriters believed iron hulls were too brittle and vulnerable to major damage when grounding—a frequent danger on the lakes. The Detroit Dry Dock Company developed a compromise between iron and wood hulls when it launched the *Fayette Brown* in 1887. She was what was called a "composite freighter" because her hull was made of an iron frame and oak planking covered by iron plates. These bulk carriers had the strength to carry large, heavy cargoes like iron or copper ore. It was, however, the launching of the *Spokane* in 1886 by the Globe Iron Works that was the true signpost to the future. At 310 feet and thirty-four hundred tons, she was the largest vessel to float on the lakes up to that time. Her steel hull had the strength and flexibility to handle either the power of a November gale on Lake Superior or the danger of grounding in the shallow channels at the Soo or Lake St. Clair. Like the *R. J. Hackett*, the *Spokane* sprouted three masts to be used in case of emergency or in favorable wind conditions.[18]

The expansion and design creativity of lake shipping took place as that trade was becoming deeply integrated in the expansion of heavy industry in the heartland. A trend began, one that continues into the present, to build vessels capable of bearing greater and greater tonnage. Vessel size grew from the three-hundred-footers of the late 1880s to the five-hundred-footers at the turn of the century. Wooden steamers continued to be built.

The shipyard of James Davidson in Bay City, Michigan, employed as many as one thousand workers and was solely devoted to wooden ship construction. In 1900 they celebrated the launching of the *Pretoria*, a 350-foot schooner. Three years later the yard produced two giant schooner barges, the *Montezuma* and the *Chieftain*. They were among the largest wooden vessels ever built on the Great Lakes at 352 feet in length (the *David Dows* built in 1881 was 365 feet in length). Although wooden construction persisted, steel clearly was the preferred material for the design of lake freighters. But unlike wood, which remained readily available along the lakes as late as 1900, steel vessels required much greater capital investment. Therefore, the creation of fleets of steel freighters reflected the integration of the lake marine into the emerging and increasingly concentrated industrial capitalist order of Gilded Age America.[19]

The great figures of late nineteenth-century American industry all became deeply involved in Great Lakes shipping in the 1890s. John D. Rockefeller, not content with the millions of dollars his Standard Oil Trust brought him, became a key figure in the consolidation of lake shipping and heavy industry into a maritime-industrial complex. In 1893 he expanded into iron mining when he used the tremendous leverage of his capital reserves and questionable ethical maneuvers to secure control over the rich Mesabi Iron Range in Minnesota. Rockefeller owned a railroad that brought the ore from the interior to the Lake Superior port of Duluth. What he needed was a fleet of ships to bring the ore to the mills along the lower lakes. Control of transportation had been one of the keys to Rockefeller's success in the oil business, and he saw that as the demand for iron ore grew, so too would the demand for shipping. As early as 1888 he invested in the American Steel Barge Company that was formed to build steel lakers. In 1895 he took an even bigger step into Great Lakes shipping—it was in fact the biggest investment ever made up until that time. He formed the Bessemer Steamship Company and, despite a continuing economic depression, commissioned twelve new steel vessels, the largest of which was 475 feet in length. When those commissions were launched, he ordered twelve more new ships. Within five years Rockefeller grew his fleet of massive steel freighters to fifty-six vessels.[20]

It did not take long for the leading iron- and steelmakers in the U.S. to wake up to the fact that the nation's most infamous monopolist was gaining a stranglehold over the mining and shipping of iron ore. Andrew Carnegie, who had previously scoffed at investing in Lake Superior mines and lake shipping, scrambled to escape the grasp of Rockefeller's iron grip. Belatedly, he began to work with partners to purchase mines. As Rockefeller's giant fleet began to take shape, he wasted no time in raising shipping rates, and mills in need of ore had no choice but to pay his price. Rumors also abounded that the oil tycoon was looking to establish his own steel plants somewhere on the lakes. All of this prompted Andrew Carnegie, the nation's largest steel magnet, to seek a rapprochement that would forestall the entry of a dangerous new competitor. In December 1896 the robber barons agreed to an alliance. Carnegie would purchase most of Rockefeller's ore and ship it on the latter's vessels at a rate determined by the market. For his part Rockefeller agreed not to establish his own steelmaking plants. The immediate result of the alliance was a consolidation of Lake Superior mines in the hands of Carnegie and Rockefeller. The two giants were able to set the price for iron ore at ruinous levels until they forced smaller producers to sell out. As Carnegie acquired more mines in northern Michigan's Gogebic and Menominee ranges, he also sought to establish an independent shipping capability. Even Rockefeller's vast Bessemer Steamship Company could not handle all the ore Andrew Carnegie's mills required. Rather than contract with smaller shipping lines, Carnegie elected to follow Rockefeller's example and form his own fleet of ore carriers. In 1899 he purchased six freighters and ordered five new vessels built for what he called the Pittsburgh Steamship Company. The actions of industrial giants like Rockefeller and Carnegie set off a boom in Great Lakes shipbuilding that would continue virtually unabated until the Great Depression. By that time the number of Great Lakes vessels, 90 percent of which were American, was greater than the commercial fleets of any nation in the world save Germany and Great Britain.[21]

One of the by-products of John D. Rockefeller's initial involvement in Great Lakes shipping was the development of a unique type of steel ship known as the whaleback. The design

022839 HENRY CORT (WHALEBACK) AND BARGE MANDA

Figure 13. Whaleback steamer *Henry Cort*, ca. 1900.
Source: Library of Congress.

was the brain child of Alexander McDougall, an experienced inland seas mariner who thought he had come up with the perfect type of ore carrier. His unconventional concept was a flat-bottomed steel hull with curved sides and an upturned bow that aided in cutting through the water. In fact, the whaleback's sloped deck was so close to the waterline that it was often awash even in moderate seas. Secure space topside was provided by two turrets, one forward and a second aft, which contained the pilothouse. By sitting low in the water, McDougall believed his vessels would be safer in heavy seas and more fuel efficient. Rockefeller provided the key investment for McDougall to establish the American Steel Barge Company in 1889. Over the next ten years McDougall built forty-two whaleback freighters and barges.[22]

The whaleback's cigar-shaped hulls and snub-nosed bow caused some sailors to mockingly dub them "pig boats." They were unloved by their crews because of the noise and vibrations that made sleep difficult when underway. They also faced difficulties in filling their designed role as ore carriers. While initially successful, McDougall could not expand the length of his hulls to keep up with the rapidly growing size of ore freighters. Most whalebacks were between two hundred and three hundred feet in length, and the largest ever constructed, the *Christopher Columbus*, was a passenger ship, not a freighter. Another problem that could not be overcome was the vessel's small cargo hatches, a necessity since the decks were often awash. Yet when machine-operated unloaders came into use at iron ports, whalebacks became cumbersome and time consuming to unload. Nor did the ships turn out to be as effective in riding out storms as McDougal had hoped. Nonetheless, although whalebacks were only built for ten years, many of those put into service enjoyed long careers. The *Frank Rockefeller*, for example, steamed the lakes for seventy-three years and endures today as a museum ship. While the whalebacks turned out to be a dead end in Great Lakes ship design, they were an eye-catching example of the boldness and ingenuity of the lake marine.[23]

George Hulett was in part responsible for the demise of the whaleback freighters. He was a Cleveland merchant who, rather late in life, became involved in the construction of equipment for coal and ore handling. In a few short years, he invented several devices that greatly improved the efficiency of moving large amounts of bulk cargoes. These included a type of conveyor belt and a machine that emptied rail cars loaded with coal or ore. He was most famous, however, for his 1899 invention of what became known as the Hulett Unloader. Giant steel walking beams lowered a self-filling bucket into the hold of a ship and scooped out the ore and then raised it up and deposited it in a rail car. Where it had previously taken days to manually unload a lake freighter, Hulett's unloader could do the job in a matter of hours. After Carnegie Steel authorized the first one for the ore docks in Cleveland, they soon became a feature of all Great Lakes ports. The unloaders further enhanced the accelerating efficiency of lake shipping at the turn of the century.[24]

Because iron ore was such a heavy commodity, no ship could be loaded in the same way that grain was loaded, which was poured into the hold to the very top of the cargo hatches. Iron ore had to be carefully trimmed to rest evenly in the ship, seldom filling more than three-quarters of the hold. Too much iron ore in a ship would push her dangerously deep in the water. When a vessel was being loaded with ore, it was the mate's job to carefully watch the draft marks on the stem and stern posts to ensure the ship was not too heavily loaded. Inevitably, steelmakers demanded bigger and bigger vessels whose size could compensate for larger and heavier loads of iron ore. The growing fleets of large, steel lake freighters changed navigation on the lakes. The size of these vessels and their ability to carry larger and weightier cargoes increased the draft of the typical lakes vessel. The intimate integration of lake shipping with the burgeoning steel industry put pressure on the federal government to increase the depth of shipping channels such as the St. Clair Flats and all major harbors. This also had an impact on lighthouse design. Vessels needing deeper water necessarily sailed farther from shore. Taller towers were needed to ensure that coastal light station flashes were visible out on the lake.[25]

In 1895 the Cleveland shipping firm of Pickands Mather launched the first of what became known as the "400 footers." Actually, the *Victory* was only 398 feet in length, but she was big enough to earn the title "Queen of the Lakes" as the largest vessel on inland waters. She did not hold that title for long. When Rockefeller was building up his fleet, some of the new commissions were classed as "500 footers." By 1900 designers at the American Shipbuilding Company in Lorain, Ohio, yet another affiliate of the multifaceted Rockefeller empire, were planning for "600 footers." In the decade that followed, 176 steel ore freighters between five hundred and six hundred feet in length were built on the Great Lakes. There were so many vessels engaged in the thousand-mile route between mills of Ohio and Pennsylvania and the Lake Superior mining district that the Lake Carriers' Association estimated that "one vessel is rarely ever out of the sight of another." The importance of this modern steel fleet to the nation's economy can best be understood when it is realized that it would have taken 240 railroad cars to carry the cargo of a single six-hundred-foot freighter.[26]

The size, speed, and especially the cost of these new lake leviathans demanded more precise and rigorous navigators in the pilothouse. The regularly updated charts provided by the U.S. Lake Survey were invaluable, as were the system of lighthouses that graced the lakes. It became the mate of the watch's duty to regularly take bearings on key features such as lighthouses, set the course of the vessel for another known point, and calculate the time it would take to be abreast of that feature. Each bearing would be recorded in the log along with the time that bearing was reached. The helmsman attempted to keep to the proscribed course and had the aid of a binnacle to do so. This impressive piece of late nineteenth-century marine navigation consisted of a waist-high case of polished hardwood and brass solidly secured to the pilothouse deck. Protected within it was a mariner's compass suspended on a gimbal ring that ensured it remained level even when the lake buffeted the vessel. The helmsman could see the compass course he had been assigned by the mate and could constantly check it against the "lubber line," a vertical indicator of the actual heading of the ship. All helmsmen strayed somewhat from the course, particularly when out on the open lake, but small variations could be easily corrected. Fred Dutton, who served as a helmsman on lake steamers before the advent of electronic aids, recalled that as a young man he was embarrassed to admit he had strayed off course. When the mate was taking a bearing, it was critical that the ship was "right on the mark." Several times Dutton tried to cover up the fact that he had strayed until it was impressed upon him that it would lead to an improper bearing that could set the ship "on the rocks" instead of safely past them. "I quickly learned to tell the truth about it," Dutton said. "Always as soon as the mate prepared to take a bearing, it was time to steady the ship on her course, and it became a matter of pride to have the ship exactly on course when the mate sang out."[27]

Each time shipbuilders made a new leap in the size of their steel creations, pressure was put on the U.S. Army Corps of Engineers to dredge deeper channels and harbors, lest the ambitions of marine architects and their robber baron bosses be constrained. When the Civil War ended, only a handful of major harbors had the ability to handle a vessel drawing as much as thirteen feet of water. Between 1881 and 1884 the corps was able to establish a sixteen-foot channel for the larger ports and the Sault Ste. Marie Canal. The iron ore trade, which boomed after the war, drove the demand for larger vessels. Between 1865 and 1884 the gross tonnage of iron ore shipped increased from 278,796 tons to 2.5 million tons. Larger vessels would be able to carry more ore per trip and, with powerful new engines, make more trips per season. No sooner was the sixteen-foot channel completed than the steel industry joined the Lake Carriers' Association to lobby the government for a twenty-foot channel. Far from the controversy over such improvements in the antebellum era, Congress in September 1890 quickly approved the dredging of a twenty-foot channel. The U.S. Army Corps of Engineers estimated the cost of this to be $3.3 million, and between 1892 and 1897 most channels were improved. Ship captains, however, had to be aware that natural fluctuations in the water level of the lakes often meant that the water in some channels, particularly on shallow Lake Erie, was much lower. By the first decade of the twentieth century, all the major harbors on the lake had been dredged to twenty feet. Because of these infrastructure investments, a lake vessel in 1905 could carry 6,000 tons more than a similar vessel back in the 1870s, when a fourteen-foot channel was the rule.[28]

The growing size of Great Lakes vessels and the massive scale of steel industry plants gave rise to several new ports. The narrow and shallow Chicago River that meandered through the heart of that city's commercial district had long been both the port and the center for manufacturing. By 1880, however, that began to change, and both shipping and steel production began to migrate twelve miles south to the Calumet River. Since 1869 the Corps of Engineers had made improvements to this sluggish stream surrounded by massive marshes. The first rolling mill came in 1880 along with a railroad branch line and a giant grain elevator. By 1909 the area had developed into one of the greatest industrial concentrations in the world, and it was decided that Calumet would become Chicago's principal harbor. As the maritime-industrial complex's growth accelerated, Detroit also gave birth to a specialized port with the creation of an industrial harbor at River Rouge, one mile south of the city limits. The naturally deep river required less engineering than the Calumet, and industry began to gravitate there in the 1880s. A major shift away from the downtown Detroit waterfront followed the 1903 opening of the

Detroit Iron and Steel Company plant on River Rouge. Henry Ford completed the transformation of the area to a bustling heavy industry workshop in 1917 when he began work on a giant automobile plant that was for a time the largest integrated factory site in the world. The Corps of Engineers made this possible by deepening the River Rouge to a depth of twenty-one feet.[29]

Many of the key navigational choke points required something more than dredging. A second canalized channel was completed through the St. Clair Flats, and the dredging of the lower reaches of the Detroit River made an additional shipping lane in and out of Lake Erie. The bigger problem, however, was at Sault Ste. Marie. The canal once decried in the Senate as "beyond the farthest bounds of Civilization, if not the moon," was now key to the operation of the world's largest iron and steel industry. In the twenty years after 1880, traffic through the canal increased by nearly twenty times. In 1895 it was typical for ships to be kept waiting five hours before they could be locked through. A second lock on the Canadian side helped somewhat, as did the completion by the Corps of Engineers of the Poe Lock at Sault Ste. Marie in 1896. Ship traffic, nonetheless, was still congested until a third U.S. lock was authorized by Congress in 1907. By that time the canal was handling nine times the tonnage of the Suez Canal in its eight-month season, and a vessel was, on average, day or night, passing through its chambers every six minutes.[30]

The Lumber Trade:
Twilight of the Schooners

While the magnets of iron and steel were building five-hundred-footers and discussing the merits of triple expansion steam engines, a large percentage of the vessels on lake waters remained sail powered. Few wooden sailing ships were built after 1886, yet the vast majority of those launched in the decades before remained in active service. Some remained in the iron ore trade, but most were employed in the transport of lumber. Lumber was a perfect cargo for the aging schooner fleet. Industry in the nineteenth century was relentlessly extractive. While the iron mines were also extractive, they operated on a scale that kept them open for decades, and they developed a small number of heavily used

ports, such as Marquette, Escanaba, Ashland, and especially
Duluth. Lumber companies in the Great Lakes resisted the consolidation of resources that typified the iron ranges, and the industry was dominated by a large number of relatively small
companies that rather quickly cut through their timberland hold-
ings. The lumber frontier, therefore, created a large number of
small ports that were busy for a relatively short time and received
limited infrastructure investment.

Scores of sawdust towns sprang up along the shores of the
inland seas. Lake Huron and Lake Michigan were the real heart
of the region's lumber frontier because they were adjacent to the
best forested lands. For a decade or two, small Michigan ports
flourished, such as Nahma, Manistique, Menominee, Ludington,
Frankfort, Grand Marais, Bay Mills, Port Crescent, and Huron
City. The federal government improved twenty-eight small harbors on Lake Michigan alone. When mills closed, communities
shrank or, in the case of Nahma and Port Crescent, were completely abandoned and the harbor works allowed to erode. The
biggest lumber ports, such as Muskegon, Manistee, Bay City,
and Saginaw, kept mills busy into the twentieth century and
then found new industries. On Lake Ontario, Oswego thrived on
timber carried across from the wild Canadian shore. The Buffalo
suburbs of Tonawanda and North Tonawanda became the great
lumber entrepôt on the eastern end of the lakes. In 1888 there
were forty-five mills there buzzing with busy circular saws.
However, the Buffalo area was too far away from the prime forest lands of the upper lakes to long endure as a milling center.
For a few years the mills kept busy by having large rafts of logs
towed from Lake Huron. The use of rafts and the mills they supplied both died out in the mid-1890s. Sailing ships, however,
continued to bring loads of finished lumber from Michigan and
Canadian mills, which were transshipped from Tonawanda
down the Erie Canal. In its peak year of 1890 Tonawanda received 718,650,000 board feet of lumber via ship and raft from
Michigan and Canada.[31]

The greatest lumber port on the Great Lakes (indeed, the
largest lumber center in the world) was Chicago. When the Civil
War ended, Chicago was in the best possible position to dominate
the lumber trade. Its location in the Lake Michigan basin gave it
easy access to the best pine and hardwood forests in the U.S. The

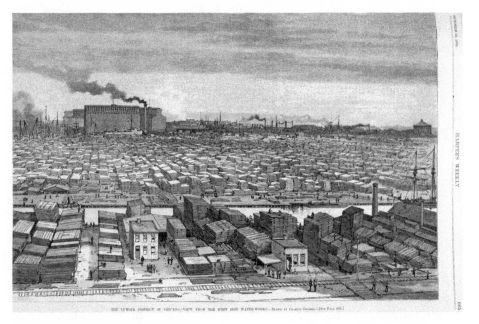

Figure 14. Chicago Lumber District.
Source: *Harper's Weekly*, October 1883.

economic problem with forest products was their considerable weight and bulk, either as timber in the forest or lumber at a sawmill, and therefore, they were costly to move effectively. The rivers of Michigan and Wisconsin were damned and channelized to carry timber to lakeshore mills, and the vast fleet of sailing ships on the lake could then take the cargo to market. Chicago became that market because of its eight railroad lines running into the city and its Illinois and Michigan Canal link to the Mississippi valley. Postwar railroad construction improved access to the West even more. At the vast lumberyards that covered the West Side of Chicago, buyers from the treeless prairie met the lumber barons of the north in a lucrative embrace. An English visitor in 1887 noted that "the timber yards are a considerable part of the city's surface, there appear to be enough boards and planks piled up to supply [a] half-dozen States."[32]

In 1867 the historian James Parton visited the Chicago lumber district. He found "miles of timber yards extended along one of the forks of the river." The harbor was "chocked with arriving timber vessels; timber trains snort over the prairie in every direction." When he ventured to the lakefront, he was greeted by a blue horizon dotted with the white canvas of arriving schooners. In one afternoon "a favorable wind blew into port two hundred and eighteen vessels loaded with timber." Throughout the shipping season, hundreds of schooners were kept in constant motion ferrying lumber cargoes from mill towns like Muskegon, at the mouth of Michigan's longest river, to the city. Some of the product of Muskegon and the Green Bay region went to Milwaukee, but the market was bigger, and prices were generally better, at Chicago. In Muskegon's peak year of 1879, Chicago, only a day's sail away, captured 86 percent of her lumber.[33]

Great Lakes schooners persisted, in part, because they stood at the apex of thousands of years of development of sail technology. Their simple design was remarkably efficient, and they could be successfully operated with a crew of only a half-dozen men. As new technology became available, schooners adapted to it. Late nineteenth-century schooners might employ steel cables for rigging and occasionally a steam donkey engine to operate the windlass. The amount of tonnage on the Great Lakes classified as "sail" actually increased by nearly 10 percent between 1886 and 1897. Long after schooners were driven from the grain trade by steam freighters, the vessels persisted in lumber because the cargo was impervious to the leaky hulls of older ships, and the short distance traveled made the trade less time sensitive than grain or ore. The vessels were cheap to buy and readily available as other trades moved on to steam and steel. A few of the major logging companies, such as Hackely & Hume based in Muskegon, invested in stout, well-maintained vessels and trusted vessel masters, but much of the lumber trade was carried by tramp schooners, ships that were owned and managed from behind the ship's wheel.[34]

Many schooners served out their final days as barges. It brought tears to the eyes of experienced sailors to see a once-proud top-sail schooner "stripped of her masts and sails" and "reduced" to a "menial task." John Noyes of Buffalo first began the practice of converting outmoded vessels into barges. In 1861 he stripped two former passenger steamers of their elaborate upper decks and used a tug to tow them across Lake Erie with timber for the mills of Tonawanda and Buffalo. On the upper lakes, it was old schooners that were subject to conversion as lumber barges. Often the vessels would retain their masts and some of their rigging, but they would be shorn of their top sails and the crew reduced to a skeleton complement. Steam propeller tugs would haul two or three such barges, the holds and decks of which would be stacked high with board lumber. In fair weather, tugs and barges could transport a larger amount of lumber faster than the old clipper schooners. Yet tragedy could result when the consorts were caught in a storm and the tugs could not maintain headway with their heavy tows. It was common practice then to cut loose the schooner barge. Ideally the barge crew would deploy their anchors and ride out their storm. Too often, however, the anchor cables, old and rotted, would separate and the barge would be driven to wreck and ruin. Typical of the end of many a schooner was the destruction of the *Plymouth* in the great storm of 1913. Caught on northern Lake Michigan when the gale struck, the tug *Martin* parted its tow cable and left the *Plymouth* to weather the storm in the lee of Gull Island. A week later a message in a bottle was found washed up on a Michigan beach. It read: "Dear Wife and Children: We were left up here in Lake Michigan by McKinnon, captain of the *James Martin*; tug at anchor. He went away and never said goodbye or anything to us. Lost one man yesterday. We have been out in the storm forty hours. Goodbye dear ones. Might see you in heaven. Pray for me. Chris K." Chris Keenan and the entire crew perished.[35]

The most common cause of mishaps for lake schooners was to be caught in unprotected waters and driven on to charted shoals or points of land when their anchors failed to hold. Thick fog was another frequent and almost unavoidable source of marine casualties. Yet as the fate of the hapless *Plymouth* demonstrated, greater attention to crew safety was needed, and in the 1890s there were regular calls for the government to inspect sailing ships and tow barges. Steamboats faced regular government inspections, but sail vessels were not covered by that legislation. In 1896 one veteran lake captain lamented, "I have seen many schooners go out of the Chicago River which were totally unfit for anything but the junkshop. They were literally sailing coffins, but the government inspectors could do nothing." Experienced schooner captains often balked at taking the helm of rotted vessels, and barges were routinely commanded by inexperienced sailors. This caused no difficulty if the weather conditions were ideal and the vessel stayed under tow. But if a tow was parted, many of these would-be masters lacked the skill to manage their craft and often steered them directly to the nearest shore and hoped for the best. In 1894 the schooner *J. D. Sawyer* broke loose from its tow on Lake Michigan. The captain was disoriented even though he was within sight of "one of the best known lighthouses on the lakes." A fine protected harbor was located just down the shore, yet in a panic the man instead guided his schooner strait for shore and smashed it on the rocks; only the arrival of a fishing boat saved him and his crew from "certain death." A vessel owner had the right to put any lubber in charge of a sailing vessel, and in the last days of the schooners too often they did just that.[36]

Although many were rotted and even lacked life preservers, wooden sailing ships maintained a grip on a portion of the lake trade as long as the lumber industry in the region flourished. As lumber production declined, so too did the role of the schooner. In 1882 the Saginaw valley of Michigan, once the cockpit of the lumber barons, reached its peak production, and within a decade, mills in the region were importing logs to cut. The Lake Michigan sawdust towns on the Michigan peninsula continued to increase production until 1890. Then lumbermen moved farther west into Wisconsin, which led the nation in production by 1900. Thereafter, there was a rapid falloff in lake states lumber. Newer mills in the region were located far from the lakeshore and moved their boards by rail. As a sign of the times, in 1915 the Lighthouse establishment agreed to allow the U.S. Forest Service to undertake replanting operations on lighthouse reservations. Many of the most successful lumbermen either quit the business or moved to the South or Pacific Northwest, where virgin forests yet awaited the saw. With the demise of the Great Lakes logging frontier came the end of the white-winged wind jammers that had once crowded the horizon with their sails. With their passing, lake communities lost a living and romantic connection to their maritime past. Lost as well was the tendency to give lake vessels the personal names of wives or mothers or bold sobriquets that conjured up far-off places, great battles fought, or heroes of old, such as *Moonlight, Persia, Austerlitz, Invincible,* or *Tempest.* The corporate fleets of the iron barons were giant, hulking hulls of great efficiency with the banal names of the rich, soft men who presided over their board rooms.[37]

Emperor of the North:
The Rise of the Port of Duluth-Superior

The site destined to be America's greatest grain port is located incongruously more than twenty-three hundred miles from the ocean. The southwestern end of Lake Superior had long played an important role in the fur trade with American Indians. Canoes were replaced by sailing ships and steamers after the Sault Ste. Marie Canal was completed. Prospective town sites were quickly established to cash in on the anticipated boom that would come with ships. Where the St. Louis River enters the lake, a long sandbar stretches nine miles and encloses a large natural harbor, nineteen square miles in size. At the narrow opening through this bar, the town of Superior, Wisconsin, was founded in 1853. Farther up the bay on the Minnesota side of the harbor, Duluth was founded a year later. The two towns sharing the same bay became both rivals and partners. Kegs of salted lake trout and whitefish were among the first cargoes shipped from the west end of Lake Superior. It was grain and iron ore, however, that would prove to be the foundation for Duluth's dynamic growth as a maritime hub.[38]

Numerous speculators, developers, and legislators saw the potential of the Duluth-Superior location. From the beginning, plans were floated for railroads and harbor improvements. Resolutions were passed by civic, state, and federal bodies, but nothing got done until the Philadelphia financier Jay Cooke stepped in and began to transform pipe dreams into iron horses. In 1863 he funded the construction of a railroad from St. Paul to Duluth. It was Cooke who insisted that the terminus be that city and not its sister Superior. In 1870 that railroad, the Mississippi and Lake Superior, was completed. Wasting no time, Cooke broke ground just west of Duluth on the Northern Pacific Railroad, a route that was projected to extend from Lake Superior to Tacoma, Washington, on Puget Sound. The route would have a long and troubled gestation, punctuated by bankruptcy and reorganization following the Panic of 1873. The Northern Pacific would not be completed until 1883. Other railroads would follow in the future, but these first two railroads became the conduits connecting Duluth with the growing wheat farms of the northern Plains. The first grain elevator was constructed in 1870, and a year later the first cargoes of wheat left the harbor. The grain trade of Duluth-Superior grew quickly after that. Chicago retained its primary position in grain shipments, with Milwaukee in second place, but by the 1890s Duluth had surpassed all other ports and moved into the third position. Wheat, corn, and flaxseed shipped from Lake Superior were sent to Buffalo for transshipment to the coast. A small portion went via Canada's Welland Canal to Oswego or Montreal.[39]

In 1906 Duluth finally bested Chicago and became the nation's greatest primary grain port. It emerged in part because of its superior access to the wheat-growing states of the Dakotas and Nebraska, but changes in maritime technology also played a role. The four-hundred- and five-hundred-footers that dominated the carrying of grain, ore, and coal in the early twentieth century required deep harbors, broad channels, and specialized docking. Chicago's harbor, like most early lake ports, was its river, a slack stream barely one hundred yards wide. Its size was not a serious obstacle when most lake vessels were one hundred to two hundred feet in length, but when the size of shipping doubled, Chicago's river port was doomed. For years marine interests advocated the building of a modern outer harbor on the lakefront, but little action was taken. In 1909 the city adopted a plan by architect Daniel Burnham to dedicate most of the lakefront to parks and recreation. Belatedly, both heavy industry and modern shipping were shunted south to the Calumet River, where a new harbor was created. Cleveland's Cuyahoga River port was modified to handle the four- and five-hundred-foot freighters, but when vessel size increased to six hundred feet in 1906 with the launch of the *J. Pierpont Morgan*, those giants required an outer harbor to unload. Duluth, on the other hand, had a natural, superb harbor, and the U.S. Army Corp of Engineers improved the ship canal that connected it to Lake Superior. The grain and ore docks of Duluth-Superior were built to service the giant lake freighters. The Great Northern elevator opened in 1901, towered 243 feet over the waterfront of Superior, Wisconsin, and was one of the largest in the world. When the iron ore dock there was enlarged in 1902, it was the largest in the world. Grain boats at Duluth typically took on cargoes of four hundred thousand bushels, which was nearly double the size of cargoes shipped from less modern ports.[40]

The Port of Duluth-Superior's efficiency was increased after 1892 when iron ore shipments began to flow through the harbor.

Figure 15. Lake steamer preparing to load iron ore, Allouez, Wisconsin, 1941.
Source: Library of Congress.

By 1900 five million tons of ore were loaded at her terminals. Within five years that number had tripled, and by 1913 Duluth-Superior was shipping thirty million tons of ore annually. Lake vessels carried 80 percent of the region's iron ore. Without this fleet the U.S. could not have emerged as the world's leader in steel production. Ships carrying grain or ore east to Lake Erie returned with cargoes of anthracite coal that went into the bins of the big freighters to fuel another four-day journey east. Buffalo was Duluth's partner in this trade. Its elevators took on western grain. The big freighters were then repositioned to the trestles where the trains that brought coal from Pennsylvania could empty their cars. In the 1880s and 1890s, one and a half million tons of coal left Buffalo annually to ballast the grain and ore boats. This east to west traffic, however, could not match the volume of tonnage sent down the lakes.[41]

In 1907 Duluth became the site of an experiment designed to take advantage of the ability of lake freighters to inexpensively supply the Lake Superior city with coal and limestone. By this time, the Rockefeller and Carnegie interests in mines, shipping, and mills had been merged with Eber Brock Ward's original mills to form in 1901 the world's first billion-dollar business—the U.S. Steel Corporation. Under the leadership of J. P. Morgan, the company built a model workers' community at Duluth, Morgan Park, and a fully integrated steel plant. The enterprise had the added benefit of appeasing the State of Minnesota that had previously threatened to put a tax on ore shipped out of state. The mill turned out steel rails for western railroads and attracted immigrants to the city in search of industrial jobs.[42]

By 1910 Duluth was an urban center of more than seventy-eight thousand citizens, and its sister city Superior, which had more than forty thousand people, was Wisconsin's second-largest city. The rapid rise of these twin cities and their dominant place in inland seas navigation had been made possible by a massive federal investment in channel and harbor improvements, which totaled $7.4 million. Yet the payoff for the nation would be worth the investment in the more efficient movement of grain and iron ore to feed growing cities and mills and to fuel the nation's booming international trade. During World War I, Duluth-Superior harbor handled fifty-two million tons of cargo, a staggering 1,700 percent increase over shipments less than twenty years before.[43]

The rise of Duluth-Superior on the American side of Lake Superior was mirrored in the emergence of twin ports on the Canadian side of the border. Fort William originated as a fur-trade depot, while Port Arthur had enjoyed modest growth as a mining center. Together they shared sheltered anchorage of Thunder Bay. Neither of these ports was of more than local importance until the Canadian Pacific Railroad began to build track west from Lake Superior and out into the vast prairies of western Canada. Those lands were the world's last great wheat growing frontier, and they became a magnet for immigrants from eastern and northern Europe. The population of the rolling grasslands of Manitoba and Saskatchewan surged from a mere four hundred thousand at the turn of the century to more than one million a decade later. Trains that brought agriculturalists west returned with hopper cars laden with the golden grain. Elevators and terminals sprouted on the Superior shore of Thunder Bay, and the demand rose for ships to bear the grain to market. The bulk of the existing Canadian-flagged commercial vessels were inadequate in both size and number. To keep U.S. freighters from securing the majority of the trade, Canadian shipping companies began a massive investment in large new steel ships. Between 1896 and 1914, the number of Canadian lakers increased by fourfold, from 27 vessels to 124. At first the scale of this new fleet did not match the behemoths launched at U.S. shipyards. The combined tonnage of Canadian-flag grain ships increased from just over thirty-one thousand gross tons in 1899 to nearly three hundred thousand gross tons in 1914. The size of the Welland Canal locks at first limited the size of the Canadian fleet, but after 1905 they also began to add large vessels that would stay on the upper lakes. Even though the number of Canadian ships began to grow, U.S. vessels also played a role in servicing the Thunder Bay ports. The cities and prairie towns of the Canadian west relied on American coal carried by U.S. hulls. Vessels would embark from Ohio ports like Ashtabula, with good rail links to Pennsylvania coal country, and deposit the coal at a Thunder Bay port before heading down the lakeshore to Duluth-Superior for a shipment of iron ore bound for Lake Erie mills.[44]

Lighthouses and the Expansion of the Lake Marine

The rise of Duluth-Superior and the establishment of other smaller iron ports at Ashland, Wisconsin, and Two Harbors, Minnesota, made Lake Superior the most heavily trafficked of the lakes by the dawn of the twentieth century. Its 1906 shipments totaled more than forty-one million tons, more than half of all traffic on the inland seas. Two Harbors was the outlet for ore from the Vermillion Iron Range, which was the first of the Minnesota mining districts to open in the early 1880s. The town, however, never developed into being more than a point for loading ore carriers. Ashland, Wisconsin, located east of Duluth-Superior at the bottom of Chequamegon Bay, looked for a time as if it might emerge as the principal port on Lake Superior. Ashland was the outlet for the myriad lumber camps in northwest Wisconsin's vast pinery. Then in 1872 hematite iron ore was discovered south of the town. A rush followed to what became known as the Penokee-Gogebic Iron Range, a narrow geological formation that stretched for eighty miles from the Upper Peninsula of

Michigan into northern Wisconsin. British and eastern investors poured money into mines, confident that the range would "take first rank as a producer of Bessemer ore." Several great ore docks were built at Ashland reaching more than a quarter of a mile out into the bay. By 1887 there were twenty-four mines on the range, and ships were carrying more than 1.3 million tons of ore from Ashland's docks. That, however, was the peak. The Penokee-Gogebic formation was both expensive to work and less rich than first believed. When the Mesabi Range in northern Minnesota was put into production, Gogebic mines could not compete, and Ashland quickly declined and lost its bid to be the great "future city on the inland sea."[45]

Navigation through western Lake Superior was challenged by a series of peninsulas and archipelagos that eventually required the U.S. Lighthouse Board to construct a constellation of lighthouses to guide vessels past the Apostle Islands, Isle Royale, and the Keweenaw. Large steel freighters passed like a conveyor belt on the Duluth-Soo lane during the busy shipping season, making Lake Superior one of the main arteries of the U.S. economy. Millions of American jobs depended on the grain and ore in the steel holds of lake steamers. Navigational aids were erected, and older ones maintained, all along that route, from the Duluth-Superior breakwater lights (1885), to Devil's Island in the Apostles (1891), to range lights at Vidal Shoals (1899) marking safe passage into the St. Mary's River. The Canadian government faced a similar challenge to secure navigation into Thunder Bay. In 1867 the first Canadian light station on Lake Superior was lit at Talbot Island just off Lake Superior's northern shore. The site was so remote that two of the first three keepers perished just trying to leave at the end of the shipping season. The station became known as the "Lighthouse of Doom." Wheat shipments from the Canadian prairies to Lake Superior at Port Arthur began in 1868 and steadily increased thereafter. This made it necessary to provide more navigational aids for vessels taking the northerly track across Superior from Sault Ste. Marie to Thunder Bay. Between 1872 and 1873 three new lights were erected at Porphyry Island near the entrance to Thunder Bay and at Michipicoten Island at the east end of the lake, where two lights helped mark the entrance to a natural harbor of refuge.[46]

There remained a particularly dangerous passage for ships on the northern Lake Superior track—Isle Royale. The largest island on the lake stood astride the approach to and out of Thunder Bay. More vexing yet was a small island three and a half miles off the northeast tip of Isle Royale that is known today as Passage Island. Between this rocky islet and Isle Royale was a fine deep-water channel. Yet threading the needle between the islands could be a formidable challenge in heavy seas or the frequent pea-soup fogs of the region. Clearly a lighthouse and fog signal were required at Passage Island. The territory belonged to the U.S., but the bulk of the ship traffic were Canadian vessels bound for a Canadian port. So necessary was a light here to the Canadian lake marine that the Dominion government was urged to purchase Passage Island from the U.S. Eventually a compromise was reached. The U.S. would build a light station on Passage Island if the Canadians would put a permanent navigational aid at the Colchester Reef on Lake Erie. American ship masters had tried to mark this trouble spot with a privately funded lightship with no consistent success. Passage Island Lighthouse became operational in 1882. The Canadian authorities initially failed to keep their end of the bargain. Lamely they first attempted to contract with a private party to operate a lightship at the reef. Yet in 1881 the lightship was, without prior warning, removed and the American steamer *Antelope* plowed onto the reef. It was not until 1885 that a permanent lighthouse was established there by the Dominion government.[47]

Great Lakes Lightships

Where hazards lurked but lighthouses were not possible, lightships were anchored on station. Lightships had been deployed on the lakes as early as 1833. The *Louis McLane*, a purpose-built forty-six-foot sloop, was typical of Pleasonton-era projects. The vessel was simply not stout enough even with a heavy anchor to weather a storm at its very exposed posting at the Waugoshance Shoal in northern Lake Michigan. After being repeatedly driven ashore and repaired, it was moved to the shelter of the Detroit River. In 1852 a lighthouse was placed at the shoal. It would be more than a generation before another lightship was posted on the Great Lakes, but by the 1890s it was clear that certain busy channels required additional marking. The waters where lakes Michigan and Huron come together are among the most ship congested and tricky to navigate on the inland seas. Numerous islands, peninsulas, and shoals challenge the navigator. It is understandable, therefore, that five lightships were eventually posted in those waters.[48]

Although the Lighthouse Board had recommended in 1852 that lightships be built of iron for durability's sake, early Great Lakes light vessels were made of wood. This was in part because the marine community suspected that iron would be too rigid to withstand the regular pounding lightships withstood on station. Two important improvements to lightships made a big difference in helping them remain in place in all weather conditions. The board increased the weight of the anchors designed to hold the vessels. The *Louis McLane,* which Pleasonton had sent to Waugoshance Shoal, had only an eight-hundred-pound mushroom anchor, and she was continually blown off station. By the 1880s the Lighthouse Board was securing its vessels with five-ton anchors. The other innovation was the use of vessels equipped with steam engines. In 1891 the Lighthouse Board launched three new lightships. Each of the new vessels was given a number instead of a name. Lightships *No. 55, No. 56,* and *No. 57* were all built in Toledo, Ohio, by the Craig Shipbuilding Company. The vessel's oak hulls were 102 feet in length with a 20-foot beam and had two stubby masts from which to suspend signal flags and their beacon light. The steam engines were a significant innovation, tested by the Lighthouse Service for the first time on the Great Lakes. The engine dramatically improved a lightship's ability to remain in place because during storms they could reduce strain on their anchor cables, and if they were blown off station they could reposition themselves. The vessels were deployed to the Straits of Mackinac, where they went on station at Simmons Reef, White Shoal, and Gray's Reef. Kerosene lanterns hung from each of their two masts and a large brass bell and a steam fog signal provided ample warning to mariners of the hazards they guarded.[49]

Unfortunately, the three new-style lightships got off to an unimpressive start in November 1891. For reasons that were never satisfactorily explained, the three ships left their stations several weeks before the close of navigation. They used their steam engines to dock at Cheboygan, Michigan—their winter quarters. The inspector for the Ninth Lighthouse District was quickly informed of this dereliction of duty. Commander Nicoll Ludlow ordered the vessels back on station. That winter he held a formal inquiry, and the officers and men, with one exception, were discharged from the service. That black mark was more than redeemed by the long record of vigilance that followed. The three lightships served mariners for more than a generation. Other steam-powered lightships followed. Lightship *No. 60* was launched in 1893, and she spent her entire thirty-two-year career at Eleven Foot Shoal on Lake Michigan. Eventually, there were twelve lightships stationed on the Great Lakes, with the bulk of them near the Straits of Mackinac.[50]

Lightships were commanded by the vessel master. These men were usually drawn from the ranks of the commercial lake marine, and in the 1880s and 1890s that meant former schooner captains. Soren Kristiansen was typical in that regard. He had been a sailor since the age of sixteen and spent a jack-tar's life on the oceans of the world and the Great Lakes. What was untypical is that he stayed on his lightship for twenty years. When he left the roving life of the lake schooner behind, he noted in his diary: "It was an important day for me. I had spent about 25 years sailing on vessels and now I should help to guide our modern merchant fleet safely in and out of harbors." From 1893 to 1913 he commanded *LV 60* stationed at Eleven Foot Shoal near the entrance to Little Bay De Noc on Lake Michigan. When he felt he was too old to tend the bobbing lightship any longer, he became keeper of the nearby Escanaba lighthouse and worked another dozen years. Life aboard a lightship was often unpleasant. With a complement of six men—four officers and two crew—the vessels offered few comforts. Crew quarters on early vessels were below decks. This arrangement was later modified to provide a deck house amidships, which contained a galley, separate rooms for the officers, and a shared berth for the seamen. Tethered in place in often tempestuous seas, their home rocked and bobbed, sometimes with a violence that could throw a man from his berth. Even veteran seamen succumbed to *mal de mer* during a prolonged storm. Nor was there any escape from the wail of the fog signal when visibility became obscured. Their daily tasks were conducted with monotonous regularity, maintaining the ship, cleaning reflectors, trimming lamps, fetching fuel, and lighting and hoisting the lanterns up the mast. Ships usually had a small library, and for sailors inclined to make use of it, there usually was plenty of spare time, especially in calm weather.[51]

Over time, the design of lightships improved in an effort to make them more stable while tethered and to upgrade the quarters for the crew. One of the new ships was *LV 82*, built in Muskegon by the Racine Truscott-Shell Company for just under $50,000. She was steel built, with a sloping hull similar to a whaleback freighter. This was thought to help her weather heavy seas by shedding oncoming waves. In 1912 *LV 82* was anchored on station outside Buffalo harbor guarding a shoal that had proved a hazard to shipping for a generation. The six-man crew was highly satisfied with the improved galley, cabins, and leather chairs. A steam-powered windlass and sanitary system made life aboard much more pleasant. Yet within a year *LV 82* was fated to be the first U.S. lightship to be lost with all hands. What became known as the Great Storm of 1913 bore down on the lakes on November 7. It mauled shipping on Lakes Superior, Michigan, and Huron as it made its way east. By November 10 it was Lake Erie's turn. Winds of eighty miles per hour ripped across the Buffalo waterfront. The men on *LV 82* knew a killer storm was bearing down on them, but they also knew that it was in such hazardous conditions that their navigational aid was most needed. Leaving their post was against the high standard of duty fostered by the Lighthouse Board. Sometime on the awful night of November 10 thirty-five-foot waves drove the *LV 82* off station breaking windows, smashing hatches, and ripping away ventilators. Amid the snow and surf, the lightship foundered. Only one crewman's body was ever recovered and that after a year in the water. In 1914 a new vessel was placed at the Buffalo harbor station, but within four years the need for a lightship there was ended by an improved system of buoys.

One of the most important functions of a lightship was to provide a sound signal when visibility of the light was impaired by fog, smoke, or haze. The fog signal equipped for the earliest Great Lakes boats was a simple bell that would be rung at regular intervals. In the 1890s steam whistles were the common fog signal. Diaphragm horns, also powered by steam, were deployed on some vessels as well. The trouble with these steam devices is that they burned up large amounts of coal, especially on Lake Superior, where fog was very common. This kept Lighthouse Board tenders busy with resupply runs. More of a problem was the havoc atmospheric conditions could play with signals as sound waves traveled through the air. Dense air could make even a powerful fog horn inaudible to someone on the deck of a vessel while a crew member aloft might hear it clearly. Too often a vessel lookout only heard the fog signals when they were almost on top of the navigation hazard.[52]

Lighthouse Board lightships played a key role in introducing the use of electricity to make a better fog signal and also a new method to execute accurate navigational bearings. As early as 1883 the board funded experiments in underwater signaling. It was a private company, however, the Submarine Signal Company pioneered by the Bostonian A. J. Moody, that perfected the device. In 1903 the board put this system through several trials on Atlantic coast lightships. In 1906 the system was deemed a success, and it was gradually deployed on most lightships. The system relied on one of the oldest methods of sound communication, the bell, and one of the newest, the telephone. The lightship suspended a large brass bell about twenty-five feet below the surface of the water. The sound of the bell could actually register over a greater distance through the water than it could ever be heard in the air. A pulse of compressed air sent from the lightship's engine room would ring the bell. Eventually, each lightship would have its own unique ring sequence to aid identification. The sound waves passed through the water to approaching vessels equipped with receivers, basically underwater microphones. A vessel had two receivers, suspended from the port and starboard bows, respectively. The receivers were connected to the bridge by a telephone line. If the signal came from the starboard receiver, the captain knew the lightship was in that direction. If the signal was from both receivers simultaneously, he knew that the lightship was straight ahead of the ship. While normal fog signals in good conditions were heard only a mile or two away, the submarine signals could be picked up as much as ten to fifteen miles from the lightship. A "veteran lake sailor" testified to the utility of these radio direction signals in thick fog. "I watched the mate take a bearing on a lightship in thick weather," he recalled, "and upon reaching the vicinity of the lightship, it would appear dead ahead, on the nose." By 1909 the system was deployed on eight Great Lakes lightships and one land-based station at DeTour, Michigan, on Lake Huron.[53]

Building a Better Buoy

One by one the lightships on the Great Lakes were replaced by either lighthouses or buoys. Minor navigational aids like buoys played a major role in improving safe shipping on the inland seas. The last decades of the nineteenth century were a fruitful period for the development and improvement of buoys. The first buoys in the Great Lakes region were put in place by private individuals or local authorities. In 1839 federal authorities placed a buoy at the mouth of the Fox River near the modern city of Green Bay; many others followed in short order. The early buoys were crude affairs. Typical were spar buoys that were little more than painted cedar logs weighted so as to float vertically in the water. Cask buoys were simple barrels anchored in place to mark a channel or hazard. Initially the placement of buoys was the duty of a local collector of customs. These patronage employees of the Treasury Department usually outsourced the placement and maintenance of buoys to local private contractors who decided where and how the buoys were to be put in place. Sometimes the contractors were experienced mariners with a vested interest in marking safe channels for commerce. In 1850 Congress attempted to bring some order to buoy placement. It ordered that channel markers should be color coded, allowing vessels passing up a channel to position themselves so that red-painted buoys would be to their starboard side while black-colored buoys would be on the port side of the channel.[54]

By the end of the Civil War, an extensive system of minor navigational aids was in place along the inland seas. In 1869 the Lighthouse Board reported that 106 buoys (barrels, cans, and spar) were in place on the Upper Great Lakes and connecting waters. The St. Mary's River, leading from Lake Superior to Lake Huron, was by far the most heavily marked, with 47 buoys indicating the navigation channel. Green Bay and the mouth of the

Fox River as well as Saginaw Bay and the mouth of the Saginaw River, waters heavily used by lumber ships, were also closely marked. However, the critical Mackinac Straits had only 2 buoys, although the board had authorized the deployment of 4 more. On Lakes Ontario and Erie an additional 110 buoys were deployed. While the number might seem impressive, only 8 spar buoys were in place on the Detroit River, a channel thronged by all vessels passing from the upper lakes to Lake Erie. None of these early Great Lakes buoys were lit to aid night navigation.[55]

Because of winter ice on the Great Lakes in the nineteenth century, most buoys, particularly the costly iron buoys, were removed at the end of the navigation season. Temporary wood buoys were put in their place over the winter. Great care had to be used when replacing them in the spring. In 1874 the propeller steamer *Nebraska* was stranded on Lake Michigan's Racine Reef. The master complained that the buoy marking the reef had been shifted from the middle of the reef to its edge and that "no notice" had been given of the change. While his complaint may have been an attempt to shift blame from his own risky course close to a known reef, it did underscore how mariners relied on the proper placement of buoys. Generally, when a buoy or lightship was repositioned, this fact was announced in the federal government's hydrographic division "sailing directions," which were published annually. These guides were the bible of the careful mariner, as they described the placement of all navigational aids and issued directions on how to avoid water hazards. In dangerous waterways, such as the St. Mary's River or the busy entrances to Duluth-Superior's harbors, tugs were assigned the task of inspecting the position of buoys on a daily basis.[56]

Buoys served two principal purposes. They were used to mark navigation hazards, such as shoals and reefs, and they were used to indicate the shipping channels between lakes or at the entrance to rivers or harbors. As sentinels guarding dangerous waters, buoys were often less than satisfactory owing to their size and visibility. Aware of this issue, the Lighthouse Board often used buoys as a stopgap until such time as a lighthouse or lightship could be put in position at a shoal. In 1869, for example, the Lighthouse Board approved buoys for St. Helena Island and Whale's Back Reef, both in Lake Michigan. Yet by 1874 a new lighthouse station was in place on St. Helena and another recommended for

Whale's Back Reef. One of the biggest problems with buoys was that they were very difficult to see at night, in fog, or during heavy seas. The challenge faced by the Lighthouse Board in the 1880s and 1890s was to find a way to improve buoy recognition.[57]

There were two strategies pursued to help mariners recognize buoys. One was to equip them with sound signals and the second was to install lights on these navigational markers. Anchored in isolated waters often far from shore, lighted buoys proved a major challenge, and experiments from the 1850s into the 1870s failed to meet the challenge. Sound proved easier. In 1855 Brown's Bell Buoy was adopted by the Lighthouse Board. The simple effective device suspended a bell with four clappers from the top of the float. Even waves a few inches in height were adequate to set the device clanging. Whistle buoys, operating on a similar principle, were introduced in the 1870s. By that time progress was finally being made on lighted buoys. The board first experimented with Great Lakes buoys lighted by oil lamps. These proved less than reliable, running out of fuel or being extinguished by wave action. A better light system was needed, and that came in 1887 with the Foster buoy. It was lit by acetylene, a hydrocarbon gas. Unfortunately, while the slow-burning acetylene somewhat solved the fuel problem for buoys, Foster buoys continued to be extinguished by heavy seas. Finally, a design by the Prussian Richard Pintsch solved the problem of both a long-lasting fuel and protection from wave action. After the first lighted buoy on the Great Lakes was placed in Cleveland harbor in 1895, they were quickly deployed, particularly to the crowded connecting channels between the lakes. The Detroit River alone had eighteen Pintsch gas buoys.[58]

In the early twentieth century, the use of acetylene was further refined for navigational aids through the work of the Swedish scientist Gustav Dalen. He developed a device that safely stored and gradually released the explosive gas so that a buoy could be left untended for as long as a year and still be kept burning. His other great innovation was the sun valve, which had a sensor so the gas could be shut off when not needed in daylight. Acetylene came with its own problems, as it was a volatile pressurized gas. Accidents most commonly occurred when filling or testing the pressure of the buoy. The danger was graphically illustrated in 1905 when the Canadian tender *Scout* was ripped by a massive explosion. It turned out that a buoy being filled with gas had a structural defect and that escaping gas eventually reached the vessel's fire box. The explosion ripped apart *Scout*'s superstructure and wrecked its engine room, and only the fact that she was tied up at the Kingston, Ontario, dock prevented her from sinking. In 1910 the U.S. Lighthouse Service tender *Amaranth* suffered a deadly explosion that killed a machinist and sent the buoy through the vessel's deck. Among the worst incidents was a deadly 1929 explosion that occurred off Red Cliff Point in the Apostle islands. Three crew members of the tender USLHS *Marigold* were killed while trying to repair a gas buoy. In spite of the dangerous qualities of acetylene, it was by far the best solution to the challenge of lighting buoys. The pressurized gas also was employed to begin the process of automating lighthouses. In 1916 the Charity Island Lighthouse on Saginaw Bay became the first Great Lakes lighthouse to be fully automated. Using Dalen's devices, lights at Baileys Harbor (1923) and Green Island (1935) in Wisconsin were automated. Widespread automation, however, awaited ready access to electricity.[59]

6

The Inland Seas
in War and Peace

1910–1945

On a snowy March morning in 1906, a new city began to rise from the sandy soil at the south end of Lake Michigan. It was soon dubbed the "Magic City" for the remarkable speed in which it emerged from the dunes and grew to a city of one hundred thousand residents. Gary, Indiana, took its name from the president and chairman of the Board of the U.S. Steel Corporation, the world's largest business. At the time of its creation, the massive corporation was the amalgamation of 213 separate industrial plants and transportation companies. At the site of Gary, the company built the largest integrated steel plant in the world. It eventually enclosed twelve blast furnaces and employed more than sixteen thousand workers. To make this possible, U.S. Steel completely remade the landscape of the site. The Grand Calumet River was "bodily moved . . . a half mile south of its ancient bed and given a new channel." Where once wild deer were stalked by Chicago sportsmen, the lakefront was filled in and a new

Figure 16. Bird's-eye view of U.S. Steel Gary Works, 1908.
Source: Library of Congress.

harbor dug over a mile in length and thirty feet deep. A broad turning basin allowed big ore carriers to maneuver without the assistance of tugs and to dock alongside derricks and automatic shovels that would rapidly unload a ship. To move raw materials and products to and from furnaces and processing plants, 160 miles of railroad track was laid. In a single day more than 130 separate trains traversed those tracks. All this environmental and industrial engineering was part of a major realignment of the American steel industry. Not only did the U.S. Steel Corporation represent the future in terms of its vertical integration of all aspects of production, from ore and coal mines to ships, coke-processing plants, and limestone quarries, but it also signaled a shift away from the Ohio River valley as the largest steel-producing region and to the Great Lakes. The region had played an important role since the Civil War, but for a generation its plants could not match the scale of Pittsburgh's or Bethlehem's operations in Pennsylvania. The founding of Gary changed everything. Most of the nation's other leading steelmakers followed U.S. Steel's lead, and in the decade that followed, they also located new plants in Gary or at adjacent South Chicago. The south end of Lake Michigan emerged as the world's greatest iron- and steel-producing region.[1]

Lake Shipping was the reason for the creation of the Gary works and the emergence of the Calumet region of Lake Michigan as a steelmaking center. Lake vessels were the most cost-effective way to bring iron ore from Lake Superior as well as the other materials needed for processing. The production of a ton of pig iron required 2,000 pounds of iron ore, 1,500 pounds of coke (refined coal), 600 pounds of limestone, and a vast amount of water. The principal source of limestone was northeastern Michigan, where deep rock formations were conveniently close to the Lake Huron shore. Pittsburgh, where the modern American steel industry had been born, declined in the face of the greater efficiency offered by mills built adjacent to lake ports. The so-called Steel City had benefited from its proximity to the anthracite coal mines but was far from sources of limestone and iron ore. Gary, Indiana, became the greatest of the lake mill centers, and along with the Chicago mills, it absorbed 20 percent of all ore shipped on the lakes. Much of the rest of the iron ore went to Detroit and the production centers along Lake Erie, especially Cleveland, Erie, Buffalo, and Tonawanda. So efficient was the maritime-industrial complex for shipping bulk cargoes that Kentucky coal was brought by railroad to Toledo, Ohio, and then loaded on lake freighters for shipment to Gary. Indiana's "Magic City" was also one of the first of a new type of port carved out of the shore wholly or in part by private industry. Government provided navigation aids, but giant steel corporations would purpose-build harbors to suit their ever-growing fleets of giant freighters. Andrew Carnegie's Conneaut, Ohio, port was an early example. Others would follow in the twentieth century, including Bethlehem Steel's Burns Harbor in Indiana and Taconite Harbor in Minnesota by the Pickands Mather & Company. In the wake of Gary's founding, what one contemporary described as an "avalanche" of orders for new ships followed. Eighty new vessels were built between 1906 and 1908, and another sixty-seven were ordered by 1910, all of which were big five-hundred- to six-hundred-footers. Lake shipping in the twentieth century was gradually dominated by the business of making steel. This would prove a boon in times of prosperity or war when the fate of nations hung on the reliability of the lake marine, but thousands of sailors and mill workers would learn that too much reliance on a single industry could prove painful in hard times.[2]

By the beginning of the twentieth century, a maritime-industrial complex had been impressed on the landscape of the North American lake country. The ports of the northern portion of the lakes were the raw material exporters. At Duluth-Superior,

Ashland, and Escanaba, red iron ore poured into the hulls of lake freighters. At Rogers City, Michigan, the limestone of the northern Lake Huron mines thundered into the dull, gray holds of the Bradley Transportation Company ships. At Manistique, Manistee, and Menominee, lumber hookers were burdened with boards that overflowed their holds and were piled high on the decks. All these ships journeyed to the great cities of the southern shore of the inland seas, where raw materials were transformed into products in great industrial workshops. The production and population centers eagerly consumed much of what came into the ports and out of the mills, from skyscraping steel beams, auto frames, and reinforcing bars to the steel rails, junction plates, spikes, and wooden ties that were the tentacles of the industrial city. There was, nonetheless a growing surplus ready for export east and to the world.

Great Lakes navigation in the first half of the twentieth century transcended the national significance it had achieved in helping build the modern American industrial economy of the post–Civil War era. The role it played in the construction of the great fortunes of John D. Rockefeller and Andrew Carnegie and other so-called robber barons had laid the foundation for the North American heartland to play a critical role in the global economy and global conflicts. To meet this rising global significance, the Great Lakes maritime industries and the federal agencies dedicated to navigation had to embrace new technologies and organizational structures. The maritime-industrial complex along the inland seas was sustained by cooperation between business and the federal government. This allowed Great Lakes navigation to reach standards of efficiency that would have astounded men who crewed lakers only a generation earlier. By 1916 there were 2,865 vessels engaged in lake commerce, only a slight increase over the number recorded in 1889. Yet such was the increased size of those vessels and the efficiency with which they were able to navigate the lakes that they were able to carry almost 400 percent more cargo than the carriers from 1889. This indicates the degree to which the pace of change and innovation had quickened since the 1880s. Global conflicts would put this maritime-industrial complex and its navigational infrastructure to the test in a contest on which would hang the fate of nations.[3]

The Birth of the Lighthouse Bureau

Even in an era of tremendous innovation in maritime technology, the oldest element in the navigational infrastructure, the lighthouse, continued to play a critical role. However, in the first decade of the twentieth century, lighthouse administration underwent a major change. In 1903 the Lighthouse Board was transferred from the Department of the Treasury, where navigational aids had been administered since the presidency of George Washington, to the new Department of Labor and Commerce. This was a prelude to a more significant shift brought on by the emergence of the so-called Progressive Movement. At the dawn of the twentieth century, the nation was undergoing considerable social and political upheaval as it transitioned from being a largely rural agricultural nation to one that was urban and industrial. The self-styled Progressives were a political response to these changes. Dominated by educated, middle-class professionals, the movement focused on social and political reform with an emphasis on efficiency and economic regulation. At first little changed in the world of lighthouses as a result of the change of departments. In 1910, however, the progressive mania for reorganization swept over and sunk the existing lighthouse service. Reformers were critical of the divided authority of the Lighthouse Board and the central role played by army and navy officers in a civil agency. As a result, the board was abolished, and a new Bureau of Lighthouses was created to be headed by a commissioner of lighthouses.[4] Historically, the Bureau of Lighthouses is also known as the Lighthouse Service because that term was used in the legislation, and it is more commonly known by that name.[5]

The new Bureau of Lighthouses was fortunate to inherit a system of navigation aids that two generations of navy and army officers and civilian scientists had built into one of the largest and most efficient in the world. Since its creation in 1852, the board had focused on the scope and technical proficiency of U.S. lights and markers. Just in the period between 1860 and 1885, the number of lighthouses alone had increased by 84 percent. The board introduced new construction techniques, moving away from heavy masonry to cutting-edge steel frame and concrete lighthouses. Through their efforts, Great Lakes ships in a single season safely delivered enough cargo that if put into rail cars would have required a train that spanned the entire globe, with another two thousand miles to spare.

The creation of the Lighthouse Bureau had once more returned the administration of a significant part of the Great Lakes maritime infrastructure to the control of one man. Fortunately, the commissioner was not a penny-pinching bureaucrat like Stephen Pleasonton. George Rockwell Putnam was an energetic man of science and adventure. He was a twenty-year veteran of the U.S. Coast and Geodetic Survey. During that time, he had surveyed the mouth of the Yukon River during the 1898 gold rush, participated in one of Admiral Robert Peary's Arctic expeditions, and charted the labyrinthine coast of the Philippines archipelago. Born in the Midwest, he knew the Great Lakes well from two years living in Chicago and from work on a boundary survey from the St. Lawrence to Lake Superior. He owed his appointment as commissioner to his broad experience and his acquaintance with President William Howard Taft, whom he had met during his six years in the Philippines, where Taft had been governor-general. Many observers in both Congress and the military predicted that the new Lighthouse Bureau would become a patronage dumping ground. Admiral Robley Evans, the former commander of the Great White Fleet and hero of the Spanish-American War, predicted that the "lustre" of the Lighthouse Service would be dimmed by the "fog of party patronage." Putnam took notice of the criticism and moved with great deliberation to find the right men to serve as district superintendents. He kept some of the naval officers who had held that position under the Lighthouse Board on duty for as long as two years until he could find the civilians with the proper experience and character. This judicious approach to his charge allowed the transition from military to civilian leadership to take place smoothly.[6]

Putnam blended genuine concern for the men and women of the Lighthouse Service with his insistence on efficiency. He frequently traveled to distant light stations to see how his people lived and worked. This knowledge gave him the confidence to request and receive salary increases for the service. In 1917 he noted that there were more than ninety keepers older than seventy, and that although some of them had served well for forty years, it became harder for them to ascend tall towers to do their duty. Yet he did not institute a program of retiring the elderly keepers until he could secure a federally funded pension. He had to overcome congressional objections because the lightkeepers were civilians and, thus, did not qualify for federal pensions. Putnam countered that they were eligible to be put into the military in time of national emergency. He also pointed out that each year more than one hundred of the five thousand lightkeepers were injured in the performance of their duties, which included undertaking lifesaving rescues. Not only was Putnam able to secure pensions for long-serving keepers, but he also was able to get Congress to approve the General Lighthouse Act of 1918, which provided pay raises for service staff. This accomplishment underscored the credibility that Putnam was able to maintain with the Congress throughout his tenure. Putnam earned this trust because he was able to demonstrate that he ran the service like a "tight ship." By the time he retired in 1935, fewer than 1 percent of Lighthouse Service personnel were engaged in administrative duties in Washington, D.C. He did this despite doubling the number of navigation aids during his tenure. Putnam had his men and women where they could do the most good to mariners, on duty along the nation's navigable waterways.[7]

Like Gifford Pinchot in the Forest Service, Putnam was a model of the progressive bureaucrat. He moved socially in the capital's highest circles, winning support for his service at private dinners and through elite social clubs such as Washington's Cosmos Club, where he served as president. He was a founding board member of the National Geographic Society and participated in international conferences on marine safety. He was not too proud to court the capital's leaders. When Woodrow Wilson's secretary of the treasury, William C. Redfield, took a cruise on the Great Lakes, he proudly flew a departmental ensign from the ship's masthead. As he sailed by each lighthouse, he was impressed to see that each lighthouse keeper saluted his passing. Redfield was "loud in his praise of the alertness of the light keepers." He never knew that Putnam had forewarned his Great Lakes keepers of the secretary's itinerary. He also was not afraid to stand up to elected officials if he thought their actions threatened the efficiency of his department, but he did so tactfully. Once he noticed a rider on an appropriation bill that directed several thousand dollars to the Lake Michigan Lighthouse depot for a new barge. Upon investigation, he discovered no such request was made or wanted by the service but was inserted to gratify a local shipbuilder. Putman sequestered the funds. After some months, the congressman who had inserted the bit of "pork" asked Putnam why the barge contract had not been given. Putnam explained the barge was not needed. When the congressman objected, Putnam offered to write a full explanation and send it to the House Committee on Appropriations. "The Representative," Putnam later recounted, "promptly asked that the barge matter be dropped, and it was never heard of again." Putnam also kept the name of the service before the public through the publication of well-written books and articles. In all venues, he made it clear that he stood for efficiency and scientific management, watchwords of the era. His time managing the nation's lighthouses is one of great technical advancement in navigation and navigational aids.[8]

The Lake Carriers' Association

By the end of the nineteenth century, the growth and sophistication of bureaucracy in government was paralleled by the birth of modern management structures in private industry and the coordination of diverse business through industrial associations. On the inland seas, a key element in the maritime-industrial complex was a powerful association of shipowners, the Lake Carriers' Association. The creation of this industrial association was long complicated by the fact that the lake marine was initially made up of a large number of small operators, some of whom owned a single vessel. Hence, early operator organizations began on the local level, among shipowners who could meet face to face to discuss common problems. The problem that most commonly brought vessel owners together was labor. In the post–Civil War era, it was common for both vessel owners and working sailors to try to use collective action to control wages. Owners usually had the upper hand in the spring when sailors were eager to secure a paying berth after the long winter layoff. Masters and vessel owners often met before navigation began to set a standard wage for that port. As the season progressed, the advantage shifted to the sailors. By September the end of the shipping season was only a couple of months away, and grain harvests were beginning to arrive at Lake Michigan and Erie elevators. Wildcat strikes by sailors demanding a raise had the vessel owners at a disadvantage and often yielded an increase in wages. This localized game of give-and-take between sailors and owners lasted until the Great Strike of 1877. This was a national job action that began with railroad workers and gradually spread to others in the labor market. In Chicago the Seamen's Benevolent Union, which had started as a social welfare organization, now committed itself to the men's "financial improvement." With more than one thousand members, it was able to dictate wages to the owners, and branches quickly spread from west to east, including Milwaukee, Cleveland, and Buffalo. In 1880 men invested in shipping in Cleveland came together to create the "Cleveland Vessel Owners Association" with the object of guarding its members from "the hostility of sailors" and to "resist" the "illegal assaults and demands of the 'Sailors Union.'" A year later a convention was held in Chicago to create an owner's association that spanned "the Inland Seas." It was essentially a means of coordinating the various owner associations in each port. That convention laid the foundation for the Lake Carriers' Association that was formally created in 1885.[9]

The initial focus of the Lake Carriers' Association was labor relations. With the help of experienced strikebreakers and the downturn in the economy in the 1890s, they were gradually able to set wages for common sailors on the lakes. However, no sooner did the association have the seamen well in hand than it faced labor trouble from an unexpected source. The Masters and Pilots Association, which also included ship engineers, went on strike for higher wages. The job action began against U.S. Steel Corporation's Pittsburgh Steamship Company but soon spread to most powered vessels on the lakes. The job action continued through the winter, with the Masters and Pilots Association adding the important safety issue of vessel overloading to their demands. When spring came, the job action heated up, and the Lake Carriers' Association brought on replacement officers to get up to fifty vessels back in service. The strikers responded by hurling stones and rotten eggs at the scabs, and they beat up one vessel owner who strayed too close to their picket line. The Masters and Pilots Association negotiated with the American Federation of Labor to strengthen their position for a long strike.

Although they were fortified by supporting referendums by union members in two of the largest posts, Chicago and Buffalo, support for the strike was not as strong in all lake ports. In June, a dozen Milwaukee masters broke with the union and returned to work. Within a week other captains returned to their ships and the strike was finished. Thereafter, the Lake Carriers' Association signed annual contracts with the sailors, masters, and longshoremen unions, usually at terms dictated by the owners.[10]

With the labor front under control, the Lake Carriers' Association moved to claim a broad mandate "to consider and take action upon all general questions relating to the navigation and carrying business of the Great Lakes." They were among the first to raise the warning about the impact on lake levels when the City of Chicago began its massive diversion of Lake Michigan water in 1900. Early in its existence, it invited officials from the Lighthouse Service and the Army Corps of Engineers to its meetings to discuss the need for new light stations or buoys. In later years, they established a standing committee of veteran lake captains to opine on navigational issues and had a rotating "Navigation Committee" of current masters meet each January to make recommendations for the coming season. The broad membership of the association, which spanned the lakes from Buffalo to Duluth, made them an effective lobby with the Congress to keep river and harbor improvements flowing. In 1920 they played a key role in the passage of the Jones Act, which among other things mandated that cargo carried between U.S. ports must be carried on American flagged vessels. This was a huge asset to the association's owners since it excluded Canadian ships from a large portion of the lake trade.[11]

On other issues, the Lake Carriers' Association worked as an effective liaison with shippers on the Canadian side of the lakes. Initially they hoped to incorporate Canadian owner-operators into their organization, but they had little success. In 1903 shipowners in British North America joined together in the Dominion Marine Association. Like their American counterparts, the Canadian shipowners were both interested in navigational issues and influencing government legislation that might affect their operations. The Lake Carriers' Association sent a representative to Dominion Marine meetings, and the Canadians had a representative when the American owners met. This was critical because as a vessel maneuvered up the Detroit or St. Mary's River, it inevitably crossed over into the territorial waters of the other country. It was therefore highly desirable for a common set of navigational rules to be developed and enforced. As a result of cooperation between the two owner associations, the U.S. in 1895 adopted a set of regulations written in consultation with the Canadians. The Canadian Parliament then adopted a corresponding set of rules the next year.[12]

In its bylaws, the Lake Carriers' Association committed itself to "improve the character of the service rendered to the public." There were many safe sailing practices that they tried to standardize. One of these was the use of steam whistle signals. At an 1895 meeting of the association, they voted on a protocol for when two vessels approached one another: "One blast to mean: I am directing my course to starboard. Two blasts to mean: I am directing my course to port." In the era before radar, navigation in fog was fraught with danger and especially tricky because there were so many vessels using the lakes. Whistle signals were an essential means for a vessel to notify others of their presence. A steamer captain with a load of iron ore from Escanaba, Michigan, recounted how proper whistle signals in "a dense fog" made for a safe passage: "We shaped our course to six miles off Seul Choix point and when about 1-½ hours past [sic] Poverty Isle, we picked up a deep whistle on our port bow. I at once stopped and reversed my engines and decided it must be a car ferry out of Manistique, which it proved to be, so we came to an understanding and passed safely on two whistles." In some years as many as two hundred ship collisions occurred on the lakes, so the standardization of whistle signals was a significant advance in safe navigation.[13]

While the association generally promoted sound navigation procedures, they were a private organization of vessel owners, and very often they opposed and delayed safety measures that would reduce the profitably of the owner's maritime investments. A sterling example was the issue of vessel overloading brought up by the Masters and Pilots Association during their strike. As ships are loaded with cargo, they ride lower in the water, reducing the "freeboard" between the water and the deck. Historically, going back to ancient times, this had been a major factor in maritime disasters. In 1876 a crusading British parliamentarian,

Samuel Plimsoll, persuaded Her Majesty's government to address the issue by having painted on the midships of every vessel a series of lines that marked the safe level to which it could be loaded with cargo. The so-called Plimsoll Line had an immediate and salutary effect on marine safety. The U.S. Congress sought to adopt this regulation in 1889 but was strongly opposed by the Lake Carriers' Association. On the lakes, vessel overloading continued, something that was especially prevalent early or late in the year when steel companies were anxious about their supply of iron ore. Most of the time calm water allowed a ship to successfully complete a transit while overloaded, but as the example of the steamer *S. R. Kirby* demonstrates, heavy seas would result in a tragic outcome. The *Kirby* was loaded with iron ore in Ashland, Wisconsin, in May 1916. She was so heavily loaded that she had only two feet of freeboard, when a safe load would have afforded her seven feet. In addition, the *Kirby* was towing a barge that was equally overloaded. One day out on Lake Superior the *Kirby* was hit by a spring gale. Thirty-foot waves battered the ship and finally broke the hull and sent the ship and twenty of her crew to the cold lake bottom. The *Kirby*'s fate was shared by scores of overloaded vessels, but economically, overloading made dollars and cents for the owners. Every successful overloaded trip increased a vessel's profitability, while if a boat came to grief because of its load level, the owner would be protected by insurance. Indeed, some owners purposely overinsured vessels, in which case a sinking could actually result in a profit. The Lake Carriers' Association successfully warded off attempts to impose Plimsoll Lines and load limits on lake vessels until 1936, more than sixty years after the safety measure was first introduced.[14]

Another area where the Lake Carriers' Association eschewed safer sailing procedures was in its resistance to standardized sailing courses on the crowded lakes. Captain J. S. Dunham of Chicago proposed that shippers adopt a page from the railroad industry, which built double tracks in congested areas to allow trains to safely pass each other. If a navigation course for up-bound vessels could be separated by several miles from that proscribed for down-bound ships, the danger would be much reduced, and captains could travel at a higher speed in confidence. This was especially important for the busy waters where Lakes Michigan, Huron, and Superior came together. Collisions there between vessels were all too common, especially in the summer season, when fog was frequent and when as many as one hundred vessels passed through those waters every hour. Although Dunham was a veteran of more than thirty years as a shipowner and the president of the Lake Carriers' Association, the members rejected the plan because the proposed navigation courses took ships slightly off the most efficient track. It was not until 1914 that Dunham's proposal was finally adopted, and then only after a special committee made up solely of vessel captains made the recommendation. The first year it was implemented there was only a single total loss due to collision in the fog. On the other hand, there was no mechanism to enforce the rule, and for several years after Dunham's plan was adopted, some old skippers continued to sail the courses they wanted to sail, when they wanted to sail them. The sentiment among captains of this ilk was: "I don't want our office telling me how I shall steer my boat."[15]

The Unfulfilled Promise
of Electrical Navigational Aids

The wonder of the late nineteenth and early twentieth century was electricity. Through the work of Nikola Tesla, Thomas Edison, and George Westinghouse, what for generations had been feared as a strange and uncontrollable source of power was harnessed to bring light to homes, illumination to city streets, music without orchestras, moving picture images to theaters, and cheap energy to industry. The application of electricity to navigational aids was well underway before the creation of the Lighthouse Bureau, but in the first three decades of the twentieth century, the bureau expanded its application in new and unanticipated directions.

The submarine fog signal initially deployed in 1901 was the first successful harnessing of electric power for navigational aids. Earlier attempts using electricity for navigation had not been crowned with success. In 1888 the Lighthouse Board thought they had found a way to light channel buoys with incandescent lights connected by a cable to a shoreline power source. Although initially impressed with the results, the electric buoys were abandoned as impractical in 1903. Too often ships' propellers inadvertently severed the electrical cables. It was in the field of wireless telegraphy that the potential of electricity to revolutionize navigation made an international impact. In 1898 Guglielmo Marconi, an Italian inventor working in Great Britain, succeeded in effecting the first ship-to-shore wireless Morse code message. Thomas E. Clark, an inventive, self-taught electricity wizard and capitalist based in Detroit, was not far behind. In 1899 Clark erected an antenna atop a Detroit skyscraper, and within a year was sending messages to ships of the Detroit and Windsor Ferry Company. By 1903 Clark's company was able to expand into transmitting voice messages as well as Morse code. Passengers on the steamers could call friends on land for the rather steep fee of five dollars. Clark eventually built six transmitting stations along the U.S. shore and one in Canada and expanded his service to other shipping lines. He transmitted music and news, although only a handful of people at a time huddled around a receiver could hear what was being sent. The same year that Clark began to send ship-to-shore messages, the Marconi Company contracted with the Ann Arbor Railroad to set up wireless communication between Frankfurt, Michigan, where the railroad terminated, and its car ferry, which crossed Lake Michigan to connect the line to the Upper Peninsula town of Menominee, Michigan. By 1912 wireless technology had advanced to the point that it could have, and should have, been standard on Great Lakes commercial vessels. Before that would happen, however, a bitter lesson had to be learned.[16]

In 1913 the greatest of the feared "gales of November" swept across the Great Lakes and reaped a terrible harvest in lives and ships. As the month began, a low-pressure system bore down from Alaska, and by November 7 it slammed into the unseasonably warm air of a midwestern "Indian summer." That a storm would result was no surprise to the Weather Bureau. They had charted the low-pressure system since it had formed over the Bering Sea. Bureau officials in Cleveland placed courtesy phone calls to shipping companies on the lake warning them of a likely storm. The warnings were by and large dismissed. They were preparing vessels for what might be their final run of the season, trips that were critical to clients eager to build up inventories before the shipping season closed. Some vessel captains were determined to end the season by making a good impression on the owners, and the prospect of bonuses may have influenced others. Both mariners and their corporate masters had faith in the strength and durability of the big modern steel ships that made up the backbone of the grain and iron ore trade on the lakes.[17]

The storm that struck Lake Superior on November 7 exceeded the expectations of the most experienced lake sailors. The Alaskan low-pressure system mixed with the warmer waters of the lakes and a storm front moving in from the southeast in a witch's brew, creating something unprecedented in the region—a hurricane. The Weather Bureau issued an updated warning of this new and greater threat, but it did not get to many vessels already out on the lakes or those just preparing to depart. The reason was that most of the "modern" steel freighters had not been equipped with the wireless communication systems that had been perfected over the previous decade. While they knew storm warnings had been issued, they had no idea they would be facing hurricane force winds. That was not true of the vessels operated by the Shenango Shipping Company, a subsidiary of a Pittsburgh-based steelmaker. The company operated some of the newest and best-equipped vessels on the lakes. In 1911 they launched the *James M. Schoonmaker*, a 617-foot monster that was at the time the biggest vessel on the lakes. It was also the first to be equipped with a wireless telegraph. By 1913 all vessels in the Shenango line had wireless telegraph capability. This enabled them to receive immediate weather updates and thereby to avoid the great November hurricane.[18]

The ships that lacked wireless receivers were caught out on the lake, and many were unable to find a sheltered place to drop anchor. Most were devastated by the storm. Nineteen vessels were sunk by the heavy seas whipped up by winds surging between seventy and ninety miles per hour. Another nineteen ships were driven ashore. Between 235 and 250 mariners and passengers were killed. The worst losses were on Lake Superior, where the storm first broke, and Lake Huron, where the storm built up tremendous power as it swept the uninterrupted two hundred miles toward its Lake St. Clair outlet. Ships that managed to bear the gale all the way down Huron's furious surface faced great danger as they approached the narrow mouth of the St. Clair River. They were in whiteout conditions, with visibility down to a few hundred feet at best. One vessel in that position was the *J. H. Sheadle*, a 530-foot vessel loaded with grain from the prairies of western Canada. Captain Stephen A. Lyons struggled to ascertain his position. In vain his lookouts strained to catch sight of either the Fort Gratiot Lighthouse or the lightship *LV 61*. Lyons tried to navigate by his Lake Survey charts. Every fifteen minutes, he took depth soundings and then tried to compare them to the depth recorded on the chart. This was hardly foolproof. After proceeding this way for more than an hour and still failing to see the lighthouse at Lake Huron's outlet, Lyons felt he was forced to make a dangerous change of course. The storm was driving him to ruin on Huron's southern shore. The only way to avoid this was to turn around and head north until the gale blew itself out. Yet to do this he would have to run broadside in the heaviest seas he had ever seen. Other vessels that tried the broadside maneuver that day were capsized, but without navigational aids to show him the way to the shelter of the St. Clair River, Lyons felt he had no choice. Fortunately, he was able to make the maneuver successfully. Another ship in the same predicament, the *H. B. Hawgood*, declined to make the dangerous maneuver and beached itself.[19]

Other vessels being driven toward the Lake Huron outlet relied on the light and fog signal of the lightship *LV 61*. Unfortunately, the severe winds drove the lightship several miles off station. This problem was compounded when the keeper insisted on keeping the beacon and steam whistle in operation, lamely claiming he needed permission from Washington, D.C., to extinguish them. By doing this he lured two passing ships to destruction. With no wireless equipment, there was no way to warn these vessels that they were being guided by an errant beacon.[20]

The Wireless Ship Act of 1910 could have mitigated some of the storm losses, which exceeded $4 million dollars. However, the Lake Carriers' Association lobbied to be exempt from the act. As written, the act only applied to passenger vessels. In 1912 Congress extended the requirement to all cargo vessels, but again the Lake Carriers' Association won an exemption for lakers. The association's spokesman assured Congress that because his ships were almost constantly within sight of land, they were never in danger and that ship-to-ship communication via wireless was unnecessary because the tremendous volume of shipping on the lakes meant that vessels were seldom out of visual observation by other ships. He made no mention of storm or fog conditions. Even after the bitter lessons of 1913, Great Lakes shipping companies resisted calls for modern communication equipment on the grounds of cost. The equipment was one problem, but an even bigger cost was hiring two skilled Morse code operators for each vessel. Nor were vessel masters eager to be in twenty-four-hour contact with their employers. Many opposed the new equipment on the grounds it would tend to give "too much control over the operation of the ships to the home office." The upshot of this was that it was not until after World War II that wireless telegraph or radiotelephones became standard on Great Lakes freighters.[21]

The penny-pinching by shipowners that retarded the adaption of wireless communication was sparked by real economic worries. The period from 1909 to 1917 was one of consolidation on the Great Lakes. The tremendous shipping boom that John D. Rockefeller had set off in the late 1890s had led eventually to an overbuilding of lake vessels, so by the time of the great storm in 1913, there were too many vessels chasing too few cargoes. In 1909 there were 597 vessels enrolled with the Lake Carriers' Association, which did not count many of the older wooden steamers or sailing ships that still tramped the lakes. As vessels were taken out of service in the next five years, the fleet of elite ships was reduced to 438, a reduction of 25 percent. Sailing ships underwent an even deeper decline. From a peak of more than 1,600 in 1880, the graceful old schooners were reduced to half that number by the turn of the century, and by 1930 the last commercial sailing ship, *Our Son*, foundered in Lake Michigan.[22]

The Chicago Diversion and the International Joint Commission

On January 2, 1900, a group of workmen broke open a dam on the Chicago River and flooded a newly excavated canal that linked the Great Lakes with the Mississippi River Valley. They worked in secret. Although the canal was the largest and most expensive project ever undertaken by an American municipality up to that time, there was no civic celebration. The inglorious action was taken to avoid a legal injunction from the U.S. Supreme Court. Since 1889 the city of Chicago, through its Sanitary District, had been excavating a twenty-eight-mile waterway designed to divert water from Lake Michigan to flush the city's raw sewage into the upper reaches of the Illinois River. It was the "big dig" of its day, requiring the excavation of forty-three million cubic yards of dirt and stone. Since the Illinois River entered the Mississippi just above St. Louis, the "Gateway City" protested that its drinking water supply would be tainted with Chicago's filth, so St. Louis filed a restraining order with the court. In response, Chicago opened the waterway and presented Missouri with a fait accompli.

The canal had been a pet project of Chicago since the 1860s when they tried to get Abraham Lincoln to fund it as a navigation improvement needed for national defense. The city's problem was that its drinking water came from Lake Michigan while its sewers emptied into the Chicago River, which in turn flowed into the lake. In the 1860s Chicago thought it solved the issue by digging fresh-water-intake cribs two miles out into the lake and by using steam pumps on the Chicago River to siphon its polluted waters into the old Illinois and Michigan Canal, which was also deepened in an early attempt at reversal. The effect was to temporarily induce the flow of the Chicago River away from the lake and the drinking water supply. Unfortunately, as Chicago's population soared to over a half-million toilet-using souls, and its stockyards slaughtered meat for the nation, the volume of filth in the river often became too great for the steam pumps and the narrow Illinois and Michigan Canal to manage, and the river then followed its natural course back into the lake, with disastrous health effects on the populace. Inspired by the idea that "the solution to pollution is dilution" the city fathers dug into the taxpayers' pockets and planned a deep canal that when completed would suck Lake Michigan water into the Chicago River and out of the metropolitan area down to the tributaries of the Illinois River. A secondary purpose of the canal was navigation. The 160-foot wide, 21-foot-deep canal would be able to handle larger vessels than the old Illinois and Michigan Canal. It was hoped that it would be the first link in an improved inland waterway system between Chicago and New Orleans.[23]

The Sanitary and Ship Canal was not the first diversion of Great Lakes water. In 1825 the Erie Canal diverted water from Lake Erie to help flood the man-made waterway, as did the later Miami and Erie Canal in Ohio. Great Britain also diverted Lake Erie water to Lake Ontario when it opened the Welland Canal. Chicago's first diversion had been in 1848 when the Illinois and Michigan Canal was built. What made the Sanitary and Ship Canal special was indicated in its name. Navigation concerns were secondary to the pursuit of clean drinking water for a city. The sanitary goal necessitated a diversion on a scale never attempted on the Great Lakes, and that was bound to elicit controversy. The Chicago diversion was an indication of a subtle but nonetheless significant shift in the way the Great Lakes were viewed and used. Hitherto, commercial navigation had been the use that had defined policy toward the inland seas. Chicago's bold and unilateral action placed drinking water for its increasing population ahead of the needs of the lake shipping industry. The city's marine links had been crucial to its growth but were deemed secondary to the economic necessity of public health. Lake Michigan for Chicago was more than an economic highway—it was itself a life-giving force.

The virtually dark-of-the-night opening of the Chicago Sanitary and Ship Canal could not remove Chicago's canal from Supreme Court jurisdiction. It did, however, allow Chicago to show that, with the diversion of lake water, the city's bacteria were destroyed long before reaching St. Louis, and Missouri's suit was dismissed. The U.S. Army Corps of Engineers issued Chicago a license to divert 4,167 cubic feet of water per second from Lake Michigan. Not content with this victory, Chicago immediately began to plan another diversion canal. This one would provide a sixteen-mile channel from Lake Michigan at South Chicago harbor into the Calumet industrial region before linking up with the new Sanitary and Ship Canal. Named the Calumet and Sag Canal, the waterway would solve sewage disposal problems and flood control issues for the southern section of the metropolitan region. Just as important, it would create miles of new industrial sites along a navigable waterway. Already much of Chicago's heavy industry had located to the region. However, this was one diversion too many for the states and municipalities that shared the lakes. There was already concern among shipping interests that the Sanitary Canal had lowered the level of water available to vessels in harbors and channels. Accordingly, in 1907 the U.S. Army Corps of Engineers refused to grant Chicago a permit for their new canal. In response, Chicago sued the federal government. Chicago lost the suit, but in 1911 still forged ahead with the construction of the Calumet-Sag Canal. It also boldly announced plans to more than double the diversion of lake water to 10,000 cubic feet per second (the equivalent of nearly 6.5 billion gallons per day). Wisconsin, Minnesota, Michigan, Ohio, Pennsylvania, and New York all filed suit in the U.S. Supreme Court to stop the Chicagoans. Also entering the fray was the Dominion of Canada, which between 1912 and 1924 filed six formal protests with Washington over what Chicago was doing. To complicate matters more, Chicago's request for an additional diversion was supported by states that relied on the Mississippi River for commercial navigation. The attorneys general for Missouri, Kentucky, Tennessee, Louisiana, Arkansas, and Mississippi understood that water taken by Chicago from Lake Michigan would raise the navigation channels for downstream river traffic.[24]

The lengthy and complicated litigation came to a head in 1929. Chicago tried to argue that the case was about the health of the citizens of the nation's second largest city. The other Great Lakes states contended it was about interstate commerce and presented evidence that since the diversion had begun, harbors on all the lakes save Superior had been lowered by several inches. This hit every industry invested in lake commerce. The loss of even an inch of harbor or channel depth reduced the carrying capacity of lake vessels by nearly one hundred tons. This meant more ships were needed to make more trips at greater cost to companies and consumers. The Lake Carriers' Association conducted a survey of the cost this imposed on other cities. Just between 1905 and 1911, Milwaukee required more than $100,000 of additional dredging. Harbors across the lakes that had finally been built with a massive post–Civil War federal investment required similar work. The mayor of Tonawanda on Lake Erie expressed the feeling of most municipal leaders when he complained to Secretary of War H. L. Stimson: "Chicago has already done more than her share of damage to our lake channels, on which the government has spent so much money." The problem was magnified by the fact that in the early twentieth century, lake shipping was undergoing a major change. Between 1900, when the Chicago diversion began, and 1910, the number of lakers over three hundred feet in length increased from 190 to 443. The court ruled that while Chicago's diversion of Great Lake water for sanitation purposes was illegal, it was legal for navigation purposes and drinking water but needed to be limited to 3,200 cubic feet per second (or 1.1 billion gallons). Further, Chicago had to construct a lock at the mouth of the Chicago River to control the rate of diversion as well as to begin to treat its sewage. That, however, was not quite the end of the matter. For the rest of the century, Chicago appealed to the court to increase its diversion, and Great Lake states have fought back on each occasion so that some aspect of the Chicago diversion has been before the federal courts for nine consecutive decades, something that continues to the present.[25]

The impact of Chicago's Sanitary Canal on lake navigation was partially mitigated in 1900 by a chain of accidents on Lake St. Clair that raised water levels on Lakes Huron and Michigan. This happened when a series of collisions occurred that led to the sinking of the 231-foot schooner *Fontana* and the 220-foot schooner *John Martin* directly in the mouth of the St. Clair River. The vast waters of the upper lakes are here confined to an eight-hundred-foot-wide channel and surge through the river mouth faster than the waters of the Grand Canyon. The impact of the ships resting at the bottom of the river at this narrow point was to back up the flow of water and raise the level of Huron and Michigan by at least one inch. This event should have been a warning to the maritime community that the St. Clair River channel was as important as the Chicago diversion in maintaining lake levels on those two lakes. It was unfortunately a warning not heeded.[26]

There was a salutary development resulting from the Chicago diversion controversy that went far beyond the quality of drinking water for Windy City residents. In 1909 an International Joint Commission was created to formulate a process of mutual consultation and resource management for the Great Lakes. Canada had been deeply troubled by the Chicago diversion. Its commerce was injured by the lower water levels in lake channels and the reduction of waterpower at Niagara Falls. More alarming was the implication that the unilateral action of an American city could diminish the Great Lakes and Canada would have no say in the matter. The International Joint Commission came into being through the Boundary Waters Treaty of 1909, negotiated between the U.S. and Great Britain—acting those days as the steward of Canadian interests. Its provisions pointedly did not include the possibility of international arbitration of the Chicago diversion but did establish that no future diversions would go forward without the approval of the Joint Commission. The treaty also established three priority uses of the Great Lakes and enumerated them in their order of importance: drinking water, navigation, and water power. A farsighted article of the treaty also stated that the lakes "shall not be polluted on either side to the injury of health or property on the other," thus making it the first international treaty to address environmental degradation.[27]

The Joint Commission was an important addition to the management software of the Great Lakes maritime infrastructure. Among the most persistent of the international issues it addressed was the depth of water in lake navigation channels and harbors. In the years ahead, the commission would have before it a plethora of plans to manipulate the levels of the lakes. Choke points like the St. Clair and Detroit Rivers were favorite places for such schemes, where it was thought works might counteract the loss of water at Chicago. Another often-discussed site was the outlet of Lake Erie, where a dam could back up water throughout the Upper Great Lakes. However, the scheme that garnered the most attention from the Joint Commission was the 1911 proposal to solve the sewage and clean water problems of Buffalo, New York, with a Chicago-like diversion of Lake Erie water.[28]

Buffalo sewage passed from Lake Erie into its Niagara River outlet and then fouled the drinking water supply for the entire Niagara frontier area of New York State and the Province of Ontario. A private New York company called the Eire & Ontario Sanitary Canal Company proposed to prevent this pollution by digging a canal and tunnel from Buffalo Creek to Lake Ontario. The effect would be to reverse the flow of Buffalo Creek from Lake Erie to Lake Ontario. The scheme would require taking six thousand cubic feet per second of Erie water. Proponents claimed that by the time the water reached Lake Ontario it would be "purified." They also promised that the scale of their diversion would be too small to affect Lake Erie navigation. They projected the cost at $30 million dollars, or half the expense of the Chicago Sanitary and Ship Canal. In 1911 the company applied to the U.S.

War Department for a permit to undertake the diversion. Needless to say, the very idea set off alarm bells at the Lake Carriers' Association and in the Dominion of Canada, neither of which wanted a repeat of the Chicago precedent.[29]

The new diversion scheme affected both navigation and drinking water issues on both sides of the international border and was referred to the International Joint Commission. For more than a decade the project was proposed, modified, debated, and investigated by the Joint Commission and the U.S. Army Corps of Engineers. The proposal was initially endorsed by the City of Buffalo, but soon after, the municipality put in place a cheaper and simpler method of securing clean drinking water. The proposal, however, stayed alive for a time as a commercial scheme. Proponents were interested in the electrical power that could be generated through their waterway as it fell 312 feet between the two lakes. The diversion was finally rejected when the Joint Commission found that the canal would not succeed in purifying Buffalo's sewage before it entered Lake Ontario.[30]

Another diversion was prevented, but the Buffalo proposal once again raised the issue of pollution. Beginning in 1912 the Joint Commission set about investigating to what extent and by what means the lakes, as a source of fresh water, were being compromised. It was at best a preliminary effort, with field work focused on the Detroit River and Niagara River areas. The principal result of their study was the recommendation that federal government leadership was needed to intervene among the many states and municipalities. There was on the books the 1899 Refuse Act, which required a U.S. Army Corps of Engineer permit to discharge any "refuse" into navigable waters or harbors. Unfortunately, the corps interpreted refuse to mean solid objects that would pose a danger to ship hulls or propellers. Liquid waste was deposited into the lakes freely. By diverting water from the Great Lakes, Chicagoans had made their city the healthiest on the inland seas. Typhoid fever was a reoccurring problem in Milwaukee, Buffalo, and Detroit. The latter city had twice as many cases as Chicago. Lake shipping was affected by this rising concern. Vessels commonly took on ballast water in polluted harbors or urban waters and then discharged it when it was not needed. In 1922 the Lake Carriers' Association released a circular to its members warning them not to dump ballast water before entering the Sault Ste. Marie locks. The small communities there on both the Canadian and U.S. side of the border were suffering "dangerous" health conditions because of the transfer of city pollution by ship ballast.[31]

The Chicago diversion ushered in a new age that would greatly expand the way the inland seas were subject to human management and engineering. The Joint Commission and the experience of the U.S. and Canada as vital allies in the world wars of the twentieth century heightened the perception of the inland seas as international waters that transcended boundary lines and that were part of an integrated North American maritime-industrial complex.[32]

The Great War on the Great Lakes

In January 1919 a group of very self-satisfied shipowners met at a downtown Detroit hotel. Their goal was to plan the coming navigation season on the Great Lakes. They reviewed the insurance rates that had been set by underwriters and listened to steelmakers who offered projections on the year's likely production goals. With this in mind they could determine how many ships would be put into service in the coming season. There also was considerable discussion of what had transpired since their last meeting, in January 1918. At that time, the U.S. was deeply involved in the greatest war the world had ever seen. The challenge of projecting U.S. military and industrial power across the Atlantic absorbed virtually the entire nation. To meet the demands of a military mobilization that eventually included three million men, and to supply that force as well as American's overseas allies, the federal government took unprecedented action. In December 1917 President Woodrow Wilson ordered the establishment of the U.S. Railroad Commission to administer the nation's rail network. On the ocean, the government took similar action through the Emergency Fleet Corporation, which embarked on a massive shipbuilding program and managed the U.S. Merchant Marine. On the Great Lakes, however, there was no government takeover. The independent members of the Lake Carriers' Association continued to transport the bulk of America's iron ore, limestone, and coal without regulation. By November 1918 Germany and its Austrian and Turkish allies had been defeated, and the executives of America's inland seas fleet gave themselves a hearty pat on the back for the role the lake marine played in making that happen.[33]

In some ways, World War I came at a fortuitous time for lake shippers. There was a glut of vessels engaged in the iron ore and grain trade on the lakes. However, when Europe went to war in August 1914, there was an ever-escalating need for shipping on the Atlantic as Great Britain and France came to rely on food and manufactured goods produced in the U.S. Instead of having vessels idled in lake ports, shippers found their surplus freighters in great demand on saltwater. During the course of the war, 149 vessels were transferred from the lakes to the Atlantic trade. Virtually all the modern ships on the inland seas, whose size would allow them to pass through the Welland and St. Lawrence locks, went east and dared the war-torn waters around Britain and France. Dozens of Great Lakes freighters too large for the Canadian canal locks were cut in half, passed through the canals, and were then reattached for Atlantic duty. The lake marine contribution became even greater after the U.S. directly entered the war in April 1917. The nation embarked on a massive program of shipbuilding. The Germans had engaged in unrestricted submarine warfare, with the belief their U-boats would be able to so inhibit the deployment of the U.S. military that they could win the war in France before American participation could change the balance of power. President Wilson and his administration realized that to upset that logic would require more than the marshalling of the nation's existing merchant marine. A constant flow of new vessels was required to make up for the loss of ships to torpedo attacks. The federal Emergency Fleet authority contracted extensively with Great Lakes shipyards to produce these vessels. A full 25 percent of all ships produced by that authority slipped out of the stocks of Great Lakes shipyards. In only twenty-eight months, Great Lakes shipbuilders produced 374 cargo vessels to get U.S. men and matériel "Over There."[34]

The produce of the American heartland, especially steel and food, were beleaguered Europe's greatest need. Unfortunately, a poor harvest in 1916 caused a near panic among the intended recipients. The price of grain soared as a result, reaching heights not seen since the American Civil War. Nonetheless, the British purchased 203 million bushels of the 1916 wheat harvest, twice as much as the U.S. normally exported to all countries. By April 1917 the need for grain in Europe was acute, even though the price continued to spiral upward, increasing by nearly threefold within a year. As soon as ice left the Straits of Mackinac, Great Lakes grain ships set off for the Buffalo terminals. That first day of the shipping season in 1917, 4.3 million bushels alone set sail from Chicago, with 17 million bushels awaiting shipment. The high demand ensured that by 1917 midwestern farmers were plowing up every possible bit of acreage to secure a bumper crop. Expectations of a great profit were high, and across the region farmers, brokers, and shippers followed with great interest the fluctuations of the military campaigns.[35] Steel prices increased by threefold between 1914 and April 1917. When the U.S. entered the war, that action triggered a further price escalation. In 1917 and 1918 the Great Lakes ore fleet operated at near record levels, delivering thirty-three million tons.[36]

For the first time in their shared use of the Great Lakes, Canada and the U.S. also shared a common enemy. Close cooperation during World War I was facilitated by a century of largely harmonious relations along the lakes. In the wake of the Civil War, the Reciprocity Treaty for free movement of goods was ended, but the two nations had agreed to continue the navigation provisions that allowed vessels from both countries to operate freely anywhere on the inland seas or St. Lawrence River. Formal denationalization followed in 1909 with the signing of the Boundary Waters Treaty. Significantly, both countries retained the right to protect their commercial interests. American cargoes moving from one American port to another had to be carried by an American vessel, and the same regulation applied to the north at Dominion ports. The spirit of cooperation was manifest in the lighthouse projects and the maintenance of navigation channels in tight, heavily trafficked border waters such as the Detroit and St. Mary's Rivers. In the latter case American army engineers carried out projects located on the Canadian side of the border that were desired by both nations' shippers.[37]

As in any war, a certain amount of hysteria rolled over the lakes. Both in the U.S. and Canada, the region boasted a very large German immigrant population. Actual acts of sabotage by German agents in the U.S., such as the 1916 Black Tom Island explosion at a New Jersey munitions plant, helped fuel fears in the Great Lakes region. In the summer of 1917, the U.S. War and Justice departments announced with great fanfare their belief that German agents, aided by American citizens, were behind a series of "accidents" designed to disrupt the movement of grain and iron ore. In May the collision and sinking of two steamers near the Sault Ste. Marie locks was suspected of having been an attempt to block that critical choke point. Then the sinking of a vessel in the Detroit River raised similar suspicions. Soon every engine failure or boiler explosion was being chalked up to German agents. When two colliers caught fire in Little Sodus Bay, the fact that the coal they were carrying was bound for a Canadian munitions plant seemed reason enough to infer sabotage. Close investigation, however, could not substantiate enemy action on the inland seas.[38]

Following the war's end in November 1918, a victory celebration of sorts was held at a series of Great Lakes ports. A German submarine, the *UC-97*, had been awarded to the U.S. as a prize of war, and in 1919 she was brought to the inland seas to stimulate a war bond drive. After attracting considerable crowds, the former terror of the high seas was moored in the murky Chicago River for nearly two years. The German vessel's final voyage was to the bottom of Lake Michigan. On June 7, 1921, the *UC-97* was towed out into the lake and sunk in a naval gunnery exercise. Ten shells from the USS *Wilmette* riddled her hull and she plunged 250 feet to the lake bottom. In the protected waters of North America's Great Lakes, this was the only vessel lost to hostile fire on account of the war.[39]

One result of the inland seas' strong support for the war on the Atlantic was that from 1914 to 1919 there was virtually no new shipping added to the lake marine. Lake shipyards were focused on war contracts, and the only aid they gave lake shipping was occasionally patching up one of the busy freighters. Thus, when the war ended, there was a tremendous glut of shipping on the nation's seacoast but a pent-up demand for new vessels on the inland seas. This enabled Great Lakes shipbuilders to immediately transition into new commercial contracts. By 1921 there were twelve new lakers under construction.[40]

Although the America's actual involvement as a belligerent in World War I only lasted a year and a half, the conflict had many long-lingering impacts. One of the longest lasting was the impact on American agriculture. The dizzying heights to which grain prices had climbed because of the war induced famers to over-extend themselves. Between 1915 and 1918 the prices farmers received for crops and livestock had doubled. The dislocation caused by World War I and the Russian Revolution and civil war that followed it kept international demand elevated until 1921. By then Europe had recovered, and U.S. harvests faced many global competitors. Prices plunged by 40 percent for farm products, and after eight years of spectacular growth, the incomes of American farmers fell sharply. The rural U.S. entered its own depression, and hundreds of farmers, particularly those in marginal areas like the Great Lakes cutover lands, lost their homes. The lake marine was inevitably impacted by the slowdown in production that followed. There was also, however, a positive impact for lake shippers. The crisis in rural America inspired calls for government action. One plan endorsed at a White House conference called by President Warren G. Harding supported the building of a new Great Lakes–St. Lawrence Waterway. The war had shown the inadequacy of the Canadian-owned Welland and St. Lawrence Canals. Their antiquated locks prevented most lakers from being able to move into Atlantic waters. If American grain could be shipped abroad directly from Duluth or Chicago terminals, midwesterners would have enhanced access to the world market. Thus was implanted in the public mind a new internal improvement project that would have a long, and in the end unsatisfying, life.[41]

A Deepwater Access to the Sea, 1920–39

The idea of opening the Great Lakes to oceangoing vessels had blossomed and withered many times in the history of the inland seas. As early as 1848, it was possible for small schooners to make the transition from the Atlantic Ocean to the Great Lakes through locks on the St. Lawrence River and the Welland Canal. In the 1850s, trans-Atlantic voyages to and from lake cities were an annual, if not a frequent, feature. In the mid-1860s, a few Norwegian immigrant ships brought new settlers from the fjords to

Lake Michigan. But in the post–Civil War era, as ship size increased on both the oceans and the lakes, such trips dwindled. The small size of the ships that could navigate the St. Lawrence locks simply could not justify the cost of an ocean transit. In 1887 the Canadian government updated the Welland Canal to a 14-foot depth and 270-foot length, but the upgrade came just as Great Lakes ship size was increasing, and the best ships on the inland sea still could not use the waterway. On the eve of World War I, the Canadian government commissioned yet another attempt to enlarge the Welland Canal. At the same time, U.S. interest in an effective lake-to-ocean connection was high. In 1913 the U.S. Senate voted unanimously to support negotiations to develop a cooperative plan with Canada. The idea was to build commercially viable locks on the St. Lawrence River and, at the same time, develop the river's hydroelectric potential. President Woodrow Wilson supported the initiative. Unfortunately, budget issues caused Canada to balk, and when the Dominion was drawn into war with Germany, the opportunity for action vanished.[42]

When the project was revisited in the 1920s, the two nations had a legacy of cooperation on which to build. From 1909 they had the International Joint Commission to resolve any issues that arose from disputes over water resources shared by both nations. The Great Lakes–St. Lawrence passage was the most important of those shared waters, and the Joint Commission's formal conferences every two years became a forum in which to promote cooperation on waterway improvement. Military planners also had before them the ridiculous spectacle of World War I, when scores of Great Lakes ships had to be cut in half so that they could be put into service on the Atlantic. Yet there also were powerful forces in both countries aligned against a lake-to-ocean waterway.

Plans for deepwater access through the St. Lawrence reopened the rivalry between New York's Hudson River and the St. Lawrence River that went back to the French and Indian Wars. Canada was founded on the St. Lawrence, the natural outlet of the Great Lakes, yet New York's Erie Canal had diverted the bulk of the lake commerce to the Hudson River route to the sea. New York would not sit back and watch the Canadians secure Uncle Sam's help at their expense. Another old rivalry was reopened by the St. Lawrence plans. Mississippi River ports wanted federal support for improvements, and they gained an important ally in Chicago, at that point still one of the most important ports on the Great Lakes. Chicago's Sanitary and Ship Canal was the first link in an emerging and reengineered waterway link between the Great Lakes and the Gulf of Mexico. The city lobbied the U.S. Army Corps of Engineers to expand the lock and dam network on the Illinois River. The prospect of diverting the bulk of Lake Michigan's trade away from the Great Lakes and to the Mississippi River allied some Chicagoans with the business community in St. Louis and New Orleans. In 1906 a major convention was held to form the Lakes-to-the-Gulf Deep Waterway Association. This galvanized southern and middle border opposition to a St. Lawrence deepwater project. There were also significant opponents in Canada, with the Prairie provinces preferring to see government investment in the Hudson Bay Railroad as a better way for them to reach Atlantic markets, while the Maritime provinces saw the seaway as a plan to bypass their ports. Montreal, which at that time was the head of oceanic navigation into Canada, worried it might lose traffic to its despised rival Toronto, which in the 1920s was already building a deepwater harbor in anticipation of having direct access to the sea. On top of that there was recurring interest in an all-Canadian or all-American waterway that could be pursued unilaterally by either country.[43]

Buffalo and Oswego, New York, were the two lake ports most strongly opposed to the proposed improvements on the St. Lawrence. Their prosperity rested on their function as gateways to the Erie Canal. They readily understood that, if ships could easily transit from the lakes to the sea, their fair cities would lose their vital functions as transfer points. In 1923 a journalist interviewed some of the leading businessmen and politicians in Buffalo. He found each eager to point out that their opposition to the proposed waterway "is not a selfish one." Rather, the proposed locks and channels were either too expensive as planned, too small as planned, unlikely to be used, and not necessary because of the money the State of New York invested in improving the old canal into the wider and deeper New York State Barge Canal. A veteran politician piously claimed, "We are trying to save the country from the selfish sectionalism of the Middle West."[44]

It was true that the newspapers and politicians of the Midwest had relentlessly beat the drum for the project, and despite an array of opponents, the logic of an improved waterway from the heartland to the tidewater had won significant support in the U.S. The Midwest's agriculturalists had long believed that their prosperity was held hostage by the railroads. While lake vessels provided a very healthy check on the rates the railroads could charge to get grain from Chicago or Duluth to Buffalo, rates rose steeply from that point east to the sea. Advocates for a deepwater access to the sea claimed that one-half of the cost of shipping grain from Duluth to Liverpool was incurred between Buffalo and the wharves of New York City. In addition to that economic argument, there was the issue of what one journalist diagnosed as ambition, "our eternal American ambition to become greater than we are: the ambition of Duluth to be greater than Milwaukee, of Milwaukee to outstrip Detroit, of Detroit to be a second Chicago by some magic of water transport, of freedom to the markets of the world." A Duluth businessman exulted, "Do you think a few rocks and shallows" in the St. Lawrence "can bar us from our rightful outlet to the sea? Never!" Like many in the heartland, he acted as if access to the sea was a panacea. The election to the presidency of the midwesterner Herbert Hoover in 1928 seemed to be the turning point. He had been a longtime supporter of the project, and his administration entreated Canada to commit to a joint seaway. Negotiations on a treaty, however, dragged on until 1932, which coincided with both a presidential election and a deepening of the Great Depression. A Great Lakes Waterway Treaty was finally signed, but its ratification was placed on the back burner by the new Franklin Roosevelt administration that was committed to fighting the Depression. The treaty also had a provision that proved to be a poison pill. The agreement contained clauses that limited the amount of water that could be diverted by Chicago for its Sanitary and Ship Canal. This was opposed by Illinois congressmen and U.S. senators responsive to Mississippi navigation, which benefited from the extra water taken by Chicago. When finally put to a vote, the treaty failed to garner the necessary two-thirds approval for passage. Canada never even submitted the treaty to Parliament for approval.[45]

One person neither surprised nor dismayed by the failure of the treaty was the new president, Franklin D. Roosevelt. He regarded the treaty as flawed but its goal laudable. "Just as sure as God made little green apples," he remarked, a St. Lawrence Seaway would be built and within days of the Senate vote, he had the State Department back working on a new treaty. On Roosevelt's watch, however, waterpower development at Niagara and on the St. Lawrence became as important as a deepwater shipping channel. The native New Yorker understood the Empire State's appetite for electricity and how important it was for industrial growth. It took until 1938 for diplomats from both countries to hammer out a new treaty, but no action was taken on it because of Canadian Prime Minister William Mackenzie King's unwillingness to confront domestic opponents of the project.[46]

The outbreak of World War II in 1939 reanimated Canadian interest in the project, and personal consultations between the prime minister and the president led to the signing of a Canadian-American executive agreement in 1941. The U.S. Congress, however, refused to affirm the deal, as sectional opposition once more asserted itself. This setback put further consideration of a Great Lakes–St. Lawrence construction project on the back burner for the duration of the war. There was one concrete result for Great Lakes navigation. The 1941 agreement had called for the U.S. to build a new, larger, and deeper lock at Sault Ste. Marie. In the wake of the Pearl Harbor attack, Congress approved the project, and by July 1943 the eight-hundred-foot MacArthur lock was busy with ore boats bound for bustling defense plants.[47]

Navigational Aid Improvements between the Wars

The twenty-one years between World Wars I and II saw important technological and organizational improvements in the management of inland seas navigation. The resulting increase in marine safety was due, in part, to war, which sped up the adoption of existing technologies, such as electricity for direction finding and illumination. It was due also to the stimulus that a military emergency often gives to technological innovation. An example of both of these was the adoption of radio beacons by lake vessels and lighthouses. As early as 1899 Guglielmo Marconi, the inventor of

wireless telegraphy, described how radio waves could be broadcast by "lighthouses and lightships, so as to enable vessels in
foggy weather to locate dangerous points around the coasts."
Here again it was the federal government that took the lead in
adapting new technology to marine safety. The U.S. Navy conducted experiments with radio beacons during World War I. The
Bureau of Standards and the Lighthouse Service paid close attention to this work, and by the early 1920s radio towers were installed at several Atlantic stations. In 1920 the U.S. Lake Survey
assisted the navy in choosing the location for a series of radio
beacon stations on Lakes Superior, Michigan, and Huron. In 1925
the first radio beacon was placed on the Great Lakes lightship
LV Huron stationed at Gray's Reef in Lake Michigan. The U.S.
system was simple and reliable. A transmitter was installed on a
lightship or lighthouse, and it sent a simple Morse code signal
unique to its location. A vessel equipped with a radio compass
could receive the signal and determine its position vis-à-vis the
light station. By registering the direction of other beacons, a navigator could, by triangulation, accurately plot a vessel's exact position. The radio beacon also allowed lightkeepers to aid ships
equipped with radio direction finders miles from the sound of a
fog horn or the sight of a light. Fog-bound vessels near a station
could get an even better fix on their positions when the radio
beacon sent a signal at the same time a fog horn was sounded. A
captain on the bridge of a ship could time the span between
when the radio signal was received and when he heard the horn
and calculate how far he was from the station.[48]

Tests on Lake Michigan in 1933 demonstrated the advantages
of mobile radio navigation systems to aid late-season navigation
on the lakes. Car ferries between Michigan and Wisconsin often
ran after the regular navigation season closed at the end of November. Low-powered radio beacons were installed on ten car
ferries. Car ferries were an important part of lake traffic, and several railroads operated these boats to transfer railroad cars across
the lake and thus avoid the rail bottleneck at Chicago caused by
the need of east-west rail tracks to dip below the southern extension of Lake Michigan. The experimental system allowed the
vessels to make radio bearings on each other and thus avoid collisions. The captain of the Pere Marquette Railroad's ferry *P.M. 22*
reported:

On December 19 when on route to Manitowoc, with strong west winds and winter fog so heavy I could not see the water from the bridge, I picked up a mobile radio signal of *P.M. 21* [a sister ship] nearly ahead. She was coming from Manitowoc. I ported one point. The bearings of the radio compass constantly changed until I had *21* abreast of me. We probably passed within a mile of each other. We did not see or hear her, but we knew by the bearings that we were going clear and also when we passed her. I consider it a perfect demonstration of the value of the mobile radio beacon.

Head of the Lighthouse Bureau George Putnam was a firm believer in the efficacy of this new technology, and he budgeted for it to be widely employed. He examined the number of ship groundings on the Great Lakes in the four years that preceded the installation of radio beacons and the four years that followed. He estimated a 50 percent decrease in stranded vessels. By 1942 there were fifty-eight radio beacons in service on the American side of the lakes and seven operated by the Dominion of Canada. Although the U.S. and Canada drafted regulations for radio communication and navigation as early as 1938, it was not until 1954 that radios were required on all commercial vessels. Beacons and radio direction finders were a popular, low-cost, electronic aid to navigation, and their use continued for the rest of the twentieth century. As late as 1991, there were nearly seven hundred thousand units still in use.[49]

Radio beacons were a product of electricity. The potential of electrical currents had been known and studied for centuries. The true power of electricity to produce a new industrial revolution was realized and enacted in the late nineteenth century. It was not, however, until the 1920s that reliable power grids had been laid out so that lighthouse electrification could became widespread. As early as 1886 the Lighthouse Board had experimented with electricity when it installed arc lights in the Statue of Liberty. In the late 1880s and into the 1890s, incandescent electric lamps were experimented with at several Atlantic stations. The Navesink Lighthouse on the Jersey shore was electrified in 1898, but it required its own independent generator. In 1913 *LV 97*, anchored off the Virginia coast, successfully operated its electric light from a battery system. One of the first Great Lakes lighthouses to use electricity was the breakwater light and fog signal at Ashland,

Wisconsin. Installed in October 1915, the fourth-order lens was lit by a sixteen-hundred-candle-powered bulb and powered by the Ashland city power grid through a two-mile-long underwater cable. It was not until 1924 that the Grosse Point Lighthouse in Evanston, Illinois, and the Wind Point Lighthouse near Racine, Wisconsin, were electrified. However, electricity gradually spread to the other Great Lakes stations during the 1920s, and it became a revolution in the 1930s.[50]

The move to incandescent lights and electrical power had a major impact on the men and women who kept Great Lakes stations. The new lights burned bright and clean without the smoke that had dirtied lenses and lantern room windows in the past. The daily task of cleaning and polishing the glass was tremendously reduced. Instead of lugging fuel up the steep steps of the tower each day, a keeper only had to flip a switch and the beacon was in service. Even this became redundant when light timers could be installed. In 1921 a rotating fixture that contained three bulbs was tested at the Ashland breakwater light. When one bulb burned out, an electromagnet rotated a new bulb in place. Also given a trial was a small emergency generator that could be activated if the power grid failed. Stations once manned by four or five keepers were reduced to two, and in some cases automation eliminated the keepers altogether. Those who were kept had to be able to deal with increasingly sophisticated electrical equipment, something many old veterans of the oil lamps could not manage.[51]

The promise (or, as some old timers saw it, the threat) of automation was demonstrated in 1934 when *LV-75*, a lightship that dated from 1902, was converted to unmanned use. Anchored at the critical Lake St. Clair choke point, she was a key navigational aid in one of the world's busiest shipping channels, passed by fourteen thousand vessels annually. All of *LV-75*'s equipment was installed in duplicate so that if a device failed its function, it could be carried on by a replacement started by remote control from a land-based station at St. Clair Flats. Radio-telephone signals allowed the lightship's operations to be accurately monitored. An astronomical clock turned the beacon light on and off. The remote operator could override automatic systems when weather conditions such as fog so required. *LV-75* was an experiment, and while she clearly pointed the way to the future, she only remained on station until 1939. At that time, a permanent off-shore lighthouse was installed. Like the lightship, the new St. Clair Light Station was unmanned and fully automated. Yet in spite of these successful early automations, manned stations were only phased out very gradually. The lighthouse service carefully tried to balance the cost of installing and maintaining new technology with the efficiency it promised. Nonetheless, by the mid-1930s George Putnam of the Lighthouse Establishment estimated that automated light stations had saved the U.S. more than $1 million annually.[52]

Another new technology that was widely adopted between the wars was the radio-telephone. The Lake Carriers' Association and many vessel masters had successfully fought off federal efforts in the period before World War I to mandate wireless telegraphs on all Great Lakes commercial vessels. But during the 1920s the use of radio-telephones was perfected, and this offered a simplified and less costly method of effecting ship-to-shore communication. In 1922 the *Carl D. Bradley* of the Michigan Limestone and Chemical Company was equipped with a radio-telephone. At the limestone company's home base in Rogers City, Michigan, the Central Radio Telegraph Station had set up a broadcast operation just before World War I. The experiment went well enough that the following year the *B. F. Taylor* was also so equipped. The ship's device was installed by the Radio Corporation of America (RCA) and allowed the vessels to receive updated directions from the home office, weather reports, and occasionally music from a shore-based record player. This successful experiment was not quickly embraced. As late as 1937 only two hundred Great Lakes vessels were capable of receiving and sending radio-telephone messages. However, most of the large carriers, such as the Pittsburgh Steamship Company, had all its vessels so equipped. That same year a formal weather forecast began to be broadcast from the government locks at Sault Ste. Marie.[53]

Another major step in improving Great Lakes navigation was made in 1922 when the *Daniel J. Morrell*, a steamer launched fourteen years earlier, was equipped with an electric-powered gyrocompass. Unlike traditional compasses that operated on the basis of magnetism, the new device was a mechanism that used gravity and inertia to point north. The gyrocompass was more accurate because it pointed to true north—the pole—not magnetic north, which was south and west of the North Pole. More important for Great Lakes navigators, the gyrocompass spared them from having to account for deflections caused by the rich iron ore deposits in the Lake Superior basin or even from the iron in the hulls of their vessels. Despite the obvious advantages of the new technology, the cost of the gyrocompass and its need for a reliable source of electricity ensured that it would take a full generation for the device to be standard on lakers. The gyrocompass kept helmsmen on their toes. It was typical for the man at the wheel to stray a bit off course when the vessel was on a broad section of open lake and then correct by steering back. The gyrocompass would make such errors obvious to anyone in the pilothouse. Helmsman Fred Dutton recalled, "The gyro repeater emits a faint *click* six times for each degree the lubber mark moves on the compass card." The skill of a helmsmen was further insulted when many vessels were equipped with the steering engine that could be connected to the gyrocompass and function as an autopilot. Such devices lessened the course deviation on the open lake, but the experienced helmsman at the wheel still earned his salary when his ship navigated narrow channels and rivers. All lake vessels continued to carry magnetic compasses, but the go-to source for directional orientation was hereafter the gyrocompass.[54]

The increased safety to lake vessels brought by this new technology was matched by continuing improvements via good old-fashioned civil engineering. While trade groups like the Lake Carriers' Association often dragged their feet on expensive new shipboard navigational aids, they were active in advocating for publicly funded improvements to harbors and channels. An important, if difficult, project championed by shipowners was a widening of the Detroit River channel to create separate transit lanes for up-bound and down-bound ships. This proved a formidable undertaking. A coffer dam nearly six thousand feet long was built across a shallow stretch of the river, and a new twenty-one-foot-deep channel was blasted out of the granite bedrock. No sooner was the first phase of this undertaking completed in 1912 than the Lake Carriers' Association wanted to have the deep channel extended. The association's prominent role in lobbying Congress for these projects was memorialized when the new channel was named the Livingston Channel after a president of the shipowners' group. By 1928 the Army Corps had spent $160 million

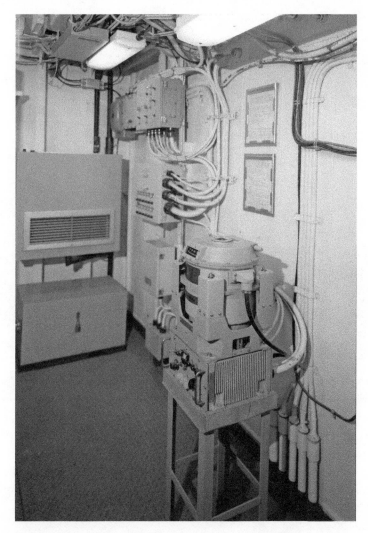

Figure 17. Gyrocompass on the USCG icebreaker *Mackinac*.
Source: Library of Congress.

on the project, which had become, in the words of one contemporary, "the largest and most expensive of any similar work ever undertaken by the U.S. within its boundaries." Further improvements were authorized in the 1930s, with the effect of greatly improving safety and the speed of ships on the river but at the cost of destroying the once thriving whitefish fishery in the river. This project, like others between the wars, was paid for by the

Figure 18. Livingston Channel, Detroit River, opening day, 1912.
Source: Library of Congress.

American taxpayer but took place in Canadian waters. In that regard, it was a testament to cooperation between the two countries and an indication of the asymmetrical nature of Great Lakes navigation, with the overwhelming majority of vessels flying the stars and stripes.[55]

A Changing of the Guard:
The Demise of the Lighthouse Bureau

In 1935 George Rockwell Putnam, the chief of the U.S. Lighthouse Bureau, retired after twenty-five highly regarded years. He had successfully combined Stephen Pleasonton's cost consciousness with the old Lighthouse Board's interest in technological efficiency and innovation. With nearly thirty thousand aids to navigation, the U.S. operated the largest lighthouse service in the world. Yet while Putnam presided over a doubling of such aids, he managed to decrease the number of personnel in his agency by 20 percent. Under Putnam the nation had been in the forefront of lighthouse automation and international maritime cooperation. Yet less than five years after he left Washington, the U.S. Lighthouse Service was no more.[56]

The change was sparked by President Franklin D. Roosevelt's desire to modernize the operations of the executive branch of the federal government. In the wake of his reelection in 1936, Roosevelt had embarked on a wholesale revision of how White House and Executive Department staff were organized and managed. One of the reorganization plans had a major and enduring impact on the Great Lakes maritime infrastructure by terminating the Lighthouse Service and vesting its functions in the U.S. Coast Guard, which then became the preeminent marine safety agency for the U.S. The Coast Guard was by far the larger entity, with more than ten thousand officers and men, while the Lighthouse service had just over four thousand civilian employees (as well as eleven hundred part-time workers), including some female keepers.[57]

The merger was a logical consolidation of marine safety functions. The modern Coast Guard was formed in 1915 when the Revenue Cutter Service was merged with the U.S. Life-Saving Service. However, the merger of civilian agencies like the Life-Saving Service and the Lighthouse Service with a military organization was a major cultural change for the men and women who did their duty on the shores of the lakes. Some lighthouse keepers were summarily fired by the Coast Guard commandants of their districts. Most were given a choice of quitting, retiring if they were longtime veterans, or staying on as civilian lighthouse keepers. There also was the offer of enlistment in the Coast Guard. Experienced keepers, who were asked to stay, were brought in at the relatively high rank of petty officer. The establishment of a peacetime draft in September 1940 made enlistment in the Coast Guard an attractive option for a young lighthouse man leery of service in the army. Some lighthouse employees, particularly those with large families at light stations, felt that the Coast Guard officers were arbitrary in their personnel decisions. For such employees, there was little recourse for appeal. Lighthouse Commissioner Harold King was initially given the rank of captain and made an assistant to the commandant of the Coast Guard, Rear Admiral Russell R. Waesche. In reality, King had little input on the transition, and he was out of the service altogether in a matter of months. Also out were most of the former lighthouse district inspectors. They were dry-docked after a brief term as "assistants" to the Coast Guard division commanders. A decade after the merger, one former lighthouse man still complained about the Coast Guard's "brassy" officers, and he contended, perhaps a bit too harshly, that "no good blood ever existed between either group."[58]

Another important change in federal navigational management came in 1942 when the Steamboat Inspection Service and the former Bureau of Navigation, both in the Commerce Department, were merged with the Coast Guard. This was important because for the first time there was a single federal authority for marine safety on all domestic waters, from buoys, lighthouses, beacons, vessel inspection, and operational safety to emergency rescue.[59]

A factor in the absorption of the Lighthouse Bureau by a branch of the military was the looming prospect of war. The official date of the merger was July 7, 1939. Fewer than sixty days later Adolph Hitler's Germany invaded Poland and World War II began. The Roosevelt administration had been trying to build up the nation's defenses despite a Congress that was reluctant to take any action that might move the U.S. closer to another war in Europe. The merger was seen as way to increase the military budget without raising fears that it would facilitate aggressive action, since the Coast Guard had a major role in enforcing observance of the nation's neutrality laws. On November 1, 1941, even before the U.S. was formally at war, President Roosevelt transferred the Coast Guard from its peacetime home of the Treasury Department to the Navy Department. The business of navigation on the inland seas was once more a part of the enterprise of war.

World War II on the Inland Seas, 1941–1945

The role of American industry in the winning of World War II has rightly been dubbed a "production miracle." At the time, it seemed all the more miraculous because it came on the heels of the Great Depression. The vast U.S. steel industry centered on the Great Lakes reached its prewar production peak in 1929 with an output of some 63 million tons. Yet by 1932, the Depression's low point, the industry was limping along at a mere 20 percent of capacity. Nearly half the inland seas fleet of 405 ore carriers never even left port that year; scores of vessels that did only made one or two runs before being shut down for the year. As late as 1938 the steel industry could not reach half of what it produced in the years before the Great Crash. World War II's impact on industry, in the words of the economic historian Hugh Rockoff, "was the obverse of the Great Depression." Only a year after the war started in Europe, the somnolent steel industry had awoken and forged eighty-one million tons. By the end of the conflict in 1945, U.S. furnaces were producing ninety-six million tons.[60]

The lake marine that emerged from the Great Depression was significantly changed from the one that had thrived in the decades of the 1910s and 1920s. When the U.S. economy roared in the twenties, as many as 350 companies operated commercial vessels on the inland seas. Hard times had the effect of drastically winnowing the competition. A premium was placed on efficiency, and many small operators whose fleets were composed of smaller, older vessels found themselves at a significant disadvantage when trying to secure shipping contracts. The larger, well-capitalized firms had been able to invest in newer, large vessels, some six hundred feet in length, equipped with a large boom that enabled them to unload their bulk cargo without any shore-based equipment. Although such vessels were rare in the prewar lake marine, they pointed the way to the future. Self-unloaders could arrive in a port at night, discharge their cargo, and be underway again by dawn. Gradually, more and more of the lake fleet was owned by fewer and fewer mammoth corporations. By the late 1930s these tended to be the vertically integrated steel companies that consolidated control over mines, railroads, shipping lines, and mills. On the American side of the lake, a mere twenty-one companies operated 308 vessels engaged in the iron ore trade. The U.S. Steel Corporation's Pittsburgh Steamship Company, not surprisingly, was the largest lake fleet, with seventy-five vessels in operation. As the Depression's cold grip on the economy loosened and the prospect of war heated investment, the industrial giant launched four new mammoth bulk carriers in anticipation of the busy times ahead.[61]

The impact of war on heavy industry in the U.S. was immediate and unmistakable. America's gross national product doubled in the last quarter of 1939 as car and truck makers increased their production goals by more than a million units. Suddenly, every steel producer wanted to increase their inventory of ore, limestone, and coal in anticipation of a busy winter in the manufacturing sector. Mothballed vessels were hastily refitted and dispatched to the Lake Superior mines to bring back as much of the red rock as possible before December's ice and storms closed navigation for the year.

In December 1940 President Roosevelt devoted his weekly "fireside chat" to the issue of defense preparedness. "We must be the great arsenal of democracy," he declared. "For us this is an emergency as serious as war itself." Two months later those words were transformed into action when the president signed an emergency naval appropriation of nearly $1 billion. The navy needed new vessels, and shipyards on the seaboard as well as on the lakes were soon bustling with construction contracts. For years, the Rush-Bagot Agreement, made in the wake of the War of 1812, had limited the ability of both Canada and the U.S. to build and operate military vessels on the Great Lakes. With the British Empire locked in an existential struggle and the U.S. preparing to join the conflict, there was no trouble in getting that treaty's limitations suspended. The immediate need was for anti-submarine vessels to help keep convoys of Atlantic merchant ships safe from U-boat attack. Orders for sixty-six submarine chasers went to Great Lakes yards in 1941 as well as for numerous mine sweepers and patrol boats.[62]

Following the Japanese attack on Pearl Harbor in December 1941, the Great Lakes were fully mobilized for war. The first step toward victory over both Japan and Germany was to secure naval control over the sea-lanes connecting the U.S. with its overseas allies. In 1942 the allies lost more than one thousand ships to U-boat attack. Between the Germans, Italians, and Japanese, 8.3 million tons of shipping was sent to the bottom of the world's oceans. The need to replace these losses strained U.S. shipyards. The folly of the Canadian and U.S. governments' failure to build a modern waterway via the St. Lawrence and the Great Lakes was painfully realized. The size of the Welland and St. Lawrence locks once again limited what types of vessels could be built on the inland seas. In desperation, the federal War Shipping Administration requisitioned twenty small Great Lakes freighters for ocean service. In July 1942 fourteen passenger-packet vessels used for excursions and the transport of miscellaneous cargoes were removed from the lakes for Atlantic duty. Of greater importance was the remarkable contribution of Great Lakes shipyards to the ever-growing allied navies. The Manitowoc Shipbuilding Company executed contracts for twenty-eight 311-foot submarines. The Bay City, Michigan, Defoe Shipbuilding Company contracted to build twenty-eight 307-foot destroyer escorts. Shipyards in Minnesota and Illinois contributed frigates, mine sweepers, cargo vessels, some up to 340 feet in size, as well as a complete assortment of landing craft from the 400-foot LST (Landing Ship Tank) to the small LCVP (Landing Craft Vehicle, Personnel). Even Chris-Craft of Michigan, famous for their elegant pleasure boats, joined in the effort and devoted production to military contracts. Because of the small size of the St. Lawrence locks, all these vessels made their way into the two-ocean war against the Axis powers via the Chicago Sanitary Canal, the Illinois Waterway, and the Mississippi River. The rivers only had on average a nine-foot depth, so some new ships had to be floated on pontoons or dry docks. A bigger problem were the numerous bridges that spanned waterways, particularly in the Chicago area. The Navy solved this with a $3 million investment in converting many fixed spans into lift bridges. The Chicago diversion was also manipulated to raise the water level when a few feet more of depth were needed or to reduce it when trying to fit a ship under a bridge. This backdoor to the Great Lakes had been made possible only by the controversial Chicago diversion and the New Deal's investments in new locks and dams along the Illinois and Mississippi Rivers in the 1930s. Both proved an unexpected bonus to national security.[63]

Of all the Great Lakes, it was Lake Michigan that was most affected by the emergency measures of the world war. Large portions of the lake were closed off from civilian use for military exercises. The submarines coming off the slips at Manitowoc had to be tested, and sailors at the Great Lakes Naval Training Station north of Chicago had to be trained, but most disruptive of all

Figure 19. USS *Robalo* ready to launch in Manitowoc, Wisconsin, 1943. A floating dry dock would take it from Lake Michigan to the Gulf of Mexico via the Illinois Waterway. Source: Naval History Center.

was the operation of two aircraft carriers on the lake during the war. World War II, at sea, was won by aircraft carriers and, specifically, by the pilots of the U.S. Navy. During the war, the U.S. was able to train sixty-five thousand naval aviators. While not all were destined for aircraft carrier duty, of those who were, 17,820 were trained on Lake Michigan's aircraft carriers. In addition, better than 22,000 flight deck crew members were trained on the lake. The idea of establishing a carrier force on the inland seas is generally credited to Commander Richard Whitehead of the Great Lakes Naval Training Station. Even before Pearl Harbor, he suggested that a Great Lakes vessel be refitted to serve as a training carrier. He was aware of the danger submarines posed to capital ships even in home waters, save, of course, for the

Figure 20. Aircraft carrier USS *Wolverine* in 1942 after being converted from a passenger steamer.
Source: Naval History Center.

Great Lakes. It was not until March 1942 that action was taken and two side-wheel-powered excursion vessels, the *Seeandbee* and the *Greater Buffalo*, were converted into the USS *Wolverine* and the USS *Sable*. By September the *Wolverine* had successfully trained its first pilot.[64]

Pilots attempted to qualify for carrier duty only after months of classroom instruction and flight training at terrestrial airfields. After that came the challenge to succeed in making ten (later eight) carrier landings and thus be awarded the wings of a naval aviator. Takeoffs from the converted carriers could be tricky. The *Wolverine* and *Sable* had flight decks only twenty-six feet above the water, much lower than the big fleet carriers, so when planes took off and dipped as they cleared the deck, pilots had to be

careful not to sink right on the waves. The danger of carrier landings for inexperienced pilots is amply demonstrated by the existence of more than 250 World War II–era warplanes on the bottom
of the lake. Most novices who splashed were quickly rescued,
but twenty-one young men lost their lives. Winter flights were
particularly risky owing to the harsh weather. Because the danger
of crashing into the lake was so great, pilots were required to
keep their cockpit canopy open so that if they hit the water, they
would have an easier time getting out of the sinking plane. The
weather made a strong impression on Lieutenant Junior Grade
George H. W. Bush, who later would pilot a torpedo plane in the
Pacific and become president of the U.S.: "I remember those
Great Lakes flights very well in the open cockpit that winter.
Coldest I ever was in my life."[65]

Lake Huron also became a practice war zone. The U.S. Army
operated aerial gunnery and aerial bombing training out of
Harbor Beach, Michigan, and Macomb County's Selfridge Field.
The Air National Guard base at Selfridge played a key role in
training a variety of squadrons that played a critical role in the
air war over Germany, among them the famed Tuskegee Airmen.
The Navy operated pilot training out of the Grosse Point Naval
Air Station. Many pilots who qualified for carrier landings on
Lake Michigan came there to practice attacking moving targets
on the open water. Of course, these same waters were heavily
trafficked by freighters supplying vital war industries. Fortunately, pilots were instructed not to interdict any large vessels.
Small craft were warned off by patrol boats and low-flying planes,
which would waggle their wings to warn operators that they
were straying into a live fire area.[66]

The major security concern on the Great Lakes were the locks
of the Sault Ste. Marie Canal. That waterway was the principal
outlet for the strategic iron ore deposits in northern Michigan
and Minnesota. Getting shiploads of that commodity to the steel
mills along the lower lakes was crucial to the ability of the U.S. to
function as an "arsenal of Democracy." Early in the war, the Lake
Carriers' Association petitioned the secretary of war to protect
the vital choke point from enemy sabotage. When the vulnera-
bility of the canal was finally investigated by the military, there
was an overreaction. Among the scenarios that emerged from an
army assessment was the fear of a German U-boat bringing a
dive bomber into Hudson's Bay and from there launching an

assault on the locks. Another outlined the possibility of a para-trooper attack on Sault Ste. Marie. As a result, in March 1942 the War Department hurried the 100th Coast Artillery to northern Michigan. They were joined there by the 131st Infantry Regiment and 399th Barrage Balloon Battalion as well as antiaircraft units. Army engineers began construction of airfields for fighter squadrons to protect the locks from the air. After a year of war, however, a more sober assessment of risk reduced the force guarding Sault Ste. Marie to a military police battalion.[67]

The Coast Guard was guilty of a similar overreaction in managing security of lake shipping. Early in 1942 it ordered that all lake freighters must have four armed guards aboard so that a twenty-four-hour watch could be mounted. This proved unpractical when it was discovered the Coast Guard had nowhere near enough manpower to staff such a guard and that few lake boats had the extra facilities to bunk four extra hands. A poor compromise was arrived at with the Coast Guard providing weapons to lake carriers' crews. This lasted a single season and resulted in "some unfortunate experiences" when poorly trained sailors unwisely used their rifles. Other measures included issuing a Coast Guard identity card to every verified U.S. citizen serving on the lakes and removing all enemy aliens from the boats, regardless of how long they had been in the country. By 1943 most lake masters had been made captains in the Coast Guard Reserve, with mates and engineers commissioned with the rank of lieutenant junior grade.[68]

Security was again a major concern on the Upper Great Lakes when President Roosevelt elected to take a fishing trip to Lake Huron in August 1943. Roosevelt had loved a summer break to fish and sail in the Bay of Fundy near his family retreat at Campobello Island, but the danger of German U-boat attack made that impractical in time of war. Instead, it was suggested that the islands and coves of Georgian Bay might prove a worthy substitute. The president brought with him a number of his most important military and civilian advisers. Between meetings regarding planning for the upcoming Quebec Conference with Winston Churchill and fishing excursions, Roosevelt was able to relax. The gun boat USS *Wilmette* was sent up from Lake Michigan to protect the party and to facilitate their fishing sorties. It did not seem to occur to any of the planners how inappropriate the *Wilmette* might be for that task. The ship had previously been known as the *Eastland*, and in 1915 she capsized in the Chicago River, killing 844 passengers in the worst disaster in Great Lakes history, hardly a recommendation for a presidential escort. The only security scare, however, came from another source. A German prisoner of war escaped from the Gravenhurst, Ontario, internment camp and was rumored to be moving in the direction of the presidential party. However, Canadian police picked up the Luftwaffe Oberleutnant as he tried to board a train. Hans Peter Krug was the closest the Nazi's ever came to the Sault Ste. Marie locks.[69]

That waterway was never busier than during World War II. The nation's political and military leaders, however, were keenly aware of how utterly dependent the war economy was on the operation of the Sault Ste. Marie locks. As early as December 1940 President Roosevelt ordered a study of a plan to construct an "overland ship railway." This hare-brained idea proposed to winch fully loaded ore freighters onto a special railway that would transport them around the twenty-foot differential between Lake Superior and the St. Mary's River. Sober analysis killed that idea, but it led to a plan to add a new lock to the two existing modern chambers that were already in use. The demand for a new lock was based on two considerations. A new facility could be made deeper than the other locks. A deeper lock would suit wartime demands by allowing ships to carry more iron ore in their holds, thereby delivering more each trip. A new lock would also help to ensure against any accidents or sabotage that might disrupt the existing canal structures. Congress approved the project in February 1942 and in short order more than one thousand workers were put to the task of building the lock. By July 1943 the facility was in operation. Named the MacArthur Lock, it played an important role in the lake marine's World War II performance.[70]

The Lake Carriers' Association made a useful if belated contribution to the safety of vital war shipping by introducing and supporting the adoption of fixed navigation courses on the lakes. Earlier in the century the association had dragged its feet for thirteen years after its own president had proposed separating up-bound vessels from the course taken by down-bound traffic. Such a plan was adopted in 1911 for Lake Huron. During World War II, the Lake Carriers' Association established a new series of navigational courses designed to create separate lanes for traffic on Lake Michigan, Lake Superior, and Lake Erie. To encourage compliance, the association reported deviations from the proscribed course to the head office of the company that owned the ship. The association appreciated that vessel masters needed a degree of latitude when directing their boats. Their guidelines read, "It is understood that masters may exercise discretion in departing from courses when ice and weather conditions are such as warrant it," but all such deviations had to be explained. Proscribed courses allowed vessels without radar to proceed with great confidence and speed when their vision was obscured, which in turn sped the delivery of cargoes strategic to the war effort.[71]

Special emergency regulations helped facilitate the movement of lake vessels. Peacetime load levels were expanded to increase the amount of ore or stone a boat was allowed to carry. The average cargo increased from 9,883 gross tons in 1940 to 10,170. A seven-day, twenty-four-hour schedule was established at docks so that loading and unloading proceeded with greater celerity. An emphasis on speed and efficiency reduced the average time spent in port discharging cargoes from fifteen to thirteen hours. Efficiency was critical because lake shipping was the best way to move iron ore, but that shipping halted each winter of necessity. By 1942 the average ore boat on the lakes traveled forty-five thousand miles during the 220-day-long shipping season. By contrast, the average railroad freight car only traveled between fifteen thousand and twenty thousand miles in 365 days of service. "As in the case of the tortoise and the hare," observed Alexander Wood, Lake Carriers' Association president, "the rate of speed, though low, is sufficient to win the race."[72]

During World War II, a half-billion tons of iron ore was torn from the Lake Superior ranges and hauled to mills along the lower lakes. Ore freighters were virtually in constant motion during the conflict. In 1939 the Pittsburgh Steamship Company, the maritime arm of U.S. Steel Corporation, had a fleet of more than seventy vessels—a bigger fleet of large ships than the U.S. Navy. They were put to maximum use for the war effort. Ship-to-shore radios, so long opposed by the Lake Carriers' Association, were employed to minimize any delays. Dispatchers monitored docking facilities and could redirect approaching vessels to ports prepared to accept immediate delivery. Throughout the war, the age-old battle with Mother Nature continued on the Great Lakes. Spurred by the heavy war production demands, shippers tried to push the start of the navigation season. In peacetime that meant April, but throughout the war attempts were made to begin shipping in March. In 1942 mild weather allowed the ore carriers to cast off on March 23. Unfortunately, a cold snap in early April led to a near disaster on Lake Superior. An ice blockage formed on Whitefish Bay and 120 vessels were stuck in a limbo between ice and a dangerous lee shore. It took weeks to restore the normal flow of vessels through the locks. Ice breaking became an increasingly important task for the Coast Guard. The service employed its cutters and tenders to the task as well as tug boats. The best icebreakers available from 1940 to 1944 were actually car ferries chartered by the Coast Guard. These unimpressive looking vessels were designed to carry rail cars across openwater stretches such as the Straits of Mackinac all year round. The best of these, such as the *Chief Wawatam* of the Mackinac Transportation Company, had spoon-shaped bows and three propellers (two aft and one in the bow) that allowed them to break through ice barriers. It was not until the fall of 1944 that a purpose-built icebreaker, the *Mackinaw*, was available to the Coast Guard.[73]

World War II saw a significant upgrading of freighters in the Great Lakes fleet. Vessels taken off the lakes and onto the ocean tended to be older, either obsolete packet-passenger ships or hulls laid down by the U.S. Maritime Commission in World War I. In September 1941 the Maritime Commission proposed to subsidize the construction of new ore carriers. The Office of Production Management had predicted there would not be enough ships available to meet the wartime demand for iron ore. Within a month, the commission had contracted with two shipbuilding firms to produce sixteen new 604-foot ore carriers. When the ships were launched, they were purchased by private lake carriers and put into service. At the same time, the government ensured the industry would not be stuck with excess capacity after the war by buying thirty-six older vessels, most of which were forty years old, from the companies and then leasing them back until the end of the war, when they would be scrapped.[74]

Great Lakes shipping was fundamental to U.S. military production during World War II. Detroit and Chicago led all American industrial centers in the value of war goods produced, topping $24 billion. Detroit-based Ford and Chrysler corporations between them produced more than a million trucks and tanks. Ford and Toledo-based Willys Overland factories churned out 647,343 jeeps for the military. Soviet, British, Canadian, Polish, as well as U.S. troops rode to victory on vehicles produced in the Great Lakes region and made from Lake Superior iron processed in foundries on Lake Michigan and Lake Erie. From Duluth to Buffalo, factories built the engines, ordinance, and chassis that made mechanized warfare possible. Generations of public investment in lighthouses, buoys, charts, canals, locks, and radio beacons allowed the Great Lakes to move the bulk raw materials that would be forged into the shield and then sword of the nation.[75]

7

May Their Lights Continue to Shine

1945–2000

In 1995 the U.S. Coast Guard put the Marblehead Lighthouse and sixteen other stations up for sale. The Marblehead sale in particular set off a wave of concern across the Great Lakes region. Built in 1821 on a point jutting into Lake Erie's Sandusky Bay, the Marblehead Light was the oldest on the inland seas. Cost cutting prompted the Coast Guard to privatize ownership of this and many other lighthouses as a way to transfer the maintenance and upkeep of the aged and exposed structures. To people who lived near the light towers, as well as the many thousands of maritime enthusiasts in the region, it seemed that privatization was the first step to extinguishing the lights altogether. While it was true that modern satellite systems were the state of the art in navigational aids, lighthouses were still treasured by the American people. To Dick Moehl of the Great Lakes Lighthouse Keepers Association, the lighthouses along the continent's waterways

Figure 21. Marblehead Lighthouse in Marblehead, Ohio. Photo taken by John
McCarty on April 9, 2005.
Source: Wikimedia Commons.

were to North America what castles are to Europe: scenic, romantic reminders of our relationship with the past.[1]

Inspired by that notion, Great Lakes folk singer and historian Lee Murdock penned a salute to the lighthouses of the inland seas. Titled "Deep Blue Horizon," the ballad is narrated from the perspective of the Marblehead Lighthouse, recalling the ever-changing boat traffic it had guided in its more than one hundred years of standing guard on Lake Erie's shores:

> I've seen the tall ships that have passed by the shore,
> the side wheeled steamers, the whale backs and more,
> the passenger packets, the self-unloaders,
> and even those noisy cigarette boaters,
> but all that I ask is don't let me go blind,
> let my light continue to shine.

Murdock captured a growing sentiment among the people of the Great Lakes region. For many, lighthouses had become landmarks in more than a navigational sense. They were symbols of a people's relationship with the lakes, a reminder of a heritage inspired by the thousands of men and women who lived and died on their waters. As the twentieth century drew to a close, the sweep of a lighthouse beacon became less important to those in peril on the water and more significant to those who lived on the land.[2]

Postwar Navigational Advances

The demise of the light tower as a critical navigational aid was accelerated by new maritime technologies, many of which were the result of wartime innovations. Ship-to-shore radio was fully embraced by 1945 after the Lake Carriers' Association finally gave up their resistance to government safety mandates. The ship-owners' association then boasted that the lakes had the largest and most integrated system of nonmilitary radio communication in the world. The Great Lakes had 580 vessels connected to seventy-five Coast Guard stations, fourteen commercial stations, fifty-seven radio beacons, and five weather bureau stations. Even before the war, such new navigational technologies prompted old-time sailors to complain that machines were taking the skill out of navigating the inland seas. In 1933 Charles Leach opined:

> There ain't no more real sailors no more. Hell, anybody who can drive a horse can drive one of them steamboats up and down here. B'god, they've got every little bend and bump in the bottom of the whole damn string of lakes and rivers marked for 'em and they carry electric range finders and radio an' every damn thing they can think of to help 'em; still, they run aground, have collisions and founder in storms.

Yet while old-timers reminisced about sailing in waters without buoys in "in all kinds of weather," even newer electronic equipment was making its way onto the modern steel freighters. Radar was the most important of these navigational devices made available in the wake of World War II.[3]

By and large the Lake Carriers' Association embraced the opportunity to bring the new wartime navigational aids to the Great Lakes. The organization played an active role in the Radio Technical Commission for Marine Services that the federal government created to coordinate "all phases of marine communications and electronic navigation systems." As early as the summer of 1944, the Lake Carriers' Association had a committee studying radar systems, with an eye for developing a system suited for the closed waters of the inland seas. That same year the U.S. Coast Guard deployed the first radar-equipped vessel on the lakes when its new ice-breaker cutter, the *Mackinaw*, was launched. Despite early interest by commercial shippers, the private sector proceeded cautiously, ever mindful of the cost involved in buying and operating sophisticated equipment.[4]

It was not until 1946 that a series of tests were conducted of the various civilian radar systems available. Indeed, there was stiff competition between electronics companies for the association's imprimatur. Six different radar systems were put through their paces. Some of the nation's leading companies, including Western Electric, General Electric, Westinghouse, Sperry, and Raytheon, sought to prove their systems. During the test period, no one radar system seems to have gained an upper hand. Certainly, the Western Electric radar designed by Bell Labs received the most press attention when it was installed on the SS *John T.*

Hutchinson, with the aid of an attractive Buffalo, New York, woman who won the contest to be "Miss Radar of the Great Lakes." Raytheon, despite not having a "Miss Radar" of their own, likely sold more units. Cost was a factor, as always, with units varying between $7,000 and $12,000 depending on range and sensitivity. In 1947 the Lake Carriers' Association announced something the U.S. Navy already knew, that radar was destined to become "not only an important safety device but a major instrument for navigation."[5]

Radar worked by bouncing a beam off objects in its path, be it an island, another ship, or a lighthouse. The return signal was captured by a dishlike antenna and displayed on a cathode ray radarscope. While a few small shipping companies were deterred by the cost of equipment, installation, and training, most Great Lakes shippers grasped the savings that could be accrued by employing this new type of navigational aid. Radar gave ship captains the confidence to maintain their cruising speed in spite of weather events such as fog. Radar made night navigation in tight passages such as the St. Mary's River or the St. Clair Flats safer and faster. In a 1947 test of a radar system designed for the Great Lakes, a U.S. Navy hydrographer was impressed with the way radar not only warned of approaching vessels but also indicated approaching squalls that, with a slight change of course, might be avoided. One shipping line estimated that the use of radar saved nearly forty hours of sailing time per month. Insurance costs were also lowered because of radar's ability to reduce the risk of both collision and groundings. The Pere Marquette Railway's car ferries were among the first fleets to fully adopt radar, gyrocompasses, and electronic direction finders. With these aids the fleet enjoyed an unbroken run of twenty straight years without a major accident. It is probable that no navigational aid from the first lighthouse to the present made a more significant impact on marine safety than the installation of radar on Great Lakes vessels.[6]

Veteran lake helmsman Fred Dutton was duly impressed the first time he worked in a pilothouse equipped with radar. He had begun his career at the ship's wheel in the days when a magnetic compass was the only navigational tool. His vessel, the *John T. Hutchinson*, was laboring through a fog-shrouded stretch of the Detroit River. "Although the visibility was only two or three hundred feet," he recalled, "the radar screen showed a clear out-line of the river, plainly depicting the shoreline on both sides and all islands and buoys—even spar buoys—as well as other vessels, in all directions." In his estimate, "radar hasn't taken all the danger out of piloting a ship, but it has eliminated a great deal of it." Of course, extreme weather conditions could create distortions on the radarscope. Snow, for example, could create interference, and heavy seas could sometimes result in distortion.[7]

Radar and ship-to-shore radio communication made Great Lakes navigation easier and safer but not risk free. The postwar years saw a number of notable disasters that reminded mariners and shipping companies that the inland seas on which they lived their lives were still a dangerous, even deadly, element. This was especially true in the weeks before the shipping season closed when the "witch of November" haunted the lakes. In November 1958, the crew of the 639-foot *Carl D. Bradley* found this out when they were caught in a gale off Lake Michigan's Gull Island. With awful suddenness, heavy seas broke the vessel in half. Only two members of the crew of thirty-five survived. Lake Huron was the site of a November gale that took the *Daniel J. Morrell* in November 1966. Seventy-mile-per-hour winds and seas running twenty-five feet in height battered and then broke apart the *Morrell*, leaving only a single man on a frozen life raft to tell the story of her sorry end. Most famous of the November wrecks was the 1975 sinking of the *Edmund Fitzgerald*. Celebrated in art, literature, and especially in song, the *Fitz* was an example of the way improved maritime technology was still not enough of an edge when a major gale locked its jaws on a vessel. The *Edmund Fitzgerald*'s ship-to-shore radio allowed it to receive updated weather forecasts and adjust its course accordingly. It had radar, although as the storm reached its peak, wind and waves tore off the antenna and the screens went dark. Still, radio allowed the *Fitzgerald* to stay in contact with another storm-tossed vessel, the *Arthur Anderson*, which shared its radar readings. One theory of the *Fitzgerald*'s sinking points to a piece of technology the ship did not have. Fathometers indicate the depth of the water through which a ship was passing. The lack of this device would have been fatal if the ship, as has been speculated, had briefly grounded while passing over the shoals north of Caribou Island. Canadian lake charts, it turned out, did not accurately indicate the location and extent of these shoals. In any event, the marine technology that the *Fitzgerald* had, and that allowed it to make 748 safe round-trips on the Great Lakes, logging more than a million miles, was not good enough on the night of November 10.[8]

The loss of the *Carl D. Bradley*, the *Daniel J. Morrell*, and the *Edmund Fitzgerald* achieved legendary status because they were spectacular exceptions to the increasing safety and enhanced reliability of Great Lakes shipping thanks to the new technology. In the postwar period, such events were subjected to detailed forensic investigation by the Lake Carriers' Association and by the U.S. Coast Guard in an effort to prevent future losses. Of course, lesser accidents still occurred, such as vessels grounding on shifting sandbars or minor collisions in harbors or while docking, but all such incidents had to be reported to the Coast Guard so that a series of minor problems did not lead to an unexpected major failure. The introduction of Coast Guard aircraft patrols also enhanced the speed of lifesaving response. All these factors ensured that the loss of life so common in the nineteenth and early twentieth centuries became increasingly rare in the postwar period.[9]

The World War II military emergency led to another system for enhancing navigation of ships that complemented radar. The Long Range Navigation system, nicknamed LORAN, was an outgrowth of Royal Air Force and U.S. Navy innovations. LORAN was a timing-based navigation system that worked by measuring the time between when a signal was sent and when it was received. If a ship could receive signals simultaneously from a series of diverse land-based stations, then it could determine its exact position on the basis of its distance from the signal stations. The Navy used it for convoys during the Battle of the Atlantic, where heavy storms often made it difficult for vessels to stay on course. The system was even more important in the Pacific, where convoys often had to make rendezvous amid the vast distances of that ocean. Early systems with numerous vacuum tubes and bulky steel housing made them too heavy for anything but shipboard use. By 1943, however, more compact systems were developed, and LORAN-A units played a major role in guiding B-29 bombers on their long-distance raids on the Japanese home islands. In the 1950s an improved LORAN system was developed with much greater daytime reach. This was LORAN-C, which for many years was reserved strictly for military use.

In the 1970s LORAN-C became a widely used aid to civilian navigation. The new system was highly accurate (to better than 0.25 nautical mile), highly accessible (99.7 percent availability), available twenty-four hours a day, and functional in all weather conditions. A chain of LORAN stations along the lakes was operational by 1967. Originally, LORAN receivers only provided the navigator with time difference calculations, and it was necessary to consult a chart that was overlain with LORAN so the time difference could be converted to longitude and latitude. This allowed a vessel's exact position to be plotted. By the late 1980s, however, the best shipboard LORAN receivers were able to convert the time difference data and pinpoint a vessel's actual location. Advanced systems also allowed the mariner to enter established waypoints into the system, such as the vessel's home berth, channel markers, buoys, dangerous shoals, and even shipwreck sites. Receivers also were equipped with alarms that sounded when fixed waypoints were approached. The last generation of LORAN-C units could even determine course and average speed of a vessel, all of which automated the task of navigation. Amateur users of LORAN, however, were often unaware of some of the system's limitations, such as the degree to which electrical high-tension wires or steel bridges might throw off a location reading by several hundred yards. Nonetheless, LORAN-C was a remarkable tool for the sailor. By the 1990s there were an estimated one million LORAN users in the U.S., of whom better than 80 percent were maritime related.[10]

The master LORAN station for the Great Lakes region was in Dana, Indiana, a community in the east-central part of the state, 150 miles from the shores of the inland seas. The secondary, or slave station, at Baudette, Minnesota, was more than 200 miles from Lake Superior. The secondary station at Seneca, New York, was actually the closest to the Great Lakes, being only about 50 miles from Lake Ontario. The remaining two secondary stations at Malone, Florida, and Boise City, Oklahoma, were not even in the region. Each of these stations were operated by Coast Guard crews, although for a time in the late 1960s they were assisted by U.S. Air Force personnel, while more "Coastie" technicians were being trained to handle the expanding system. They performed a task that was just as vital, if not more so, than the original lighthouse keepers perched in towers above the surf. Originally, LORAN stations had fairly large crews of between fifteen and twenty men. In the 1980s, automated equipment was installed, and generally a crew of five men or women ensured that the station continued to send its thirty-three-and-a-half pulses per second from the seven-hundred-foot skeletal transmission tower. Stations consisted of crew housing, a generator building (which was necessary in case there was a disruption to the electrical grid), the tower, and the transmitter building. Crew members would spend their "watch" monitoring computer screens in windowless rooms surrounded by rows of machines. Boredom was a real problem that was only relieved by coffee while on duty and outdoor recreation when off the job. Like the lightkeepers of old, they were diligent in their duty. If, on rare occasions, the station's signal went dead, the crew could spring into action and, often in less than a minute, get it "back on air and in tolerance." Failure to do so could lead to stiff reprimands. Serious transmission interrupts were rare and usually only occurred when old and outdated equipment broke down. While LORAN duty was relatively easy, it was not popular with most Coast Guard men who expected duty near blue water. Unfortunately, it was not fully realized until the 1990s that some landlocked "Coasties" had been exposed to dangerous levels of radiation from high-powered vacuum tubes. LORAN crews won no lifesaving medals, but their remote service came at the hidden cost of an elevated risk of cancer later in life.[11]

As effective as LORAN was, it was no substitute for an experienced captain and attentive deck crews. Apparently neither was present in December 1997 when the $25 million 634-foot freighter *MV Buffalo* made the turn to leave the Detroit River and enter Lake Erie, promptly plowing head-on into the Detroit River Lighthouse. The light had been guarding the key navigation point since 1885. The *MV Buffalo* had been passing it on a regular basis for better than twenty years. The seas were calm that morning and the weather was clear. The *Buffalo's* radar and LORAN systems were fully functional. The lighthouse lantern was flashing at its normal six-second intervals, although a buildup of ice may have dimmed the beam. Unfortunately, the *Buffalo's* bridge crew, which had set their automatic pilot toward the lighthouse, had gone below to collect mail that had just been delivered. One crewman noticed the impending collision but could not alert the wheelhouse in time. The vessel hit the lighthouse with a sickening sound as steel bent and buckled. Amazingly, the well-built, spark-plug-style lighthouse that sat atop cement caissons sunk twenty feet into a shoal was undamaged save for a few minor cracks. The proud modern vessel limped away with a bow "pushed in like a tin can," a twenty-foot gash, and $1.2 million in needed repairs. Past met present that morning, and the lighthouse, listed on the National Register of Historic Places, a symbol of another century's commitment to navigational safety, came away neither bloodied nor bowed. The hapless crew of the *MV Buffalo* was discharged by the chagrined owners of the damaged vessel.[12]

Such negligence was rare because of the increased rigor of training received by the officers of lake vessels. Government examinations were required before deck officers or engineers were given the licenses necessary to serve on a Great Lakes vessel. Beginning in 1975 the Coast Guard operated a school to train Great Lakes crew in the proper use of radar, the gyrocompass, and later LORAN-C. Increasingly after 1970 ships' officers were graduates of the Great Lakes Maritime Academy in Traverse City, Michigan, which eventually offered a four-year Bachelor of Science degree program. The sophisticated technology available after World War II ensured the demise of the old tradition of crew members working their way up from deck hand to mate to master of the vessel. Yet even with formal education and high-tech navigation tools, there still was a need for seamanship and experience. Historian and former able seaman J. C. Martin was on the bridge of a lake steamer headed for the Straits of Mackinac when all electronic navigational aids suddenly went out just as the vessel needed to make a course correction at the entrance to the fog-shrouded straits. The captain, a veteran of a life on the lakes, took the helm and, relying on his long familiarity with the channel, guided the ship past several rocky reefs and safely into the Straits.[13]

The reign of LORAN as the most widely used navigational aid on the Great Lakes was brief—over in less than a generation. In 2010 the U.S. Coast Guard ordered the closing of all of its twenty-four signal stations. Crews were reassigned from their landlocked stations and the equipment was sold off. The sudden demise of this highly successful and widely used navigation tool was caused by the rise of a satellite-based navigation system known as the Global Positioning System or GPS. Like LORAN, GPS employed a time-difference radio navigation technique, but instead of a chain of land-based transmission stations, communication satellites in low Earth orbit provided the necessary signals.[14]

Like LORAN before it, GPS was a system developed by the military. Its origins were directly tied to the Cold War. In 1957 the Soviet Union launched the first space satellite, Sputnik. Scientists at Johns Hopkins University's Applied Physics Laboratory measured the Doppler shift as Sputnik passed over the U.S.[15] This allowed them to determine the satellite's orbit, but conversely, those same measurements indicated their exact position on Earth. The finding immediately opened up the possibility of using satellites as navigational aids. The U.S. Navy first explored this possibility in the early 1960s with the goal of locating ballistic missile submarines on long-range patrols. There was also the hope that satellite systems might help improve the accuracy of naval and air force weapon systems. A system called Transit was developed that used seven polar orbiting satellites and several land-based stations to send navigational signals. By 1967 Transit was made available to civilian users and enjoyed some popularity with the commercial marine and a few elite pleasure craft operators. Transit satellites had no timing devices aboard, and so land-based receivers had to do the calculations, which could take as long as fifteen minutes. Transit's significance was that it proved the efficacy of satellite-based navigation. At the same time, the U.S. Air Force and Army were working on satellite-based navigation programs that included the use of atomic clocks. The Department of Defense eventually united the research efforts under an interservice program, which between 1974 and 1979 tested something they called the NAVSTAR Global Positioning System. The early orientation of the program was toward monitoring atmospheric nuclear tests. Then in 1983 Soviet jet fighters cravenly shot down a Korean civilian airplane that had strayed into the USSR's air space. In response, President Ronald Reagan offered the use of GPS to civilian airlines as soon as it was fully operational. Unfortunately, the system's development was hindered by the 1986 explosion of the space shuttle *Challenger*, which was the principal means the U.S. had to launch new satellites. Nonetheless, by 1994 GPS was operational when the twenty-fourth NAVSTAR satellite was successfully put into orbit. By the beginning of the twenty-first century, seventeen thousand U.S. military aircraft were outfitted with GPS and sixty thousand portable military receivers were deployed. In 2000 accurate GPS receivers were, for the first time, made available to individual consumers for personal use. Within a decade so-called smart phones equipped with GPS apps provided sophisticated navigational assistance to the ordinary consumer.[16]

In 1999 the U.S. Coast Guard, in cooperation with the Department of Transportation and the U.S. Army Corps of Engineers, introduced a modified GPS system to the Great Lakes region, Differential GPS (DGPS). This was an augmented GPS system that corrected the small variation that can occur in signals sent from outer space. It allowed vessels to receive their position to within one to five meters of their actual location. This highly accurate plotting was seen as necessary for ships in confined waters or in approaching harbors. Differential GPS was only for use in U.S. coastal waters and the Great Lakes. To support DGPS, stations were established throughout the U.S. to correct the signals sent from the orbiting GPS satellites. Eleven of these stations in the U.S. and two in Canada provide the corrected signals to lake mariners, while eighty-five stations were needed to provide coverage over the entire land mass of the U.S. and Puerto Rico. These new technologies revolutionized the task of piloting a Great Lakes vessel. Satellite data was fed into an electronic chart that allowed sailing plans to be loaded and reused for an entire season. An automatic identification system connected to the electronic chart allowed a vessel master to also see the name, location, direction, and speed of all other lakers.[17]

The Unrealized Promise of the St. Lawrence Seaway

The long-dreamed-of, the often-planned, the ever-frustrated St. Lawrence Seaway was finally born on June 26, 1959. President Dwight D. Eisenhower and Queen Elizabeth II presided over the opening, justly proud of the largest such project ever completed through the joint efforts of two countries. The queen described the new waterway as "one of the outstanding engineering accomplishments of modern times." Eisenhower recalled the long struggle to build the seaway and celebrated the "culmination of the dreams of thousands of individuals on both sides of our common Canadian–U.S. border." The royal yacht *Britannia* passed through six new locks on the St. Lawrence River, being lifted a full sixty-nine meters before cruising across Lake Ontario to the Welland Canal and its eight chambers. Improvements on the Detroit River and Lake St. Clair, as well as the already enlarged Sault Ste. Marie Canal, completed the seaway system.[18]

The press celebrated it as "one of the most incredible engineering and construction jobs . . . ever attempted." Economists predicted the Midwest would experience "an unprecedented boom of industrial expansion." One Chicago magazine went so far as to predict 890,000 new industrial jobs for that Lake Michigan city alone. Within a few weeks, as many as thirty ships per day were moving through the new system of locks. By the end of the shipping season it was estimated that six thousand commercial vessels had made the passage between the Great Lakes and the Atlantic Ocean, as well as an additional six hundred smaller pleasure craft. The largest vessel to do so was the Norwegian tanker *Solviken* at 610 feet. The long-deferred seaway seemed to be on its way to justifying its optimistic boosters. To international strategists, the seaway represented the triumph of a global strategic and economic vision on the part of the U.S. and Canada, in which local concerns were pushed aside in favor of a new prosperity based on international trade. Two world wars in the twentieth century had transformed both countries, but especially the U.S., from isolationism to economic and military activism.[19]

Amid the celebrations and anticipations, there were disquieting voices raised. Despite the tremendous publicity for the seaway, traffic that first year fell five thousand vessels short of what had been projected. George Horne, transportation reporter for the *New York Times*, predicted trouble ahead when he noted, "Many experts now fear that the seaway was underbuilt; that new and larger locks will be needed in the future." This fear was warranted. While the locks of the Panama Canal were 1,000 feet long and 110 feet wide, the seaway chambers were only 766 feet by 80 feet. The seaway project had been badly retarded by its long gestation and botched legislative delivery. "Few projects have been so bitterly opposed," one political insider recalled, "or inspired so many opinions, arguments, legal battles, treaties and inter-government memoranda." The navigational advantages of the seaway were less important to many of the project's supporters than the hydroelectric energy and cheap power that would be generated by the dams that needed to be built along the St. Lawrence. Railroad lobbyists as well as Gulf Coast and Atlantic seaboard representatives saw their special interests threatened by the seaway's potential impact on transportation patterns. While they eventually lost the battle to get the seaway built, their continued opposition ensured that the waterway languished. Their political influence diverted federal cargoes that could have been more cheaply shipped via the lakes to rails and East Coast ports. Even the Lake Carriers' Association, which normally supported all navigation improvements, was cool to the seaway and the prospect of oceangoing competition. The seaway offered cheaper transportation to heartland manufacturers shipping products abroad. However, it also was a slower route. Even one extra week in transit was regarded as an unacceptable burden by some businesses that instead used the railroad to get their goods to saltwater ports. Interstate trucks were another factor that siphoned off traffic from the waterway. While the St. Lawrence Seaway was being built, the U.S. Congress was funding another major construction project of greater transformative power—the Interstate Highway System that knitted the interior and coastal regions of the country together with high-speed roads. The seaway opened when cloverleafs had only just started sprouting. By the mid-1970s most interstate highways were in operation and the seaway began to experience a steady decline in ship traffic. In the late 1980s, it was hoped that the development of container traffic would revive the flagging seaway. Containers are large steel boxes that are loaded with general cargo and protected from damage and pilfering. Chicago, Duluth, and other Great Lakes ports invested in new container terminals to capitalize on the trade, only to be frustrated by aggressive competition from the railroads and the development of giant container ships that could not fit in the undersized locks of the seaway.[20]

Such were the problems following the opening of the seaway that as early as 1961 seaway executives adopted an apologetic tone when meeting with veteran lake mariners. "At times I have felt, that some people believed the seaway was created for the avowed purpose of ruining their livelihood," said Harry C. Schriver of the Seaway Development Corporation to a Lake Carriers' meeting. "There are perhaps shipmasters who at times have felt the seaway was designed as a hazard to navigation." Both propositions were to a certain extent true. In the first year of the seaway's operation, the shipment of grain by lake freighters was quickly reduced by half of its past volume by the arrival of foreign flag ships at the elevators in Duluth-Superior. That first year also saw a flood of ships with no experience on the lakes pushing into its broad waters and narrow channels without the use of experienced pilots. The result should have been predictable, with one vessel sunk, several collisions, numerous near misses, and many lake sailors shaking their fists at the oblivious newcomers. A common complaint about the saltwater ships was that they ran too fast in narrow channels, creating a heavy wash for riparian property owners and complicating navigation for lake freighters, but because of their hull structure, some ocean vessels could not maintain steerage at a slower speed. The worst was the loss of the Liberian-flagged freighter *Monrovia*. As was typical of ships sailing under a flag of convenience, the *Monrovia* lacked radar, and amid thick mist and rising seas became confused and strayed from its proper heading and into the downbound lake traffic. The Canadian vessel *Royalton* slammed into her port side. While the crew were all rescued, the *Monrovia* went under Huron's green seas. A year later a second Liberian ship met its end on Lake Michigan. The *Francisco Morazan* was trying to escape the lakes before the onset of winter. With an inexperienced master, a crew of only twelve, engine problems, and again no radar, the ship departed Chicago on November 28—destined for trouble. As she entered the Manitou Passage, the captain became confused by heavy snow and piloted the ship onto the rocks at South Manitou Island, where she still sits to this day, a total loss. As unprepared for the lakes as the ocean ships often were, Great Lakes ports were too often unprepared to handle their international customers. Only a handful of ports were deep enough in 1959 to accept the draft of ocean ships. Even those that could lacked the dock space for more than a couple of ships at a time, which resulted in the foreign-flagged ships sometimes having to wait more than a week to tie up. It took a couple of years before harbor improvements were completed, and eventually lake pilots were assigned to get the "salties" safely through the lakes.[21]

Not only did the seaway fail to deliver on its promised boon to the Great Lakes economy, but it actually hurt some Great

Lakes ports. Since 1826 and the opening of the Erie Canal, Buffalo had been the great transit terminal for the grain trade. But with the improvement of locks along the St. Lawrence River, a large share of the trade began to move north through Canada. International vessels from Baltic or Black Sea ports picked up grain at Duluth-Superior and took it directly to saltwater through the seaway, diverting shipments that in the past went first to Buffalo's elevators. The seaway also greatly improved Montreal's position in the trade, as the enhanced St. Lawrence waterway was, for some cargoes, a more efficient conduit than Buffalo's barge or rail connections to New York City. Eastbound vessels might make port at Duluth, Chicago, Detroit, or Cleveland but bypass Buffalo as they passed through the Welland Canal, Lake Ontario, and the seaway to Montreal. Buffalo's civic leaders anticipated this result, and they had vigorously lobbied against the 1954 legislation that funded seaway construction. When the grain shipments to Buffalo tailed off, the flour mills and breweries, once major employers, declined. Waterfront industries, such as shipbuilding and repair, closed when vessel traffic declined. Buffalo's population, which had grown in every decade since the opening of the Erie Canal, began a decline that continued in every decade since the opening of the seaway. Once the "Queen City of the Lakes," Buffalo was dethroned by the seaway.[22]

Automobile manufacturing and steelmaking were twin pillars of heartland industry in 1959 America. Steelmakers saw the seaway as an avenue to access new iron ore mines in Quebec and as an inexpensive way to ship their steel abroad. An Interstate Steel executive enthused, "You can ship from Chicago to Antwerp for the same price you can truck a ton of steel from Pittsburgh to Chicago—about $13." Unfortunately for U.S. steelmakers, the opposite was also true. The seaway reduced the cost of foreign steelmakers to compete in the American market. The mammoth mill complexes along the south shore of the lakes found themselves losing market share to more modern, government-subsidized plants in Asia and South America. In time steel became one of the main imports brought into the industrial heartland by foreign-flagged vessels. In this regard, the seaway hurt rather than helped the regional economy. Detroit also was disappointed by the impact of the seaway. In the heady days when the waterway was under construction, Chrysler Motors had predicted that

80 percent of its exports could now go out to the world on ships using the lakes; instead, American automakers received an unwelcome surprise when cargo ships from Germany began to unload Volkswagen Beetles, the "Love Bug" of the 1960s, onto Great Lakes wharves. The first year of the seaway, ships brought 1,620 Volkswagens to Chicago. A year later Windy City importers expected 8,000 of the Nazi-era "people's car." At Kenosha, Wisconsin, more than one thousand Beetles were unloaded at a dock adjacent to an American Motors Corporation plant that built small, fuel-efficient American cars. By 1988 the plant was closed, throwing fifty-five hundred workers, 10 percent of the town's population, out of a job. During the 1980s, in part because of the seaway's failure to live up to expectations, what had been America's industrial engine declined and the region became disparaged as "the rust belt."[23]

The seaway had a more salutary impact on the Canadian side of the lakes. The Canadian lake fleet had always been smaller than the American in terms of numbers of vessels but also the size of those vessels. If Canadian shippers wanted to reach their nation's great port at Montreal, their hulls could not exceed the modest size of the St. Lawrence locks. The seaway increased the size of those locks from 261 feet in length to 766 feet, and this led to a revolution in Canadian shipbuilding. Sixty-two new ships slipped into the water from northern dry docks. Other older vessels were lengthened to seaway size, and together, the carrying capacity of Canadian shipping more than doubled, almost equaling that of the American fleet by 1970. The design of these new ships sailing under the maple leaf impacted the future of inland seas navigation. The majority of these new lakers did away with the distinctive double superstructure of the inland seas that featured a pilothouse forward and crew's quarters in the stern. Like the newer vessels on saltwater, the next generation of lake ships had a single stern mounted superstructure.[24]

The Changing Environment of Great Lakes Navigation

The 1970s and 1980s were hard times on the Great Lakes, and across the region thousands of people still shiver in the cold shadow of those years. Instead of a panacea, the seaway was more the harbinger of a new era of global competition and environmental problems that would reshape navigation on the inland seas. Industrial plants, particularly steel and automobile, which were built early in the twentieth century and which operated at such a high level during World War II, were outdated and inefficient by the 1970s. Labor contracts and work rules that made sense during boom years became a burden in the face of foreign competition and corporate leaders' failure to invest in modernization. Heavy industry did not die in Chicago, Detroit, Buffalo, Toledo, Erie, or Cleveland, but those cities did lose market share and shed workers like an autumn oak. Since the beginning of the nineteenth century, the region had grown dramatically in population, production, and wealth. It now had to adjust to an era of circumscribed growth, altered expectations, and limited natural resources.

The shipping of iron and coal on the Great Lakes had made the region the great "arsenal of Democracy." Yet in the 1970s both of these backbones of the lake marine underwent profound shifts. Coal was the fuel that powered industrial production and generated urban electrical grids. The transport of coal had traditionally been a commodity transfer from east to west. Railroads brought coal from the Appalachian mines to Lake Erie ports such as Ashtabula, Erie, or Toledo where it was loaded on vessels bound for cities and production centers on the upper lakes. Yet new efficiencies by railroads made it increasingly more economical to move coal west by rail. Unit trains assembled near the mines and composed completely of coal cars destined for terminals at Midwest power plants began to take a large share of the trade. In this way, the Lake Erie ports were completely bypassed. At the same time that the east-to-west coal trade declined, new environmental regulations in the 1970s made western low-sulphur coal preferable to the output from some West Virginia mines. Coal began to move from west to east as great open-pit mines in Wyoming sent their product by train to Duluth-Superior, from where it was taken by lakers to Lake Michigan or Huron ports. Changes in the federal Clean Air Act of 1970, therefore, helped alter one of the major commodity trades on the lakes.[25]

The transport of iron ore for steel production also experienced a profound shift in the 1970s. For nearly one hundred years, the iron ranges of the Lake Superior region had provided high-quality ore for the forges of the ever-expanding American economy. By the 1950s, however, high-grade ore deposits neared exhaustion, and mining companies began to turn their attention to processing formations that previously had been regarded as dross. Their attention focused on taconite, a sedimentary rock in which iron ore was intermixed with quartz, chert, or dolomite. Unlike high-grade ore, which was as much as 90 percent pure iron, taconite was 70 percent non-ore rock. Early in the twentieth century, mining companies had experimented with trying to process taconite, which was much more abundant than high-grade ore. The cost of doing so, however, could not be justified while the Mesabi Range was still producing an abundance of its quality ore. After the intensive production of the World War II years, the situation was vastly different, and it was clear that the future of Lake Superior mining depended on making taconite processing pay. The key breakthrough was made by E. W. Davis, a University of Minnesota scientist who found a way to pulverize the taconite, separate the ore, and roll it into small, high-grade pellets. While this procedure was costly, once the taconite was in pellet form it could be more economically employed in steel-making. The creation of taconite pellets also greatly affected the transportation of iron ore on the lakes.[26]

Two new ports were created on Lake Superior to produce and transport taconite. Both Silver Bay, fifty miles northeast of Duluth, and Taconite Harbor further up the coast were company towns and privately built ports. Silver Bay was constructed by the Reserve Mining Company, with a capacity to service four to five iron boats a day. Lake Superior provided the large amount of water needed to roll taconite ore into the small round pellets, and it proved a convenient and unfortunate dumping ground for the large amount of tailings left over from pellet production. For twenty-five years, the Reserve Mining Company dumped tailings into the lake, contaminating its pure waters with cancer-causing asbestos particles. The dumping was not stopped until 1980 amid great controversy and numerous lawsuits. Taconite Harbor did not dump tailings into Lake Superior, as its pellets were processed inland. Taconite pellets also helped lead to a new generation of Great Lakes freighters. Taconite pellets can be more easily loaded or discharged than the red hematite ore that once was the mainstay of the Mesabi Range. The uniform, small, round pellets are moved easily from hopper cars to vessel holds and discharged via conveyor belts. Because taconite is a refined and concentrated iron product, it has much greater density and, therefore, can constitute a heavier burden than traditional cargoes like hematite or coal. In this way, the specific properties of taconite and a renewed emphasis on efficiency helped to give birth in the 1970s to a new generation of superfreighters on the American side of the lakes, many of them one thousand feet in length, specializing solely in taconite transport.

Canadian mills adopted a different solution to the decline of high-grade ore in the Lake Superior mines. Northern Quebec had ample supplies of quality ore, and transporting the iron to mills along the northern rim of the lakes created a new traffic flow for Canadian ships. A steady stream of six- to seven-hundred-foot Canadian ore carriers transited the St. Lawrence Seaway and docked at the port of Sept-Iles in the Gulf of St. Lawrence. Sept-Iles quickly became one of the most heavily trafficked ports in the Dominion. The port's excellent rail connections to the heavily forested interior also made it a source of newsprint for Great Lakes cities. The seaway was a boon to Canada's steel industry, which became the largest foreign rival to the troubled American mills.

In 1969 the U.S. Army Corps of Engineers opened a new twelve-hundred-foot-long lock at Sault Ste. Marie. In anticipation of this, the Bethlehem Steel Company announced it would build a one-thousand-foot freighter to supply taconite to its new steel plant at Burns Harbor, Indiana. The *Stewart J. Cort* was the first of a new class of giant lake vessels. Indicative of the decline of Great Lakes industries, this new supership did not roll off the stocks of an inland seas shipbuilder. The bow and stern sections were built on the Mississippi Gulf Coast, brought under their own power along the Atlantic Coast and up the St. Lawrence Seaway to Erie, Pennsylvania, where the huge midship cargo hold was attached. The construction process took nearly three years, but when it was done, the steel company had a ship that could carry fifty-eight thousand tons of taconite, two and a half times more cargo than the seven-hundred-foot vessels the *Stewart J. Cort* replaced. As big as she was, the *Cort* was fairly nimble thanks to its twin screws, twin rudders, and bow and stern thrusters that allowed her to move in and out of port unassisted. Unlike previous bulk carriers, such as the famed *Edmund Fitzgerald*, the *Cort* traveled "light," with its hold empty from Indiana to Lake Superior. This was in part because of the decline in the movement of Appalachian coal from east to west but also because the *Cort* was tailormade for taconite. Between 1972 and 1981 a dozen more one-thousand-footers were put into service on the American side of the lake. Their size prevented them from transiting the Welland Canal or the St. Lawrence, which in part explained why Canadian shipping companies did not embrace the design. The superfreighters rendered a large number of older, smaller vessels obsolete. Between 1966 and 2006, the number of U.S.-flagged vessels engaged in bulk transportation on the lakes declined from 154 to a mere 51. This was a far cry from the 2,400 cargo vessels that crisscrossed the lakes at the start of the twentieth century. It is ironic that the safer the lakes became to navigate, the fewer the vessels that did so. In some ways it was that safety that made it economical to invest the vast sums needed to build a thousand-footer.[27]

The move from hematite to taconite also impacted the length of the navigation season on the Great Lakes. Natural ore contained moisture, and in cold weather it would freeze in ore cars when being transported to the loading docks and could not be dumped into the holds of ships. Low winter temperatures could also freeze ore in the hold of a vessel, making it impossible to unload until warm weather. Taconite pellets are dry and could be transported in any weather. This created a demand for extending the navigation season on the lakes into the winter months. This had been attempted with very mixed results during World War II. At the end of 1944, the government deployed to the lakes a new Coast Guard cutter, the *Mackinaw*, reputed to be the "most powerful icebreaker in the world." Yet the *Mackinaw*'s duties were largely restricted to clearing late spring ice from harbor approaches. The new superfreighters that came into use in the 1970s were all equipped with reinforced bows for ice breaking. Between 1971 and 1979 the Corps of Engineers and the Coast Guard cooperated in a congressionally authorized experiment of keeping the lakes open for navigation into February. During the mild 1974–76 winters, Great Lakes shipping operated continuously. However, a serious recession in 1980 brought an end to the program as demand for iron and coal declined. Environmentalists expressed reservations regarding winter navigation's impact on shoreline erosion and the increased chance of accidents and oil spills, nor was the Lake Carriers' Association entirely sold on the prospect of year-round operation. The winter months were an important time to lay vessels up for maintenance and upgrades. Yet when the economy rebounded, the Coast Guard was charged with several regular programs of winter ice breaking. Operation Taconite was the program to keep Lake Superior and the St. Mary's River open to ore boats shuttling between the mines and mills. The smaller Operation Coal Shovel kept open a navigation channel between Toledo's coal docks and Detroit power plants, and Operation Oil Can ensured the occasional delivery of oil in the Green Bay and Grand Traverse Bay area. Winter became an especially busy season for the Eighth Coast Guard District. In addition to ice breaking, the service had to retrieve 1,282 buoys and replace about half of those with smaller lighter wintermarks that could withstand ice damage. The government also had to manage ice fenders at locks and bubbler systems at key locations, like the St. Mary's River. These tubes, placed on the lake bottom, agitated the water and inhibited ice formation. While global climate change also became a factor in enabling winter navigation, the economics of the steel industry generally did not support the extra cost entailed by year-round sailings. Freighters frequently sailed into January but typically laid up for February and March.[28]

From the 1970s onward, concern over the broader ecological impact of lake shipping became an increasingly important factor in the Great Lakes Region. The Environmental Protection Agency was the lead department assessing the environmental and social impact of winter navigation. That agency, created by President Richard Nixon in 1970, also came to play a major role in the planning of harbor and channel improvements. Since the beginning of heavy industry along the Great Lakes, the waterways had been used as a dump site for unwanted by-products and wastewater. As a result, the bottoms of harbors and rivers became coated with toxic sediment. The deepening of heavily used water courses, therefore, was not just a navigational issue but also one fraught with public health implications. The bottom of the Detroit River, one of the most heavily trafficked stretches of the Great Lakes system, was polluted with the waste from the heavily industrialized Rouge River. The Calumet and the Cuyahoga Rivers similarly were beset by polychlorinated biphenyls (PCBs) and other heavy metals from generations of coke and steel production. Dredging such waterways created two major environmental problems: where would the toxic sediment be deposited, and what would be the impact of dredging on downstream waters? As much as environmentalists would have loved to see a river bed or harbor cleaned of dangerous deposits, the process of doing so inevitably stirred up sediments that could be carried to new, less polluted areas and into drinking water. These were issues that came up every time it was necessary to undertake dredging to maintain the twenty-seven-foot channel required by current lake vessels. Millions of dollars of new costs became necessary to safely landfill toxic sediment. One impact of these new environmental protection realities was to make prohibitive the deepening of lake channels to a thirty- or thirty-five-foot depth necessary for a projected new generation of even bigger superfreighters. In many ways, winter navigation was a preferable way to increase the volume of shipping without having to reengineer the channels.[29]

The growing complexity of something like harbor dredging, which has been going on regularly since the 1830s, illustrates the way navigation issues on the Great Lakes no longer took precedence. In the 1960s and 1970s, commercial use of the lakes increasingly took a secondary or tertiary position to issues of drinking water, recreation, and ecosystem health. A turning-point moment came in the fight over the Indiana Dunes on Lake Michigan. Since the 1920s, environmentalists had advocated the creation of a national park to protect thirty-five miles of shoreline dunes and bogs. In the 1950s Bethlehem Steel Corporation and the Indiana General Assembly selected the area as the site of a major new industrial harbor and state-of-the-art steel processing plant. In 1966 a "compromise" national park unit was created, but right in the middle of it was Burns Harbor (aka Port of Indiana) with its huge steel plant and mountains of coal. Economics won out over environmental amenities at Indiana Dunes, but the fight played a major role in activating public concern for the latter. The public "woke up" to the fact that 86 percent of Lake Michigan's shoreline and 70 percent of Lake Erie's was covered by housing or industry. In the wake of the fight, large sections of the Great Lakes were set aside as national lakeshores and state parks. These included Sleeping Bear Dunes on Lake Michigan and Apostle Islands and Pictured Rocks on Lake Superior as well as scores of smaller state parks. The growing use of the lakes as a source of recreation would eventually play an important role in the perception and preservation of lighthouses along the inland seashore.[30]

Redundant Sentinels:
Lighthouse Automation and Decommissioning

With radar providing mariners an electronic picture of what was in front and around their vessels, and LORAN and later DGPS providing pinpoint plotting of their exact position, the beacon of a lighthouse was regarded by some as a redundant aid to navigation. Yet the lighthouse towers and paper charts that for centuries had been used by mariners to locate their position and steer clear of hazards still had a role to play. Not every sport fisherman who put a small boat onto the lakes was willing or able to invest in the latest technology. Storms or accidents could disable electronic systems when they were most needed. Under such circumstances, a lighthouse or pier-head beacon remained a saving sight to the beleaguered boater. While some lighthouses still performed a valuable function, by the late 1970s the rationale for staffing them with keepers became tenuous.

The automation of lighthouses, while not common, went back to the period after World War I and the introduction of the acetylene lights and automated clock mechanisms that could light or extinguish beacons. These systems were hardly foolproof, and while such stations might not require a twenty-four-hour keeper, they did still need some monitoring and occasional cleaning. When the Sand Island Lighthouse on Lake Superior was fitted out with the acetylene system in 1921, the light became the responsibility of the keeper of the Raspberry Island Lighthouse located about seven miles away. In the wake of World War II, the Coast Guard began in earnest to automate its light stations. Electrification proceeded faster than actual automation. As late as 1962, 327 lighthouses were still manned in the U.S. In 1968 the Coast Guard began the Lighthouse Automation and Modernization Program (LAMP). Over the next twenty years, the process of automating lighthouses increased as more than $26 million was invested in new technology. Solar power was experimented with in the 1980s, and by the end of the decade, the Coast Guard was far advanced in making it standard for most of the sixteen thousand minor lights in American waters as well as many of the Great Lakes lighthouses. One by one, lighthouses equipped with electric lights and solar panels were stripped of their crews and automated. The job of lighthouse keeper had gone the way of other once crucial trades such as blacksmith, carriage maker, and typist.[31]

Most lighthouse keepers were reluctant to give up their stations. "I really hated to see it done," complained Fred Dornhecher, the last keeper of the North Manitou Shoal Lighthouse. "It was really kind of a symbol of the area." By 1981 only five Great Lakes lighthouses remained with full crews. At this handful of manned stations, the old vigil of watchful waiting continued. One Coast Guard man was on duty at all times to monitor if the beacon was on and if it was sending out the proper flash characteristic—a red or a white flash emitted at a set interval of seconds. The station's radio beacon also had to be monitored so that it also gave out the prearranged transmission on time. Finally, there was the least popular navigational aid with the crew of the light—the fog horn. It was activated whenever visibility dropped to under five miles. Its deep, sonorous sound could shake the light tower with its vibrations and render sleep all but impossible. Such audible warnings usually ended when automation took over. The last manned station on the American side of Great Lakes was the Sherwood Point Lighthouse in Wisconsin. It stood guard over the passage from Green Bay to Sturgeon Bay on the Door Peninsula. At the end of the 1983 season, Sherwood Point was fitted with light sensors and automatic gauges. The tower was locked, and the last keeper, Mike Ritchie, drove away. On the Canadian side of the lakes, manned stations endured a bit longer. The last station to be automated was Cove Island in Georgian Bay, which was stripped of its keeper in 1991.[32]

Technology made automation possible, but federal budgets played a role in the pace of the process. A lighthouse crew of three Coast Guard men required an outlay of $80,000 annually. Between 1968 and 1983, the penny-wise Department of the Treasury that administered the Coast Guard saved $18 million dollars by replacing crews with sensors and solar panels. This type of cost savings made the ending of the manned lighthouses a priority for the service. Yet as the automation program went forward, the question of what would become of the housing and outbuildings that made up a lighthouse complex was left unexamined.[33]

Privatization of these federally built structures seemed a logical solution, especially as post–Vietnam War America turned increasingly conservative in its political inclinations and budget cutting became an annual exercise. In the 1980s Congress and the administration of President Ronald Reagan nudged the Coast Guard away from its navigation safety mission and toward illegal drug interdiction. As far back as 1963, the Coast Guard had turned over surplus lighthouses to local interest groups. The Michigan City Lighthouse was an early example on the Great Lakes. The Coast Guard sold the structure to the city, which in turn granted a lease to the Michigan City Historical Society on the condition that they restore the building and operate it as a museum.[34] The saga of the Michigan City Lighthouse was a forerunner to the joys and frustrations that many later lighthouse preservationists would encounter. Schemes to secure funds and labor for the project ran the gamut from imaginative to desperate. They sold construction bonds for $1 apiece and at one point used Indiana state prisoners for construction work. It was not until 2014 that a new lantern room was installed. Yet the long effort seemed worth it to the hundreds of volunteers who devoted themselves to the old lighthouse. The lighthouse became a civic "shrine" to residents and a beacon of tourist marketing from the Lighthouse Restaurant to the Lighthouse Outlet Mall.[35]

Another early experiment in privatization of automated and unmanned lighthouses took place in Chicago. The Chicago Harbor Lighthouse, which dated from 1917, was a prominent feature of the Windy City lakefront. Located a quarter of a mile off Navy Pier, it was automated in 1978. Unexpectedly, the Coast Guard was contacted by Sterling Bemis, a thirty-seven-year-old salesman. Bemis was an avid boater, who had fallen in love with the idea of making the abandoned lighthouse his home. This was no small challenge, in part because the lighthouse could only be reached by boat. Bemis spent several years at the lighthouse. He paid only $1,050 a year in rent for the tower, but he made himself useful by taking on the repair of windows damaged by birds or storms. Bemis was eventually able to find a partner to share the beacon with, and his wave-washed bride-to-be and a Cook County marriage court justice braved heavy seas on the day of the wedding to say "I do" at the lighthouse. However, Bemis's time as a lightkeeper would not last long. In 2004 the City of Chicago named the structure a city landmark and began proceedings to have the Coast Guard transfer ownership to municipal authority.[36]

The reason the Coast Guard eventually yielded to Sterling Bemis's request for occupancy of the Chicago lighthouse was because in the short time the light had been abandoned, it suffered considerable deterioration due to lack of upkeep. Bemis took on the not inconsiderable job of making the basic repairs necessary to keep out the environment. The Coast Guard soon discovered that without such ongoing maintenance, lighthouses that were automated and unmanned would quickly deteriorate. Lighthouses survived for decades because an on-site keeper made immediate repairs to the minor wear and tear faced by structures. Even back in the pecuniary days of Stephen Pleasonton's administration of U.S. lighthouses in the first half of the nineteenth century, half the cost of lighthouses went to annual repairs. Another problem was vandalism. The Coast Guard should have expected that its abandoned light stations would become magnets for break-ins. The St. Helena Island Lighthouse in northern Lake Michigan could have served as a lesson of the danger posed by vandals. St. Helena was the first Michigan station to be automated when it was fitted with a sun-valve system in 1922. Over the decades that followed, even though the light was on a remote island, everything that could possibly be taken away was looted — doors, banisters, floor boards, and even bricks. Fires were carelessly set and allowed to burn while outbuildings were all but demolished. So bad did the site become that the Coast Guard ordered the demolition of the ruined complex but then lacked the funds to do so. Fortunately, in 1986 the Great Lakes Lighthouse Keepers Association, a group dedicated to lighthouse history and preservation, took on the salvation of the wrecked St. Helena station, and with the help of the Boy Scouts of Michigan began a long and ongoing restoration project.[37]

The New Keepers of the Light

The Coast Guard was mandated to cooperate with historic preservation organizations because of the growing importance of cultural heritage in late twentieth-century America. Beginning with the passage in 1966 of the National Historic Preservation Act, a system of federal and state, private and public organizations had ensured that potential effects on historic sites were—in the words of the act—"taken into account" in federal government actions. In 1971 President Richard Nixon deepened the federal government's commitment to historic preservation when he issued Executive Order 11593, which ordered all agencies of the national government to inventory and administer significant cultural resources under their control in such a way that they be "preserved, restored and maintained." The Coast Guard then set about assessing which of its 481 light stations nationwide were historically significant under the terms of the National Historic Preservation Act. Eventually, most lighthouses would qualify for the National Register of Historic Places, with more than 450 being listed. This status ensured that most lighthouses would receive careful local and federal attention. By the late twentieth century, experience had taught the Coast Guard that the preservation of individual lighthouses would be better ensured if they were occupied by tenants charged with the maintenance of the historic property. The agency was encouraged in this direction by a variety of private organizations of lighthouse enthusiasts, who were committed to the preservation of historic navigational aids.[38]

Lighthouse preservationists played a key role in raising awareness of the growing danger of deterioration to the nation's navigational aids. Their efforts led in 2000 to a significant amendment to the National Historic Preservation Act. Titled the National Historic Lighthouse Preservation Act, the new law laid out a procedure by which local groups could preserve light stations critical to community heritage while at the same time relieving the Coast Guard of the burden of maintaining hundreds of obsolete navigational aids. Under the legislation, the Coast Guard would work with lighthouse preservationists, the National Park Service, and the General Services Administration to dispose of lighthouses that no longer met the requirements of the Coast Guard. The first step in the procedure was for the Coast Guard to declare the lighthouse "excess" to its mission. At that point, the National Park Service would aid in determining if the lighthouse was eligible for listing on the National Register of Historic Places. If a light was not historically significant, it would be transferred to the General Services Administration and disposed of like any other piece of redundant government property, usually by sale to a private party. A lighthouse determined to be eligible for historic status, as most light stations are, is first made available to not-for-profit groups or local government entities dedicated to history and preservation. Such groups must prepare a plan for the care of the structure and pledge to make it available to the public for education and tourism. While the act moved preservation groups to the head of the line when it came to property disposal, it did little to actually help individual groups carry out the work of restoration and public education. In keeping with the spirit of the times, it effectively privatized the continued maintenance for a vast system of historic navigational aids that had once been the pride of the federal government.[39]

North of the border, the Canadian Coast Guard was also eager to be relieved of the burden of lighthouse maintenance. Here again it was necessary for citizen preservationists to advocate for the old light towers. In 2008 public pressure from communities interested in protecting lighthouses important to local identity and tourism finally pressured Parliament to address the issue. The Heritage Lighthouse Protection Act set up a process by which a select group of light stations could be afforded protected status. Initially, fourteen Great Lakes lighthouses were designated under this legislation. Like the laws in the U.S., the parliamentary act allocated no new funds for preservation of lighthouses. Unfortunately, in 2010 the Canadian Coast Guard declared most of the remaining lighthouses surplus and a rapid privatization process was set in motion.[40]

In peril on both sides of the border, the lighthouses of the inland seas were not without friends. Across the region scores of grassroots organizations sprang into being committed to preserving a lighthouse in their area. By 2015, 25 of the approximately 124 lighthouses in the state of Michigan alone had been transferred from federal control, while across the country many more lighthouses had been either donated or sold. A handful of lighthouses have been repurposed as bed-and-breakfast inns, most others as historic sites. One group that received a donated lighthouse was the Friends of Point Betsie Lighthouse, which was formed when the Coast Guard transferred the site to Benzie County, Michigan, in 2004. The light had been among the last manned stations on Lake Michigan and was not automated until 1983. The light tower and outbuildings soon began to suffer from neglect, and when the transfer took place, extensive work was needed for all structures. Yet within a decade, an aggressive capital campaign in the region and timely state and federal grants allowed the "friends" to completely restore the complex, install interpretative exhibits and a gift shop and develop a two-bedroom vacation apartment in the assistant keeper's quarters to help sustain the operation of the historic site. The fact that Benzie County is a popular summer tourist destination was a significant aid to the Friends of Point Betsie Lighthouse efforts. Visitation helped generate income, community interest, and donations.

A more difficult preservation challenge has been the Port Austin Reef Light, which is located a mile and a half off shore in Lake Huron. The station was automated in 1953 and suffered the inevitable deterioration over the next three decades until it found a savior in the person of Lou Schillinger, a resident of Port Austin. Schillinger negotiated a five-year lease from the Coast Guard with the promise he would do his best to stabilize the structure. His efforts and those of his family and friends led in 1988 to the formation of the Port Austin Reef Light Association, Inc. For several decades they acted as caretakers for the lighthouse. In the face of repeated vandalism, they invested thousands of dollars in repairs and rehabilitation. Finally, in 2011 federal authorities acting under the National Historic Lighthouse Act turned over ownership of the structure to the association. Yet access to the offshore light is problematic, and public interpretation largely takes place at Port Austin History Center on the mainland.[41]

Great Lakes lighthouses can be popular tourist attractions and touchstones of local identity. The private and governmental institutions that have rushed into the maintenance void created by Coast Guard decommissioning have done a considerable public service by their restoration activities. Unfortunately, lighthouse restoration never terminates—the job is never done. Every storm, every winter, every malicious vandal demands renewed attention and dollars. If the light towers on the inland seas are going to continue to endure, they will require long-term care, decade after decade. These lights were born out of a national commitment to a public good. In the nineteenth and twentieth centuries, that commitment was to safe navigation and commerce. In the twenty-first century, that public good is a common heritage that can help bind together the peoples of the Great Lakes region and enable them to be better stewards of more than 20 percent of the world's most precious resource—fresh water. Local governments, private citizens, and nonprofits are the new keepers of the lights. Their long-term success requires both love and money. The new private keepers of the lights mean well, but the most poorly funded cultural institutions in the U.S. are local historical museums, and these are the very institutions—along with local governments—that the National Lighthouse Preservation Act entrusted to rescue the Coast Guard from the heavy burden of long-term maintenance. If that vision has any hope for enduring success, then a federal annual fund or endowment is required to help the new lightkeepers sustain these tangible reminders of our maritime heritage.[42]

Afterword

In May 1976 I attended a concert by Canadian folksinger Gordon Lightfoot at Chicago's Auditorium Theater. To the disappointment of many in the audience, who wanted to hear Lightfoot sing some of his best-known ballads, he went through the playlist of his latest album, *Summertime Dream*. However, he paused before starting one of those new songs. The folksinger was famously "crotchety" with reporters and occasionally audiences. Perhaps sensing some restlessness among his fans, Lightfoot launched into a lecture berating Chicagoans for living on the shores of the Great Lakes but knowing nothing of their nature or history. He pointed out that just the year before, a November gale had destroyed a giant lake freighter. All hands had been lost, yet the tragedy barely received a ripple of public attention. "Those lakes are part of your heritage," he said, and he then began to sing "The Wreck of the Edmund Fitzgerald."[1]

Lightfoot's song became a phenomenon that stimulated renewed awareness of the lakes and the Midwest region's maritime heritage. It spawned television documentaries, museum
exhibits, plays, even a beer: the Great Lakes Brewing Company's
Edmund Fitzgerald Porter. "The Wreck of the Edmund Fitzgerald" burst on the scene at a time when the lakes were just
beginning to mount a recovery from industrial pollution, mis-
management, and the first wave of invasive species. In the late
1960s and early 1970s, Great Lakes beaches were annually beset
with waves of dead fish washing ashore. The invasive sea lam-
prey destroyed the natural food chain in the lakes, which let
populations of silvery little alewives grow exponentially, only to
die off in huge numbers. In 1967 six billion of the herringlike fish
washed ashore on Lake Michigan alone. The smell of rotting fish
or giant algae blooms spawned by phosphate pollution kept
thousands of people away from the region's beaches and harbors. By 1976, when the song was released, the introduction of
salmon to attack the alewives and the regulations brought by the
1972 Clean Water Act began to make the lakeshore once more a
desirable place for recreation. There was a boom in resort development along the lakes and a surge in recreational boating.
During these same years, foreign competition wreaked havoc
on the region's industrial economy. Lightfoot's song paid tribute
to blue-collar crews that worked the lakes, while its mournful
dirgelike melody memorialized a way of life that was—if not dis-
appearing entirely—certainly being eclipsed.

The decline of the Great Lakes steel industry had a shatter-
ing impact on inland seas shipping. Typical of the trend at the
time was the Bethlehem Steel Company plant in Buffalo. During
World War II, more than twenty thousand workers labored there
in what was the largest single steel plant in the world. Its blast
furnaces and forges produced steel plate for battleships, tanks,
and other implements of war. After the war, production hardly
slowed. As late as 1981, the plant produced a record profit of
$8 billion. That marvelous return, however, was just corporate
management wringing the last drops of value out of a facility
they refused to modernize. Just two years later, the plant was
closed. Today what was once one of the densest concentrations
of industry in the world is an empty brownfield. Across the lakes
the same cold wind blew. The people of Lake Michigan's Calumet

District shuddered as their biggest plants closed: Wisconsin Steel, Republic Steel, Pressed Steel, and, most devastating of all, U.S. Steel's South Works and its twenty thousand jobs. As steel plants closed or were cut back, ships were idled. In 1981 U.S. Steel separated from the Pittsburgh Steamship Company, its maritime arm and the largest fleet of vessels on the lakes. The still profitable fleet then passed through the hands of several investment firms seeking short-lived profits. Within a decade, the once mighty array of freighters that in 1939 numbered more than eighty boats was reduced to a mere dozen.[2]

Ironically, many of the problems that beset the Great Lakes from the mid-twentieth century to today have been connected with navigation improvements. If the nineteenth-century lake suffered from a lack of improvements, the contemporary watershed has suffered from too many ill-considered engineering interventions. The oversold and underbuilt St. Lawrence Seaway has been the prime culprit in transforming the waters of the inland seas for the worse. Ships from the Black and Baltic Seas regularly visited the lakes to take on cargoes of wheat or corn. Before filling their holds, ship captains emptied the ballast water they had taken on in home waters. What they unwittingly dumped into the inland seas were numerous nonnative species that quickly spread throughout the basin. It is estimated that 70 percent of the forty-three exotic species that have entered the Great Lakes since the opening of the St. Lawrence Seaway have done so via ballast water transfers. Gallingly, only voluntary ballast guidelines were instituted in 1989, and it was not until 1993 that mandatory rules were put in place. Those rules were easily and willfully circumvented by foreign-flagged vessels, and the problem got worse, not better. In the 1980s the zebra mussel, native to the Black Sea, was introduced in this way. This prolific alien produces a million eggs per year, so once it found a home in the lakes, it spread rapidly. The fingernail-sized mussels latched on to everything in the water. Soon water intake pipes for power plants or water works were clogged with thousands of mussels. Since their introduction, this one species has caused more than $5 billion in damages. That does not count the mischief caused by its close cousin, the quagga mussel, or the way it combines with other invaders such as the round goby to cause avian botulism. The guagga mussel today literally blankets the bottom of the lakes. Like all mussels, they are filter feeders. In their billions they take in the zooplankton that are the basis of the fishery food chain. This destroyed native fish stocks but clarified the water, which at first seemed a silver lining. For a time, Great Lakes beaches rivaled the Caribbean in their crystal-clear visibility. Unfortunately, the extra sunlight reaching into the depths of the lake triggered algae blooms when interacting with fertilizer that had run off farm fields. The algae fouled beaches, while out in the lake the dying green weeds stole the oxygen from the water, creating large dead zones where no life can linger. The toxic algae even began to threaten the region's human population. In 2014 a giant bloom engulfed Toledo's water-intake crib, and the city's entire water supply was poisoned. The toxin contained in the blue-green algae was microcystin, which can cause skin rashes, GI problems, and, more seriously, deadly liver and kidney damage. This was a high price to pay for a waterway that allowed foreign flag vessels to bring in steel to compete with the most important industrial product of the region. As the ecological costs continue to escalate, the St. Lawrence Seaway's negative impacts seem to outweigh any of its realized economic advantages.[3]

Other navigation improvements have played serious mischief with the environment of the inland sea. When preparing the St. Clair River channel for what was thought to be the increased traffic of the seaway, the U.S. Army Corps of Engineers dredged two million cubic yards of sand and stone from the river bottom. Together with channel dredging done since the mid-nineteenth century, a total of thirty-three million cubic yards had been scooped out of the choke point. Unfortunately, the last round done for the seaway was one scoop too many. Unwittingly the Army engineers had removed a strata of rock that protected the bottom of the river. Once removed, the rush of the St. Clair's current began to erode away the soft sand that was beneath. As a result, parts of the channel were deeper than intended, and the deeper river began to pull a much larger flow of water out of Lake Huron. Lakes Michigan and Huron make up one basin, so the effect of the ill-conceived dredging was to lower their levels nearly two feet, more than the controversial Chicago diversion. This was a major unintended impact of navigation improvements. It passed largely without public notice because the region entered a period of increased precipitation in the 1960s. Yet the unnatural diversion could have long-term consequences for both shipping and industry on the lakes.[4]

During high-water years, which naturally occur every decade or so, navigation dams become a subject of controversy. The dam at the Sault Ste. Marie locks controls the amount of water sent from Lake Superior to Lakes Michigan and Huron. Shoreline property owners on Superior naturally want the dam to let out the extra water to prevent shoreline erosion. This elicits protests from lakefront property owners on the lower lakes, who are threatened by rising water levels. The Moses-Saunders Dam on the St. Lawrence Seaway has the same effect on Lake Ontario water levels. Control boards established by the International Joint Commission have the authority to regulate flows, often to the dissatisfaction of either or both the upstream or downstream property owners.[5]

The history of Great Lakes navigation and navigational aids is a mixed legacy. Global urban centers and industries were born in the heart of North America because of the government's ability to shape the inland seas into an integrated and coherent economic entity. Yet maritime commerce has also contributed to ecosystem-altering cycles of pollution and the introduction of invasive species. Billions of dollars of damage to the lake region and beyond has been a result. By the late twentieth century, the cost of dealing with the problems created by lake navigation exceeded the money spent on maintaining the maritime infrastructure. This reflects the growing reality that the lakes are now much more valued as a natural resource than as a means of navigation. The Great Lakes represent 98 percent of the fresh surface water in the U.S. Clean drinking water is the world's most valuable resource, and the combination of invasive species and agricultural runoff threaten the safety of drinking water for lakeshore cities. Safe beaches and sport fishing are amenities that both Canadian and American citizens value more than lake shipping, especially the oceangoing traffic brought by the St. Lawrence Seaway. Compared with the oversized promises made by seaway proponents in the 1950s, the waterway has been an abject failure. In terms of tonnage, it represents a mere 5 percent of commercial navigation on the Great Lakes, yet it has been the corridor for billions of dollars of environmental damage.[6]

The changing perception of navigation by political leaders along the inland seas is well illustrated by the example of Chicago's two Mayor Daleys. Richard J. Daley was Chicago's mayor in 1959 when the seaway opened. When the Dutch freighter *Prins-Johan Willem Frisco* docked at the city's Navy Pier, the first Mayor Daley personally greeted the vessel with fireworks, bands, and a parade down Michigan Avenue. Speaking at a gala luncheon in honor of the vessel's captain, the mayor proclaimed: "Seaway traffic would make Chicago one of the great cities of the world." Some four decades later, with a seaway-spawned invasive species invasion costing Chicago and other lake cities millions of dollars, Richard J. Daley's son occupied city hall. Disgusted with the unwanted expense, Mayor Richard M. Daley told a reporter that all oceangoing vessels should be prevented from even entering the seaway, should "off load their cargo in Nova Scotia and ship it down by rail." The cost of such a radical change to navigation was estimated in 2005 to be $55 million annually in increased transportation costs, yet the environmental damage caused by the seaway exceeds $200 million each year. This was not the economic impact anticipated in 1959 when the waterway opened.[7]

While the seaway has been a source of endless frustration and ecological mischief, navigation between Great Lakes ports has continued to play an integral role in the North American economy. The inland maritime system still accounts for $33.5 billion in business investment and 226,000 jobs. Shipping products on the Great Lakes is a green alternative to other means of transportation. The movement of bulk products like iron, coal, and stone on the lakes is nearly seven times more fuel efficient than truck transportation. That same truck would emit six times more greenhouse gasses. Even if the nation's rail system could handle the extra burden, its trains would emit one-and-a-half times more greenhouses gases than a Great Lakes vessel. Inland seas shipping plays an important role in creating a "greener" North America. The inland seas at the heart of the continent remain a marvelous economic asset in global competition for the U.S. and Canada. And yet the inland seas are neglected in the corridors of power in Washington, D.C., and Ottawa. Environmental remediation is a national priority in neither capital. In Canada, there is a tendency to view the lakes as Ontario's business as well as to let their bigger, louder American cousins take the lead and bear the bulk of the financial burden. In the U.S., there has been a renewed antifederalism that, like that of the antebellum era, seeks to treat one of the continent's defining and most valuable natural resources as a local concern.[8]

Nor is there a national will to maintain the maritime infrastructure developed after the Civil War that played such a vital role in the nation's twentieth-century prosperity. In 1986 the increasingly conservative federal government changed the way harbor and channel improvements were funded. Previously this work was done as needed and paid for out of the general fund. The Harbor Maintenance Tax approved by Congress passed on a large part of those costs to a pool of money raised by taxing the value of a cargo entering an American port. Ironically, this was the solution proposed in the antebellum era by James K. Polk and others, who advocated for a federal government removed from economic development. Perhaps for seacoast ports this made sense. There the tax would be paid by foreign firms exporting their wares to the U.S. For the Great Lakes, it was onerous because the bulk of lake traffic is from one American port to another, with the tax paid by American industry. In addition, Great Lakes shipping enters and exits harbors on a weekly basis, unlike globe-spanning oceanic commerce. The new policy heaped an unfair expense on lake shipping but did little to maintain the maritime infrastructure because Congress still controlled the resulting funds. The taxes flowed into something called the Harbor Maintenance Trust Fund. But legislative "budget hawks" refused to approve expenditures in the name of fiscal responsibility. So the trust fund continued to grow, and harbors continued to decay. By 2015 an independent study of Great Lakes revealed that more than half of all harbors and navigational improvements were in failing condition and were not properly serving the needs of recreational and commercial shipping. Coastal engineering works such as breakwaters are generally designed for a fifty-year lifespan. Yet half of all such navigational improvements on the lakes were built prior to World War I. Patching and repair can only prevent a major failure for so long. History may not repeat itself, but people and their governments are certainly capable of making the same errors of judgment time after time. The so-called fiscal conservatives in Congress largely hail from the "sun belt," the same region that in the antebellum era opposed building lake harbors in the first place.[9]

The Great Lakes are a unique maritime region in the heart of a continent. It is perhaps the continent's greatest natural resource, shaped and managed by a "second nature" infrastructure designed to allow population and commerce to flourish. The lighthouses, channel improvements, charts, and harbors that allowed for commercial development were generally beyond the capacity of individual capitalists and of necessity became the work of government operating for the commonweal. Even more than the building of the much-celebrated transcontinental railroads, the lakes required an activist federal government to build and manage a system of works. Compared with the boom in railroad construction in the 1870s and 1880s, the federally managed maritime infrastructure of the Great Lakes was accomplished with greater efficiency and considerably less corruption. Unlike many of those railroads, the Great Lakes maritime industrial complex was a major contributor to the growth of the North American economy in the nineteenth and twentieth centuries. That there is such a thing as midwestern maritime history needs to cease being an oxymoron and instead appreciated as the means by which a unique region significantly shaped national and transnational history.[10]

Out on the waters of the lakes, miles off shore, out of the sight of skyscrapers or smokestacks, the vast dark expanse seems primeval and powerful—impervious to political trends that, like clouds, pass over and recede. The Great Lakes have been exploited, treasured, neglected, taken for granted by the people who call the region home, and all but forgotten by coastal elites. Imposing steel freighters and sleek fiberglass sloops ply its waters for profit and pleasure. Cities rise on its shores, thrive, decay, and seek renewal, while the blue-water horizon remains. With promise and menace, since the time of the glaciers, the lakes abide. They have been changed and channeled, but they remain resilient and untamed. As Gordon Lightfoot's song recounts, "And the iron boats go as the mariners all know, / With the gales of November remembered." Despite lighthouses and satellite GPS, the sailor who forgets the menace of untamed nature still risks the icy embrace of the inland sea.[11]

Acknowledgments

Like all my books, *Mastering the Inland Seas* began life as a public history project. The initial research was sponsored via contract by the National Park Service, Midwest Regional Office. It was occasioned by the rapid decommissioning of Great Lakes lighthouses and the agency's interest in documenting the role these navigational aids played in the broad pattern of American history. Dr. Michele Curran of the National Park Service supervised the contract and was of considerable assistance in locating research materials as well as being an attentive and patient editorial advisor. Dr. Donald J. Stevens assisted in the initial conception and scoping of the project. James Bissaillon of the Midwest Region was of considerable assistance navigating the contracting process. Many other National Park Service staff played an advisory role as readers of the various drafts. These included Dena L. Sanford, Vergil Noble, Kimberly Mann, Seth DePasqual, David Cooper, and Laura Quakenbush. Dena Sanford was particularly helpful in assisting with the recommendation of historic navigational aids for National Landmark status that was a large focus of the government report. David Cooper also devoted several days to a fascinating tour of Apostle Islands Lighthouses that advanced my appreciation of the challenges involved in lighthouse interpretation and preservation. I am grateful also to the U.S. Army Corps of Engineers Office of History, which has sponsored many of the best histories of Great Lakes maritime infrastructure.

This manuscript evolved from a public history project to a published book thanks to Gwen Walker and Sheila McMahon of the University of Wisconsin Press. Mary Magray assisted by copyediting the final text.

A number of individuals in the public history community were particularly helpful. Matthew Daley of Grand Valley State University read the draft manuscript and made many helpful suggestions. Thanks to Alan Newell, Heather Miller, and Dawn Vogel of Historical Research Associates for sharing with me their well-documented National Register nominations for Lake Superior Lighthouses. Patrick O'Bannon of Gray & Pape made available his research on Sault Ste. Marie navigation aids. Henry Barkhausen, the "dean" of Great Lakes maritime history, graciously shared his perspectives on the navigation of early lake schooners. Among the maritime historians who have come before me and helped prepare the way, few figure more prominently than Richard Wright, who helped create the Maritime Collections of the Great Lakes at Bowling Green State University.

While many research facilities were consulted during this project, several deserve more than a footnote. At the National Archives, Katie Dishman, Glenn Longacre, and Douglas Bicknese shared their knowledge of the Great Lakes Branch's maritime records. Robert Graham of the Historical Collections of the Great Lakes at Bowling Green State University was especially helpful with research at the start of the project. The Wisconsin Maritime Museum is always a great place to do research, starting with the director, Rolf Johnson, and manuscripts staff of Caitlin Clyne and Lisa Pike. At the Wisconsin Historical Society, I would like to thank Jim Draeger and Joseph DeRose of the Historic Preservation Division. Suzette Lopez of the Marine Collection at the Milwaukee Public Library helped me locate key illustrations. I also am in debt to Barbara Wyatt of the National Park Service, who facilitated my participation in the National Oceanic and Atmospheric Administration's 2015 Maritime Cultural Landscape Conference held in Madison, Wisconsin. North of the border, Sharon A. Babaian, the historian at the Canada Science and Technology Museum, shared her deep knowledge of the history of marine navigation in Canada. Closer to home, Jane Currie of the Loyola University library was a wonderful source of online databases and interlibrary loan assistance. I am always grateful for my association with colleagues at the Chicago Maritime Museum, particularly Don Glasell, Kellogg Fairbank, and Jim Jarecki.

The preparation of this manuscript was also facilitated by the modern, if informal, lighthouse establishment. This includes the

Great Lakes Lighthouse Keepers Association, whose conferences, tours, and website are invaluable; and likewise Foghorn Publishing and all the contributors to *Lighthouse Digest*, not least of whom is Terry Pepper, whose website Seeing the Light: Lighthouses of the Western Great Lakes is a ready and reliable source of lighthouse history. Patricia Wright and Larry Wright's *Great Lakes Lighthouse Encyclopedia* was another important source for both American and Canadian lighthouses. Nor could this book have been written without the aid of the late Candace Clifford's marvelous 1994 inventory of historic American light stations, which was a key part of the National Park Service's Maritime Initiative. Lee Murdock played a role in this book as well. His folk songs about the Great Lakes bring the past alive with grace and verve. There is no better way to know the inland seas than to sail on them, and for the many opportunities to do just that I thank the people of Blount Small Ship Adventures.

Closer to home I would like to thank Joseph Karamanski, who ably served as a research assistant on several trips to inspect Great Lakes Lighthouses. Finally, I am, as always, very much in debt to my dearest colleague, Dr. Eileen M. McMahon of Lewis University, who brought her sharp editorial eye to the draft manuscript and shared with me not only her own knowledge of midwestern history but also several tight berths on the inland sea.

Notes

Introduction

1. Joseph Conrad, *Lord Jim* (New York: McClure, Phillips, 1900), 199.

2. Christer Westerdahl, "The Maritime Cultural Landscape," *International Journal of Nautical Archaeology* 21, no. 1 (1992): 5–14.

3. William Cronon, *Nature's Metropolis: Chicago and the Great West* (New York: Norton, 1990), xvii; Walter Prescott Webb, *The Great Plains* (Lincoln: University of Nebraska Press, 1931, 1959).

4. Two important recent books that make that mistake are Stephen Hahn's *A Nation without Borders: The United States and Its World in an Age of Civil Wars, 1830–1910* (New York: Penguin, 2016) and Adam Arenson's *The Great Heart of the Republic: St. Louis and the Cultural Civil War* (Columbia: University of Missouri Press, 2015). Both volumes perform a valuable service reinterpreting the nature and significance of sectionalism in nineteenth-century America but overlook the important and unique role of the Great Lakes region. For a broad survey of the role of maritime history in U.S. development, see Benjamin W. Labaree, William M. Fowler Jr., John B. Hattendorf, Jeffrey J. Safford, Edward W. Sloan, and Andrew W. German, *America and the Sea: A Maritime History* (Mystic, Conn: Mystic Seaport, 1998). Anishinaabeg is the collective name for the Odawa, Potawatomi, and Ojibwe Indian peoples of the Great Lakes region who share a similar language and traditions and are known as the "Three Fires Confederacy."

5. Paul A. Samuelson, "The Pure Theory of Public Expenditure," *Review of Economics and Statistics* 36, no. 4 (November 1954): 387–89.

6. For state formation and settler colonialism in the Old Northwest region, see Bethel Saler, *The Settlers' Empire: Colonialism and State Formation in America's Old Northwest* (Philadelphia: University of Pennsylvania Press, 2015); Lawrence B. A. Hatter, *Citizens of Convenience: The Imperial Origins of American Nationhood on the U.S.-Canadian*

Border (Charlottesville: University of Virginia Press, 2016); and Andrew R. L. Cayton, "'Separate Interests' and the Nation-State: The Washington Administration and the Origins of Regionalism in the Trans-Appalachian West," *Journal of American History* 79, no. 1 (June 1992): 39–67.

7. William J. Novak, "The Myth of the 'Weak' American State," *American Historical Review* 113, no. 3 (June 2008): 752–72; Alexis de Tocqueville, *Democracy in America*, trans. George Lawrence, ed. J. P. Mayer (New York: HarperPerennial, 1988), 394–95; J. P. Nettl, "The State as a Conceptual Variable," *World Politics* 20 (July 1968): 559–92.

Chapter 1. Native Waters

1. Louis Hennepin, *A Description of Louisiana*, trans. John G. Shea (New York: John G. Shea, 1880), 95–96; Don Bamford, *Freshwater Heritage: A History of Sail on the Great Lakes, 1670–1918* (Toronto: Natural Heritage Books, 2007), 23.

2. Hennepin, *A Description of Louisiana*, 95–96. There is some debate about whether there had actually been a couple of smaller earlier vessels than *Le Griffon*, but there is no doubt that *Le Griffon* was the first named vessel on the Great Lakes, the first to travel from one lake to the next, and the first to be designed and dedicated to commerce.

3. Nathaniel Bowditch, *American Practical Navigator: An Epitome of Navigation and Nautical Astronomy*, rev. ed. (Washington, D.C.: U.S. Government Printing Office, 1939), 19.

4. Kimberly Monk, "The Development of Aboriginal Watercraft in the Great Lakes Region," *Totem: The University of Western Ontario Journal of Anthropology* 7, no. 1 (1999): 71–77; for more on canoe types, see Edwin Tappan Adney and Howard Chappelle, *The Bark Canoes and Skin Boats of North America* (Washington, D.C.: Smithsonian Institution, 1964).

5. Monk, "The Development of Aboriginal Watercraft," 71–77; Caven Clark, *Archeological Survey and Testing, Isle Royale National Park, 1987–1990 Seasons*, Midwest Archeological Center Occasional Studies in Anthropology 32 (Lincoln, Neb.: Midwest Archeological Center, U.S. National Park Service, 1995).

6. Andrew J. Blackbird, *A History of the Ottawa and Chippewa People* (Ypsilanti, Mich.: Ypsilantian Job Printing House, 1887), 32–33.

7. Virgil Vogel, *Indian Place Names in Michigan* (Ann Arbor: University of Michigan Press, 1986), 134–36.

8. Annette S. Lee, William Wilson, Jeff Tibbetts, and Carl Gawboy, *Ojibwe Giizhig Anang Masinaa'igan, Ojibwe Sky Star Map Constellation*

Guidebook: An Introduction to Ojibwe Star Knowledge (North Rocks, Calif.: Lightning Source-Ingram Spark, 2014), 1–10.

9. Claude Allouez, SJ, *The Jesuit Relations and Allied Documents,* vol. 50, ed. Ruben Gold Thwaites (Cleveland: William Burrows Company, 1896–1901), 286; Blackbird, *A History of the Ottawa and Ojibwe People,* 76–77; Serge Lemaitre, "Mishipeshu," *Canadian Encyclopedia,* accessed September 2014, http://www.thecanadianencyclopedia.com /en/article/mishipeshu/; Timothy Cochrane, *Minong—The Good Place: Ojibwe and Isle Royale* (East Lansing: Michigan State University Press, 2009), 25; Theresa S. Smith, *Island of the Anishinaabeg: Thunders and Water Monsters in the Traditional Ojibwe Life-World* (Lincoln: University of Nebraska Press, 1995), 120–21.

10. Carolyn Podruchny, *Making the Voyageur World: Travelers and Traders in the North American Fur Trade* (Lincoln: University of Nebraska Press, 2006), 102; Timothy J. Kent, *Birchbark Canoes of the Fur Trade,* vol. 1 (Ossineke, Mich.: Silver Fox Enterprises, 1997), 95–99; for more about lob trees, see Clifford Ahlgren and Isabel Ahlgren, *Lob Trees in the Wilderness* (Minneapolis: University of Minnesota Press, 1984).

11. David Chapin, *Freshwater Passages: The Trade and Travels of Peter Pond* (Lincoln: University of Nebraska Press, 2014), 41–42; Podruchny, *Making the Voyageur World,* 104–11.

12. James Axtel, *The Invasion Within: The Contest of Cultures in Colonial North America* (New York: Oxford University Press, 1985), 9; Henry Howland, "Navy Island and the First Successors to the Griffon," *Publications of the Buffalo Historical Society* 6 (1903): 18–19.

13. Howland, "Navy Island and the First Successors to the Griffon," 19–33.

14. Howland, "Navy Island and the First Successors to the Griffon," 32–33; James Fenimore Cooper, *The Pathfinder: Or, The Inland Sea* (New York: Sully and Kleinteich, 1876), 120–21.

15. Daniel Dempster and Todd Berger, *Lighthouses of the Great Lakes* (Minneapolis: Voyageur Press, 2002), 19–20.

16. Ordinance for the Government of the Territory of the United States North and West of the River Ohio, 13 July 1787, Our Documents, accessed October 2014, http://www.ourdocuments.gov/doc.php?doc= 8&page=transcript.

17. Theodore J. Karamanski, *Schooner Passage: Sailing Ships and the Lake Michigan Frontier* (Detroit: Wayne State University Press, 2000), 45.

18. For more on the three-way military struggle for the Great Lakes, see David Curtis Skaggs and Larry L. Nelson, eds., *The Sixty Years' War for the Great Lakes, 1754–1814* (East Lansing: Michigan State University Press, 2001).

19. For an analysis of the role of war in shaping the differences between the Old Northwest and Old Southwest relative to the national government, see Cayton, "'Separate Interests' and the Nation-State."

Chapter 2. A Transportation Revolution on the Lakes, 1789–1839

1. William L. Bancroft, "Memoir of Captain Samuel Ward, with a sketch of early Commerce on the Great Lakes," *Michigan Pioneer and Historical Collections* 21 (1892): 336–67; Friend Palmer, *Personal Reminiscences of Important Events and Descriptions of the City for Over Eighty Years* (Detroit: Hunt and June, 1906), 41.

2. Bancroft, "Memoir of Captain Samuel Ward," 338.

3. Bancroft, "Memoir of Captain Samuel Ward," 340–42.

4. John Lauritz Larson, *The Market Revolution in America: Liberty, Ambition, and the Eclipse of the Common Good* (New York: Cambridge University Press, 2010), 1.

5. The cornerstone of historiography on the market revolution is Charles Sellers, *The Market Revolution: Jacksonian America, 1815–1846* (New York: Oxford University Press, 1991); Daniel Walker Howe, *What God Hath Wrought: The Transformation of America, 1815–1848* (New York: Oxford University Press, 2007), 4–5; John W. Larson, *A History of Great Lakes Navigation* (Fort Belvoir, Va.: National Waterways Study, U.S. Army Engineer Water Resources Support Center, Institute for Water Resources, 1983), 6.

6. Stanley Elkins and Eric McKitrick, *The Age of Federalism: The Early American Republic, 1788–1800* (New York: Oxford University Press, 1991), 62–72; *The Lighthouse Act of 1789* (Washington, D.C.: U.S. Senate History Office, 1991), 2–3.

7. *Lighthouse Act of 1789*, 10.

8. Max Farrand, ed., *The Records of the Federal Convention of 1787*, vol. 2 (New Haven, Conn.: Yale University Press, 1911), 615–16.

9. John Seelye, *The Beautiful Machine: Rivers and the Republican Plan, 1755–1825* (New York: Oxford University Press, 1991), 251–52, 260–61.

10. Allen S. Miller, "'The Lighthouse Top I See': Lighthouses as Instruments and Manifestations of State Building in the Early Republic," *Buildings and Landscapes: Journal of the Vernacular Architecture Forum* 17, no. 1 (Spring 2010): 13–34.

11. J. B. Mansfield, *History of the Great Lakes*, vol. 1 (Chicago: J. H. Beers, 1899), 364; Larry Wright and Patricia Wright, *Great Lakes Lighthouse Encyclopedia* (Erin, Ontario: Boston Mills Press, 2011), 91, 101; Robert D. Ilisevich, *Daniel Dobbins Frontier Merchant* (Erie, Pa.: Erie Historical Society, 1993), 1–25.

12. Wright and Wright, *Great Lakes Lighthouse Encyclopedia*, 91, 101.

13. James Cooke Mills, *Our Inland Seas: Their Shipping and Commerce for Three Centuries* (Chicago: McClurg, 1910), 89–100.

14. Wright and Wright, *Great Lakes Lighthouses Encyclopedia*, 113.

15. Mills, *Our Inland Seas*, 100–108.

16. Todd R. Berger, *Lighthouses of the Great Lakes* (Minneapolis: Voyageur Press, 2002), 26; Wright and Wright, *Great Lakes Lighthouse Encyclopedia*, 21, 34.

17. Charles K. Hyde, *The Northern Lights: Lighthouses of the Upper Great Lakes* (Lansing, Mich.: Two Peninsula Press, 1986), 80–81, 98; Wright and Wright, *Great Lakes Lighthouse Encyclopedia*, 161, 166–67.

18. Joanne Grossman and Theodore J. Karamanski, eds., *Historic Lighthouses and Navigational Aids of the Illinois Shore of Lake Michigan* (Chicago: Chicago Maritime Society, 1989), 3; Alfred T. Andreas, *A History of Chicago*, vol. 1 (Chicago: A. T. Andres, 1884), 239; Hyde, *Northern Lights*, 112.

19. Larry Lankton, *Beyond the Boundaries: Life and Landscape at the Lake Superior Copper Mines, 1840–1875* (New York: Oxford University Press, 1997), 7–14; for the Horace Greeley quote, see Terry Pepper, "Whitefish Point Light Station," *Seeing the Light: Lighthouses of the Western Great Lakes*, accessed October 2014, http://terrypepper.com/lights/superior/whitefish/whitefish.htm; Hyde, *Northern Lights*, 176; Jane C. Busch, *Copper Country Survey Final Report and Historic Preservation Plan* (Houghton, Mich.: Keweenaw National Historical Park Advisory Commission, 2013), 80–86; the original keeper's dwelling from the 1849 Copper Harbor Lighthouse still stands. As of 2015 nineteen light stations established in the copper country remain extant.

20. Michael Nelson, "A Short, Ironic History of American National Bureaucracy," *Journal of Politics* 44, no. 3 (August 1982): 747–78; Charles Wilkes, *Autobiography of Rear Admiral Charles Wilkes, U.S. Army, 1798–1877*, ed. William Morgan et al. (Washington, D.C.: Naval History Division, Dept. of Navy, 1978), 316–17; F. Ross Holland Jr., *America's Lighthouses: An Illustrated History* (Brattleboro, Vt.: Greene Press, 1972), 27–29.

21. Amy K. Marshall, "Frequently Close to the Point of Peril: A History of Buoys and Tenders in U.S. Coastal Waters, 1789–1939" (MA thesis, East Carolina University, 1997), 10–11; Holland, *America's Lighthouses*, 29.

22. Hyde, *Northern Lights*, 17; Holland, *America's Lighthouses*, 29–30.

23. Robert Browning, "Lighthouse Evolution and Typology," U.S. Coast Guard Historians Office, accessed October 2014, http://www.uscg.mil/history/weblighthouses/LHevolution.asp; "Robert Stevenson," *Encyclopedia Britannica* (1911), vol. 25, accessed October 2014,

http://en.wikisource.org/wiki/1911_Encyclop%C3%A6dia_Britan
nica/Stevenson,_Robert; Holland, *America's Lighthouses*, 18–19.

24. Brian J. Faltinson, "Split Rock Light Station," National Historic
Landmark Nomination (2009), 28.

25. The masonry tower is one of the most prolific; it is estimated
that 52 percent of all extant lighthouses in the U.S. are of this type. See
Candace Clifford, ed., "Light Stations of the United States," Multiple
Property Documentation Form, 1999, 15, citing Robert L. Scheina, "The
Evolution of the Lighthouse Tower," in *U.S. Lighthouse Service Bicenten-
nial, a U.S. Lighthouse Society Event Souvenir Program* (Newport, R.I.,
September 21–24, 1999), 18; and Candace Clifford, *Inventory of Historic
Light Stations* (Washington, D.C.: Government Printing Office for the
National Park Service, 1994).

26. Clifford, *Inventory of Historic Light Stations*, 15.

27. Wright and Wright, *Great Lakes Lighthouse Encyclopedia*, 101,
166–67, 355.

28. Eber Ward, "Incidents in the Life of Mr. Eber Ward, Father of
Capt. E. B. Ward of Steamboat Fame as Related to Mrs. E. M. S. Stewart
in The Summer of 1852," *Michigan Pioneer and Historical Society, Pioneer
Collections* 6 (1884): 471–73; Bernard C. Korn, "Eber Brock Ward: Pathfinder of American Industry" (PhD diss., Marquette University, 1942),
50–53.

29. Frederick J. Starin, "Diary of a Journey to Wisconsin in 1840,"
Wisconsin Magazine of History 6, no. 1 (1922): 78–79.

30. Eber Ward, "Incidents in the Life," 471–73; Wright and Wright,
Great Lakes Lighthouse Encyclopedia, 166–67; *Commemorative and Biographical Record of the Upper Lake Region* (Chicago: J. H. Beers, 1905), 203.

31. James E. Davis, *Frontier Illinois* (Bloomington: Indiana University Press, 1998), 123–25; John Drury, *Old Illinois Houses* (Chicago: University of Chicago Press, 1977), 13–14.

32. Mansfield, *History of the Great Lakes*, 1:186; Carol Sheriff, *The
Artificial River: The Erie Canal and the Paradox of Progress, 1817–1862*
(New York: Hill and Wang, 1996), 181.

33. Ronald E. Shaw, *Erie Waters West: A History of the Erie Canal*
(Lexington: University of Kentucky Press, 1966), 57, 87, 192.

34. Timothy Flint, *The History and Geography of the Mississippi Valley*
(Cincinnati: E. H. Flint and L. R. Lincoln, 1832), 184–85; James E. Davis,
*Frontier America, 1800–1840: A Comparative Demographic Analysis of the
Frontier Process* (Glendale, Calif.: Arthur Clark Company, 1977), 46–47;
Howe, *What God Hath Wrought*, 137–39; Thomas McKenney, *Sketches of
a Tour of the Lakes* (Baltimore: Fielding Lucas, 1827), 59.

35. William H. Keating, *Narrative of an Expedition to the Source of St.
Peter's River* (Philadelphia: H. C. Carey, 1824), 166; Kenneth E. Lewis,

West to Far Michigan: Settling the Lower Peninsula, 1815–1860 (East Lansing: Michigan State University Press, 2002), 222–25; Karamanski, *Schooner Passage*, 44–46; Richard Weston quoted in Catherine Cangany, *Frontier Seaport: Detroit's Transformation into an Atlantic Entrepôt* (Chicago: University of Chicago Press: 2014), 201.

36. Sheriff, *Artificial River*, 16, 24–25.

37. Margaret Fuller, *A Summer on the Lakes* (Boston: Charles Little and James Brown, 1844), 14.

38. In the case of Chicago, half the registered voters in the city's early elections (1828–30) were by the 1850s living out on the plains with their removed Indian kinsmen. For more, see Jacqueline Peterson, "The Founding Fathers: The Absorption of French-Indian Chicago, 1816–1837," in *Ethnic Chicago*, ed. Melvin G. Holi and Peter d'A. Jones (Grand Rapids: William B. Eerdmans, 1984), 300–337.

39. Francis Paul Prucha, SJ, *Broadax and Bayonet: The Role of the United States Army in the Development of the Northwest, 1815–1860* (Lincoln: University of Nebraska Press, 1953), vii–xii; Patrick E. McLear, "The Rise of the Port of Chicago to 1848" (MA thesis, University of Missouri, St. Louis, 1967), 20.

40. For more on Indian removal in the region, see Ronald Satz, *American Indian Policy in the Jacksonian Era* (Norman: University of Oklahoma Press, 1975). A small band of Potawatomi under the leadership of Leopold Pokagon were also able to avoid removal in southern Michigan.

41. Roy M. Robbins, *Our Landed Heritage: The Public Domain, 1776–1936* (Lincoln: University of Nebraska Press, 1962), 7–8.

42. Karamanski, *Schooner Passage*, 50–52.

43. Thomas W. Symons and John Quintus, "History of Buffalo Harbor: Its Construction and Improvement in the Nineteenth Century," *Publications of the Buffalo Historical Society* 5 (1902): 240–60.

44. Todd Shallot, *Structures in the Stream: Water, Science, and the U.S. Army Corps of Engineers* (Austin: University of Texas Press, 1994), 127.

45. H. Massey, "Traveling on the Great Lakes When Detroit Was Young," *Michigan Pioneer and Historical Collections*, vol. 6 (Lansing: Thorp and Godfrey, 1886), 131–33; Jay C. Ehle, *Cleveland's Harbor: The Cleveland-Cuyahoga Port Authority* (Kent, Ohio: Kent State University Press, 1996), 6; "Origins of the Detroit District," *Great Lakes Update* (U.S. Army Corps of Engineers Detroit District), vol. 172 (July 2008), 2.

46. Nuala Drescher, *Engineers for the Public Good: A History of the Buffalo District of the Army Corps of Engineers* (Buffalo: U.S. Army Corps of Engineers, 1982), 100–109.

47. Charles J. Latrobe, *The Rambler in North America*, vol. 2 (London: R. B. Seeley and W. Burnside, 1835), 190, 202.

48. John W. Larson, *Those Army Engineers: A History of the Chicago District of the U.S. Army Corps of Engineers* (Chicago: U.S. Army Corps of Engineers, 1979), 24–25.

49. Captain James Allen quote from John W. Larson, *Those Army Engineers*, 24–37.

50. "Origins of the Detroit District," *Great Lakes Update*.

51. Francis M. Carroll, "The Search for the Canadian-American Boundary along the Michigan Frontier, 1819–1827: The Boundary Commissions under Articles Six and Seven of the Treaty of Ghent," *Michigan Historical Review* 30, no. 2 (Fall 2004): 77–104.

52. Mortimer G. Barnes, *Inland Waterways: Their Necessity, Importance and Value in Handling the Commerce of the United States and Reducing Transportation Costs* (Springfield: State of Illinois, Division of Waterways, 1920), 8; Alex Rolland, *The Way of the Ship: America's Maritime History Reenvisioned, 1600–2000* (Hoboken, N.J.: John Wiley and Sons, 2008), 145.

53. R. Douglas Hurd, *The Ohio Frontier: Crucible of the Old Northwest* (Bloomington: Indiana University Press, 1996), 389–95.

54. Ronald E. Shaw, *Canals for a Nation: The Canal Era in the United States, 1790–1860* (Lexington: University of Kentucky Press, 1990), 137–42.

55. James William Putnam, *The Illinois and Michigan Canal: A Study in Economic History* (Chicago: University of Chicago Press, 1918), 102–7.

Chapter 3. The Era of Bad Feelings, 1839–1860

1. *Buffalo Commercial Advertiser*, May 13, 1840; *Cleveland Daily Herald*, May 13, 1840; Mansfield, *History of the Great Lakes*, 1:634; for quotes on want of harbors, see Larson, *Those Army Engineers*, 54.

2. James L. Barton, *Letter to Hon. Robert McClelland Chairman of the Committee on Commerce in Relation to the Value and Importance of the Commerce of the Western Great Lakes* (Buffalo, N.Y.: Jewett, Thomas, 1846), 8–12; for quote by a future senator, see Isaac Stephenson, *Recollections of a Long Life, 1829–1915* (Chicago: privately printed, 1915), 92–93.

3. For more on the origins and demise of the "Era of Good Feelings," see Howe, *What God Hath Wrought*; for a competing perspective, particularly on the rival political forces of the era, see Sean Wilentz, *The Rise of American Democracy, from Jefferson to Lincoln* (New York: W. W. Norton, 2005).

4. John L. Larson, *Internal Improvement: National Public Works and the Promise of Popular Government in the Early National United States* (Chapel Hill: University of North Carolina Press, 2001), 183; "Democratic Party Platform, 1840," May 6, 1840, American Presidency Project, accessed

November 2014, http://www.presidency.ucsb.edu/ws/index.php?pid
=29572.

5. E. B. Ward to William Woodbridge, Senator from Michigan, December 26, 1842, printed in Larson, *Those Army Engineers*, 55.

6. "Finding Aid," Eber Brock Ward Papers, Clarke Historical Library, Central Michigan University; Larson, *Internal Improvement*, 223.

7. For the *Milwaukee Sentinel* quote, see John Gurda, *The Making of Milwaukee* (Milwaukee: Milwaukee County Historical Society, 1999), 45–48; Karamanski, *Schooner Passage*, 54–55.

8. Karamanski, *Schooner Passage*, 58–59; Larson, *Those Army Engineers*, 80–94.

9. William Chandler, *Illustrated History of the St. Mary's Falls Ship Canal* (n.p.: Chapman and Kibby, 1893), 2–8.

10. Willis F. Dunbar and George S. May, *Michigan: A History of the Wolverine State* (Grand Rapids, Mich.: William Eerdmans, 1995), 260–61.

11. Mark L. Thompson, *Graveyard of the Great Lakes* (Detroit: Wayne State University Press, 2000), 28–29; Karamanski, *Schooner Passage*, 26–29.

12. Henry N. Barkhausen, *Focusing on the Centerboard* (Manitowoc, Wis.: Manitowoc Maritime Museum, 1990); Karamanski, *Schooner Passage*, 28–29.

13. Howard Chapelle, *The History of American Sailing Ships* (New York: W. W. Norton, 1955), 219–49.

14. Keith N. Meverden and Tamara L. Thomsen, *Wisconsin's Cross-Planked Mosquito Fleet: Underwater Archaeological Investigations of the Scow Schooners* Iris, Ocean Wave, *and* Tennie and Laura (Madison: Wisconsin Historical Society, 2005), 8–12.

15. Arthur B. Strough, "Crews of Early Great Lakes Vessels," *Inland Seas* 48, no. 2 (1993): 258–60; Karamanski, *Schooner Passage*, 31–32.

16. Thompson, *Graveyard of the Lakes*, 51–52; James P. Barry, *Ships of the Great Lakes: 300 Years of Navigation* (Holt, Mich.: Thunder Bay Press, 1996), 45.

17. Frank R. Rossel, "The *Vandalia*, First Great Lakes Propeller," *Marine Review*, September 1917, 338–39. There was an earlier propeller-driven craft before *Vandalia*. The English-built *Francis B. Ogden*, however, was only a small launch. Arthur Pound, *Lake Ontario* (New York: Bobbs-Merrill, 1945), 322.

18. Thurlow Weed, "A Trip to Chicago and the Lake Harbor Convention," in *Chicago River-and-Harbor Convention*, ed. Robert Fergus (Chicago: Robert Fergus, 1882), 149.

19. Mansfield, *History of the Great Lakes*, 1:439; Karamanski, *Schooner Passage*, 59–60.

20. Joseph Dart, "The Grain Elevators of Buffalo," *Publications of the*

Buffalo Historical Society 1 (1879): 391–404; Cronon, *Nature's Metropolis*, 110–11.

21. John J. Binder, "The Transportation Revolution and Antebellum Sectional Disagreement," *Social Science History* 35, no. 1 (Spring 2011): 19–57; J. W. Hall, *Marine Disasters on the Western Lakes During the Navigation of 1871, With the Loss of Life and Property, With a Sketch of Early Marine History* (Detroit: Free Press Job Printing Office, 1872), 5–13; Stephenson, *Recollections of a Long Life*, 93; Thompson, *Graveyard of the Lakes*, 99–101; Karamanski, *Schooner Passage*, 201–4.

22. Walter Johnson, *River of Dark Dreams: Slavery and Empire in the Cotton Kingdom* (Cambridge, Mass.: Harvard University Press, 2013), 107–19; U.S. Congress, "An Act to Provide for the Better Security of the Lives of the Passengers on Board Vessels Propelled in Whole or in Part by Steam," 32nd Congress, 1st Session, 1853, 2–11; *Chicago Tribune*, January 12, 2003; Lloyd M. Short, *The Steamboat Inspection Service: Its History, Organization, and Activities* (New York: D. Appleton, 1922), 6–7.

23. Thompson, *Graveyard of the Great Lakes*, 210.

24. Harriet Martineau, *Society in America*, 2 vols. (London: Saunders and Otley, 1837), 2:6.

25. J. P. D. Dunbabin, "Motives for Mapping the Great Lakes: Upper Canada, 1782–1827," *Michigan Historical Review* 31, no. 1 (Spring 2005): 1–43; Paul H. Gibbs, ed., "Extracts from the Log of the Schooner *Augusta* April to November, Captain S. G. Gibbs, Master, Sailing Season of 1856," *Inland Seas* 45, no. 2 (Summer 1989): 117–30.

26. Timothy Kelly, Log of the *Thomas Howland*, 1876, Box 84, Timothy Kelley Papers, Wisconsin Maritime Museum, Manitowoc, Wisconsin; Timothy Kelly, Log of the Schooner *C. L. Johnson*, 1872, Box 76A, Timothy Kelly Papers, Wisconsin Maritime Museum; Kelly Diary, 1873, Box 76A, 15 November 1873, Wisconsin Maritime Museum; U.S. Hydrographic Office, *Sailing Directions for Lake Erie and Lake Ontario, St. Clair and Detroit River and Lake St. Clair* (Washington, D.C.: U.S. Government Printing Office, 1896).

27. John Kenlon, *Fourteen Years a Sailor* (New York: George H. Doran Company, 1923), 194–98.

28. William Hodge, "Recollections of Captain David Wilkeson," in *Papers Concerning the Early Navigation of the Great Lakes* (Buffalo, N.Y.: Bigelow Brothers, 1883), 6–8.

29. *Report of the Committee of Commerce*, 27th Congress, 3rd Session, Senate Document no. 234 (Washington, D.C.: Government Printing Office, 1843), 9.

30. Elizabeth Whitney Williams, *A Child of the Sea; and Life Among the Mormons* (1905; repr. St. James, Mich.: Beaver Island Historical Society, 1983), 215–16.

31. *Chicago Evening Journal*, July 5, 1847, quoted in Mansfield, *History of the Great Lakes*, 1:202.

32. Mansfield, *History of the Great Lakes*, 1:201; Mentor Williams, "The Chicago River and Harbor Convention, 1847," *Mississippi Valley Historical Association* 5, no. 4 (March 1949): 607–26.

33. Mansfield, *History of the Great Lakes*, 1:20; Robert W. Merry, *A Country of Vast Design: James K. Polk, the Mexican War, and the Conquest of the American Continent* (New York: Simon & Schuster, 2009), 282–83.

34. For Yancy quote, see Paul Paskoff, *Troubled Waters: Steamboat Disasters, River Improvements, and American Public Policy, 1821–1860* (Baton Rouge: Louisiana State University, 2007), 63–72; Merry, *A Country of Vast Designs*, 283; Joshua Saltzman, "Safe Harbor: Chicago's Waterfront and the Political Economy of the Built Environment, 1847–1918" (PhD diss., University of Illinois at Chicago, 2008), 34.

35. James Belich, *Replenishing the Earth: The Settler Revolution and the Rise of the Anglo-American World, 1783–1939* (New York: Oxford University Press, 2009), 228–29; For lighthouse quote, see Mansfield, *History of the Great Lakes*, 1:264–65; Lawrence J. Malone, *Opening the West: Federal Internal Improvements before 1860* (Westport, CT: Greenwood Press, 1998), 22–25.

36. Randy William Widdis, "'Across the Boundary in a Hundred Torrents': The Changing Geography of Marine Trade within the Great Lakes Borderland Region during the Nineteenth and Early Twentieth Centuries," *Annals of the Association of American Geographers* 101, no. 2 (March 2011): 356–79.

37. Robert W. Johannsen, *To the Halls of the Montezuma: The Mexican War in the American Imagination* (New York: Oxford University Press, 1985), 27, 64; *Chicago Daily Journal*, 19 August 1846.

38. Robert Fergus, ed., *Chicago River and Harbor Convention* (Chicago: Fergus Printing Company, 1882), 138, 141; Duff Green to John C. Calhoun, May 31, 1847, quoted in Marc Egnal, *Clash of Extremes: The Economic Origins of the Civil War* (New York: Hill and Wang, 2011), 117–18; *Mississippian* (Jackson), July 23, 1847.

39. Williams, "The Chicago River and Harbor Convention, 1847"; Gabor Boritt, *incoln and the Economics of the American Dream* (Urbana: University of Illinois Press, 1994), 131; for South Carolina's opposition to improvement of West to North communication, see Martineau, *Society in America*, 2:34, footnote; Thomas M. Leonard, *James K. Polk: A Clear and Unquestionable Destiny* (Wilmington, Del.: Scholarly Resources, 2001), 49; George Woodman Hilton, *Lake Michigan Passenger Steamers* (Stanford, Calif.: Stanford University Press, 2002), 21.

40. Paul H. Bergeron, "President Polk and Economic Legislation," *Presidential Studies Quarterly* 15, no. 4, Perspectives on the Presidency

(Fall 1985): 782–95; Richard Lawrence Miller, *Lincoln and His World*, vol. 3, *The Rise to National Prominence, 1843–1853* (Jefferson, N.C.: McFarland, 2011), 133–34.

41. Carter Goodrich, "The Revulsion Against Internal Improvements," *Journal of Economic History* 10, no. 2 (November 1950): 145–69.

42. Millard Fillmore, First Annual Address to Congress, December 2, 1850, The American Presidency Project, accessed November 2014, http://www.presidency.ucsb.edu/ws/?pid=29491; Robert Scary, *Millard Fillmore* (New York: McFarland, 2001), 229.

43. Mansfield, *History of the Great Lakes*, 1:660–61; see also J. E. Hopkins, *1850: Death on Lake Erie: The Saga of the S. P. Griffith* (Frederick, Md.: American Star Books, 2011); "Marine Disasters and Losses of Life and Property," in *Report of the Fourth Annual Meeting of the Board of Lake Underwriters Held at Buffalo, February 10th, 1858* (Buffalo, N.Y.: Clapp, Matthews, 1858), 8.

44. Millard Fillmore, Second Annual Message to Congress, December 2, 1851, The American Presidency Project, accessed November 2014, http://www.presidency.ucsb.edu/ws/?pid=29492.

45. John C. Calhoun, "Further Remarks at the Southwestern Convention," November 14, 1845, in *The Papers of John C. Calhoun*, vol. 22, ed. Clyde Wilson (Columbia: University of South Carolina Press, 1995), 286–87; Francis, Count de Castelnau, *Vues et Souvenirs de l' Amerique du Nord*, quoted in Ken Wardius and Barb Wardius, *Wisconsin Lighthouses: A Photographic and Historical Guide* (Madison: State Historical Society of Wisconsin Press, 2013), 71; Herman Melville, *Moby-Dick* (New York: Knopf, 1988), 264; Peter Zavodnyik, *The Age of Strict Construction: A History of the Growth of Federal Power, 1789–1861* (Washington, D.C.: Catholic University Press, 2007), 208.

46. U.S. Supreme Court, *The Propeller Genessee Chief v. Fitzhugh, 53 U.S. 443 (1851) 53 U.S. 443*, December Term, 1851, accessed December 2014, http://caselaw.lp.findlaw.com/scripts/getcase.pl?court=US&vol=53&invol=443.

47. Stephen A. Douglas to Governor Joel A. Matteson of Illinois, 1854, pamphlet, Washington, D.C., Library of Congress, https://archive.org/details/riverharborimprooodoug. This is a letter written after the Senate debate to further explain Douglas's plan for funding additional improvements.

48. Paskoff, *Troubled Waters*, 85–101; Victor L. Albjerg, "Internal Improvements without a Policy (1789–1861)," *Indiana Magazine of History* 28, no. 3 (1932): 168–79; Ralph G. Plumb, "Early Harbor History of Wisconsin," *Transactions of the Wisconsin Academy of Sciences, Arts and Letters* 17, pt. 1 (1911): 187–94.

49. For quote on the perception of the lakes, see Stephenson, *Recollections of a Long Life*, 92–94; for Senator Petit quotes, see Rebecca S. Shoemaker, "Michigan City, Indiana: The Failure of a Dream," *Indiana Magazine of History* 84, no. 4 (1988): 317–42; Yonatan Eyal, "Franklin Pierce, Democratic Partisan," in *A Companion to Antebellum Presidents, 1837–1861*, ed. Joel L. Silbey (Malden, Mass.: Wiley Blackwell, 2014), 360; Larson, History of Great Lakes Navigation, 15–16; Zavodnyik, *Age of Strict Construction*; *The Statutes at Large, Treaties, and Proclamations of the United States*, vol. 11 (Boston: Little, Brown, 1859), 25.

50. Charles Johnson, ed., *Proceedings of the First Three Republican National Conventions of 1856, 1860, and 1864* (Minneapolis: Harrison and Smith, 1893), 44.

51. Carter Goodrich, "Public Spirit and American Improvements," *Proceedings of the American Philosophical Society*, 92 (1948): 305–9; Horace Greeley quoted in Alan C. Guelzo, *Fateful Lightning: A New History of the Civil War and Reconstruction* (New York: Oxford University Press, 2012), 122.

52. Historian William E. Gienapp dismissed the economic issue in the creation of the Republican Party when he wrote, "In the 1850s specific economic issues played only a minor role in its attractiveness to voters." See William E. Gienapp, *The Origins of the Republican Party, 1852–1856* (New York: Oxford University Press, 1987), 354. For a strongly contrary interpretation, see Marc Egnal's *Clash of Extremes* and Peter Zavodnyik's, *Age of Strict Construction*. Egnal's volume is a notable effort to reintroduce the importance of navigation issues in the sectional conflict (see pages 205–26). For the Barksdale quote, see Yonatan Eyal, *The Young America Movement and the Transformation of the Democratic Party, 1828–1861* (New York: Cambridge University Press, 2012), 224.

53. J. H. L. Peeke, *Centennial History of Erie County, Ohio*, vol. 1 (Cleveland: Penton Press, 1925), accessed February 2017, http://history.rays-place.com/oh/erie/underground-rr.htm; Josiah Henson, *The Life of Josiah Henson, Formerly a Slave, Now an Inhabitant of Canada, as Narrated by Himself* (Boston: Arthur D. Phelps, 1849), 58.

54. Harriet Beecher Stowe, *Uncle Tom's Cabin* (Boston: John P. Jewett, 1852), 238; Jon McGinty, "Local Ties to the Underground Railroad," *Northwest Quarterly.com* (Fall 2010), accessed February 2017, http://oldnorthwestterritory.northwestquarterly.com/2010/09/local-ties-to-the-underground-railroad/.

55. Douglas H. Shepard, "G. L. Heaton: The Underground Railroad and Lake Erie" (2013), accessed February 2017, http://chautauqua.ny.us/DocumentCenter/Home/View/124.

56. Arthur M. Woodford, *Charting the Inland Seas: A History of the U.S. Lake Survey* (Detroit: Wayne State University Press, 1994), 10–14; Christopher Baruth, "Mapping the Great Lakes, 1670–2007," Wisconsin Water Library, University of Wisconsin Sea Grant Project, accessed November 2014, http://greatlakesmaps.org/Default.aspx?tabid=89.

57. C. B. Comstock, *Report upon the Primary Triangulation of the United States Lake Survey, United States Army Corps of Engineers* (Washington, D.C.: U.S. Government Printing Office, 1882), 2; *Reports of the Chief of Engineers, U.S. Army, 1866–1912*, 63rd Congress, 2nd Session, House of Representatives, Document 740 (Washington, D.C.: U.S. Government Printing Office, 1916), 2125.

58. Woodford, *Charting the Inland Seas*, 20–21.

59. John H. Foster, "Reminiscences of the Survey of the Northwestern Lakes," *Michigan Pioneer and Historical Collections* 9 (1886): 100–105.

60. Woodford, *Charting the Inland Seas*, 31–41; *Annual Report of the Chief of Engineers, United States Army and of Subordinate Engineers Upon the Improvement of Rivers and Harbors*, 59th Congress, 2nd Session, House of Representatives, Document 22 (Washington, D.C.: Government Printing Office, 1906), Appendix FFF, 2251.

61. George Gordon Meade, *The Life and Letters of George Gordon Meade* (New York: Charles Scribner's Sons, 1913), 208–10; Henry E. Borger, "The Role of Army Engineers in the Westward Movement in the Lake Huron-Michigan Basin Before the Civil War" (PhD diss., Columbia University, 1954), 180–84; W. H. Hearding, Address to the Houghton County Historical Society, n.d., Hearding Journal and Papers, Bentley Historical Library, University of Michigan, Ann Arbor.

62. George Gordon Meade to Orlando Poe, March 24, 1859, in *Michigan in Letters*, ed. John Fierst and Susan Powers, Clarke Historical Library, accessed February 2015, http://www.michiganinletters.org/2010/05/orlando-poe-and-united-states-lake.html.

63. Hugh Whiteley, "Henry Bayfield, 1795–1885," *Contributions to Professional Engineering*, accessed February 2015, http://www.engineeringhistory.on.ca/index.php?id=3; William Ratigan, *Great Lakes Shipwrecks and Survivals* (Grand Rapids, Mich.: William B. Eerdmans, 1960), 106–9.

64. *Barnet's Coast Pilot for the Lakes, on Both Shores: Michigan, Superior, Huron, St. Clair, Erie and Ontario* (Chicago: James Barnet, 1881).

65. Frederick E. Haynes, "The Reciprocity Treaty with Canada of 1854," *Publications of the American Economic Association* 7, no. 6 (November 1892): 7–70.

66. Widdis, "'Across the Boundary in a Hundred Torrents'"; John J. Bukowczyk, "Migration, Transportation, Capital and State in the Great Lakes Basin, 1815–1890," in *The Permeable Border: The Great Lakes Basin*

as *Transnational Region, 1650–1990*, ed. John J. Bukowczyk (Pittsburgh: University of Pittsburgh Press, 2005), 46–49; Nora Faires, "Leaving the 'Land of the Second Chance': Migration from Ontario to the Upper Midwest in the Nineteenth and Early Twentieth Centuries," in Bukowczyk, *The Permeable Border*, 84; Scott L. Cameron, *The Frances Smith: Palace Steamer of the Upper Great Lakes, 1867–1896* (Toronto: Natural Heritage Books, 2005), 119.

67. *Liverpool Daily Post*, 24 September 1856; *The Working Farmer* (New York), October 15, 1857; Henry Jones, "American Lake Navigation," in *Papers on Naval Architecture and Other Subjects Connected with Naval Science* (London: Wittaker, 1865), 298; Patrick Barry, *The Theory and Practice of the International Trade of the United States and Great Britain and the Trade of the United States and Canada* (Chicago: D. B. Cooke, 1858), 132.

68. Lighthouse Board, *Laws of the United States Relating to Establishment, Support, And Management of Light-Houses, Light Vessels, Monuments, Beacons, Spindles, Buoys, And Public Piers of the United States from August 7, 1789 to March 3, 1855* (Washington, D.C.: A. O. P. Nicholson, Public Printer, 1855), 128–33.

69. Stephen Pleasonton to Thomas Corwin, Secretary of the Treasury, December 14, 1850, in U.S. Bureau of Light-Houses, *Compilation of Public Documents and Extracts from Reports and Papers Relating to Light-Houses, Light-Vessels, and Illuminating Apparatus, 1789–1871* (Washington, D.C.: Light-House Establishment, 1871), 542.

70. George R. Putnam, *Lighthouses and Lightships of the United States* (Boston: Houghton-Mifflin, 1917), 42; George Weiss, *The Lighthouse Service, Its History, Activities, and Organization* (Baltimore: Johns Hopkins University Press, 1926), 7.

71. Arnold Burges Johnson, *The Modern Lighthouse Service* (Washington, D.C.: Government Printing Press, 1890), 15–17.

72. Holland, *American Lighthouses*, 29; T. Michael O'Brien, *Guardians of the Eighth Sea: A History of the U.S. Coast Guard on the Great Lakes* (Honolulu, Hawai'i: University Press of the Pacific, 2001), 15–16; Letter from the Secretary of the Treasury, Transmitting A Report of the Fifth Auditor, in relation to the execution of the act of 7th July last, for Building Light-houses, Light-boats, etc. H. Doc. 19, 19th Cong., 1st sess., 1838, Serial 131.

73. Lt. G. J. Pendergrast, "Recapitulatory Report, Erie, Pennsylvania, August 18, 1837," in United States Bureau of Light-Houses, *Compilation of Public Documents and Extracts*, 90–91.

74. Weiss, *The Lighthouse Service*, 9–11; Putnam, *Lighthouses and Lightships of the United States*, 43; Stephen Pleasonton to John P. Kennedy, Chairman, Committee of Commerce, 13 May 1842, in U.S. Bureau of Light-Houses, *Compilation of Public Documents and Extracts*, 311–16.

75. *London Times*, quoted in Carroll Pursell, *The Machine Age in America: A Social History of Technology* (Baltimore: Johns Hopkins University Press, 1995), 186.

76. "An Act making appropriations for lighthouses, lightships, buoys, &c., and providing for the erection and establishment of the same, and for other purposes, March 3, 1851," in *Laws of the United States Relating to the Establishment, Support, and Management of Lighthouses*, 155–59; *Report of the Officers Constituting The Light House Board Convened Under Instructions from the Secretary of the Treasury to Inquire Into the Condition of the Light-House Service of the United States, Under the Act of March 3, 1851*, 32nd Congress, 1st Session, Senate Executive Document 28 (Washington, D.C.: A. Boyd Hamilton, 1852), 7–10; Holland, *American Lighthouses*, 36. For details on Pleasonton's personal life, see Charles Wilkes, *Autobiography of Rear Admiral Charles Wilkes, U.S. Army, 1798–1877*, ed. William Morgan et al. (Washington, D.C.: Naval History Division, Dept. of Navy, 1978), 316–17.

77. Terry Pepper, "The Incredible Fresnel Lens: A Brief History and Technical Explanation," *Seeing the Light: Lighthouses of the Western Great Lakes*, accessed November 2014, http://www.terrypepper.com/lights/closeups/illumination/fresnel/fresnel.htm; Donald J. Terras, Grosse Point Light Station National Historic Landmark Nomination, March 1998, 13.

78. Claire Elizabeth Campbell, *Shaped by the West Wind: Nature and History in Georgian Bay* (Vancouver: University of British Columbia Press, 2005), 41; *Buffalo Daily Republic*, July 13, 1853; Wayne Sapulski, "The Imperial Towers of Lake Huron and Georgian Bay," *Lighthouse Digest* (December 1996), accessed October 2015, http://www.lighthousedigest.com/digest/StoryPage.cfm?StoryKey=156.

79. Carol P. Miller and Charles K. Hyde, United States Coast Guard Lighthouse and Light Stations of the Great Lakes, National Register for Historic Places Nomination, Historic American Engineering Record Survey, 1979, Section 8, p. 3.

Chapter 4. The Construction Era, 1860–1880

1. Comstock, *Report upon the Primary Triangulation of the United States Lake Survey*, 8–12; Meade, *Life and Letters of George Gordon Meade*, 217.

2. Meade, *Life and Letters of George Gordon Meade*, 206–9.

3. Meade, *Life and Letters of George Gordon Meade*, 212–13; David R. Goldfield, *America Aflame: How the Civil War Created a Nation* (New York: Bloomsbury Press, 2010), 1–15. Goldfield's thesis that evangelical religion caused an otherwise avoidable war has not been broadly

embraced by historians; however, a recent book by James Oakes makes the case that the destruction of slavery was at the heart of the Republican Party agenda. Most historians would accept that evangelical Christianity provided the passion and power behind the antislavery movement. For more, see James Oakes, *Freedom National: The Destruction of Slavery in the United States, 1861–1865* (New York: W. W. Norton, 2012).

4. Meade, *Life and Letters of George Gordon Meade*, 215–16; John W. Fuller, "Our Kirby Smith," in *Sketches of War History: Papers Read before the Ohio Commander of the Loyal Legion of the United States* (Cincinnati: Robert Clarke, 1888), 161–70.

5. Allan Pred, *Urban Growth and City Systems in the United States, 1840–1860* (Cambridge, Mass.: Harvard University Press, 1980), 98–101; James L. Huston, *Calculating the Value of the Union: Slavery Property Rights and the Economic Origins of the Civil War* (Chapel Hill: University of North Carolina Press, 2003), 273–76; Frank Boles, *Sailing into History: Great Lakes Bulk Carriers of the Twentieth Century and the Crews Who Sailed Them* (Lansing: Michigan State University Press, 2017), 5; John Bassett Moore, ed., *The Works of James Buchanan, Comprising His Speeches, State Papers, and Private Correspondence, 1856–1860*, vol. 10 (Philadelphia: Lippincott Company, 1911), 385.

6. Revisionist historians, starting with Charles and Mary Beard in 1930, emphasized the economic origins of the Civil War. Long discredited, the economic interpretation has been revived by the recent work of economic historians, notably Marc Egnal, who stresses the impact of the transportation revolution on exacerbating sectional tensions. What is new in my argument is the emphasis on Great Lakes infrastructure in particular as a source of intersectional division. Historians note that after the transportation revolution, the South faced a hostile Northwest, but they fail to explain why. That is where the fight over internal improvements is key. The repeated vetoes of harbor bills by Presidents Polk, Pierce, and Buchanan weakened support for the Democratic Party in the Northwest and helped spur the Republican Party to dominance in that region. For more on this, see Charles Beard and Mary Beard, *The Rise of American Civilization* (New York: Macmillan, 1930); Egnal, *Clash of Extremes*; Binder, "Transportation Revolution and Antebellum Sectional Disagreement"; Huston, *Calculating the Value of the Union*, 274; James McPherson, *Battle Cry of Freedom: The Civil War Era* (New York: Oxford University Press, 1988), 227; see also McPherson's *The Struggle for Equality: Abolitionists and the Negro in the Civil War and Reconstruction* (Princeton, N.J.: Princeton University Press, 1964), 11–18; Stephen Middleton, *The Black Laws: Race and the Legal Process in Early Ohio* (Athens: Ohio University Press, 2005), 241–49; Anna Lisa Cox, "African Americans," in *The American Midwest: An Interpretive Encyclopedia*, ed.

Andrew R. L. Cayton, Richard Sisson, and Chris Zacher (Bloomington: Indiana University Press, 2007), 199–200; Sheriff, *Artificial River*, 16, 24–25.

7. "Platform of the National Republican Convention Held in Chicago, May 7, 1860," in *Civil War Chicago: Eyewitness to History*, ed. Theodore J. Karamanski and Eileen M. McMahon (Athens: Ohio University Press, 2014), 33–36; Richard F. Bensel, *American Leviathan: The Origins of Central State Authority in America, 1859–1877* (New York: Cambridge University Press, 1990), 69–72; William A. Messe, *Abraham Lincoln: Incidents of His Life Relating to Waterways* (Moline, Ill.: Desaulniers, 1908), 1–74; *Reports of the Chief of Engineers, U.S. Army, 1866–1912*, 63rd Congress, 2nd Session, House of Representatives, Document 740 (Washington, D.C.: U.S. Government Printing Office, 1916), 2125.

8. Emerson E. Fite, "The Canal and the Railroad From 1861 to 1865," *Yale Review* 15, no. 2 (August 1906): 195–213.

9. Frederick Merk, *Economic History of Wisconsin During the Decade of the Civil War* (Madison: State Historical Society of Wisconsin, 1916), 17–19; Andrew F. Smith, *Starving the South: How the North Won the Civil War* (New York: St. Martin's, 2011), 72–87; Lee A. Craig, "Industry, Agriculture, and the Economy," in *The American Civil War: A Handbook of Literature and Research*, ed. Stephen Woolworth (Westport, Conn.: Greenwood, 1996), 506.

10. *Chicago Tribune*, August 11, 1860, August 24, 1862; Karamanski, *Schooner Passage*, 151–53.

11. *Proceedings of the National Ship Canal Convention Held at the City of Chicago June 2nd and 3rd 1863* (Chicago: Tribune Job Printing, 1863), 28; *The Niagara Ship Canal: Its Military and Commercial Necessity* (New York: n.p., 1863); *New York Times*, May 30, 1863.

12. McPherson, *Battle Cry of Freedom*, 388–91; Charles B. Stuart, *Proposed Improvements to Pass Gunboats from Tide Water to the Northern and Northwestern Lakes, Message from the President of the United States*, 38th Congress, 1st Session, House of Representatives, Executive Document 61, March 1864 (Washington, D.C.: n.p., 1864), 1–28.

13. Charles Hyde, *Copper for America: The United States Copper Industry from Colonial Times to the 1990s* (Tucson: University of Arizona Press, 1998), 40–42; Terry Reynolds and Virginia Dawson, *Iron Will: Cleveland-Cliffs and the Mining of Iron Ore, 1847–2006* (Detroit: Wayne State University Press, 2012), 42–43; D. H. Merritt, "A History of the Marquette Ore Docks," *Michigan History Magazine* 3, no. 3 (July 1919): 424–30; "History of the Iron Ore Trade," *Cleveland Memory Project*, Cleveland State University Library, accessed December 2014, http://www.cleve landmemory.org/glihc/oretrade.html.

14. Theodore J. Karamanski, *Rally 'Round the Flag: Chicago and the Civil War* (New York: Rowman and Littlefield, 2006), 172; W. Bruce Bowlus, *Iron Ore Transport on the Great Lakes: The Development of a Delivery System to Feed American Industry* (Jefferson, N.C.: McFarland, 2010), 92.

15. George A. Newett, "A History of the Marquette Iron Range," *Proceedings of the Lake Superior Mining Institute* 19 (1914): 300–301; "The Real Builders of America: Eber Brock Ward," *American Marine Engineer* 6, no. 4 (April 1914): 9–11.

16. Cronon, *Nature's Metropolis*, 86–90; James Lester Strum, "Railroads and Market Growth: The Case of Peoria and Chicago, 1850–1900" (MA thesis, University of Wisconsin–Madison, 1965); Isaac Lippincott, *Economic Development of the United States* (New York: D. Appleton, 1921), 542–43; Nuala Drescher and James Martin-Diaz, *Engineers for the Public Good: A History of the Buffalo District, Army Corps of Engineers* (Buffalo, N.Y.: U.S. Army Corps of Engineers, 1982), 154.

17. Peter D. Hall, *The Organization of American Culture, 1700–1900: Private Institutions, Elites, and the Origins of American Nationality* (New York: New York University Press, 1982), 242–45.

18. Thompson, *Graveyard of the Great Lakes*, 146–55; "Regulations for Preventing Collisions on the Water, April 29, 1864," in *The Statutes at Large, Treaties, and Proclamations of the United States*, vol. 13 (Boston: Little, Brown, 1868), 58–60.

19. Claire Prechtel-Kluskens, "'A Reasonable Degree of Promptitude': Civil War Pension Application Processing, 1861–1885," *Prologue* 42, no. 1 (Spring 2010): 26–35.

20. Jay C. Martin, *James S. Donahue, Lighthouse Keeper* (Bowling Green, Ohio: n.p., 1989), 1–29; *Biographical and Portrait Record of Kalamazoo, Allegan, and Van Buren Counties, Michigan* (Chicago: Chapman Brothers, 1892), 355–56; Timothy Harrison and Jeannette Stevie, "South Haven Lights: Pages from Their Past," *Lighthouse Digest*, October 1999; Marilyn Turk, "The Abnormal Lighthouse Keeper," *Pathways of the Heart*, accessed December 2014, http://pathwayheart.com/the-abnormal -lighthouse-keeper/.

21. Paul Taylor, *Orlando M. Poe: Civil War General and Great Lakes Engineer* (Kent, Ohio: Kent State University Press, 2009), xvii–xviii, 221–31.

22. Taylor, *Orlando M. Poe*, 286–87.

23. Taylor, *Orlando M. Poe*, 236–37; Wright and Wright, *Great Lakes Lighthouse Encyclopedia*, 184; Russ Rowlett, "Early Classic Brick Towers, 1850–1869," *The Lighthouse Directory*, accessed December 2014, https:// www.unc.edu/~rowlett/lighthouse/types/earlymodernbrick.html; Taylor, *Orlando M. Poe*, 237; Kenneth J. Vrana, ed., *Inventory of Maritime*

and Recreation Resources of the Manitou Passage Underwater Preserve (East Lansing: Michigan State University, 1995); Wright and Wright, *Great Lakes Lighthouse Encyclopedia*, 333.

24. "Spectacle Reef, MI," Lighthousefriends.com, citing the Lighthouse Board, accessed August 8, 2016, http://www.lighthousefriends .com/light.asp?ID=708.

25. The earliest application of a coffer dam is attributed to the 1873 Craighill Channel Lower Range Rear Lighthouse in Maryland. Clifford, *Inventory of Historic Light Stations*, 14, 28–30.

26. Taylor, *Orlando M. Poe*, 233–34; Wright and Wright, *Great Lakes Lighthouse Encyclopedia*, 189–90; Terry Pepper, "Spectacle Reef Lighthouse," *Seeing the Light: Lighthouses of the Western Great Lakes*, accessed December 2014, http://terrypepper.com/lights/huron/spectacle /index.htm.

27. Clifford, *Inventory of Historic Light Stations*, 28.

28. Holland, *American Lighthouses*, 187.

29. O'Brien, *Guardians of the Eighth Sea*, 20–22; Wright and Wright, *Great Lakes Lighthouse Encyclopedia*, 401–2; Hyde, *Northern Lights*, 169–71.

30. Zachariah Chandler to B. H. Bristow, July 24, 1874, printed in Victoria Brehm, ed., *The Women's Great Lakes Reader* (Duluth, Minn.: Holy Cow Press, 1998), 241–42.

31. Brenda Wheeler Williams, Arnold Alanen, and William Tishler, *Coming through with Rye: An Historical Agricultural Landscape Study of South Manitou Island, Sleeping Bear National Lakeshore, Michigan* (Omaha, Neb.: Midwest Region, National Park Service, 1986), 35; Barb Wardius and Ken Wardius, *Cana Island Lighthouse* (Chicago: Arcadia, 2006), 42–45.

32. Women made up only 3 percent of lighthouse keepers or assistants. *Biographical and Portrait Record of Kalamazoo, Allegan, and Van Buren Counties, Michigan* (Chicago: Chapman Brothers, 1892), 355–56; Kathy S. Mason, *Women Lighthouse Keepers of Lake Michigan: Heroic Tales of Courage and Resourcefulness* (Lewiston, N.Y.: Edwin Mellen Press, 2012), 30–36; Williams, *A Child of the Sea*, 213–15.

33. Mason, *Women Lighthouse Keepers of Lake Michigan*, 1–10.

34. "Isle Royale (Menagerie Island) Lighthouse," Lighthousefriends.com, accessed July 2017, http://www.lighthousefriends.com /light.asp?ID=735.

35. Thomas Tag, "The Clock without Hands," *Keeper's Log*, Spring 2008, 28–35.

36. Terry Pepper, "South Manitou Lighthouse," *Seeing the Light: Lighthouses of the Western Great Lakes*, accessed December 2014, http:// www.terrypepper.com/lights/michigan/southmanitou/southmanitou .htm.

37. Ron Bloomfield, *Legendary Locals of Bay City* (Charleston, S.C.: Arcadia Press, 2012), 15; Terry Pepper, "Saginaw River Rear Range Light," *Seeing the Light: Lighthouses of the Western Great Lakes*, accessed February 2015, http://www.terrypepper.com/lights/huron/saginaw/saginaw.htm; Wright and Wright, *Great Lakes Lighthouse Encyclopedia*, 265, 356.

38. Boles, *Sailing into History*, 33.

39. Dempster, *Lighthouses of the Great Lakes*, 28; Dennis L. Noble, *Lighthouses and Keepers: The U.S. Lighthouse Service and Its Legacy* (Annapolis: Naval Institute Press, 1997), 33–34; Mason, *Women Lighthouse Keepers of Lake Michigan*, 42–43.

40. United States Light-House Board, *Annual Report of the Light-House Board of the United States to the Secretary of the Treasury for the Year 1875* (Washington, D.C.: Government Printing Office, 1875), 99–105; Noble, *Lighthouse and Keepers*, 33–35.

41. Jim Claflin, "Collecting Lighthouse Antiques," *Lighthouse Digest*, July 1998.

42. Ralph Gordon Plumb, *History of Navigation on the Great Lakes*, Hearings of the Commerce of the Great Lakes, Committee on Railways and Canals (Washington, D.C.: Government Printing Office, 1911), 36–39; Elizabeth Sherman, *Beyond the Windswept Dunes: The Story of Maritime Muskegon* (Detroit: Wayne State University Press, 2003), 24.

43. The cornerstone of Reconstruction historiography is Eric Foner's *Reconstruction: America's Unfinished Revolution, 1863–1877* (New York: Harper & Row, 1988). Foner expanded Reconstruction to the industrial North. More recently Heather Cox Richardson in *West from Appomattox* (New Haven, Conn.: Yale University Press, 2008) included the far West in a broader narrative of national unification that set the stage for global expansion. For figures on river and harbor expenditures, see "River and Harbor Improvements," in *Dictionary of American History* (Framington Hills, Mich.: Gale Group, 2003), accessed January 2017, http://www.encyclopedia.com/history/dictionaries-thesauruses-pictures-and-press-releases/river-and-harbor-improvements.

44. John W. Larson, *Essayons: A History of the Detroit District, U.S. Army Corps of Engineers* (Detroit: U.S. Army Corps of Engineers, 1981), 74–77.

45. J. W. Larson, *Those Army Engineers*, 133–51; Terry Pepper, "Manistee Pierhead Light," *Seeing the Light: Lighthouses of the Western Great Lakes*, accessed December 2014, http://terrypepper.com/lights/michigan/manisteepier/manisteepier.htm; Plumb, "Early Harbor History of Wisconsin."

46. Terry Pepper, "Marquette Harbor Light," *Seeing the Light: Lighthouses of the Western Great Lakes*, accessed December 2014, http://

terrypepper.com/lights/superior/marquette/marquette.htm; *Report on the River and Harbor Bill by the Committee on Commerce, River and Harbor Bill*, U.S. Senate, 61st Congress, 2nd Session, Report no. 527 (Washington, D.C.: Government Printing Office, 1910), 525; Sarah Harvey, *Jubilee Annals of the Lake Superior Ship Canal: The World's Greatest Mechanical Waterway* (Cleveland: J. B. Savage Company, 1906), 19–21.

47. The Daniel Ball, 77 U.S. 557 (1870), accessed October 2015, https://supreme.justia.com/cases/federal/us/77/557/case.html.

48. "Small Towns and the Army Corps of Engineers: The Evolution of the Region," *National Archives at Chicago Bulletin*, August 2015, 1–8.

49. Symons and Quintus, "History of Buffalo Harbor"; Leigh Cutler, Duluth Harbor North Breakwater Light, National Register of Historic Places Nomination, Section 7, 1–2.

50. Mansfield, *History of the Great Lakes*, 1:299–300, 561–64; "The Buffalo Breakwater System," *The Engineering Record, Building Record and Sanitary Engineer* 47, no. 14 (April 1903): 343.

51. Boles, *Sailing into History*, 8.

52. Plumb, *History of Navigation on the Great Lakes*, 60–61, 65; Sharon A. Babaian, *Setting Course: A History of Navigation in Canada* (Ottawa, Ontario: Canada Science and Technology Museum, 2006), 44–46.

53. "A Sailor's Fare," *Inland Marine*, April 4, 1884, quoted in Jay C. Martin, "Sailing the Freshwater Seas: A Social History of Life Aboard the Commercial Sailing Vessels of the United States and Canada on the Great Lakes, 1815–1930" (PhD diss., Bowling Green State University, 1995), 61.

54. Kenlon, *Fourteen Years a Sailor*, 191–94.

55. Newspaper accounts of the wreck of the *D. A. Van Valkenberg* indicate she left Chicago on a Tuesday, but that did not stop sailors two years later from twisting her story to justify not sailing on a Friday. *Cleveland Daily Herald*, September 9, 1881.

56. "Sailor's Superstitions," Box 6, Ivan Henry Walton Collection, Bentley Historical Library, University of Michigan, Ann Arbor; *Chicago Inter-Ocean*, April 27, 1883.

57. "Sailor Customs," Box 6, Walton Collection.

58. Ivan H. Walton and Joe Grimm, *Windjammers: Songs of the Great Lakes Sailors* (Detroit: Wayne State University Press, 2002), 86, 131–32, 173, 193, 215–16.

Chapter 5. The Emergence of the Maritime-Industrial Complex, 1880–1910

1. The often-cited figure of one in four Americans visiting the World's Fair is actually a projection based on the total attendance of

twenty-seven million people, roughly 25 percent of the U.S. population. In *City of the Century: The Epic of Chicago and the Making of America* (New York: Simon & Schuster, 1996), Donald L. Miller estimates that up to fourteen million foreign visitors attended the fair (p. 488). Timothy Harrison, "Lighthouses at the 1893 World's Columbian Exposition," *Lighthouse Digest*, September 2008; J. T. Barrett, *Electricity at the Columbian Exposition: An Account of the Exhibits* (Chicago: R. R. Donnelly, 1894), 68; Theresa Levitt, *A Short Bright Flash: Augustin Fresnel and the Birth of the Modern Lighthouse* (New York: W. W. Norton, 2013), 224; Rossiter Johnson, ed., *A History of the World's Columbian Exposition Held in Chicago in 1893*, vol. 3 (New York: D. Appleton, 1898), 493.

2. Barrett, *Electricity at the Columbian Exposition*, 6–7.

3. David Swayze, "The Great Spring Gale of 1894," *Inland Seas* 48, no. 2 (Summer 1992): 99–112.

4. Swayze, "Great Spring Gale of 1894," 103–8; *Chicago Tribune*, May 19, 1894.

5. Mansfield, *History of the Great Lakes*, 1:778; Dennis L. Noble, *A Legacy: The United States Life-Saving Service* (Washington, D.C.: U.S. Coast Guard, 1976), 4–6; Irving King, *The Coast Guard Expands, 1865–1915: New Roles, New Frontiers* (Annapolis, Md.: Naval Institute Press, 1996), 193–204.

6. O'Brien, *Guardians of the Eighth Sea*, 34–36; J. B. Mansfield, *History of the Great Lakes*, vol. 2 (Chicago: J. H. Beers, 1899), 702.

7. J. H. Rogers, Assistant Inspector to Harrison Miller, Keeper of Point Betsie Station, May 11, 1889, Point Betsie Life-Saving Station Records, 1888–1931, Box 1, Sleeping Bear National Lakeshore, Empire, Michigan; O'Brien, *Guardians of the Eighth Sea*, 36–38; Marblehead Life-Saving Station Journal, November 1877, Historical Collections of the Great Lakes, Bowling Green State University.

8. Plumb, *History of Navigation on the Great Lakes*, 67.

9. Noble, *United States Life-Saving Service*, 10–13; O'Brien, *Guardians of the Eighth Sea*, 37–39; David Porter Dobbins, *The Dobbins Life Boat* (Buffalo, N.Y.: Matthews, Northrup, 1886), 29–36.

10. *Annual Report of the Operations of the United States Life-Saving Service for the Fiscal Year Ending June 30, 1881* (Washington, D.C.: Government Printing Office, 1881), 19–36; William D. O'Connor, *Heroes of the Storm* (Boston: Houghton Mifflin, 1904), 92–124; Daniel Koski-Karel et al., U.S. Government Lifesaving Stations, Houses of Refuge, and pre-1950 U.S. Coast Guard Stations, National Register of Historic Places Multiple Property Documentation Form, 2013, Section E, 9.

11. See Arthur and Evelyn Knudsen, *A Gleam Across the Wave: The Biography of Martin Knudson Lighthouse Keeper on Lake Michigan* (Ellison Bay, Wis.: Cross+Roads Press, 2006); "History of the St. Helena Island

Light Station, *Great Lakes Light Keepers Association*, accessed February 2017, https://www.gllka.com/sth-hist.html.

12. Gustav J. Person, "Captain George G. Meade and the Lake Survey," *Engineer*, September–December 2010, 43–49; "Sketch of Increase A. Lapham, LLD," *Popular Science Monthly* 22 (April 1883): 835–40; *Cleveland Morning Leader*, May 24, 1858; Rebecca Robbins Raines, *Getting the Message Through: A Branch History of the U.S. Army Signal Corps* (Washington, D.C.: U.S. Army Center for Military History, 1996), 46.

13. E. D. Townsend, "Report of the Chief Signal-Officer: Inclosure M—General Orders No. 29," March 15, 1870, in *Annual Reports of the War Department*, vol. 4, pt. 1 (Washington, D.C.: Government Printing Office, 1883), 942; "Sketch of Increase A. Lapham, LLD"; Erik D. Craft, "An Economic History of Weather Forecasting," EH.net (Economic History Association), accessed January 2015, http://eh.net/encyclopedia/an-economic-history-of-weather-forecasting/.

14. Erik D. Craft, "The Value of Weather Information Services for Nineteenth-Century Great Lakes Shipping," *American Economic Review* 88, no. 5 (December 1998): 1059–76; Erik D. Craft, *Early Weather Information, Costs That May Be Sunk, and the Ensuing Rate of Return*, Working Paper no. 15 (Chicago: Center for the Study of the Economy and the State, University of Chicago, 1996), 12–20.

15. Craft, "Value of Weather Information Services," 1065.

16. Dina M. Brazzill, *The Missing Link between Sail and Steam: Steambarges and the Joys of Door County, Wisconsin*, Research Report no. 19 (Greenville, N.C.: Program in Maritime Studies, East Carolina University, 2007), 28–30; Barry, *Ships of the Great Lakes*, 107–8.

17. Jerome King Laurent, "The Development of Harbors, Waterborne Shipping, and Commerce at Six Wisconsin Ports on Lake Michigan through 1910" (PhD diss., Indiana University, 1973), 75–82; Craft, "Value of Weather Information Services," 1061.

18. The first iron ship on the Great Lakes and the first iron ship in the U.S. Navy was the USS *Michigan* launched in 1844. An iron-hulled passenger-package steamer, the *Merchant*, was launched in 1862 at Buffalo, but wood remained the dominant material for hulls on the inland seas for another two decades. A year before the launch of the *Onoko*, the Detroit Dry Dock Company produced the *Brunswick*, which was basically a copy of the *R. J. Hackett* but with an iron hull. The ship had a short, star-crossed career, sinking with loss of life in Lake Erie after only a season of service. For more on the *Onoko* and the growing size of lake freighters, see Richard Wright, *Freshwater Whales: The American Shipbuilding Company and Its Predecessors* (Kent, Ohio: Kent State University Press, 1969), 5; and Mark L. Thompson, *Queen of the Lakes* (Detroit: Wayne State University Press, 1994), 31–33.

19. Mark L. Thompson, *Steamboats and Sailors of the Great Lakes* (Detroit: Wayne State University Press, 1991), 22–23; *Saginaw Courier-Herald*, July 25–27, 1900.

20. David A. Walker, *Iron Frontier: The Discovery and Early Development of Minnesota's Three Ranges* (St. Paul: Minnesota Historical Society Press, 1979), 170–89, 208; William D. Ellis, *The Cuyahoga* (Santa Fe, N. Mex.: Landfall Press, 1998), 249–57; Barry, *Ships of the Great Lakes*, 175–76; Thompson, *Queen of the Lakes*, 48; Wright, *Freshwater Whales*, 48–50.

21. Walker, *Iron Frontier*, 210–11, 225; Thomas Kessner, *Capital City: New York City and the Men Behind America's Rise to Economic Dominance, 1860–1900* (New York: Simon & Schuster, 2009), 300–302; Boles, *Sailing into History*, 54.

22. Neel R. Zoss, *McDougall's Great Lakes Whalebacks* (Chicago: Arcadia Press, 2007), 7–9; Wright, *Freshwater Whales*, 126.

23. Zoss, *McDougall's Great Lakes Whalebacks*, 9; Mills, *Our Inland Seas*, 219.

24. Elroy M. Avery, *A History of Cleveland and Its Environs: The Heart of New Connecticut*, vol. 3 (Chicago: Lewis Publishing, 1918), 130–31; "The Hulett Automatic Ore Unloaders," The Cleveland Memory Project, Cleveland State University Library, accessed January 2015, http://www.clevelandmemory.org/glihc/hulett/.

25. Raymond Bawl, *Superships of the Great Lakes: Thousand-Foot Ships on the Great Lakes* (Clinton Township, Mich.: Inland Expressions, 2011), 11; Fred W. Dutton, *Life on the Great Lakes: A Wheelsman's Story*, ed. William Donohue Ellis (Detroit: Wayne State University Press, 1981), 119.

26. Thompson, *Steamboats and Sailors of the Great Lakes*, 37–40; *Annual Report of the Lake Carriers' Association, 1910* (Detroit: P. N. Bland, 1911), 110; Frank Andrews, *Grain Movement in the Great Lakes Region*, U.S. Department of Agriculture, Bureau of Statistics, no. 81 (Washington, D.C.: U.S. Government Printing Office, 1910), 66–67.

27. Dutton, *Life on the Great Lakes*, 81–94.

28. *Annual Report of the Lake Carriers' Association, 1910*, 115; O. M. Poe, *Annual Report upon the Improvement of Waters Connecting the Great Lakes* (Washington, D.C.: U.S. Government Printing Office, 1893), iii–iv; Andrews, *Grain Movement in the Great Lakes Region*, 56.

29. "Chicago's Harbors: From the Chicago to the Calumet Rivers," *Encyclopedia of Chicago*, accessed December 2015, http://www.encyclopedia.chicagohistory.org/pages/300044.html; Larson, *History of Great Lakes Navigation*, 37, 42.

30. William Livingston, "The Commerce of the Lakes," *Marine Review*, July 1905, 26; James Oliver Curwood, "Commerce on the Great Lakes," *World's Work* 8, no. 6 (March 1907): 878. Congress's 1892 authorization was actually only able to lower the connecting channels to

about seventeen feet, and it took another bill in 1902 to meet the goal of a twenty-foot channel.

31. Karamanski, *Schooner Passage*, 66–69; Larson, *History of Great Lakes Navigation*, 3; Frances Hanna, *Sand, Sawdust, and Saw Logs: Lumber Days in Ludington* (Ludington, Mich.: privately printed, 1955), 14–17; George W. Hotchkiss, *The History of the Lumber and Forest Industry of the Northwest* (Chicago: George W. Hotchkiss, 1898), 661–68; James Elliott Defebaugh, *History of the Lumber Industry of America*, vol. 2 (Chicago: American Lumberman, 1907), 444–50.

32. *London Times*, October 21, 1887; Cronon, *Nature's Metropolis*, 175.

33. James Parton, "Chicago," *Atlantic Monthly*, March 1867, 330–33; James Gordon Rae, "Great Lakes Commodity Trade" (PhD diss., Purdue University, 1967), 53–54; Jonathan Eyler, *Muskegon County: Harbor of Promise* (Northridge, Calif.: Windsor Publications, 1986), 25–72.

34. Karamanski, *Schooner Passage*, 73; George Gerald Tunell, *Transportation on the Great Lakes of North America* (Chicago: University of Chicago, 1898), 97; Rae, "Great Lakes Commodity Trade," 84, 110.

35. Knut Gjerset, *Norwegian Sailors on the Great Lakes* (Northfield, Minn.: Norwegian-American Historical Association, 1928), 8; Tunell, *Transportation on the Great Lakes of North America*, 97; Chris Keenan letter quoted in Dwight Boyer, *True Tales of the Great Lakes* (New York: Dodd, Mead, 1971), 214–24.

36. U.S. Hydrographic Office, Maritime Accidents and Casualties, Port of Milwaukee, National Archives, RG 35, Series Entry 1746, Records of the U.S. Customs Service, vol. 1, p. 3; "Not Fit to Sail the Lakes: Some Vessels Little Better Than Floating Coffins," *Chicago Tribune*, January 29, 1896.

37. U.S. Bureau of Corporations, *Report of the Commissioner of Corporations on Transportation by Water in the United States*, pt. 3, *Water-Borne Traffic* (Washington, D.C.: U.S. Government Printing Office, 1909), 180; U.S. Light-House Board, *Annual Report of the Commissioners of Lighthouses of the United States to the Secretary of Commerce for the Year 1915* (Washington, D.C.: U.S. Government Printing Office, 1915), 22.

38. Norman K. Risjord, *Shining Big Sea Water: The Story of Lake Superior* (St. Paul: Minnesota Historical Society Press, 2008), 112–14.

39. Risjord, *Shining Big Sea Water: The Story of Lake Superior*, 114–15; *Detroit Tribune*, June 10, 1886; Andrews, *Grain Movement in the Great Lakes Region*, 42. It is worth noting that improvements made by the U.S. government to the Sault Ste. Marie Canal enabled Duluth to rapidly capture the grain trade. Meanwhile, Oswego, New York, on Lake Ontario lost its role as a receiver of western grain because of the failure of the U.S. to build a Niagara ship canal or the Canadian government to modernize the Welland Canal. In the 1870s Oswego received about

eleven million bushels of grain annually; by the twentieth century this had declined to fewer than five hundred thousand bushels.

40. Andrews, *Grain Movement in the Great Lakes Region*, 63; Garrett Wolf, "A City and Its River: An Urban Political Ecology of the Loop and Bridgeport in Chicago" (MA thesis, Louisiana State University, 2012), 7; Harold M. Mayer, "Prospects and Problems of the Port of Chicago," *Economic Geography* 31, no. 2 (April 1955): 95–124; William J. Brown, *American Colossus: The Grain Elevator, 1843 to 1943* (Brooklyn, N.Y.: Colossal Books, 2009), 210; "Lake Superior Iron Mines," *Iron Trade Review* 35, no. 18 (May 1902): 49.

41. *Detroit Tribune*, June 10, 1886.

42. U.S. Bureau of Corporations, *Report of the Commissioner of Corporations on Transportation by Water* (Washington, D.C.: U.S. Government Printing Office, 1910), 149–50; Grace Lee Nute, *Lake Superior* (New York: Bobbs-Merrill, 1944), 285–86.

43. J. W. Larson, *A History of Great Lakes Navigation*, 34.

44. M. Stephen Salmon, "'A Prosperous Season': Investment in Canadian Great Lakes Shipping, 1900–1914," in *A Fully Accredited Ocean: Essays on the Great Lakes*, ed. Victoria Brehm (Ann Arbor: University of Michigan Press, 1998), 107–54.

45. Eric D. Olmanson, *The Future City on the Inland Sea: A History of Imaginative Geographies of Lake Superior* (Athens: Ohio University Press, 2007), 116–25; *Chicago Times*, July 25, 1886; Walker, *Iron Frontier*, 14–15.

46. Wright and Wright, *Great Lakes Lighthouse Encyclopedia*, 358, 360, 382–84, 387, 404; Elle Andra-Warner, "Lighting the Northern Edge: Lake Superior's Ontario Lighthouses," *Lake Superior Magazine*, August 15, 2014; Wright and Wright, *Great Lakes Lighthouse Encyclopedia*, 408, 428–30, 433.

47. Thom Holden, *Above and Below: Lighthouses and Shipwrecks of Isle Royale* (Houghton, Mich.: Isle Royale Natural History Assn., 1985) 10; *Cleveland Herald*, 27, September 30, 1881; Wright and Wright, *Great Lakes Lighthouse Encyclopedia*, 133; Terry Pepper, "Passage Island Light Station," *Seeing the Light: Lighthouses of the Western Great Lakes*, accessed October 2015, http://terrypepper.com/lights/superior/passage/passage_island.htm.

48. Putnam, *Lighthouses and Lightships of the United States*, 163.

49. Noble, *Lighthouses and Keepers*, 134–35.

50. O'Brien, *Guardians of the Eighth Sea*, 23–24; Putnam, *Lighthouses and Lightships of the United States*, 163.

51. Soren Kristiansen, *Diary of Captain Soren Kristiansen, Lake Michigan Schooner Captain, 1891–1893* (Escanaba, Mich.: Delta County Historical Society, 1981), 82; Willard Flint, *A History of U.S. Lightships* (Washington, D.C.: U.S. Coast Guard Historian's Office, 1993), 5–8.

52. J. B. Millet, "Submarine Signaling by Means of Sound," *Mechanical Engineer* 20 (July 27, 1907): 114–15.

53. J. B. Millet, "Further Results of Submarine Signaling by Means of Sound," *Transactions of the Institution of Naval Architects* 49 (1907): 300–307; Submarine Signal Company, *Submarine Signals: Results of Tests Made by the United States Lighthouse Board During June and July of 1906 of the System of Submarine Signaling Controlled by the Submarine Signal Company* (Boston: Submarine Signal Company, 1906), 22–25; U.S. Navy, "Submarine Sound Signals," *Reprint of Hydrographic Information*, no. 5 (June 30, 1909): 3–7; quote from the "veteran lake sailor" in Dutton, *Life on the Great Lakes*, 85–86. The initial shore station using the submarine signal was the DeTour Lighthouse, where it was installed by the Submarine Signal Company in 1907. The water near the lighthouse, however, was not of the proper depth and so the signal was moved more than one thousand feet offshore. Great Lakes shipowners were delighted with the system, and it was quickly adopted by the large shipping companies. The system at DeTour was sold to the government in 1911.

54. Amy K. Marshall, "A History of Buoys and Tenders," p. 4, U.S. Coast Guard Historian's Office, accessed September 2019, https://media.defense.gov/2018/Jul/09/2001940267/-1/-1/0/H_BUOYS.PDF.

55. U.S. Dept. of the Treasury, *Report of the Secretary of the Treasury on the State of the Finances for the Year 1869*, 41st Congress, 2nd Session, House of Representatives, Executive Document no. 2 (Washington, D.C.: U.S. Government Printing Office, 1869), 463–70.

56. U.S. Hydrographic Office, *Sailing Directions for the Great Lakes and Connecting Waters* (Washington, D.C.: U.S. Government Printing Office, 1896), 2, 11, 60; U.S. Hydrographic Office, Maritime Accidents and Casualties, Port of Milwaukee, National Archives, RG 26, Series Entry 1746, Records of the U.S. Customs Service, vol. 1, p. 7.

57. U.S. Department of the Treasury, *Report of the Secretary of the Treasury on the State of the Finances For the Year 1874*, 43rd Congress, 2nd Session, House of Representatives, Executive Document no. 2 (Washington, D.C.: U.S. Government Printing Office, 1874), 674–76.

58. "Buoys: Signposts of the Sea," *Ponce De Leon Inlet Light Station* 31, no. 1 (October 2009): 6–9; Marshall, "Frequently Close to the Point of Peril," 40–93; "Lighting Detroit and St. Mary's Rivers," *Marine Review*, April 1916, 140.

59. Dempster and Berger, *Lighthouses of the Great Lakes*, 104; "An Acetylene Explosion," *Canadian Engineer* 12, no. 5 (May 1905): 135–36; *British Whig* (Kingston, Ontario), April 20, 1905; Marshall, "A History of Buoys and Tenders," 10–11.

Chapter 6. The Inland Seas in War and Peace, 1910–1945

1. Powell Moore, *The Calumet Region: Indiana's Last Frontier* (Indianapolis: Indiana Historical Bureau, 1959), 265; John C. Hudson, *Across This Land: A Regional Geography of the United States and Canada* (Baltimore: Johns Hopkins University Press, 2002), 219–22; Frederick William Howat, ed., *A Standard History of Lake County Indiana and the Calumet Region*, vol. 1 (Chicago: Lewis Publishing, 1915), 316.

2. Hudson, *Across This Land*, 219–21; George J. Joachim, *Iron Fleet: The Great Lakes in World War II* (Detroit: Wayne State University Press, 1994), 17; Langdon White and George Primmer, "The Iron and Steel Industry of Duluth: A Study in Locational Maladjustment," *Geographical Review* 27, no. 1 (January 1937): 82–91.

3. J. W. Larson, *History of Great Lakes Navigation*, 56.

4. "The President's Commission on Economy and Efficiency," *American Political Science Review* 5, no. 4 (November 1911): 626–28; United States President's Commission on Economy and Efficiency, *Economy and Efficiency in the Government Service: Message of the President* (Washington, D.C.: U.S. Government Printing Office, 1912), 51–74.

5. Clifford, *Inventory of Historic Light Stations*, 11, citing George R. Putnam, *Sentinel of the Coasts: The Log of a Lighthouse Engineer* (New York: W. W. Norton, 1937), 119.

6. Judi Kearney, "George Rockwell Putnam: Commissioner, Bureau of Lighthouses," *Lighthouse Digest*, July/August 2012.

7. Lighthouse Service, Hearings before the Committee on Interstate and Foreign Commerce of the House of Representatives, Sixty-Fifth Congress, Second Session, on HR 7913, February 9, 1918 (Washington, D.C.: U.S. Government Printing Office, 1918), 28–31; Robert Erwin Johnson, *Guardians of the Sea: History of the United States Coast Guard, 1915 to the Present* (Annapolis, Md.: Naval Institute Press, 1987), 162.

8. Putnam, *Sentinels of the Coast*, 284–86.

9. For sailors' efforts to organize, see Karamanski, *Schooner Passage*, 108–11; Articles of Association, Cleveland Vessel Owners Association, September 1, 1880, Box 117, Roll 24, Lake Carriers' Association Records, Historical Collections of the Great Lakes (hereafter HCGL), Bowling Green State University (hereafter BGSU); Articles of Association for the Government of Vessel Owners of the Inland Seas and Resolutions Adopted at the Chicago Convention, February 17, 1881, Box 117, Roll 24, Lake Carriers' Association Records, HCGL, BGSU.

10. *Chicago Tribune*, September 17, 1903, September 23, 1903, May 20, 1904, May 26, 1904, June 5, 1904.

11. Lake Carriers' Association Board Meeting, July 3, 1889, Box 117, Roll 24, Lake Carriers' Association Records, HCGL, BGSU.

12. Boles, *Sailing into History*, 86.

13. Minutes of Board Meeting, 1895, Lake Carriers' Association Records, Box 117, Roll 24, HCGL, BGSU; Captain Charles O. Rydholm to L. C. Sabin, June 23, 1944, Lake Carriers' Association Records, Box 116, Folder 28, HCGL, BGSU; Thompson, *Graveyard of the Great Lakes*, 167.

14. Thompson, *Graveyard of the Great Lakes*, 273–78.

15. *Chicago Tribune*, October 26, 1897; Mansfield, *History of the Great Lakes*, 1:504–5; Thompson, *Graveyard of the Lakes*, 167; "Welfare Work of the Lake Carriers' Association," *American Iron and Steel Institute Bulletin* 3 (January 1915): 150–74; *Chicago Tribune*, July 5, 1914.

16. Marshall, "Frequently Close to the Point of Peril," 40–60; Erik Barnuw, *A History of Broadcasting in the United States*, vol. 1, *A Tower of Babel* (New York: Oxford University Press, 1966), 22–34; *Western Electrician*, May 16, 1903, 385; *Electricity, a Popular Electrical Journal* 17, no. 25 (1899): 387; *Duluth Evening Herald*, September 15, 1909, July 22, 1911; *Detroit Free Press*, April 24, 1912.

17. The 1913 storm has given rise to a virtual subgenre of Great Lakes historical articles and books. Frank Barcus's *Freshwater Fury: Yarns and Reminiscences of the Greatest Storm in Inland Navigation* (Detroit: Wayne State University Press, 1986) contains many primary source accounts of mariners caught in the deadly gale. Among the strong book-length histories of the event are David G. Brown, *White Hurricane: A Great Lakes November Gale and America's Deadliest Maritime Disaster* (New York: McGraw-Hill, 2002); Robert J. Hemming, *Ships Gone Missing: The Great Lakes Storm of 1913* (Chicago: Contemporary Books, 1992); and, most recently, Michael Schumacher, *November's Fury: The Deadly Great Lakes Hurricane of 1913* (Minneapolis: University of Minnesota Press, 2013).

18. Schumacher, *November's Fury*, 6–11.

19. Schumacher, *November's Fury*, 74–77.

20. *Globe* (Toronto), November 12, 1913; "The Greatest Storm in Lake History," *Marine Review*, March 1914, 1–24; Larry Wright and Patricia Wright, *Lightships of the Great Lakes* (n.p.: privately printed, 2011), 62–64.

21. Thompson, *Graveyard of the Lakes*, 284, 341; U.S. Congress, Senate Committee on Commerce, *Safety of Navigation on Water: Hearing Before a Subcommittee, Sixty-Second Congress, Second Session* (Washington, D.C.: U.S. Government Printing Office, 1912), 238–39.

22. Thompson, *Graveyard of the Lakes*, 255.

23. David M. Solzman, *The Chicago River: An Illustrated History and Guide to the River and Its Waterways* (Chicago: Wild Onion Press, 1998), 49–52; Louis P. Cain, *Sanitation Strategy for a Lakefront Metropolis: The Case of Chicago* (DeKalb: Northern Illinois University Press, 1978), 59–76.

From its opening in 1848, the Illinois and Michigan Canal operated pumps that pulled an ever-increasing amount of water out of Lake Michigan. Originally this was only one hundred cubic feet per second. As the city grew, the amount that was pulled into the canal and out of the lake for sanitation purposes increased to five hundred cubic feet per second by the 1880s.

24. Cain, *Sanitation Strategy*, 98–101; Larson, *Those Army Engineers*, 203–5; Lyman M. Cooley, *The Diversion of the Waters of the Great Lakes By Way of the Sanitary and Ship Canal of Chicago: A Brief of the Facts and the Issues* (Chicago: Sanitary District of Chicago, 1913), iii; Bruce Barker, "Lake Diversion at Chicago," *Case Western Reserve Journal of International Law* 18, no. 1 (1986): 208.

25. Mayor of Tonawanda, New York, to Henry L. Stimson, February 23, 1912, Lake Carriers' Association Records, Box 13, Folder 1, HCGL, BGSU; Memorandum, Lake Carriers' Association, 1911, Box 13, Folder 2, HCGL, BGSU; Paul M. Janicke, "Lake Michigan Water Diversion: A Brief Legal History" (paper presented at the Institute for Intellectual Property and Information Law, University of Houston Law Center, n.d.), http://www.watercases.org/LIB_1/Lake_Michigan_Water_Diversion_Story.pdf.

26. Dan Egan, *The Death and Life of the Great Lakes* (New York: Norton, 2017), 286–88.

27. The Great Lakes are actually just one of a series of boundary waters overseen by the Joint Commission. The treaty mentions the Milk River, Lake of the Woods, the St. Croix River, and other waters along the international border. Gordon Walker, "The Boundary Waters Treaty 1909—A Peace Treaty?," *Canada–United States Law Journal* 39, no. 14 (2014): 170–86.

28. Harvey G. Goulder, General Consul, Lake Carriers' Association, to William Livingston, President, Lake Carriers' Association, April 5, 1902, Box 13, Folder 3, Lake Carriers' Association Records, HCGL, BGSU.

29. Millard F. Bowen, *The Erie and Ontario Sanitary Canal Company* (Buffalo, N.Y.: Erie and Ontario Canal Company, 1911).

30. *The St. Lawrence Waterway: Message from the President of the United States, Transmitting a Letter from the Secretary of State Submitting the Report of the International Joint Commission* (Washington, D.C.: Government Printing Office, 1922), 32.

31. Richard N. L. Andrews, *Managing the Environment, Managing Ourselves: A History of American Environmental Policy* (New Haven, Conn.: Yale University Press, 1999), 204; Frank S. Streeter and Henry A. Powell, *Pollution of Boundary Waters* (Washington, D.C.: U.S. Government Printing Office, 1913), 20–26; *Detroit News*, February 19, 1929;

Lake Carriers' Circular no. 404, September 5, 1922, Lake Carriers' Association Records, Box 13, Folder 17, HCGL, BGSU.

32. For more on this change in the perception of the Great Lakes, see Michele Dagenais and Kenneth Cruikshank, "Gateways, Inland Seas, or Boundary Waters? Historical Conceptions of the Great Lakes and the St. Lawrence River since the 19th Century," *Canadian Geographer* 60, no. 4 (Winter/hiver 2016): 413–24.

33. "Private Operation Meets the Test," *Marine Review*, March 1920, 1; "Brokers Attend Lake Convention," *Eastern Underwriter* (New York), January 23, 1920, 26; David M. Kennedy, *Over Here: The First World War and American Society* (New York: Oxford University Press, 1980), 252–54.

34. "Private Operation Meets the Test," *Marine Review*, March 1920, 1; *New York Times*, December 16, 1917.

35. Fred A. Record, "Grain Trade Upsets in 1916 Caused by War," *Chicago Tribune*, December 30, 1916, A1; *Chicago Tribune*, April 23, 1917, March 26, 1918; Tom G. Hall, "Wilson and the Food Crisis: Agricultural Price Control during World War I," *Agricultural History* 47, no. 1 (January 1973): 25–46.

36. Robert D. Cuff and Melvin I. Urofsky, "The Steel Industry and Price-Fixing during World War I," *Business History Review* 44, no. 3 (Autumn 1970): 291–306; "Traffic on the Great Lakes in 1921," *Marine Review*, February 1922, 80–83.

37. Boles, *Sailing into History*, 150; "Boundary Waters Treaty of 1909, 36 Stat 2448, T.S. No. 548," NOAA Office of the General Council, accessed April 2017, http://www.gc.noaa.gov/gcil_boundarywaters treaty.html.

38. *New York Times*, July 3, 1917.

39. Doug Bukowski, "Chicago's Other U-boat," *Chicago Tribune*, January 28, 1998.

40. "Marine Field Out of Red Ink," *Marine Review*, October 1922, 408.

41. Jason Henderson, Brent Gloy, and Michael Boehlje, "Agriculture's Boom-Bust Cycles: Is This Time Different?," *Economic Review, Kansas City Federal Reserve* (Fourth Quarter 2011): 84–85; *Iron Age* 109, no. 5 (February 1922): 330.

42. Karamanski, *Schooner Passage*, 34; Ronald Stagg, *The Golden Dream: A History of the St. Lawrence Seaway* (Toronto: Dundurn, 2010), 109–11.

43. Stagg, *Golden Dream*, 115; *Report of the Second Annual Convention of the Lakes-to-the-Gulf Deep Waterways Association* (St. Louis: Lakes-to-the-Gulf Deep Waterways Association, 1907), 63, 119.

44. Webb Waldron, *We Explore the Great Lakes* (New York: Century, 1923), 224–26.

45. Daniel Macfarlane, "To the Heart of the Continent: Canada and Negotiation of the St. Lawrence Seaway and Power Project, 1921–1954" (PhD Diss., University of Ottawa, 2010), 80–87; Waldron, *We Explore the Great*, 60, 244.

46. William R. Willoughby, *The St. Lawrence Waterway: A Study in Politics and Diplomacy* (Madison: University of Wisconsin Press, 1961), 160–80.

47. Daniel Macfarlane, "Caught between Two Fires: The St. Lawrence Seaway and Power Project, Canadian-American Relations, and Linkage," *International Journal* (Spring 2012): 465–82; Willoughby, *St. Lawrence Seaway*, 195.

48. F. W. Dunmore, "Radio Direction Finding as an Aid to Navigation," *American Shipping* 15, no. 2 (April 1922): 10–12, 16; Alan Renton, *Lost Sounds: The Story of Coast Fog Signals* (Caithness, Scotland: Whittles Publishing, 2001), 129–31; John W. Kean, "New Lighthouse Devices Safeguard Mariners," *Popular Mechanics: An Illustrated Weekly Review of the Mechanical* 36, no. 1 (July 1921): 60–61; quote from *M.P.* 22 in *News-Palladium* (Benton Harbor, Michigan), March 18, 1933; Dempster and Berger, *Lighthouses of the Great Lakes*, 104–7; Hyde, *Northern Lights*, 44.

49. Woodford, *Charting the Inland Seas*, 117; Putnam, *Sentinels on the Coasts*, 213–15; O'Brien, *Guardians of the Eighth Sea*, 69; "Title 47, Telephones, Telegraphs, and Radio Telegraphs," in *United States Code, 2000* (Washington, D.C.: U.S. Government Printing Office, 2001), 29; U.S. Coast Guard, *LORAN-C User Handbook* (Washington, D.C.: U.S. Coast Guard, n.d.), 11.

50. U.S. Light-House Board, *Annual Report of the Commissioners of Lighthouses*, 87–89; Donald J. Terras, *The Grosse Point Lighthouse, Evanston, Illinois: Landmark to Maritime History and Culture* (Evanston, Ill.: Windy City Press, 1995), 89; Terry Pepper, "Wind Point Light, Racine, Wisconsin," *Seeing the Light: Lighthouses of the Western Great Lakes*, accessed April 2015, http://terrypepper.com/lights/michigan/wind point/windpoint.htm.

51. Terras, *Grosse Point Lighthouse*, 89; Kean, "New Lighthouse Devices Safeguard Mariners," *Popular Mechanics* (July 1921): 60–61.

52. Jerry Biggs, "Candles on the Water—Bluewater Belles: The Lightships Huron, St. Clair and Their Sisters on the Lake," *Lighthouse Digest*, September 1995; "Lake St. Clair," Lighthousefriends.com, accessed April 2015, http://www.lighthousefriends.com/light.asp?ID=705; Putnam, *Sentinels of the Coasts*, 227.

53. The *Carl D. Bradley* mentioned here was not the same as the ill-fated vessel that so famously sank in Lake Michigan in 1958. That vessel was not built until 1927. The original *Carl D. Bradley* was built in 1917 and was renamed when the newer, larger steamer was launched.

For wireless telegraphy at Rogers City, see *The Wireless Age: An Illustrated Monthly Magazine of Radio* (July 1922): 53; Robert F. Crittenden, "WLF—WLC Central Radio Telegraph Company," 1947, accessed April 2015, http://www.imradioha.org/text/wlc_1947_article.txt; "Today Rogers City Is a Center of a Live, Healthy, Progressive Community," *Calcite Screenings* (Special Edition, 1950): 16; Thompson, *Graveyard of the Great Lakes*, 341–42.

54. Thompson, *Great Lakes Steamboats and Sailors*, 55–56; Dutton, *Life on the Great Lakes*, 93.

55. David A. Bennion and Bruce Manny, *The Construction of Shipping Channels in the Detroit River: History and Environmental Consequences* (Reston, Va.: U.S. Geological Survey and the U.S. Environmental Protection Agency, 2011), 5–6.

56. Noble, *Lighthouses and Keepers*, 37.

57. Matthew J. Dickinson, *Bitter Harvest: FDR, Presidential Power and the Growth of the Presidential Branch* (New York: Cambridge University Press, 1996), 86–93; Reorganization Plan No. II, 53 Statute, 76th Congress, 1st Session, May 9, 1939, p. 1431.

58. Timothy Harrison, "The Last Days of the Lighthouse Commissioner," *Lighthouse Digest*, January/February 2012; R. E. Johnson, *Guardians of the Sea*, 162–65.

59. Canada did not have a unified marine safety organization until 1962, when the Canadian Coast Guard was created. However, prior to that the Department of the Marine and Fisheries and later the Department of Transportation operated a national system of lighthouses and a handful of lifesaving stations. For a full history, see Thomas E. Appleton, *A History of the Canadian Coast Guard and Marine Services* (Ottawa, Ontario: Department of Transportation, 1968).

60. Hugh Rockoff, "The United States: From Ploughshares to Swords," in *The Economics of World War II: Six Great Powers in International Comparison*, ed. Mark Harrison (New York: Cambridge University Press, 1998), 81–121; Joachim, *Iron Fleet*, 10.

61. Joachim, *Iron Fleet*, 18–20; Al Miller, *Tin Stackers: A History of the Pittsburgh Steamship Company* (Detroit: Wayne State University Press, 1999), 131.

62. Joachim, *Iron Fleet*, 34–36.

63. Thomas B. Buell, John H. Bradley, and Clifton R. Franks, *The Second World War: Europe and the Mediterranean* (Garden City Park, N.Y.: West Point Military Series, 2002), 221; Joachim, *Iron Fleet*, 52–55; Thomas P. Ostrom, *The United States Coast Guard in World War II: A History of Domestic and Overseas Action* (Jefferson, N.C.: McFarland, 2009), 56–59; Robert D. Smith to A. T. Wood, Office of Defense Transport, October 5, 1946, Lake Carriers' Association Records, Box 13, HCGL, BGSU.

64. Matt Portz, "Aviation Training and Expansion," *Naval Aviation News*, July/August 1990, 22–27.

65. Theodore J. Karamanski and Deane Tank, *Maritime Chicago* (Chicago: Arcadia Press, 2000), 80–85.

66. Notice to Mariners, U.S. Coast Guard, May 1945, Lake Carriers' Association Records, Box 13, HCGL, BGSU.

67. David Warner, "When Michigan's Soo Locks Readied for World War II," MyNorth, February 18, 2014, http://mynorth.com/2014/02 /northern-michigan-history-when-the-soo-locks-readied-for-world -war-ii/.

68. Shore Captains Committee Minutes, December 2, 1942, Lake Carriers' Association Records, Box 116, Folder 6, HCGL, BGSU.

69. Graeme S. Mount, "Myths and Realities: FDR's 1943 Vacation on Lake Huron, August 1–7, 1943," *Northern Mariner/Le Marin du Nord* 11, no. 3 (July 2001): 23–32.

70. Joachim, *Iron Fleet*, 92–95.

71. Shore Captains Committee, 1945, Lake Carriers' Association Records, Box 116, Folder 29, HCGL, BGSU.

72. Alexander T. Wood, "Great Lakes Transport," *Annals of the American Academy of Political and Social Science* 230 (November 1943): 37–43.

73. Waring G. Smith, "Running the Ice Blockade," *Popular Mechanics* (April 1943): 50–53, 173–74; George Woodman Hilton, *The Great Lakes Car Ferries* (Davenport, Iowa: Montevallo Historical Press, 2003), 29.

74. Joachim, *The Iron Fleet*, 102–6.

75. Perry R. Duis, "World War II," in *Encyclopedia of Chicago*, ed. James Grossman, Ann Durkin Keating, and Jan Reiff (Chicago: University of Chicago Press, 2004), 897; Charles K. Hyde, *Arsenal of Democracy: The American Automobile Industry in World War II* (Detroit: Wayne State University Press, 2013), 152–54.

Chapter 7. May Their Lights Continue to Shine, 1945–2000

1. Lee Murdock, "Liner Notes," in *Voices across the Water* (Kaneville, Ill.: Depot Recordings, 1997), cassette recording; *Isthmus* (Madison, Wis.), August 1–7, 1996.

2. Murdock, "Deep Blue Horizon," in *Voices across the Water*.

3. Charles Leach quote from Walton and Grimm, *Windjammers*, 11.

4. "Radar Sought for Lake Ships: Post War Hopes Told," *Milwaukee Journal*, July 9, 1944; R. T. Brown to Lyndon Spencer, January 15, 1957, Lake Carriers' Association Records, Box 27, Folder 1, HCGL, BGSU; *Federal Communications Commission: Thirteenth Annual Report* (Washington, D.C.: U.S. Government Printing Office, 1947), 36.

5. Larry Wolters, "Begin Testing of Radar on Lake Fraters [*sic*]," *Chicago Tribune*, July 9, 1947; "Collision Warning Radar, Western Electric Radar First on Great Lakes Fleet," National Museum of American History, accessed June 2015, http://scienceservice.si.edu/pages /103066.htm; "Firm's Sale of 450 Units Shows Use of Radar in Navigation," *Chicago Tribune*, April 4, 1948.

6. Larry Wolters, "Radar Value Demonstrated on Lake Ship," *Chicago Tribune*, May 23, 1947; Thompson, *Graveyard of the Great Lakes*, 75–76; Hilton, *The Great Lakes Car Ferries*, 126.

7. Dutton, *Life on the Great Lakes*, 88–89.

8. James Hopp, *Mayday: Tragedy at Sea* (Rogers City, Mich.: James L. Hopp, 2008); Ratigan, *Great Lakes Shipwrecks and Survivals*, 150–61; for more on the *Fitzgerald*, see Frederic Stonehouse, *The Wreck of the Edmund Fitzgerald* (Gwinn, Mich.: Avery Color Studios, 1998).

9. Marine Board of Investigation, Foundering of the SS Carl Bradley in Lake Michigan, November 18, 1958, A. C. Richmond, Coast Guard Commandant, July 7, 1959, Lake Carriers' Association Records, Box 17, Folder 38, HCGL, BGSU.

10. David Wyatt and Mike Tooley, *Aircraft Communications and Navigation Systems: Principles, Operations, and Maintenance* (New York: Routledge, 2013), 175; H. T. Sherman and V. L. Johnson, "The LORAN-C Ground Station," *Navigation: Journal of the Institute of Navigation* 23, no. 4 (Winter 1976): 349–58.

11. Steve McManamen, "Coast Guard on the Wyoming Prairie Near Gillette," *Gillette News-Record* (Wyoming), February 4, 2010; Pat Glesner, "LORAN For Dummies," *Coast Guard Stories at Jack's Joint Front Page*, accessed August 2015, http://www.jacksjoint.com/loran_ for_dummies.htm; "Recreation Gear Sought to Ease Boredom at Coast Guard Station," *Star Banner* (Ocala, Florida), November 13, 1983; Peggy Revell, "Fort Native Heading Coast Guard Station," *Fort Frances Times* (Ontario), August 5, 2005.

12. Wright and Wright, *Great Lakes Lighthouse Encyclopedia*, 98; "Detroit River, MI," Lighthousefriends.com, accessed November 2015, http://www.lighthousefriends.com/light.asp?ID=160.

13. J. C. Martin, personal communication, May 7, 2017.

14. Scott Pace, Gerald P. Frost, Irving Lachow, David R. Frelinger, Donna Fossum, Don Wassem, and Monica M. Pinto, *The Global Positioning System Assessing National Policies* (Sana Monica, Calif.: Rand Corporation, 1995), 37.

15. The Doppler Effect or shift is named after Christian Doppler, a Prague-based scientist who in 1842 demonstrated that a sound wave (or later a radio wave) will be distorted for an observer relative to its

source, such as the change in the sound of a police siren when passing another automobile.

16. Pace et al., *Global Positioning System*, 237–48.

17. U.S. Coast Guard, *Light List: Great Lakes* (Washington, D.C.: U.S. Government Printing Office, 2015), xv.

18. "Remarks by the Queen and President at the Seaway Dedication," *New York Times*, June 27, 1959, 8.

19. Donald F. Wood, "Significance of the Saint Lawrence Seaway to the Great Lakes Commerce and Industry" (M.A. thesis, University of Wisconsin–Madison, 1957), 1, 26; Claire Parham, "The St. Lawrence Seaway: A Bi-National Political Marathon, a Local and State Initiative," *New York History* 85, no. 4 (Fall 2004): 359–85.

20. George Horne, "Seaway Too Small? An Analysis of Its Congestion Problems Indicates Possible Need for Expansion," *New York Times*, June 28, 1959, 60; Bob Wiedrich, "Why Does the U.S. Shun Our Port?," *Chicago Tribune*, May 7, 1979; Michael Kuby and Neil Reid, "Technological Change and the Concentration of the U.S. General Cargo Port System: 1970–88," *Economic Geography* 68, no. 3 (July 1992): 272–89.

21. Address of Harry C. Schriver, St. Lawrence Seaway Development Corporation, January 12, 1961, Lake Carriers' Association Records, Box 44, Folder 1, HCGL, BGSU; Office of Response and Restoration, *Screening Level Risk Assessment Package Monrovia* (Washington, D.C.: National Oceanic and Atmospheric Administration, 2013), 4–5.

22. Mark Goldman, *High Hopes: The Rise and Decline of Buffalo, New York* (Albany: State University of New York Press, 1983), 268–73; Egan, *Death and Life of the Great Lakes*, 23.

23. *St. Lawrence Seaway and Midcontinental Factsheet* 2, no. 2 (September 1966); Raymond Ellis, "First Volkswagen Seaway Shipment Due April 27," *Chicago Daily Tribune*, April 4, 1960, D4; John Holusha, "Time Runs Out for an Old Car Plant," *New York Times*, January 29, 1988.

24. Boles, *Sailing into History*, 70–71.

25. J. W. Larson, *History of Great Lakes Navigation*, 79–80; John Thomasian, *The Clean Air Act, the Electric Utilities, and the Coal Market* (Washington, D.C.: Congressional Budget Office, U.S. Government Printing Office, 1982), 46. Environmental regulations alone were not responsible for the growing use of western coal in the Midwest during the 1970s and 1980s. Mining practice in the west was more cost effective, which made their low-sulphur coal very competitive with low-sulphur coal from Appalachia.

26. The best sources for the rise of taconite is the memoir of E. W. Davis, *Pioneering with Taconite* (St. Paul: Minnesota Historical Society Press, 1964); see also Jeffrey T. Manuel, *Taconite Dreams: The Struggle to*

Sustain Mining on Minnesota's Iron Range, 1915–2000 (Minneapolis: University of Minnesota Press, 2015).

27. Raymond A. Bawal, *Superships of the Great Lakes: Thousand-Foot Ships on the Great Lakes* (Clinton Township, Mich.: Inland Expressions, 2011), 7–15; J. W. Larson, *History of Great Lakes Navigation*, 78.

28. Thompson, *Steamboats and Sailors of the Great Lakes*, 186–87; O'Brien, *Guardians of the Eighth Sea*, 86–89; James L. Wuebben, ed., *Winter Navigation on the Great Lakes: A Review of Environmental Studies* (Detroit: U.S. Army Corps of Engineers, 1995), 1–3.

29. William Ashworth, *The Late, Great Lakes: An Environmental History* (Detroit: Wayne State University Press, 1987), 205–8; J. W. Larson, *History of Great Lakes Navigation*, 85.

30. Kay Franklin and Norma Schaeffer, *Duel for the Dunes: Land Use Conflict on the Shores of Lake Michigan* (Urbana: University of Illinois Press, 1983), 124–49; Ashworth, *Late, Great Lakes*, 8–9.

31. "Sand Island, WI," Lighthousefriends.com, accessed October 2015, http://www.lighthousefriends.com/light.asp?ID=689; Wright and Wright, *Great Lakes Lighthouse Encyclopedia*, 396–97.

32. Bruce J. Berman, "Just Last Year a Guy Tried to Jump Off the Tower," *Chicago Tribune*, April 18, 1971, 40–44; for Fred Dornhecher quote, see Eileen Ogintz, "Last Lighthouse Loses Human Touch," *Chicago Tribune*, December 14, 1980; Art Barnum, "Automation Dims Manned-Lighthouse Era," *Chicago Tribune*, February 13, 1984, 8; Wayne Sapulski, "The Imperial Towers of Lake Huron and Georgian Bay," *Lighthouse Digest*, December 1996.

33. Ogintz, "Last Lighthouse Loses Human Touch"; Barnum, "Automation Dims Manned-Lighthouse Era," 8.

34. "Society Accepts Lease to Restore Lighthouse," *Chicago Tribune*, March 14, 1965, 2.

35. Bernard Judge, "Hope to Raise $80,000 to Restore Lighthouse," *Chicago Tribune*, October 23, 1966, Q4; "Prisoners Assist with Lighthouse in Michigan City," *Chicago Tribune*, June 11, 1967, 3; Jessica O'Brien, "New Lantern Room Not the End of Upgrades for Old Lighthouse Museum," *Michigan City News-Dispatch*, October 18, 2014; Rick Richards, "Dreams Beckon Inspiration at Michigan City Lighthouse," *Lighthouse Digest*, July/August 2011.

36. The Chicago Harbor light was built in 1893 but moved to its breakwater location in 1917. Douglas Frantz, "He Makes a Big Move That Will Light Up His Life," *Chicago Tribune*, May 18, 1980, 1.

37. Bruce Roberts and Ray Jones, *Western Great Lakes Lighthouses: Michigan and Superior* (Guliford, Conn.: Globe Pequot Press, 1994), 12; Terry Pepper, "St. Helena Island Lighthouse," *Seeing the Light: Lighthouses of the Western Great Lakes*, accessed September 2015, http://

www.terrypepper.com/lights/michigan/st-helena/st-helena.htm;
Sarah Gleason, *Kindly Lights: A History of Lighthouses of Southern New England* (Boston: Beacon Press, 1991), 87; David Reese and Robert Browning, "Lighthouse Management: A Balancing Act by the U.S. Coast Guard," *CRM-Cultural Resource Management* 20, no. 8 (1997): 37–39.

38. Executive Order 11593—Protection and Enhancement of the Cultural Environment, accessed September 2015, http://www.archives.gov/federal-register/codification/executive-order/11593.html; "Museum History and Chronology," National Lighthouse Museum, accessed November 2015, http://lighthousemuseum.org/welcome/museum-history/; William C. Hidlay, "Lighthouse Battle Is Not a Thing of the Past," *Chicago Tribune*, November 10, 1991, 1E.

39. National Historic Lighthouse Preservation Act of 2000, *Senate Report 106-380*, 106th Congress, 2nd Session, July 16, 2000. The State of Michigan, recognizing this gap, subsequently approved funds raised through the sale of special license plates to support lighthouse preservation in their Michigan Lighthouse Assistance Program. See http://www.michigan.gov/mshda/.

40. The Heritage Lighthouse Protection Act, Parks Canada, accessed October 2015, http://www.pc.gc.ca/progs/lhn-nhs/pp-hl/index.aspx; Michael MacDonald, "Canada Deciding on Heritage Status for Surplus Lighthouses," *Toronto Star*, May 28, 2015.

41. "Stewards Needed for Four Historic Great Lakes Lighthouses," News Release, General Services Administration, May 21, 2015; Friends of Point Betsie Lighthouse, "Our Restoration Story," accessed September 2015, http://www.pointbetsie.org/restoration.html; Port Austin Reef Light Association, "History," accessed September 2015, http://www.portaustinreeflight.org/?page_id=12.

42. John Dichtl, "Historical Organizations: Ubiquitous but Under-Resourced," American Academy of the Arts and Sciences, Academy Data Forum, September 25, 2015, accessed November 2015, https://www.amacad.org/content/research/dataForumEssay.aspx?i=21941.

Afterword

1. Ken Fireman, "Ballad Charts the Memory of the Edmund Fitzgerald," *Chicago Tribune*, October 7, 1976.

2. Gerald L. Halligan, *Images of America: Lackawanna* (Charleston, S.C.: Arcadia, 2011), 22–55; Boles, *Sailing into History*, 136–37; Rod Sellers, "Chicago's Southeast Side Industrial History," Southeast Historical Society, Chicago, 2006, accessed July 2017, https://www.csu.edu/cerc/researchreports/documents/ChicagoSESideIndustrialHistory.pdf.

3. David B. Fischer, "A Tale of Two Environmental Stressors on the Great Lakes," *Natural Resources and Environment* 18, no. 2 (Fall 2003): 51–55; Kristen T. Holleck, Edward L. Mills, Hugh J. MacIsaac, Margaret R. Dochoda, Robert I. Colautti, and Anthony Riccardi, "Bridging Troubled Waters: Biological Invasions, Transoceanic Shipping, and the Laurentian Great Lakes," *BioScience* 54, no. 10 (October 2004): 919–29; E. L. Mills, J. H. Leach, J. T. Carlton, and C. L. Secor, "Exotic Species in the Great Lakes: A History of Biotic Crises and Anthropogenic Introductions," *Journal of Great Lakes Research* 19 (1993): 1–54.

4. Egan, *The Death and Life of the Great Lakes*, 288–95.

5. Tony Briscoe, "Lake's Overflow Traced to Superior," *Chicago Tribune*, July 15, 2018, 1; David Figura, "Is Plan 2014 Really the Culprit behind Lake Ontario's High Water Levels," accessed July 2018, https://www.newyorkupstate.com/buffalo/2017/04/is_plan_2014_really_the_culprit_behind_lake_ontarios_high_water_levels.html.

6. Egan, *The Death and Life of the Great Lakes*, 145–46.

7. "Two Ships Dock to Make Chicago a World Port," *Chicago Tribune*, May 1, 1959; Egan, *Death and Life of the Great Lakes*, 145–47.

8. U.S. Army Corps of Engineers, *The Great Lakes Navigation System: Economic Strength of the Nation* (Detroit: U.S. Army Corps, Detroit District, 2013).

9. American Great Lakes Ports Association, "Harbor Maintenance Trust Fund," accessed April 2017, http://www.greatlakesports.org/issues/harbor-maintenance-trust-fund/; Boles, *Sailing into History*, 149.

10. For studies of the corruption and waste of western railroad expansion, see Robert W. Fogel, *Railroads and American Economic Growth: Essays in Econometric History* (Baltimore: Johns Hopkins University Press, 1964), and Richard White, *Railroaded: The Transcontinentals and the Making of Modern America* (New York: W. W. Norton, 2011).

11. Gordon Lightfoot, "Wreck of the Edmund Fitzgerald," accessed April 2017, https://www.google.com/?gws_rd=ssl#q=lyrics+to+edmund+fitzgerald&*&spf=1.

Bibliography

Newspapers

British Whig (Kingston, Ontario)
Buffalo Commercial Advertiser
Buffalo Daily Republic
Chicago Daily Journal
Chicago Evening Journal
Chicago Inter-Ocean
Chicago Times
Chicago Tribune
Cleveland Daily Herald
Detroit Free Press
Detroit Tribune
Duluth Evening Herald
Eastern Underwriter (New York)
Fort Frances Times (Ontario)
Gillette News-Record (Wyoming)
Globe (Toronto)
Iron Age (Philadelphia/New York)
Isthmus (Madison, Wisconsin)
Liverpool Daily Post (England)
London Times (England)
Marine Review (New York)
Michigan City News-Dispatch (Indiana)
Milwaukee Journal
Mississippian (Jackson, Mississippi)
New York Times
News-Palladium (Benton Harbor, Michigan)
Saginaw Courier-Herald (Michigan)
Star Banner (Ocala, Florida)
Toronto Star

Western Electrician (Chicago)
Working Farmer (New York)

Archives

Bentley Historical Library, University of Michigan, Ann Arbor
Chicago History Museum, Special Collections
Chicago Maritime Museum
Clarke Historical Library, Special Collections, Central Michigan
    University
Erie Maritime Museum, Erie, Pennsylvania
Historical Collections of the Great Lakes, Bowling Green State
    University
National Archives, Great Lakes Branch, Chicago, Illinois
Newberry Library, Chicago, Illinois
Sleeping Bear National Lakeshore, Empire, Michigan
Wisconsin Historical Society, Madison
Wisconsin Marine Historical Society, Milwaukee Public Library
Wisconsin Maritime Museum, Manitowoc, Wisconsin

Books, Reports, and Periodicals

Adney, Edwin, and Howard Chapelle. *Bark Canoes and Skin Boats of North America.* Washington, D.C.: Smithsonian Institution, 1964.
Ahlgren, Clifford, and Isabel Ahlgren. *Lob Trees in the Wilderness.* Minneapolis: University of Minnesota Press, 1984.
Albjerg, Victor L. "Internal Improvements without a Policy (1789–1861)." *Indiana Magazine of History* 28, no. 3 (1932): 168–79.
Allouez, Claude, S. J. *The Jesuit Relations and Allied Documents.* Vol. 50. Edited by Ruben Gold Thwaites. Cleveland: William Burrows Company, 1896–1901.
Andra-Warner, Elle. "Lighting the Northern Edge: Lake Superior's Ontario Lighthouses." *Lake Superior Magazine,* August 15, 2014.
Andreas, Alfred T. *A History of Chicago.* Vol. 1. Chicago: A. T. Andres, 1884.
Andrews, Frank. *Grain Movement in the Great Lakes Region.* U.S. Department of Agriculture, Bureau of Statistics, no. 81. Washington, D.C.: U.S. Government Printing Office, 1910.
Andrews, Richard N. L. *Managing the Environment, Managing Ourselves*: A History of American Environmental Policy. New Haven, Conn.: Yale University Press, 1999.
Annual Report of the Chief of Engineers, United States Army and of Subordinate Engineers Upon the Improvement of Rivers and Harbors. 59th

Congress, 2nd Session, House of Representatives, Document 22. Washington, D.C.: Government Printing Office, 1906.

Annual Report of the Lake Carriers' Association, 1910. Detroit: P. N. Bland, 1911.

Annual Reports of the War Department. Vol. 4, pt. 1. Washington, D.C.: Government Printing Office, 1883.

Appleton, Thomas E. *A History of the Canadian Coast Guard and Marine Services.* Ottawa, Ontario: Department of Transportation, 1968.

Arenson, Adam. *The Great Heart of the Republic: St. Louis and the Cultural Civil War.* Columbia: University of Missouri Press, 2015.

Ashworth, William. *The Late, Great Lakes: An Environmental History.* Detroit: Wayne State University Press, 1987.

Avery, Elroy M. *A History of Cleveland and Its Environs: The Heart of New Connecticut.* Vol. 3. Chicago: Lewis Publishing, 1918.

Axtel, James. *The Invasion Within: The Contest of Cultures in Colonial North America.* New York: Oxford University Press, 1985.

Babaian, Sharon A. *Setting Course: A History of Navigation in Canada.* Ottawa, Ontario: Canada Science and Technology Museum, 2006.

Baird, David. *Northern Lights: Lighthouses of Canada.* Toronto: Lynx Images, 1999.

Bamford, Don. *Freshwater Heritage: A History of Sail on the Great Lakes, 1670–1918.* Toronto: Natural Heritage Books, 2007.

Bancroft, William L. "Memoir of Captain Samuel Ward, with a Sketch of Early Commerce on the Great Lakes." *Michigan Pioneer and Historical Collections* 21 (1892): 336–67.

Barcus, Frank. Freshwater Fury: *Yarns and Reminiscences of the Greatest Storm in Inland Navigation.* Detroit: Wayne State University Press, 1986.

Barker, Bruce. "Lake Diversion at Chicago." *Case Western Reserve Journal of International Law* 18, no. 1 (1986): 208.

Barkhausen, Henry N. *Focusing on the Centerboard.* Manitowoc, Wis.: Manitowoc Maritime Museum, 1990.

Barnard, J. G. "Lighthouse Engineering as Displayed at the Centennial Exhibition." *Transactions of the American Society of Civil Engineering* 8 (March 1879): 55–70.

Barnes, Mortimer G. *Inland Waterways: Their Necessity, Importance and Value in Handling the Commerce of the United States and Reducing Transportation Costs.* Springfield: State of Illinois, Division of Waterways, 1920.

Barnet's Coast Pilot for the Lakes, on Both Shores: Michigan, Superior, Huron, St. Clair, Erie and Ontario. Chicago: James Barnet, 1881.

Barnuw, Erik. *A History of Broadcasting in the United States.* Vol. 1, *A Tower of Babel.* New York: Oxford University Press, 1966.

Barrett, J. T. *Electricity at the Columbian Exposition: An Account of the Exhibits*. Chicago: R. R. Donnelly, 1894.

Barry, James P. *Ships of the Great Lakes: 300 Years of Navigation*. Holt, Mich.: Thunder Bay Press, 1996.

Barry, Patrick. *The Theory and Practice of the International Trade of the United States and Great Britain and the Trade of the United States and Canada*. Chicago: D. B. Cooke, 1858.

Barton, James L. *Letter to Hon. Robert McClelland Chairman of the Committee on Commerce in Relation to the Value and Importance of the Commerce of the Western Great Lakes*. Buffalo, N.Y.: Jewett, Thomas, 1846.

Bawal, Raymond A. *Superships of the Great Lakes: Thousand-Foot Ships on the Great Lakes*. Clinton Township, Mich.: Inland Expressions, 2011.

Beard, Charles, and Mary Beard. *The Rise of American Civilization*. New York: Macmillan, 1930.

Belich, James. *Replenishing the Earth: The Settler Revolution and the Rise of the Anglo-American World, 1783–1939*. New York: Oxford University Press, 2009.

Bennion, David A., and Bruce Manny. *The Construction of Shipping Channels in the Detroit River: History and Environmental Consequences*. Reston, Va.: U.S. Geological Survey and the U.S. Environmental Protection Agency, 2011.

Bensel, Richard F. *American Leviathan: The Origins of Central State Authority in America, 1859–1877*. New York: Cambridge University Press, 1990.

Berger, Todd R. *Lighthouses of the Great Lakes*. Minneapolis: Voyageur Press, 2002.

Bergeron, Paul H. "President Polk and Economic Legislation." *Presidential Studies Quarterly* 15, no. 4, Perspectives on the Presidency (Fall 1985): 782–95.

Bierce, Ambrose. *The Collected Works of Ambrose Bierce*. Vol. 7. New York: Neal, 1911.

Biggs, Jerry. "Candles on the Water—Bluewater Belles: The Lightships Huron, St. Clair and Their Sisters on the Lake." *Lighthouse Digest*, September 1995.

Binder, John J. "The Transportation Revolution and Antebellum Sectional Disagreement." *Social Science History* 35, no. 1 (Spring 2011): 19–57.

Biographical and Portrait Record of Kalamazoo, Allegan, and Van Buren Counties, Michigan. Chicago: Chapman Brothers, 1892.

Blackbird, Andrew J. *A History of the Ottawa and Chippewa People*. Ypsilanti, Mich.: Yipsilantian Job Printing House, 1887.

Bloomfield, Ron. *Legendary Locals of Bay City*. Charleston, S.C.: Arcadia Press, 2012.

Boles, Frank. *Sailing into History: Great Lakes Bulk Carriers of the Twentieth Century and the Crews Who Sailed Them*. Lansing: Michigan State University Press, 2017.

Borger, Henry E. "The Role of Army Engineers in the Westward Movement in the Lake Huron-Michigan Basin before the Civil War." PhD diss., Columbia University, 1954.

Boritt, Gabor. *Lincoln and the Economics of the American Dream*. Urbana: University of Illinois Press, 1994.

Bowditch, Nathaniel. *American Practical Navigator: An Epitome of Navigation and Nautical Astronomy*. Rev. ed. Washington, D.C.: U.S. Government Printing Office, 1939.

Bowen, Millard F. *The Erie and Ontario Sanitary Canal Company.* Buffalo, N.Y.: Erie and Ontario Canal Company, 1911.

Bowlus, W. Bruce. *Iron Ore Transport on the Great Lakes: The Development of a Delivery System to Feed American Industry*. Jefferson, N.C.: McFarland, 2010.

Boyer, Dwight. *True Tales of the Great Lakes*. New York: Dodd, Mead, 1971.

Brazzill, Dina M. *The Missing Link between Sail and Steam: Steambarges and the Joys of Door County, Wisconsin*. Research Report no. 19. Greenville, N.C.: Program in Maritime Studies, East Carolina University, 2007.

Brehm, Victoria, ed. *The Women's Great Lakes Reader*. Duluth, Minn.: Holy Cow Press, 1998.

Bromwell, Bethany Ann. "Mothers of the Sea: Female Lighthouse Keepers and Their Image and Role within Society." MA thesis, University of Maryland at Baltimore County, 2008.

Brown, David G. *White Hurricane: A Great Lakes November Gale and America's Deadliest Maritime Disaster*. New York: McGraw-Hill, 2002.

Brown, William J. *American Colossus: The Grain Elevator, 1843 to 1943*. Brooklyn, N.Y.: Colossal Books, 2009.

Buell, Thomas B., John H. Bradley, and Clifton R. Franks. *The Second World War: Europe and the Mediterranean*. Garden City Park, N.Y.: West Point Military Series, 2002.

"The Buffalo Breakwater System." *The Engineering Record, Building Record and Sanitary Engineer* 47, no. 14 (April 1903): 343.

Bukowczyk, John J., ed. *The Permeable Border: The Great Lakes Basin as Transnational Region, 1650–1990*. Pittsburgh: University of Pittsburgh Press, 2005.

"Buoys: Signposts of the Sea." *Ponce De Leon Inlet Light Station* 31, no. 1 (October 2009): 6–9.

Busch, Jane C. *Copper Country Survey Final Report and Historic Preservation Plan*. Houghton, Mich.: Keweenaw National Historical Park Advisory Commission, 2013.

————. *People and Places: A Human History of the Apostle Islands.* Omaha, Neb.: Midwest Region, National Park Service, 2008.

Cain, Louis P. *Sanitation Strategy for a Lakefront Metropolis: The Case of Chicago.* DeKalb: Northern Illinois University Press, 1978.

Cameron, Scott L. *The Frances Smith: Palace Steamer of the Upper Great Lakes, 1867–1896.* Toronto: Natural Heritage Books, 2005.

Campbell, Claire Elizabeth. *Shaped by the West Wind: Nature and History in Georgian Bay.* Vancouver: University of British Columbia Press, 2005.

Cangany, Catherine. *Frontier Seaport: Detroit's Transformation into an Atlantic Entrepôt.* Chicago: University of Chicago Press: 2014.

Carroll, Francis M. "The Search for the Canadian-American Boundary along the Michigan Frontier, 1819–1827: The Boundary Commissions under Articles Six and Seven of the Treaty of Ghent." *Michigan Historical Review* 30, no. 2 (Fall 2004): 77–104.

Castelnau, Count de, Francis. *Vues et Souvenirs de l' Amerique du Nord.* Paris: A. Bertrand, 1842.

Cayton, Andrew R. L. "'Separate Interests' and the Nation-State: The Washington Administration and the Origins of Regionalism in the Trans-Appalachian West." *Journal of American History* 79, no. 1 (June 1992): 39–67.

Chandler, William. *Illustrated History of the St. Mary's Falls Ship Canal.* n.p.: Chapman and Kibby, 1893.

Chapelle, Howard. *The History of American Sailing Ships.* New York: W. W. Norton, 1955.

Chapin, David. *Freshwater Passages: The Trade and Travels of Peter Pond.* Lincoln: University of Nebraska Press, 2014.

Claflin, Jim. "Collecting Lighthouse Antiques." *Lighthouse Digest*, July 1998.

Clark, Caven. *Archeological Survey and Testing, Isle Royale National Park, 1987–1990 Seasons.* Midwest Archaeological Center Occasional Studies in Anthropology 32. Lincoln, Neb.: Midwest Archeological Center, U.S. National Park Service, 1995.

Clifford, Candace. *Inventory of Historic Light Stations.* Washington, D.C.: U.S. Government Printing Office for the National Park Service, 1994.

————. "Light Stations of the United States." Multiple Property Documentation Form, 1999.

Clifford, Candace, Ralph Eshelman, Michael Seibert, and Thomas A. Vitanza. *Historic Lighthouse Preservation Handbook.* Washington, D.C.: National Park Service, Maritime Initiative, 1997.

Cochrane, Timothy. *Minong—The Good Place: Ojibwe and Isle Royale.* East Lansing: Michigan State University Press, 2009.

Commemorative and Biographical Record of the Upper Lake Region. Chicago: J. H. Beers, 1905.

Comstock, C. B. *Report upon the Primary Triangulation of the United States Lake Survey, United States Army Corps of Engineers.* Washington, D.C.: U.S. Government Printing Office, 1882.

Conrad, Joseph. *Lord Jim.* New York: McClure, Phillips, 1900.

Cooley, Lyman M. *The Diversion of the Waters of the Great Lakes by Way of the Sanitary and Ship Canal of Chicago: A Brief of the Facts and the Issues.* Chicago: Sanitary District of Chicago, 1913.

Cooper, James Fenimore. *The Pathfinder: Or, The Inland Sea.* New York: Sully and Kleinteich, 1876.

Cox, Anna Lisa. "African Americans." In *The American Midwest: An Interpretive Encyclopedia,* edited by Andrew R. L. Cayton, Richard Sisson, and Chris Zacher, 199–200. Bloomington: Indiana University Press, 2007.

Cronon, William. *Nature's Metropolis: Chicago and the Great West.* New York: W. W. Norton, 1991.

Craft, Erik D. *Early Weather Information, Costs That May Be Sunk, and the Ensuing Rate of Return.* Working Paper no. 15. Chicago: Center for the Study of the Economy and the State, University of Chicago, 1996.

———. "The Value of Weather Information Services for Nineteenth-Century Great Lakes Shipping." *American Economic Review* 88, no. 5 (December 1998): 1059–76.

Craig, Lee A. "Industry, Agriculture, and the Economy." In *The American Civil War: A Handbook of Literature and Research,* edited by Stephen Woolworth, 505–14. Westport, Conn.: Greenwood, 1996.

Cuff, Robert D., and Melvin I. Urofsky. "The Steel Industry and Price-Fixing during World War I." *Business History Review* 44, no. 3 (Autumn 1970): 291–306.

Curwood, James Oliver. "Commerce on the Great Lakes." *World's Work* 8, no. 6 (March 1907): 8785–90.

Dagenais, Michele, and Kenneth Cruikshank. "Gateways, Inland Seas, or Boundary Waters? Historical Conceptions of the Great Lakes and the St. Lawrence River since the 19th Century." *Canadian Geographer* 60, no. 4 (Winter/hiver 2016): 413–24.

Dart, Joseph. "The Grain Elevators of Buffalo." *Publications of the Buffalo Historical Society* 1 (1879): 391–404.

Davis, E. W. *Pioneering with Taconite.* St. Paul: Minnesota Historical Society Press, 1964.

Davis, James E. *Frontier America, 1800–1840: A Comparative Demographic Analysis of the Frontier Process.* Glendale, Calif.: Arthur Clark, 1977.

————. *Frontier Illinois*. Bloomington: Indiana University Press, 1998.

Defebaugh, James Elliott. *History of the Lumber Industry of America*. Vol. 2. Chicago: American Lumberman, 1907.

Dempster, Daniel, and Todd Berger. *Lighthouses of the Great Lakes*. Minneapolis: Voyageur Press, 2002.

Dickinson, Matthew J. *Bitter Harvest: FDR, Presidential Power and the Growth of the Presidential Branch*. New York: Cambridge University Press, 1996.

Dixon, Conrad. "Navigation Changes Direction from Art to Science." In *Frutta di Mare: Evolution and Revolution in the Maritime World in the 19th and 20th Centuries*, edited by Paul C. van Royen, Lewis R. Fischer, and David M. Williams, 19–27. Amsterdam: Batavian Lion International, 1998.

Dobbins, David Porter. *The Dobbins Life Boat*. Buffalo, N.Y.: Matthews, Northrup, 1886.

Drescher, Nan. *Engineers for the Public Good: A History of the Buffalo District of the Army Corps of Engineers*. Buffalo: U.S. Army Corps of Engineers, 1982.

Drury, John. *Old Illinois Houses*. Chicago: University of Chicago Press, 1977.

Dunbabin, J. P. D. "Motives for Mapping the Great Lakes: Upper Canada, 1782–1827." *Michigan Historical Review* 31, no. 1 (Spring 2005): 1–43.

Dunbar, Willis F., and George S. May. *Michigan: A History of the Wolverine State*. Grand Rapids, Mich.: William Eerdmans, 1995.

Dunmore, F. W. "Radio Direction Finding as an Aid to Navigation." *American Shipping* 15, no. 2 (April 1922): 10–16.

Dutton, Fred W. *Life on the Great Lakes: A Wheelsman's Story*. Edited by William D. Ellis. Detroit: Wayne State University Press, 1981.

Egan, Dan. *The Death and Life of the Great Lakes*. New York: Norton, 2017.

Egnal, Marc. *Clash of Extremes: The Economic Origins of the Civil War*. New York: Hill and Wang, 2011.

Ehle, Jay C. *Cleveland's Harbor: The Cleveland-Cuyahoga Port Authority*. Kent, Ohio: Kent State University Press, 1996.

Elkins, Stanley, and Eric McKitrick. *The Age of Federalism: The Early American Republic, 1788–1800*. New York: Oxford University Press, 1991.

Ellis, William D. *The Cuyahoga*. Santa Fe, N.Mex.: Landfall Press, 1998.

Eyal, Yonatan. "Franklin Pierce, Democratic Partisan." In *A Companion to Antebellum Presidents, 1837–1861*, edited by Joel L. Silbey, 345–66. Malden, Mass.: Wiley Blackwell, 2014.

———. *The Young America Movement and the Transformation of the Democratic Party, 1828–1861*. New York: Cambridge University Press, 2012.

Eyler, Jonathan. *Muskegon County: Harbor of Promise*. Northridge, Calif.: Windsor Publications, 1986.

Faires, Nora. "Leaving the 'Land of the Second Chance': Migration from Ontario to the Upper Midwest in the Nineteenth and Early Twentieth Centuries." In *The Permeable Border: The Great Lakes Basin as Transnational Region, 1650–1990*, edited by John J. Bukowczyk, 78–119. Pittsburgh: University of Pittsburgh Press, 2005.

Farrand, Max, ed. *Records of the Federal Convention of 1787*. Vol. 2. New Haven, Conn.: Yale University Press, 1911.

Federal Communications Commission: Thirteenth Annual Report. Washington, D.C.: U.S. Government Printing Office, 1947.

Fergus, Robert, ed. *Chicago River and Harbor Convention*. Chicago: Fergus Printing Company, 1882.

Fischer, David B. "A Tale of Two Environmental Stressors on the Great Lakes." *Natural Resources and Environment* 18, no. 2 (Fall 2003): 51–55.

Fite, Emerson E. "The Canal and the Railroad From 1861 to 1865." *Yale Review* 15, no. 2 (August 1906): 195–213.

Flint, Timothy. *The History and Geography of the Mississippi Valley*. Cincinnati: E. H. Flint and L. R. Lincoln, 1832.

Flint, Willard. *A History of U.S. Lightships*. Washington, D.C.: U.S. Coast Guard Historian's Office, 1993.

Fogel, Robert W. *Railroads and American Economic Growth: Essays in Econometric History*. Baltimore: Johns Hopkins University Press, 1964.

Foner, Eric. *Reconstruction: America's Unfinished Revolution, 1863–1877*. New York: Harper & Row, 1988.

Foster, John H. "Reminiscences of the Survey of the Northwestern Lakes." *Michigan Pioneer and Historical Collections* 9 (1886): 100–105.

Franklin, Kay, and Norma Schaeffer. *Duel for the Dunes: Land Use Conflict on the Shores of Lake Michigan*. Urbana: University of Illinois Press, 1983.

Fuller, John W. "Our Kirby Smith." In *Sketches of War History: Papers Read before the Ohio Commander of the Loyal Legion of the United States*, 161–70. Cincinnati: Robert Clarke, 1888.

Fuller, Margaret. *A Summer on the Lakes*. Boston: Charles Little and James Brown, 1844.

Gibbs, Paul H., ed. "Extracts from the Log of the Schooner Augusta April to November, Captain S. G. Gibbs, Master, Sailing Season of 1856." *Inland Seas* 45, no. 2 (Summer 1989): 117–30.

Gienapp, William E. *The Origins of the Republican Party, 1852–1856.* New York: Oxford University Press, 1987.

Gjerset, Knut. *Norwegian Sailors on the Great Lakes.* Northfield, Minn.: Norwegian-American Historical Association, 1928.

Gleason, Sarah. *Kindly Lights: A History of Lighthouses of Southern New England.* Boston: Beacon Press, 1991.

Goldfield, David R. *America Aflame: How the Civil War Created a Nation.* New York: Bloomsbury Press, 2010.

Goldman, Mark. *High Hopes: The Rise and Decline of Buffalo, New York.* Albany: State University of New York Press, 1983.

Goodrich, Carter. "Public Spirit and American Improvements." *Proceedings of the American Philosophical Society* 92 (1948): 305–9.

———. "The Revulsion Against Internal Improvements." *Journal of Economic History* 10, no. 2 (November 1950): 145–69.

"The Greatest Storm in Lake History." *Marine Review,* March 1914, 1–24.

Grossman, Joanne, and Theodore J. Karamanski, eds. *Historic Lighthouses and Navigational Aids of the Illinois Shore of Lake Michigan.* Chicago: Chicago Maritime Society, 1989.

Guelzo, Alan C. *Fateful Lightning: A New History of the Civil War and Reconstruction.* New York: Oxford University Press, 2012.

Gurda, John. *The Making of Milwaukee.* Milwaukee: Milwaukee County Historical Society, 1999.

Hahn, Stephen. *A Nation without Borders: The United States and Its World in an Age of Civil Wars, 1830–1910.* New York: Penguin, 2016.

Hall, J. W. *Marine Disasters on the Western Lakes During the Navigation of 1871, With the Loss of Life and Property, With a Sketch of Early Marine History.* Detroit: Free Press Job Printing Office, 1872.

Hall, Peter D. *The Organization of American Culture, 1700–1900: Private Institutions, Elites, and the Origins of American Nationality.* New York: New York University Press, 1982.

Hall, Tom G. "Wilson and the Food Crisis: Agricultural Price Control during World War I." *Agricultural History* 47, no. 1 (January 1973): 25–46.

Halligan, Gerald L. *Images of America: Lackawanna.* Charleston, S.C.: Arcadia, 2011.

Handy, Moses, ed. *The Official Directory of the World's Columbian Exposition.* Chicago: W. B. Gonkey, 1893.

Hanna, Frances. *Sand, Sawdust, and Saw Logs: Lumber Days in Ludington.* Ludington, Mich.: privately printed, 1955.

Harrison, Timothy. "The Last Days of the Lighthouse Commissioner." *Lighthouse Digest,* January/February 2012.

———. "Lighthouses at the 1893 World's Columbian Exposition." *Lighthouse Digest,* September 2008.

Harrison, Timothy, and Jeannette Stevie. "South Haven Lights: Pages from Their Past." *Lighthouse Digest*, October 1999.

Harvey, Sarah. *Jubilee Annals of the Lake Superior Ship Canal: The World's Greatest Mechanical Waterway*. Cleveland: J. B. Savage Company, 1906.

Hatter, Lawrence B. A. *Citizens of Convenience: The Imperial Origins of American Nationhood on the U.S.-Canadian Border*. Charlottesville: University of Virginia Press, 2016.

Hawley, Jonathan P. *Point Betsie Lightkeeping and Life-Saving on Northeastern Lake Michigan*. Ann Arbor: University of Michigan Press, 2008.

Haynes, Frederick E. "The Reciprocity Treaty with Canada of 1854." *Publications of the American Economic Association* 7, no. 6 (November 1892): 7–70.

Hemming, Robert J. *Ships Gone Missing: The Great Lakes Storm of 1913*. Chicago: Contemporary Books, 1992.

Henderson, Jason, Brent Gloy, and Michael Boehlje. "Agriculture's Boom-Bust Cycles: Is This Time Different?" *Economic Review, Kansas City Federal Reserve* (Fourth Quarter 2011): 81–87.

Hennepin, Louis. *A Description of Louisiana*. Translated by John G. Shea. New York: John G. Shea, 1880.

Henson, Josiah. *The Life of Josiah Henson, Formerly a Slave, Now an Inhabitant of Canada, as Narrated by Himself*. Boston: Arthur D. Phelps, 1849.

Herbrandson, Carl. *Health Consultation, Mercury at a Lighthouse, Split Rock Lighthouse, Two Harbors, Lake County, Minnesota*. St. Paul: Minnesota Department of Health Environmental Health Division, 2009.

Hilton, George Woodman. *The Great Lakes Car Ferries*. Davenport, Iowa: Montevallo Historical Press, 1962.

———. *Lake Michigan Passenger Steamers*. Stanford, Calif.: Stanford University Press, 2002.

Hodge, William "Recollections of Captain David Wilkeson." In *Papers Concerning the Early Navigation of the Great Lakes*, 1–21. Buffalo, N.Y.: Bigelow Brothers, 1883.

Holden, Thom. *Above and Below: Lighthouses and Shipwrecks of Isle Royale*. Houghton, Mich.: Isle Royale Natural History Assn., 1985.

Holleck, Kristen T., Edward L. Mills, Hugh J. MacIsaac, Margaret R. Dochoda, Robert I. Colautti, and Anthony Riccardi. "Bridging Troubled Waters: Biological Invasions, Transoceanic Shipping, and the Laurentian Great Lakes." *BioScience* 54, no. 10 (October 2004): 919–29.

Holland, F. Ross, Jr. *America's Lighthouses: An Illustrated History*. Brattleboro, Vt.: Greene Press, 1972.

Hopkins, J. E. *1850: Death on Lake Erie: The Saga of the S. P. Griffith.* Frederick, Md.: American Star Books, 2011.

Hopp, James. *Mayday: Tragedy at Sea.* Rogers City, Mich.: James L. Hopp, 2008.

Hotchkiss, George W. *The History of the Lumber and Forest Industry of the Northwest.* Chicago: George W. Hothckiss, 1898.

Howat, Frederick William, ed. *A Standard History of Lake County Indiana and the Calumet Region.* Vol. 1. Chicago: Lewis Publishing, 1915.

Howe, Daniel Walker. *What God Hath Wrought: The Transformation of America, 1815–1848.* New York: Oxford University Press, 2007.

Howland, Henry. "Navy Island and the First Successors to the Griffon." *Publications of the Buffalo Historical Society* 6 (1903): 18–19.

Hudson, John C. *Across This Land: A Regional Geography of the United States and Canada.* Baltimore: Johns Hopkins University Press, 2002.

Hurd, R. Douglas. *The Ohio Frontier: Crucible of the Old Northwest.* Bloomington: Indiana University Press, 1996.

Huston, James L. *Calculating the Value of the Union: Slavery Property Rights and the Economic Origins of the Civil War.* Chapel Hill: University of North Carolina Press, 2003.

Hyde, Charles K. *Arsenal of Democracy: The American Automobile Industry in World War II.* Detroit: Wayne State University Press, 2013.

———. *Copper for America: The United States Copper Industry from Colonial Times to the 1990s.* Tucson: University of Arizona Press, 1998.

———. *The Northern Lights: Lighthouses of the Upper Great Lakes.* Lansing, Mich.: Two Peninsula Press, 1986.

Ilisevich, Robert D. *Daniel Dobbins Frontier Merchant.* Erie, Pa.: Erie Historical Society, 1993.

Janicke, Paul M. "Lake Michigan Water Diversion: A Brief Legal History." Paper presented at the Institute for Intellectual Property and Information Law, University of Houston Law Center, n.d. http://www.watercases.org/LIB_1/Lake_Michigan_Water_Diversion_Story.pdf.

Joachim, George J. *Iron Fleet: The Great Lakes in World War II.* Detroit: Wayne State University Press, 1994.

Johannsen, Robert W. *To the Halls of the Montezuma: The Mexican War in the American Imagination.* New York: Oxford University Press, 1985.

Johnson, Arnold Burges. *The Modern Lighthouse Service.* Washington, D.C.: U.S. Government Printing Press, 1890.

Johnson, Charles, ed. *Proceedings of the First Three Republican National Conventions of 1856, 1860, and 1864.* Minneapolis: Harrison and Smith, 1893.

Johnson, Robert Erwin. *Guardians of the Sea: History of the United States Coast Guard, 1915 to the Present.* Annapolis, Md.: Naval Institute Press, 1987.

Johnson, Rossiter, ed. *A History of the World's Columbian Exposition Held in Chicago in 1893*. Vol. 3. New York: D. Appleton, 1898.

Johnson, Walter. *River of Dark Dreams: Slavery and Empire in the Cotton Kingdom*. Cambridge, Mass.: Harvard University Press, 2013.

Jones, Henry. "American Lake Navigation." In *Papers on Naval Architecture and Other Subjects Connected with Naval Science*, 288–98. London: Wittaker, 1865.

Karamanski, Theodore J. *Rally 'Round the Flag: Chicago and the Civil War*. New York: Rowman and Littlefield, 2006.

———. *Schooner Passage: Sailing Ships and the Lake Michigan Frontier*. Detroit: Wayne State University Press, 2000.

Karamanski, Theodore J., and Eileen M. McMahon, eds. *Civil War Chicago: Eyewitness to History*. Athens: Ohio University Press, 2014.

Karamanski, Theodore J., and Deane Tank. *Maritime Chicago*. Chicago: Arcadia Press, 2000.

Kean, John W. "New Lighthouse Devices Safeguard Mariners." *Popular Mechanics: An Illustrated Weekly Review of the Mechanical* 36, no. 1 (July 1921): 60–61.

Kearney, Judi. "George Rockwell Putnam: Commissioner, Bureau of Lighthouses." *Lighthouse Digest*, July/August 2012.

Keating, William H. *Narrative of an Expedition to the Source of St. Peter's River*. Philadelphia: H. C. Carey, 1824.

Kenlon, John. *Fourteen Years a Sailor*. New York: George H. Doran Company, 1923.

Kennedy, David M. *Over Here: The First World War and American Society*. New York: Oxford University Press, 1980.

Kent, Timothy J. *Birchbark Canoes of the Fur Trade*. Vol. 1. Ossineke, Mich.: Silver Fox Enterprises, 1997.

Kessner, Thomas. *Capital City: New York City and the Men Behind America's Rise to Economic Dominance, 1860–1900*. New York: Simon & Schuster, 2009.

King, Irving. *The Coast Guard Expands, 1865–1915: New Roles, New Frontiers*. Annapolis, Md.: Naval Institute Press, 1996.

Knudsen, Arthur, and Evelyn Knudsen. *A Gleam Across the Wave: The Biography of Martin Knudson Lighthouse Keeper on Lake Michigan*. Ellison Bay, Wis.: Cross+Roads Press, 2006.

Korn, Bernard C. "Eber Brock Ward: Pathfinder of American Industry." PhD diss., Marquette University, 1942.

Kristiansen, Soren. *Diary of Captain Soren Kristiansen, Lake Michigan Schooner Captain, 1891–1893*. Escanaba, Mich.: Delta County Historical Society, 1981.

Kuby, Michael, and Neil Reid. "Technological Change and the Concentration of the U.S. General Cargo Port System: 1970–88." *Economic Geography* 68, no. 3 (July 1992): 272–89.

Labaree, Benjamin W., William M. Fowler Jr., John B. Hattendorf, Jeffrey J. Safford, Edward W. Sloan, and Andrew W. German. *America and the Sea: A Maritime History*. Mystic, Conn: Mystic Seaport, 1998.

"Lake Superior Iron Mines." *Iron Trade Review* 35, no. 18 (May 1902): 49.

Lankton, Larry. *Beyond the Boundaries: Life and Landscape at the Lake Superior Copper Mines, 1840–1875*. New York: Oxford University Press, 1997.

Larson, John Lauritz. *Internal Improvement: National Public Works and the Promise of Popular Government in the Early National United States*. Chapel Hill: University of North Carolina Press, 2001.

———. *The Market Revolution in America: Liberty, Ambition, and the Eclipse of the Common Good*. New York: Cambridge University Press, 2010.

Larson, John W. *Essayons: A History of the Detroit District, U.S. Army Corps of Engineers*. Detroit: U.S. Army Corps of Engineers, 1981.

———. *A History of Great Lakes Navigation*. Fort Belvoir, Va.: National Waterways Study, U.S. Army Engineer Water Resources Support Center, Institute for Water Resources, 1983.

———. *Those Army Engineers: A History of the Chicago District of the U.S. Army Corps of Engineers*. Chicago: U.S. Army Corps of Engineers, 1979.

Latrobe, Charles J. *The Rambler in North America*. Vol. 2. London: R. B. Seeley and W. Burnside, 1835.

Laurent, Jerome King. "The Development of Harbors, Waterborne Shipping, and Commerce at Six Wisconsin Ports on Lake Michigan through 1910." PhD diss., Indiana University, 1973.

Laurent, Jerome K. "Trade, Transport, and Technology: The American Great Lakes, 1866–1910." *Journal of Transport History* 4 (1983): 1–3, 12.

Lee, Annette S., William Wilson, Jeff Tibbetts, and Carl Gawboy. *Ojibwe Giizhig Anang Masinaa'igan, Ojibwe Sky Star Map Constellation Guidebook: An Introduction to Ojibwe Star Knowledge*. North Rocks, Calif.: Lightning Source-Ingram Spark, 2014.

Leonard, Thomas M. *James K. Polk: A Clear and Unquestionable Destiny*. Wilmington, Del.: Scholarly Resources, 2001.

Levitt, Theresa. *A Short Bright Flash: Augustin Fresnel and the Birth of the Modern Lighthouse*. New York: W. W. Norton, 2013.

Lewis, G. Malcom. "First Nations Mapmaking in the Great Lakes Region." *Michigan Historical Review* 30, no. 2 (Fall 2004): 1–34.

Lewis, Kenneth E. *West to Far Michigan: Settling the Lower Peninsula, 1815–1860*. East Lansing: Michigan State University, 2002.

Lighthouse Board. *Laws of the United States Relating to Establishment, Support, And Management of Light-Houses, Light Vessels, Monuments, Beacons, Spindles, Buoys, And Public Piers of the United States From August 7, 1789 to March 3, 1855*. Washington, D.C.: A. O. P. Nicholson, Public Printer, 1855.

Lighthouse Service. Hearings before the Committee on Interstate and Foreign Commerce of the House of Representatives. Sixty-Fifth Congress, Second Session, on HR 7913, February 9, 1918. Washington, D.C.: U.S. Government Printing Office, 1918.

"Lighting Detroit and St. Mary's Rivers." *Marine Review*, April 1916, 140.

Lippincott, Isaac. *Economic Development of the United States*. New York: D. Appleton, 1921.

Livingston, William. "The Commerce of the Lakes." *Marine Review*, July 1905, 26.

Macfarlane, Daniel. "Caught between Two Fires: The St. Lawrence Seaway and Power Project, Canadian-American Relations, and Linkage." *International Journal* (Spring 2012): 465–82.

———. "To the Heart of the Continent: Canada and Negotiation of the St. Lawrence Seaway and Power Project, 1921–1954." PhD diss., University of Ottawa, 2010.

Majher, Patricia. *Ladies of the Lights: Michigan Women in the Lighthouse Service*. Ann Arbor: University of Michigan Press, 2010.

Malone, Lawrence J. *Opening the West: Federal Internal Improvements before 1860*. Westport, Conn.: Greenwood Press, 1998.

Mansfield, J. B. *History of the Great Lakes*. 2 vols. Chicago: J. H. Beers, 1899.

Manuel, Jeffrey T. *Taconite Dreams: The Struggle to Sustain Mining on Minnesota's Iron Range, 1915–2000*. Minneapolis: University of Minnesota Press, 2015.

"Marine Disasters and Losses of Life and Property." In *Report of the Fourth Annual Meeting of the Board of Lake Underwriters Held at Buffalo, February 10th, 1858*, 8. Buffalo, N.Y.: Clapp, Matthews, 1858.

"Marine Field Out of Red Ink." *Marine Review*, October 1922, 408.

Marshall, Amy K. "Frequently Close to the Point of Peril: A History of Buoys and Tenders in U.S. Coastal Waters, 1789–1939." MA thesis, East Carolina University, 1997.

Martin, Jay C. *James S. Donahue, Lighthouse Keeper*. Bowling Green, Ohio: n.p., 1989.

———. "Sailing the Freshwater Seas: A Social History of Life Aboard the Commercial Sailing Vessels of the United States and Canada on the Great Lakes, 1815–1930." PhD diss., Bowling Green State University, 1995.

Martineau, Harriet. *Society in America*. 2 vols. London: Saunders and Otley, 1837.

Mason, Kathy S. *Women Lighthouse Keepers of Lake Michigan: Heroic Tales of Courage and Resourcefulness*. Lewiston, N.Y.: Edwin Mellen Press, 2012.

Massey, H. "Traveling on the Great Lakes When Detroit Was Young." In *Michigan Pioneer and Historical Collections*, vol. 6, 131–33. Lansing, Mich.: Thorp and Godfrey, 1886.

Mayer, Harold M. "Prospects and Problems of the Port of Chicago." *Economic Geography* 31, no. 2 (April 1955): 95–124.

McKenney, Thomas. *Sketches of a Tour of the Lakes*. Baltimore: Fielding Lucas, 1827.

McLear, Patrick E. "The Rise of the Port of Chicago, to 1848." MA thesis, University of Missouri, Kansas City, 1967.

———. "Rivalry between Chicago and Wisconsin Lake Ports for Control of the Grain Trade." *Inland Seas* 24, no. 3 (1968): 225–31.

McPherson, James. *Battle Cry of Freedom: The Civil War Era*. New York: Oxford University Press, 1988.

———. *The Struggle for Equality: Abolitionists and the Negro in the Civil War and Reconstruction*. Princeton, N.J.: Princeton University Press, 1964.

Meade, George Gordon. *The Life and Letters of George Gordon Meade*. New York: Charles Scribner's Sons, 1913.

Melville, Herman. *Moby-Dick*. New York: Knopf, 1988.

Merk, Frederick. *Economic History of Wisconsin During the Decade of the Civil War*. Madison: State Historical Society of Wisconsin, 1916.

Merritt, D. H. "A History of the Marquette Ore Docks." *Michigan History Magazine* 3, no. 3 (July 1919): 424–30.

Merry, Robert W. *A Country of Vast Design: James K. Polk, the Mexican War, and the Conquest of the American Continent*. New York: Simon & Schuster, 2009.

Messe, William A. *Abraham Lincoln: Incidents of His Life Relating to Waterways*. Moline, Ill.: Desaulniers, 1908.

Meverden, Keith N., and Tamara L. Thomsen. *Wisconsin's Cross-Planked Mosquito Fleet: Underwater Archaeological Investigations of the Scow Schooners* Iris, Ocean Wave, *and* Tennie and Laura. Madison: Wisconsin Historical Society, 2005.

Middleton, Stephen. *The Black Laws: Race and the Legal Process in Early Ohio*. Athens: Ohio University Press, 2005.

Miller, Al. *Tin Stackers: A History of the Pittsburgh Steamship Company*. Detroit: Wayne State University Press, 1999.

Miller, Allen S. "'The Lighthouse Top I See': Lighthouses as Instruments and Manifestations of State Building in the Early Republic." *Buildings and Landscapes: Journal of the Vernacular Architecture Forum* 17, no. 1 (Spring 2010): 13–34.

Miller, Donald L. *City of the Century: The Epic of Chicago and the Making of America*. New York: Simon & Schuster, 1996.

Miller, Richard Lawrence. *Lincoln and His World*. Vol. 3, *The Rise to National Prominence, 1843–1853*. Jefferson, N.C.: McFarland, 2011.

Millet, J. B. "Further Results of Submarine Signaling by Means of Sound." *Transactions of the Institution of Naval Architects* 49 (1907): 300–307.

———. "Submarine Signaling by Means of Sound." *Mechanical Engineer* 20 (July 27, 1907): 114–15.

Mills, E. L., J. H. Leach, J. T. Carlton, and C. L. Secor. "Exotic Species in the Great Lakes: A History of Biotic Crises and Anthropogenic Introductions." *Journal of Great Lakes Research* 19 (1993): 1–54.

Mills, James Cooke. *Our Inland Seas: Their Shipping and Commerce for Three Centuries*. Chicago: McClurg, 1910.

Monk, Kimberly. "The Development of Aboriginal Watercraft in the Great Lakes Region." *Totem: The University of Western Ontario Journal of Anthropology* 7, no. 1 (1999): 71–77.

Moore, John Bassett, ed. *The Works of James Buchanan, Comprising His Speeches, State Papers, and Private Correspondence, 1856–1860*. Vol. 10. Philadelphia: Lippincott Company, 1911.

Moore, Powell. *The Calumet Region: Indiana's Last Frontier*. Indianapolis: Indiana Historical Bureau, 1959.

Mount, Graeme S. "Myths and Realities: FDR's 1943 Vacation on Lake Huron, 1–7 August 1943." *Northern Mariner / Le Marin du Nord* 11, no. 3 (July 2001): 23–32.

Murdock, Lee. *Voices across the Water*. Kaneville, Ill.: Depot Recordings, 1997. Cassette recording.

Murray, John C. *Course of Instruction for Navigation School of the Lake Carriers' Association*. Cleveland: John C. Murray, 1957.

Nelson, Michael. "A Short, Ironic History of American National Bureaucracy." *Journal of Politics* 44, no. 3 (August 1982): 747–78.

Nettl, J. P. "The State as a Conceptual Variable." *World Politics* 20 (July 1968): 559–92.

Newett, George A. "A History of the Marquette Iron Range," *Proceedings of the Lake Superior Mining Institute* 19 (1914): 300–301.

The Niagara Ship Canal: Its Military and Commercial Necessity. New York: n.p., 1863.

Noble, Dennis L. *A Legacy: The United States Life-Saving Service*. Washington, D.C.: U.S. Coast Guard, 1976.

———. *Lighthouses and Keepers: The U.S. Lighthouse Service and Its Legacy*. Annapolis, Md.: Naval Institute Press, 1997.

Noble, Dennis, and T. Michael O'Brien. *Sentinels of the Rocks: From "Graveyard Coast" to National Lakeshore*. Marquette: Northern Michigan University Press, 1979.

Novak, William J. "The Myth of the 'Weak' American State." *American Historical Review* 113, no. 3 (June 2008): 752–72.

Nute, Grace Lee. *Lake Superior*. New York: Bobbs-Merrill, 1944.

Oakes, James. *Freedom National: The Destruction of Slavery in the United States, 1861–1865*. New York: W. W. Norton, 2012.

O'Brien, T. Michael. *Guardians of the Eighth Sea: A History of the U.S.*

Coast Guard on the Great Lakes. Honolulu, Hawai'i: University Press of the Pacific, 2001.

O'Connor, William D. *Heroes of the Storm*. Boston: Houghton Mifflin, 1904.

Odle, Thomas "Entrepreneurial Cooperation on the Great Lakes: The Origin of the Methods of American Grain Marketing." *Business History Review* 38, no. 4 (Winter 1964): 439–55.

Office of Response and Restoration. *Screening Level Risk Assessment Package Monrovia*. Washington, D.C.: National Oceanic and Atmospheric Administration, 2013.

Olmanson, Eric D. *The Future City on the Inland Sea: A History of Imaginative Geographies of Lake Superior*. Athens: Ohio University Press, 2007.

"Origins of the Detroit District." *Great Lakes Update* (U.S. Army Corps of Engineers, Detroit District) 172 (July 2008): 2.

Ostrom, Thomas P. *The United States Coast Guard in World War II: A History of Domestic and Overseas Action*. Jefferson, N.C.: McFarland, 2009.

Pace, Scott, Gerald P. Frost, Irving Lachow, David R. Frelinger, Donna Fossum, Don Wassem, and Monica M. Pinto. *The Global Positioning System Assessing National Policies*. Santa Monica, Calif.: Rand Corporation, 1995.

Palmer, Friend. *Personal Reminiscences of Important Events and Descriptions of the City for Over Eighty Years*. Detroit: Hunt and June, 1906.

Parham, Claire. "The St. Lawrence Seaway: A Bi-National Political Marathon, a Local and State Initiative." *New York History* 85, no. 4 (Fall 2004): 359–85.

Parton, James. "Chicago." *Atlantic Monthly*, March 1867, 330–33.

Paskoff, Paul. *Troubled Waters: Steamboat Disasters, River Improvements, and American Public Policy, 1821–1860*. Baton Rouge: Louisiana State University, 2007.

Person, Gustav J. "Captain George G. Meade and the Lake Survey." *Engineer*, September–December 2010, 43–49.

Peterson, Jacqueline. "The Founding Fathers: The Absorption of French-Indian Chicago, 1816–1837." In *Ethnic Chicago*, edited by Melvin G. Holi and Peter d' A. Jones, 300–337. Grand Rapids, Mich.: William B. Eerdmans, 1984.

Plumb, Ralph Gordon. "Early Harbor History of Wisconsin." *Transactions of the Wisconsin Academy of Sciences, Arts and Letters* 17, pt. 1 (1911): 187–94.

———. *History of Navigation on the Great Lakes*. Hearings of the Commerce of the Great Lakes, Committee on Railways and Canals. Washington, D.C.: U.S. Government Printing Office, 1911.

Podruchny, Carolyn. *Making the Voyageur World: Travelers and Traders in the North American Fur Trade*. Lincoln: University of Nebraska Press, 2006.

Poe, O. M. *Annual Report upon the Improvement of Waters Connecting the Great Lakes*. Washington, D.C.: U.S. Government Printing Office, 1893.

Portz, Matt. "Aviation Training and Expansion." *Naval Aviation News*, July/August 1990, 22–27.

Pound, Arthur. *Lake Ontario*. New York: Bobbs-Merrill, 1945.

Prechtel-Kluskens, Claire. "'A Reasonable Degree of Promptitude': Civil War Pension Application Processing, 1861–1885." *Prologue* 42, no. 1 (Spring 2010): 26–35.

Pred, Allan. *Urban Growth and City Systems in the United States, 1840–1860*. Cambridge, Mass.: Harvard University Press, 1980.

"The President's Commission on Economy and Efficiency." *American Political Science Review* 5, no. 4 (November 1911): 626–28.

"Private Operation Meets the Test." *Marine Review*, March 1920, 1.

Proceedings of the National Ship Canal Convention Held at the City of Chicago June 2nd and 3rd 1863. Chicago: Tribune Job Printing, 1863.

Prucha, Francis Paul, SJ. *Broadax and Bayonet: The Role of the United States Army in the Development of the Northwest, 1815–1860*. Lincoln: University of Nebraska Press, 1953.

Pursell, Carroll. *The Machine Age in America: A Social History of Technology*. Baltimore: Johns Hopkins University Press, 1995.

Putnam, George R. *Lighthouses and Lightships of the United States*. Boston: Houghton-Mifflin, 1917.

————. *Sentinels of the Coast: The Log of a Lighthouse Engineer*. New York: Norton, 1937.

Putnam, James William. *The Illinois and Michigan Canal: A Study in Economic History*. Chicago: University of Chicago Press, 1918.

Rae, James Gordon. "Great Lakes Commodity Trade, 1850 to 1900." PhD diss., Purdue University, 1967.

Raines, Rebecca Robbins. *Getting the Message Through: A Branch History of the U.S. Army Signal Corps*. Washington, D.C.: U.S. Army Center for Military History, 1996.

Ratigan, William. *Great Lakes Shipwrecks and Survivals*. Grand Rapids, Mich.: William B. Eerdmans, 1960.

"The Real Builders of America: Eber Brock Ward." *American Marine Engineer* 6, no. 4 (April 1914): 9–11.

Reese, David, and Robert Browning. "Lighthouse Management: A Balancing Act by the U.S. Coast Guard." *CRM-Cultural Resource Management* 20, no. 8 (1997): 37–39.

"Regulations for Preventing Collisions on the Water, April 29, 1864." In

The Statutes at Large, Treaties, and Proclamations of the United States, vol. 13, 58–60. Boston: Little, Brown, 1868.

Renton, Alan. *Lost Sounds: The Story of Coast Fog Signals.* Caithness, Scotland: Whittles Publishing, 2001.

Report of the Committee of Commerce. U.S. Senate, 27th Congress, 3rd Session. Senate Document no. 234. Washington, D.C.: Government Printing Office, 1843.

Report of the Second Annual Convention of the Lakes-to-the-Gulf Deep Waterways Association. St. Louis: Lakes-to-the-Gulf Deep Waterways Association, 1907.

Report on the River and Harbor Bill by the Committee on Commerce, River and Harbor Bill. U.S. Senate, 61st Congress, 2nd Session, Report no. 527. Washington, D.C.: Government Printing Office, 1910.

Reports of the Chief of Engineers, U.S. Army, 1866–1912. Washington, D.C.: U.S. Government Printing Office, 1916.

Reynolds, Terry, and Virginia Dawson. *Iron Will: Cleveland-Cliffs and the Mining of Iron Ore, 1847–2006.* Detroit: Wayne State University Press, 2012.

Richards, Rick. "Dreams Beckon Inspiration at Michigan City Lighthouse." *Lighthouse Digest,* July/August 2011.

Richardson, Heather Cox. *West from Appomattox.* New Haven, Conn.: Yale University Press, 2008.

Risjord, Norman K. *Shining Big Sea Water: The Story of Lake Superior.* St. Paul: Minnesota Historical Society Press, 2008.

Robbins, Roy M. *Our Landed Heritage: The Public Domain, 1776–1936.* Lincoln: University of Nebraska Press, 1962.

Roberts, Bruce, and Ray Jones. *Western Great Lakes Lighthouses: Michigan and Superior.* Guliford, Conn.: Globe Pequot Press, 1994.

Rockoff, Hugh. "The United States: From Ploughshares to Swords." In *The Economics of World War II: Six Great Powers in International Comparison,* edited by Mark Harrison, 81–121. New York: Cambridge University Press, 1998.

Rolland, Alex. *The Way of the Ship: America's Maritime History Reenvisioned, 1600–2000.* Hoboken, N.J.: John Wiley and Son, 2008.

Rossel, Frank R. "The Vandalia, First Great Lakes Propeller." *Marine Review,* September 1917, 338–39.

Saler, Bethel. *The Settlers' Empire: Colonialism and State Formation in America's Old Northwest.* Philadelphia: University of Pennsylvania Press, 2015.

Salmon, M. Stephen. "'A Prosperous Season': Investment in Canadian Great Lakes Shipping, 1900–1914." In *A Fully Accredited Ocean: Essays on the Great Lakes,* edited by Victoria Brehm, 107–54. Ann Arbor: University of Michigan Press, 1998.

Saltzman, Joshua. "Safe Harbor: Chicago's Waterfront and the Political Economy of the Built Environment, 1847–1918." PhD diss., University of Illinois at Chicago, 2008.

Samuelson, Paul A. "The Pure Theory of Public Expenditure." *Review of Economics and Statistics* 36, no. 4 (November 1954): 387–89.

Sapulski, Wayne. "The Imperial Towers of Lake Huron and Georgian Bay." *Lighthouse Digest*, December 1996.

Satz, Ronald. *American Indian Policy in the Jacksonian Era*. Norman: University of Oklahoma Press, 1975.

Scary, Robert. *Millard Fillmore*. New York: McFarland, 2001.

Schiffer, Michael Brian. "The Electric Lighthouse in the Nineteenth Century: Aid to Navigation and Political Technology." *Technology and Culture* 46, no. 2 (April 2005): 275–305.

Schumacher, Michael. *November's Fury: The Deadly Great Lakes Hurricane of 1913*. Minneapolis: University of Minnesota Press, 2013.

Seelye, John. *The Beautiful Machine: Rivers and the Republican Plan, 1755–1825*. New York: Oxford University Press, 1991.

Sellers, Charles. *The Market Revolution: Jacksonian America, 1815–1846*. New York: Oxford University Press, 1991.

Shallot, Todd. *Structures in the Stream: Water, Science, and the U.S. Army Corps of Engineers*. Austin: University of Texas Press, 1994.

Shaw, Ronald E. *Canals for a Nation: The Canal Era in the United States, 1790–1860*. Lexington: University of Kentucky Press, 1990.

———. *Erie Waters West: A History of the Erie Canal*. Lexington; University of Kentucky Press, 1966.

Sheriff, Carol. *The Artificial River: The Erie Canal and the Paradox of Progress, 1817–1862*. New York: Hill and Wang, 1996.

Sherman, Elizabeth. *Beyond the Windswept Dunes: The Story of Maritime Muskegon*. Detroit: Wayne State University Press, 2003.

Sherman, H. T., and V. L. Johnson. "The LORAN-C Ground Station." *Navigation: Journal of the Institute of Navigation* 23, no. 4 (Winter 1976): 349–58.

Shoemaker, Rebecca S. "Michigan City, Indiana: The Failure of a Dream." *Indiana Magazine of History* 84, no. 4 (1988): 317–42.

Short, Lloyd M. *The Steamboat Inspection Service: Its History, Organization, and Activities*. New York: D. Appleton, 1922.

Skaggs, David Curtis, and Larry L. Nelson, eds. *The Sixty Years' War for the Great Lakes, 1754–1814*. East Lansing: Michigan State University Press, 2001.

"Sketch of Increase A. Lapham, LLD." *Popular Science Monthly* 22 (April 1883): 835–40.

"Small Towns and the Army Corps of Engineers: The Evolution of the Region." *National Archives at Chicago Bulletin*, August 2015, 1–8.

Smith, Andrew F. *Starving the South: How the North Won the Civil War*. New York: St. Martin's, 2011.

Smith, Theresa S. *Island of the Anishinaabeg: Thunders and Water Monsters in the Traditional Ojibwe Life-World*. Lincoln: University of Nebraska Press, 1995.

Smith, Warring G. "Running the Ice Blockade." *Popular Mechanics*, April 1943, 50–174.

Snow, Edward Rowe, and Jeremy D'Entremont. *The Lighthouses of New England*. Carlisle, Mass: Commonwealth Editions, 2003.

Solzman, David M. *The Chicago River: An Illustrated History and Guide to the River and Its Waterways*. Chicago: Wild Onion Press, 1998.

Stagg, Ronald. *The Golden Dream: A History of the St. Lawrence Seaway*. Toronto: Dundurn, 2010.

Starin, Frederick J. "Diary of a Journey to Wisconsin in 1840." *Wisconsin Magazine of History* 6, no. 1 (1922): 78–79.

The Statutes at Large, Treaties, and Proclamations of the United States. Boston: Little, Brown, 1863–69.

Steamboat Inspection Service. *Great Lakes: General Rules and Regulations Prescribed by the General Board of Supervising Inspectors*. Washington, D.C.: U.S. Government Printing Office, 1916.

Stephenson, Isaac. *Recollections of a Long Life, 1829–1915*. Chicago: privately printed, 1915.

"Stewards Needed for Four Historic Great Lakes Lighthouses." News Release, General Services Administration, May 21, 2015.

St. Lawrence Seaway and Midcontinental Factsheet 2, no. 2 (September 1966).

The St. Lawrence Waterway: Message from the President of the United States, Transmitting a Letter from the Secretary of State Submitting the Report of the International Joint Commission. Washington, D.C.: Government Printing Office, 1922.

Stonehouse, Frederic. *The Wreck of the Edmund Fitzgerald*. Gwinn, Mich.: Avery Color Studios, 1998.

Stowe, Harriet Beecher. *Uncle Tom's Cabin*. Boston: John P. Jewett, 1852.

Streeter, Frank S., and Henry A. Powell. *Pollution of Boundary Waters*. Washington, D.C.: U.S. Government Printing Office, 1913.

Strough, Arthur B. "Crews of Early Great Lakes Vessels." *Inland Seas* 48, no. 2 (1993): 258–66.

Stuart, Charles B. *Proposed Improvements to Pass Gunboats from Tide Water to the Northern and Northwestern Lakes, Message from the President of the United States*. 38th Congress, 1st Session, House of Representatives, Executive Document 61, March 1864. Washington, D.C.: n.p., 1864.

Strum, James Lester. "Railroads and Market Growth: The Case of Peoria and Chicago, 1850–1900." MA thesis, University of Wisconsin–Madison, 1965.

Submarine Signal Company. *Submarine Signals: Results of Tests Made by the United States Lighthouse Board During June and July of 1906 of the System of Submarine Signaling Controlled by the Submarine Signal Company.* Boston: Submarine Signal Company, 1906.

Swayze, David. "The Great Spring Gale of 1894." *Inland Seas* 48, no. 2 (Summer 1992): 99–112.

Symons, Thomas W., and John Quintus. "A History of Buffalo Harbor: Its Construction and Improvement in the Nineteenth Century. *Publications of the Buffalo Historical Society* 5 (1902): 240–60.

Tag, Thomas. "The Clock without Hands." *Keeper's Log*, Spring 2008, 28–35.

Taylor, Paul. *Orlando M. Poe: Civil War General and Great Lakes Engineer.* Kent, Ohio: Kent State University Press, 2009.

Terras, Donald J. *The Grosse Point Lighthouse, Evanston, Illinois: Landmark to Maritime History and Culture.* Evanston, Ill.: Windy City Press, 1995.

Thomasian, John. *The Clean Air Act, the Electric Utilities, and the Coal Market.* Washington, D.C.: Congressional Budget Office, U.S. Government Printing Office, 1982.

Thompson, Mark L. *Graveyard of the Great Lakes.* Detroit: Wayne State University Press, 2000.

———. *Queen of the Lakes.* Detroit: Wayne State University Press, 1994.

———. *Steamboats and Sailors of the Great Lakes.* Detroit: Wayne State University Press, 1991.

Tocqueville, Alexis de. *Democracy in America.* Translated by George Lawrence. Edited by J. P. Mayer. New York: HarperPerennial, 1988.

"Today Rogers City Is a Center of a Live, Healthy, Progressive Community." *Calcite Screenings* (Special Edition 1950): 16.

"Traffic on the Great Lakes in 1921." *Marine Review*, February 1922, 80–83.

Truman, Stephen, Grace Truman, and Joel Truman. *Storm Sands: A Story of Shipwrecks and Big Sable Point Coast Guard Station.* Grand Rapids, Mich.: Pine Woods Press, 2012.

Tunnell, George Gerald. *Transportation on the Great Lakes of North America.* Chicago: University of Chicago, 1898.

United States Bureau of Light-Houses. *Compilation of Public Documents and Extracts from Reports and Papers Relating to Light-Houses, Light-Vessels, and Illuminating Apparatus, 1789–1871.* Washington, D.C.: Light-House Establishment, 1871.

United States Code, 2000. Washington, D.C.: U.S. Government Printing Office, 2001.

United States Light-House Board. *Annual Report of the Light-House Board of the United States to the Secretary of the Treasury for the Year 1875.* Washington, D.C.: Government Printing Office, 1875.

United States President's Commission on Economy and Efficiency. *Economy and Efficiency in the Government Service: Message of the President*. Washington, D.C.: U.S. Government Printing Office, 1912.

U.S. Army Corps of Engineers. *The Great Lakes Navigation System: Economic Strength of the Nation*. Detroit: U.S. Army Corps, Detroit District, 2013.

U.S. Hydrographic Office. *Sailing Directions for Lake Erie and Lake Ontario, St. Clair and Detroit River and Lake St. Clair*. Washington, D.C.: U.S. Government Printing Office, 1896.

Vogel, Virgil. *Indian Place Names in Michigan*. Ann Arbor: University of Michigan Press, 1986.

Vrana, Kenneth J. ed. *Inventory of Maritime and Recreation Resources of the Manitou Passage Underwater Preserve*. East Lansing: Michigan State University, 1995.

Waldron, Webb. *We Explore the Great Lakes*. New York: Century, 1923.

Walker, David A. *Iron Frontier: The Discovery and Early Development of Minnesota's Three Ranges*. St. Paul: Minnesota Historical Society Press, 1979.

Walker, Gordon. "The Boundary Waters Treaty 1909—A Peace Treaty?" *Canada–United States Law Journal* 39, no. 14 (2014): 170–86.

Walton, Ivan H., and Joe Grimm. *Windjammers: Songs of the Great Lakes Sailors*. Detroit: Wayne State University Press, 2002.

Ward, Eber. "Incidents in the Life of Mr. Eber Ward, Father of Capt. E. B. Ward of Steamboat Fame as Related to Mrs. E. M. S. Stewart in the Summer of 1852." *Michigan Pioneer and Historical Society, Pioneer Collections* 6 (1884): 471–73.

Wardius, Barb, and Ken Wardius. *Cana Island Lighthouse*. Chicago: Arcadia, 2006.

Weed, Thurlow. "A Trip to Chicago and the Lake Harbor Convention." In *Chicago River-and-Harbor Convention*, edited by Robert Fergus, 147–71. Chicago: Robert Fergus, 1882.

Weiss, George. *The Lighthouse Service, Its History, Activities, and Organization*. Baltimore: Johns Hopkins University Press, 1926.

"Welfare Work of the Lake Carriers Association." *American Iron and Steel Institute Bulletin* 3 (January 1915): 150–74.

Westerdahl, Christer. "The Maritime Cultural Landscape." *International Journal of Nautical Archaeology* 21, no. 1 (1992): 5–14.

White, Langdon, and George Primmer. "The Iron and Steel Industry of Duluth: A Study in Locational Maladjustment." *Geographical Review* 27, no. 1 (January 1937): 82–91.

White, Richard. *Railroaded: The Transcontinentals and the Making of Modern America*. New York: W. W. Norton, 2011.

Widdis, Randy William. "'Across the Boundary in a Hundred Torrents': The Changing Geography of Marine Trade within the Great Lakes

Borderland Region during the Nineteenth and Early Twentieth Centuries." *Annals of the Association of American Geographers* 101, no. 2 (March 2011): 356–79.

Wilentz, Sean. *The Rise of American Democracy, from Jefferson to Lincoln.* New York: W. W. Norton, 2005.

Wilkes, Charles. *Autobiography of Rear Admiral Charles Wilkes, U.S. Army, 1798–1877.* Edited by William Morgan et al. Washington, D.C.: Naval History Division, Dept. of Navy, 1978.

Williams, Brenda Wheeler, Arnold Alanen, and William Tishler. *Coming through with Rye: An Historical Agricultural Landscape Study of South Manitou Island, Sleeping Bear National Lakeshore, Michigan.* Omaha, Neb.: Midwest Region, National Park Service, 1986.

Williams, Elizabeth Whitney. *A Child of the Sea; and Life Among the Mormons.* 1905. Reprint, St. James, Mich.: Beaver Island Historical Society, 1983.

Williams, Mentor. "The Chicago River and Harbor Convention, 1847." *Mississippi Valley Historical Association* 35, no. 4 (March 1949): 607–26.

Williamson, Samuel H. "The Growth of the Great Lakes as a Major Transportation Resource, 1870–1911." *Research in Economic History* 2 (1977): 173–248.

Willoughby, William R. *The St. Lawrence Waterway: A Study in Politics and Diplomacy.* Madison: University of Wisconsin Press, 1961.

Wilson, Clyde, ed. *The Papers of John C. Calhoun.* Vol. 22. Columbia: University of South Carolina Press, 1995.

Wolf, Garrett. "A City and Its River: An Urban Political Ecology of the Loop and Bridgeport in Chicago." MA thesis, Louisiana State University, 2012.

Wood, Alexander T. "Great Lakes Transport." *Annals of the American Academy of Political and Social Science* 230 (November 1943): 37–43.

Wood, Donald F. "Significance of the Saint Lawrence Seaway to the Great Lakes Commerce and Industry." MA thesis, University Wisconsin-Madison, 1957.

Wood, Gordon. *What God Hath Wrought: The Transformation of America, 1815–1848.* New York: Oxford University Press, 2007.

Woodford, Arthur M. *Charting the Inland Seas: A History of the U.S. Lake Survey.* Detroit: Wayne State University Press, 1994.

Wright, Larry, and Patricia Wright. *Great Lakes Lighthouse Encyclopedia.* Erin, Ontario: Boston Mills Press, 2011.

———. *Lightships of the Great Lakes.* n.p.: privately printed, 2011.

Wright, Richard. *Freshwater Whales: A History of the American Shipbuilding Company and Its Predecessors.* Kent, Ohio: Kent State University Press, 1969.

Wuebben, James L., ed. *Winter Navigation on the Great Lakes: A Review of Environmental Studies.* Detroit: U.S. Army Corps of Engineers, 1995.

Wyatt, David, and Mike Tooley. *Aircraft Communications and Navigation Systems: Principles, Operations, and Maintenance*. New York: Routledge, 2013.

York, Eugene V. "The Architecture of the United States Life-Saving Stations." MA thesis, Boston University, 1983.

Zavodnyik, Peter. *The Age of Strict Construction: A History of the Growth of Federal Power, 1789–1861*. Washington, D.C.: Catholic University Press, 2007.

Zoss, Neel R. *McDougall's Great Lakes Whalebacks*. Chicago: Arcadia Press, 2007.

Index